Telecommunications Strategy

T0304190

The telecommunications industry is one of the most influential and significant global industries and is fundamental to the health of the modern economy. Yet it is currently facing strategic challenges ranging from globalization and cross-border alliances to changing technologies and consumer demands.

This innovative text provides a comprehensive analysis of representative key players in this industry and uses their experiences to illustrate the strategic decisions and dilemmas that have led to both notable successes and infamous failures. The book includes in-depth case studies of global companies, including AOL Time Warner, AT&T, Vodafone and WorldCom, to illustrate the industry's key strategic concepts, which include:

- Managing ascent and decline
- Convergence and specialization
- Protecting core markets
- Managing industrial restructuring

Combining in-depth analysis with discussions of the wider strategic contexts, this study will be of interest to students on specialist telecommunications and information management courses as well as MBA students interested in the strategic analysis of this evolving global industry.

Peter Curwen is Visiting Professor of Telecommunications at Strathclyde University. **Jason Whalley** is Lecturer in Management Sciences at Strathclyde University.

Telecommunications Strategy

Cases, theory and applications

Peter Curwen and Jason Whalley

Routledge
Taylor & Francis Group

LONDON AND NEW YORK

First published 2004
by Routledge
2 Park Square, Milton Park, Abingdon, Oxfordshire, OX14 4RN

Simultaneously published in the USA and Canada
by Routledge
711 Third Avenue, New York, NY 10017

Routledge is an imprint of the Taylor & Francis Group

Transferred to Digital Printing 2005

Typeset in Baskerville by Exe Valley Dataset Ltd, Exeter, Devon

British Library Cataloguing in Publication Data
A catalogue record for this book is available from the British Library

Library of Congress Cataloging-in-Publication Data
Curwen, Peter J.
  Telecommunications strategy : theory and applications / Peter Curwen
  and Jason Whalley.
    p.   cm.
  Inclues bibliographical references and index.
  1. Telecommunication–Management–Case studies.   2. Strategic planning–
  Case studies.
  I. Whalley, Jason.   II. Title.
HE7661.C87 2004
384´.068´4–dc22   2004000698

ISBN 0–415–34239–2 (hbk)
ISBN 0–415–34238–4 (pbk)

To Hilary, for her endurance in the face of a scribbler's tantrums

To Nils, for a continuous supply of new dishes

Contents

Illustrations

Figures

Tables

Preface

This is a book of case studies with a difference – or, more correctly, differences. In the first place, it concentrates upon a single sector, albeit a very large one. This is often known in its broadest sense as TMT – technology, media and telecommunications – although all of the case studies bar one fall into the latter two categories. This is partly to keep the length of the book under control, but mainly because the connection between these categories is at heart very straightforward: the telecommunications cases are primarily concerned with networks and the delivery of data, while the media cases are primarily concerned with the content that, aside from voice, constitutes the data that are conveyed. Insofar as technology is relevant, it is primarily in the context of companies that manufacture equipment for telecommunications use, as in the case of Marconi. The choice of media and telecommunications barely needs justification: No other industry has undergone so much radical change in such a short period of time in the entire history of world industry. Although the cases delve back somewhat further at times, the stories laid out in the cases largely cover a period no longer than the past decade, with the key events falling on either side of 2001 when the so-called 'meltdown' took place.

The second difference is that the case studies are highly detailed rather than the typical snapshots that are presented as cases in most strategy texts. We do not believe that such snapshots are sufficient for detailed analysis, nor do we believe that the provision of a detailed set of accounts is in any way sufficient to understand how companies have arrived at where they are today. We believe not only that a good deal of historical analysis is needed, but also that an overview of the environment that encompasses simultaneously all of the companies is essential. One of the virtues of concentrating upon telecommunications is that it becomes possible to do both of these things.

The third difference lies in the method of dealing with the strategic analysis. Normally, textbooks on strategy deal in detail with large numbers of strategic concepts, some of which are then applied briefly and hurriedly to real world cases. This book largely reverses this process. What it does is to introduce all of the most relevant concepts in an introductory chapter – with relevance to the recent circumstances of the TMT sector the critical driver in making the selection. At the beginning of each group of case studies one strategic model is applied to one of the cases in order to illustrate how this is done in a specific case study context. Beyond that, readers – who are presumed primarily to consist of students of strategy – are expected to apply the other models for themselves under the guidance of their tutors. The choice of models, and the points in the case studies where these are to be applied, is initially up to individual readers to decide for themselves.

However, it may be added that these cases are also written to be of general interest to anyone who works in, or has an interest in, what has happened to the telecommunications sector over the past decade, but who understandably does not have the time to keep up to date across the whole range of companies.

It is anticipated that the book will find its primary markets in Europe and the USA, in part because of the use of English as the teaching medium. Of the ten cases examined, seven are largely about telecommunications and three about the media, although there are lots of overlaps. Three of the cases are primarily located in the USA (AOL Time Warner, AT&T and WorldCom) and five in Europe (BT, Marconi, Vivendi Universal, Kirch and Telecom Italia), while two have a more international dimension (Vodafone and Cable & Wireless). However, this distinction needs to be treated with care, and is not used as the basis for the structure of the book. Rather, the first division is between the telecommunications and media cases, with the latter being put together in one of the four sections. In another section, BT and AT&T are placed together because they share the same essential characteristic – that of apparently unassailable domestic incumbents that tried to diversify away from their core businesses only to end up much where they began, with Telecom Italia added in to provide the contrast of an incumbent that managed to avoid this fate. In a third section are to be found Marconi and Cable & Wireless. Here the main thrust is to do with an attempt by these companies to transform themselves into different industrial animals, with largely disastrous results. This, incidentally, is a story that is shared in many ways by Vivendi Universal so the sectoral groupings are not intended to be seen as self-contained. The fourth section contains WorldCom and what is strictly the Vodafone Group. The common theme is the attempt to become world beaters in their respective fields. The contrast lies in the collapse of WorldCom and the success (for the moment as much, if not more, relative rather than absolute) of Vodafone.

The one theme that runs consistently throughout these case studies is change and the (mis)management of change. It is the job of senior management to manage change, and hence they should be held liable for the often monumental mistakes that they make. However, it is much easier to view events retrospectively rather than prospectively, so one of the tasks for readers is to judge for themselves whether the traumatic events at the turn of the millennium could reasonably have been foreseen, and hence the extent of the culpability of management. To assist them in this task, an introductory chapter sets out a detailed statistical analysis of the telecommunications and media sector as a whole, with the companies analyzed in this book highlighted to facilitate cross-referencing to the individual case studies.

Acknowledgements

The authors wish to acknowledge the assistance of Tony Fowler of Sheffield Hallam University in the preparation of the case study on KirchMedia. They also wish to thank Colin Blackman, editor of telecoms journal info, for his input into initial versions of certain of the cases.

Abbreviations

3G	Third-generation mobile telephony
ADSL	Asynchronous digital subscriber line
AGM	Annual general meeting
AOL	America Online
AOLTW	AOL Time Warner
ARPU	Average revenue per user
ASP	Application service provider
AT&T	American Telegraph & Telephone
AWE	AT&T Wireless
BT	British Telecommunications
CEO	Chief executive officer
CFO	Chief financial officer
CLEC	Competitive local exchange carrier
COO	Chief operating officer
CWC	Cable & Wireless Communications
DSL	Digital Subscriber Line
EBITDA	Earnings before interest, taxes, depreciation and amortisation
EDGE	Enhanced data [rates] for GSM evolution
FCC	Federal Communications Commission
FT	Financial Times
GAAP	Generally accepted accounting principles
GEC	General Electric Company
GPRS	General packet radio service
GSM	Global system for mobile
IP	Internet protocol
IPO	Initial public offer
IRS	Internal Revenue Service (USA)
ISP	Internet service provider
M&A	Mergers & acquisitions
MMS	Multimedia messaging service
MoU	Memorandum of understanding
MVNO	Mobile virtual network operator
OFTEL	Office of Telecommunications (UK)

PC	Personal computer
PCN	Personal communications network
RBOC	Regional Bell operating company
SDH	Synchronous digital hierarchy
SEC	Securities & Exchange Commission
TDMA	Time division multiple access
TIM	Telecom Italia Mobile
TMT	Technology, media & telecommunications
TWE	Time Warner Entertainment
UK	United Kingdom
UMTS	Unversal mobile telecommunications system
US	United States
VUE	Vivendi Universal Entertainment
WAP	Wireless application protocol
W-CDMA	Wideband code division multiple access

Chapter 1

Structural overview

And when they were up, they were up

Introduction

The purpose of this introductory chapter is to 'set the scene' for the ten case studies that form the bulk of the book. One of the obvious drawbacks to books involving case studies is that there are no links at all between them – different industries, different time periods and different levels of detail are involved. This book sets out to overcome these difficulties by covering a single, albeit substantial, industrial sector, a common time period and a very similar level of detail. However, it is still possible to get so involved with the specifics of individual cases as to lose sight of the bigger picture: at the end of the day, not only must all of the companies have been responding in part to the same set of external pressures, but they must in many cases have been interacting with one another either as partners or competitors.

Although it is not possible in an introductory chapter to cover all of these matters in detail, the discussion that follows, which contains a rich data base, should help to clarify a number of issues for the reader, and, in particular, make it possible to cross-reference back from the case studies in respect of events such as mergers. Where entries are important in relation to the case studies, they appear in bold. It may be noted that one company, Kirch, does not appear in any of the tables. Without going into a lengthy discussion of why that is at this stage, it should simply be borne in mind that not all significant developments involve large quoted companies.

The industrial sector into which all of the case studies fall is generally known as Technology, Media and Telecommunications (TMT). However, the former is largely excluded from the list of case studies here, partly to maintain focus and partly because the term 'technology' covers such a wide range of possibilities, including all kinds of software and hardware, with most relevant companies having only a tenuous relationship to the telecoms and media industries. Put crudely, the media companies are included because they provide the content, and the telecoms companies (known generally as operators or carriers) because they provide the networks that carry that content to the users. This distinction was historically fairly clear-cut, but has become much less so in recent years because of the Internet, as is shown in the case studies. However, our case studies can be clearly divided into these two categories for analytical purposes. The relationship between content providers and operators is necessarily very close, although one of the most interesting, and as yet unresolved, questions is whether operators need content more or less than media companies need operators.

Ranking the companies

It is not possible to provide a definitive overview of the TMT sector because, among other issues, those who seek to sell this information at high prices have a vested interest in defining their terms somewhat differently from everyone else seeking to do the same thing. What is crucial, when all is said and done, is to have a set of data that is consistently defined and covers the period under investigation. Given the industries under review, the critical period is from the beginning of 1997 to the present day, which in this case is December 2003 – although it is not possible to be quite so up to date because most data are only published once a year. For this reason, we have chosen to utilize the annual data that encompass the 500 largest companies as defined by the *Financial Times*. The broad picture presented by the relevant sections of the FT500 is laid out in Table 1.1.[1] As can be seen, size is defined here by reference to the capital values of the companies listed. There are several reasons for this. In particular, capitalization (market value) is easily measured and can be adjusted on a daily basis to allow for a rolling comparison. In addition, while concepts such as revenue or profit are conventionally used in this context – for example, *Fortune* magazine's US500 is based upon revenue – they are increasingly unhelpful in a 'virtual' world where there can be (and, indeed, have been, although few cases currently exist) a significant number of companies that earn negligible revenues and make ongoing losses, yet have capital values running into the billions of dollars. A particular problem with both revenue and profit data is that they are only declared a few times each year, in arrears and, generally, with more than an element of imprecision (as some case studies demonstrate). In contrast, capital values are available from stock markets on a daily basis, and, in theory at least, take account of all known facts about a company as well as its future prospects, suitably discounted to the present day.

Table 1.1 concentrates upon what in 1998 were classified as 'telephone companies' and from 1999 onwards as 'telecoms', but is intended to be representative of all links in the supply chain from the creation of content to the delivery of data, encompassing a sample of companies in the broadcasting media, computer software and services, communications equipment and other sectors. Hence, although only one case study is of a 'technology' company, the most relevant of these in the sense of, for example, specialising in the provision of telecomunications equipment, are included in this overview to indicate their place in the greater scheme of things. The choice of companies is necessarily somewhat arbitrary because the telecommunications sector, if defined as TMT, encompasses a range of very different types of business, both 'old economy' and 'new economy', and mergers and acquisitions (M&A) activity during the period 1998 to 2001 had significant structural consequences. However, given that our purpose is to examine reasonably broad trends which would not be affected by the inclusion or exclusion of a handful of companies, the sample is more than adequate for our purposes.

Table 1.1 ranks companies at the end of six successive periods of roughly one calendar year, encompassing the beginning of 1997 to the end of March 2003 inclusive. All of the companies in the main section of the table were numbered among the FT500 in the year to 28 March 2003, but not necessarily in every previous period. It is rare, in practice, for a TMT company to return to the FT500 once having fallen below the minimum size to qualify, but it is of importance for our analysis to include those companies that have ceased to be listed during the period of TMT decline commencing at the beginning of 2000. In the table, accordingly, 54 companies are listed for 2002 (strictly, 28 March 2002 to 28 March 2003) compared to 57 companies for 2001 (in this – exceptional – case a 15-month period). Of the 54, three were new entries, while six had disappeared from the 2001 list. In contrast, the new entrants in 2001 were massively outweighed by those departing which numbered 23 of the 76 listed in 2000, as was true of the 21 listed in 1999 which failed to make the list in 2000. Overall, therefore, it is clear that there has been considerable attrition during the period January 1999 to March 2003, but also that the process slowed sharply between March 2002 and March 2003. It may naturally be argued that as the residual number of surviving companies shrinks, the attrition rate must sooner or later slow down, but as noted the reduction in the attrition rate during 2002 was very marked.

What this indicates strongly, and this can readily be borne out by looking backwards rather than forwards from 1999, is that 1999 was a clearly defined peak year for the TMT sector. In that year, 87 of the largest 500 companies qualified for the data set, whereas in 1997 there were a mere 36. Furthermore, 67 of the 87 were listed in the top 250. In other words, companies in the TMT sector literally burst upon the scene during a two-year period in a manner that has no historical precedent. This immediately leads to one initial conclusion. No set of companies can actually grow internally at such a rate as to overtake companies in every other industrial sector in so short a time. Hence, one of two things must have happened: Either there was an extraordinarily large and speedy process of M&A activity during these two years or the market values of this particular group of companies were raised much faster than for others on the grounds that its future prospects had suddenly improved beyond all expectation. We will return to these matters in due course. Suffice it to say for now that, if anything, the situation was even more extreme than it appeared to be since M&A activity which is launched in a particular year may often not reach fruition until a later year because of the delays in the obtaining of regulatory approvals. Nevertheless, a word of

Table 1.1 Telecommunications companies in the FT500, December 1997–March 2003

Company	Country	Sector			Rank					
		1998	1999/2000	2001/2002	2002[a]	2001[b]	2000[c]	1999[c]	1998[d]	1997
Vodafone Group[e]	UK	223	673	100	13	17	8[e]	24	81	226
NTT DoCoMo	Japan	–	678	100	19	14	16	3	–	–
Verizon Communications[f]	USA	–	673	100	22	19	21	–	–	–
Cisco Systems	USA	533	938	200	24	20	2	4	19	51
Nokia	Finland	551	938	200	31	30	12	11	62	108
SBC Communications	USA	223	673	100	35	18	17	23	30	35
Comcast	USA	474	543	300	40	149	137	137	219	453
AOL Time Warner[g]	USA	482	974	400	55	31[g]	36	16	145	–
Deutsche Telekom[h]	Germany	223	673	100	56	51[h]	40	10	27	44
Telefónica	Spain	223	673	100	57	69	61	55	77	101
Telecom Italia[i]	Italy	223	673	100	59	64	84	67	80	84
BellSouth	USA	223	673	100	64	47	53	54	35	58
China Mobile (HK)[j]	Hong Kong	223	673	100	66	59	34	51	198	–
Samsung Electronics	South Korea	–	938	200	67	85	225	146	–	–
Orange[k]	France	–	–	100	71	133	–	–	–	–
Telecom Italia Mobile	Italy	223	678	100	82	95	74	65	74	127
NTT	Japan	223	673	100	93	55	29	7	11	7
Telstra	Australia	223	673	100	96	108	115	70	79	–
Qualcomm	USA	–	938	200	101	156	80	41	–	–
Liberty Media[l]	USA	495	542	300	120	133	136	72	308	–
France Télécom	France	223	673	100	132	116	39	29	75	57
Hutchison Whampoa	Hong Kong	223	240	500	133	107	91	90	179	68
BT Group[m]	UK	223	673	100	140	122	81	22	25	64
Teléfonos de Mexico	Mexico	223	673	100	156	137	130	180	211	234
Swisscom	Switzerland	–	673	100	164	193	286	200	–	–
BSkyB	UK	474	543	300	166	192	167	224	249	305
Motorola	USA	551	938	200	171	141	102	49	134	62
Cox Communications	USA	474	543	300	177	201	194	221	244	–
AT&T Wireless[n]	USA	–	678	100	180	180	103	–	–	–

Company	Country								
Saudi Telecom	Saudi Arabia	223	—	100	181	—	—	—	—	—
BCE	Canada	223	673	100	185	310	232	94	208	192
KPN	Netherlands	—	673	100	215	355	326	130	252	202
Vivendi Universal[o]	**France**	—	**543**	**300**	**222**	**94**	**66**	—	—	—
Yahoo!	USA	482	974	400	232	416	324	40	293	—
TeliaSonera[p]	Finland	—	673	100	238	431	344	—	—	—
Alltel	USA	223	673	100	241	255	249	239	287	—
Singapore Telecom[q]	Singapore	223	673	100	248	288	223	176	139	129
AT&T[r]	**USA**	**223**	**673**	**100**	**259**	**63**	**54**	**18**	**17**	**26**
KDDI[s]	Japan	—	673	100	263	419	293	186	—	—
Nextel Communications	USA	—	678	100	271	—	257	178	—	—
Ericsson	Sweden	533	938	200	313	124	43	30	46	—
Sprint FON[t]	USA	—	673	100	325	307	252	107	—	—
SK Telecom	South Korea	—	673	100	331	221	270	217	—	—
KT Corp.[u]	South Korea	—	673	100	349	328	297	115	—	—
Etisalat	UAE	—	—	100	362	486	—	—	—	—
Alcatel	France	533	938	200	404	250	67	121	217	169
Japan Telecom[v]	Japan	—	673	100	405	459	395	232	—	—
Olivetti[w]	**Italy**	—	**673**	**100**	**408**	**418**	**342**	**442**	—	—
America Móvil[x]	Mexico	—	—	100	413	279	—	—	—	—
Portugal Telecom	Portugal	—	—	100	415	496	—	—	—	—
Wanadoo[y]	France	—	—	400	439	—	—	—	—	—
Nortel Networks	Canada	533	938	200	457	313	30	31	167	—
T-Online International[z]	Germany	—	974	400	458	321	339	—	—	—
NTT Data	Japan	223	972	100	468	375	289	78	364	351
Excluded during 2002									
WorldCom[aa]	**USA**	**223**	**673**	**100**	—	**215**	**87**	**26**	**24**	—
Lucent Technologies	USA	533	938	200	—	276	95	9	21	45
Qwest Communications[bb]	USA	533	678	100	—	324	59	198	371	—
China Unicom[cc]	China	—	678	100	—	386	280	—	—	—
Telecom Carso Global	Mexico	—	—	100	—	466	—	—	—	—
Sprint PCS[dd]	USA	—	678	100	—	480	238	134	—	—
Excluded during 2001									
Time Warner[ee]	**USA**	**474**	**535**	—	—	—	**57**	**57**	**54**	**96**
Corning	USA	—	938	—	—	—	99	192	—	—

Table 1.1 (Continued)

Company	Country	Sector			Rank					
		1998	1999/2000	2001/2002	2002[a]	2001[b]	2000[c]	1999[c]	1998[d]	1997
JDS Uniphase	USA	—	936	—	—	—	118	133	—	—
Juniper Networks	USA	—	932	—	—	—	131	326	—	—
Cable & Wireless[ff]	**UK**	**223**	**673**	**■**	**■**	**■**	**133**	**143**	**153**	**187**
Marconi[gg]	**UK**	**541**	**938**	**■**	**■**	**■**	**182**	**120**	**186**	**210**
VoiceStream Wireless[hh]	USA	—	678	—	—	—	183	482	—	—
Tellabs	USA	533	938	—	—	—	204	229	491	428
Ciena	USA	—	938	—	—	—	207	—	—	—
Matsushita Communication	Japan	—	938	—	—	—	218	108	—	—
Nextel Communications[ii]	USA	—	678	—	—	—	257	178	—	—
Seat-Pagine Gialle	Italy	—	547	—	—	—	273	451	—	—
Global Crossing[jj]	USA	—	673	—	—	—	278	155	—	—
Comverse Technology	USA	—	938	—	—	—	306	—	—	—
Palm[kk]	USA	—	932	—	—	—	336	—	—	—
Colt Telecom	UK	—	673	—	—	—	340	182	—	—
ADC Telecommunications	USA	—	938	—	—	—	364	—	—	—
Pacific Century Cyber[ll]	Hong Kong	—	974	—	—	—	370	261	—	—
Sonera[mm]	Finland	—	673	—	—	—	373	114	—	—
Level 3 Communications	USA	533	673	—	—	—	399	210	393	—
Energis	UK	—	673	—	—	—	448	376	—	—
Sycamore Networks	USA	—	938	—	—	—	486	243	—	—
Exodus Communications	USA	—	974	—	—	—	494	374	—	—
Excluded during 2000										
Mannesmann[nn]	**Germany**	**563**	**678**	**■**	**■**	**■**	**—**	**39**	**83**	**216**
Bell Atlantic[oo]	USA	223	673	—	—	—	—	52	33	29
GTE[pp]	USA	223	673	—	—	—	—	79	51	61
MediaOne[qq]	USA	474	543	—	—	—	—	113	127	282
C&W HKT[rr]	**Hong Kong**	**223**	**673**	**■**	**■**	**■**	**—**	**168**	**151**	**119**
US West[ss]	USA	223	673	—	—	—	—	172	130	197
Yahoo! Japan	Japan	—	974	—	—	—	—	236	—	—
Equant[tt]	France	—	673	—	—	—	—	248	—	—

Company	Country					
EchoStar Communications	USA	—	543	—	258	—
C&W Communications[uu]	**UK**	223	673	—	**264**	**382**
UPC Communications	Netherlands	—	543	—	320	—
TDC (Tele Danmark)	Denmark	223	673	—	335	357
Terra Networks[vv]	Spain	—	543	—	344	—
Canal Plus[ww]	**France**	543	—	—	**349**	—
3 Com[xx]	USA	533	938	—	354	349	208
@Home[yy]	**USA**	974	—	—	**399**	—
C&W Optus	Australia	673	—	—	426	—
OTE	Greece	673	—	—	440	314	359
NTL	USA	673	—	—	445	—
Telewest Communications	UK	673	—	—	456	—
Telekom Malaysia	Malaysia	673	—	—	474	—

Source: Financial Times (1999, 2000, 2001, 2002, 2003). See also www.ft.surveys@ft.com.

Notes:

[a]28 March 2003. [b]28 March 2002. [c]4 January 2001 and 2000 respectively. [d]28 September 1998. [e]Vodafone bought Mannesmann. [f]A merger between Bell Atlantic and GTE. [g]Prior to 2001, the entry was for America Online only. [h]Having acquired the former VoiceStream Wireless of the USA. [i]In the process of being merged with Olivetti. [j]The Hong Kong listed arm of China Mobile. [k]Divested from, but still largely owned by France Télécom. [l]Until 2001 listed as AT&T Liberty Media. [mm]Divested mmO2. [n]Divested from AT&T. [o]Incorporated Canal Plus and Seagram. [p]Formed when Telia acquired Sonera. [q]Acquired C&W Optus. [r]AT&T bought MediaOne and subsequently divested AT&T Wireless and AT&T Broadband. [s]KDDI was formed by a three-way merger between DDI, KDD and IDO in October 2000. [t]Divested from Sprint together with Sprint PCS. [u]Formerly Korea Telecom. [v]A subsidiary of Vodafone. [w]To be merged with Telecom Italia. [x]Divested from Teléfonos de México. [y]Partially divested but still largely owned by France Télécom. [z]Partially divested, but also still largely counted as part of Deutsche Telekom. [aa]Into Chapter 11 bankruptcy. [bb]Into Chapter 11 bankruptcy. [cc]The listed arm of China United in Hong Kong. [dd]Divested from Sprint together with Sprint FON. [ee]Taken over by AOL. [ff]C&W Optus acquired by SingTel. [gg]Subsequently restructured. [hh]Acquired by Deutsche Telekom - now T-Mobile USA. [ii]One of the few telcos to reappear in the rankings (in 2002). [jj]Into Chapter 11 bankruptcy. [kk]Divested from 3Com. [ll]Acquired C&W HKT. [mm]Taken over by Telia to form TeliaSonera. [nn]Bought by Vodafone. [oo]Merged with GTE. [pp]Merged with Bell Atlantic. [qq]Bought by AT&T. [rr]Bought by Pacific Century Cyberworks. [ss]Bought by Qwest Communications. [tt]Bought by France Télécom. [uu]Split up and sold. [vv]Now Terra Lycos. [ww]Canal Plus became a subsidiary of Vivendi Universal. [xx]Palm was divested from 3Com in 2000. [yy]Became part of Excite@Home.

Sector codes are as follows: The FT did not supply its own for 2001 and 2002, so they were assigned by the author to match the altered terminology used by the FT to describe the sectors: 1998: 223 = telephone companies; 474 = broadcasting media; 482 = computer software/services; 495 = retail – misc. & specialist; 533 = communications equipment; 541 = electrical equipment; 551 = electronics; 563 = machinery. 1999 and 2000: 240 = diversified industrials; 535 = home entertainment; 542 = broadcasting contractors; 543 = cable & satellite; 547 = publishing & printing; 673 = fixed-wire telecoms; 678 = wireless telecoms; 932 = computer hardware; 936 = semiconductors; 938 = telecoms equipment; 972 = computer services; 974 = Internet. 2001 and 2002: 100 = telecommunications services; 200 = information technology hardware; 300 = media & entertainment; 400 = software & computer service; 500 = diversified industrials.

caution is also in order because sectoral dominance of this kind is not a unique phenomenon, having been even more marked with respect to the railway and banking industries in earlier periods even if it took much longer to appear.

It is worth observing that only 37 of the 2002 entries appear in the top 250 compared to 67 companies in 1999. In other words, more than one in four of the most highly capitalized 250 companies in the world in 1999 were in some way associated with telecommunications, whereas in 2002 it was nearer one in eight. It is also notable that 23 companies are listed across all six years of the table, and a further eight are listed over the most recent five years. On the face of it, this represents only a modest rump of longer-term survivors, and raises a question mark over the prospects for the sector. Given that there is so much talk – but much less action – in relation to consolidation, it must be borne in mind that if this takes the form of M&A activity among the larger companies then the TMT presence among the FT500 will probably continue to decline, whereas M&A activity involving second-tier companies may create new entrants.

Another interesting aspect of Table 1.1 is what it tells us about the geographical dispersion of the major TMT companies. In 1999, 37 of these were based in the USA, and almost as many in 2000. However, of the 54 companies listed in 2002, only 16 were domiciled in the USA compared to 20 in Western Europe and 11 in the Far East. It is noteworthy that four of the six departures during 2002 were from the USA as well as 15 during 2001 and eight during 1999 – 27 in total. This can be compared with the zero, six and nine departures respectively by European companies – 15 in total but mostly at the beginning of the period. In other words, the TMT sector in the USA has borne the brunt of the attrition since the beginning of 2000 and this process must inevitably slow down given how few US-based companies are left in the list, not to mention the previous status of the departures which in 2002 were WorldCom, Qwest Communications – both in Chapter 11 bankruptcy – Lucent Technologies, once a top ten entry, and Sprint PCS, once worth more than its fixed-wire counterpart Sprint FON.

Effects upon market values

Table 1.2 is less comprehensive than Table 1.1 with a view to presenting a more concise picture while ensuring that the full range of experiences over the entire period is represented. The capital values on five specific dates corresponding to the end dates of the periods in Table 1.1 are given in sequence, starting with the most recent. These are followed by the four corresponding annual rates of change and the rate of change covering the entire period. The first point to note is the general increase in capital values during 1999 (A to B) when every single entry is positive in sign. The minimum for inclusion in 1998 was a capital value of $7.6 billion, whereas it was $11.3 billion in 1999, a rise of just under 50 per cent. However, this was not particularly notable as Yahoo! rose by 769 per cent and three-figure increases were fairly commonplace. Nevertheless, it is possible to make a distinction of sorts between the 'new economy' and 'old economy' elements in the table with the latter generally growing more slowly. As ever, there were some exceptions such as Deutsche Telekom and France Télécom, but these were state-owned incumbents with a gridlock on the local loop, and even they need to be considered in relation not merely to the growth of Internet companies but of equipment manufacturers. During 1999, for example, Qualcomm grew by an astonishing 3,276 per cent, while Nortel Networks grew by 537 per cent, Nokia by 345 per cent and Cisco Systems by 279 per cent. These huge increases in capitalization reflected such factors as the growth in mobile networks and the need to upgrade fixed networks to make them Internet-ready. In the case of Cisco, it also reflected the 18 significant takeovers set in hand in 1999 – to which it added a further 22 in 2000 before running out of steam in 2001.

Equity markets are by their very nature somewhat volatile, and Table 1.2 necessarily provides only a point-in-time snapshot. It must also be borne in mind that comparisons over a period of years should be treated with caution since between the dates specified a company may have altered the number of shares in issue, perhaps to finance a takeover bid, or demerged part of its activities. Nevertheless, there can be no doubting the overall picture depicted by the table. As can be seen, 11 companies listed in Table 1.2 lost over half their value during 2000 (B to C) – with the worst performers respectively Yahoo! and Lucent Technologies – while only a modest number rose in value, among whom a handful made good progress bearing in mind the general downward trend. More notably, there is not a single plus sign to be seen during the 15-month period to 28 March 2002 – the exact opposite of the situation during 1999 when there were no minus signs. Superficially, the figures do not appear to be all that bad, but that is largely a statistical illusion since a rise of 100 per cent is exactly compensated by a subsequent fall of only 50 per cent and the largest possible fall is 100 per cent. Furthermore, although there are a fair number of increases during the period (A to D), these are often the result of acquisitions (as in the cases of Cisco, SBC Communications and Vodafone). If 1998 is excluded, and the period (B to D) is examined, then every entry is negative during this 27-month period. Furthermore, the extent of some of the reductions is hard to comprehend: for example, Cisco Systems fell in value by $242 billion – yes, billion! – the mighty NTT DoCoMo by $228 billion, Lucent Technologies by $219 billion, NTT by $208 billion, Deutsche Telekom by $152 billion, WorldCom by $130 billion and Nortel Networks by $122 billion. In other words, a mere six TMT companies saw roughly one trillion dollars disappear from their joint market values.

Not surprisingly, this could not continue – at least not at this pace. Nevertheless, 30 of the entries for March 2002 to March 2003 (D to E) are negative (including WorldCom) and only five are positive. Among the latter, the

Table 1.2 Telecommunications and related companies' capital values, 31 December 1998–28 March 2003

Company	Capital values ($bn)					Change in value (%)				
	(E) 28/03/03	(D) 28/03/02	(C) 04/01/01	(B) 31/12/99	(A) 31/12/98	(D to E)	(C to E)	(B to C)	(A to B)	(A to E)
Vodafone Group[a]	**122.9**	**126.5**	**227.2**	**153.8**	**35.5**	**−3**	**−44**	**+48**	**+333**	**+346**
NTT DoCoMo[b]	101.1	137.8	175.4	366.2	—	−27	−21	−52	—	—
Cisco Systems	94.0	124.0	304.7	366.5	96.6	−24	−59	−17	+279	−3
Nokia	70.1	102.2	197.5	208.5	46.9	−31	−48	−5	+345	+51
SBC Communications[c]	67.7	125.5	174.8	166.3	81.5	−46	−28	+5	+104	−17
Comcast[f]	64.4	29.8	38.5	35.9	17.3	+116	−23	+7	+107	+272
Deutsche Telekom[d]	47.3	63.7	94.7	215.6	83.7	−26	−33	−56	+158	−43
Telefónica	47.2	53.7	75.5	81.1	36.7	−12	−29	−7	+121	+29
Telecom Italia[e]	**45.8**	**55.5**	**57.8**	**73.7**	**35.6**	**−17**	**−4**	**−22**	**+107**	**+29**
China Mobile (Hong Kong)	40.6	57.5	102.3	92.1	18.6	−29	−44	+11	+395	+118
Telecom Italia Mobile[e]	**35.9**	**41.6**	**64.7**	**73.8**	**38.0**	**−14**	**−36**	**−12**	**+94**	**−6**
NTT[b]	31.7	62.6	116.7	271.2	117.6	−49	−46	−57	+131	−73
AT&T/AT&T Wireless[f]	**31.4**	**55.6**	**79.0**	**162.2**	**102.5**	**−44**	**−30**	**−51**	**+58**	**−69**
Telstra	31.2	36.9	46.7	68.8	35.8	−15	−21	−32	+92	−13
Qualcomm	29.6	28.9	59.5	114.8	3.4	+2	−51	−48	+3276	+770
France Télécom[a]	24.1	35.5	96.7	134.8	58.1	−32	−63	−28	+132	−59
Teléfonos de Mexico	20.9	32.4	40.6	32.7	17.6	−35	−20	+24	+86	+19
BSkyB	19.7	22.5	31.0	27.7	14.5	−13	−27	+11	+91	+36
Motorola[g]	19.1	31.6	50.4	89.7	25.6	−40	−37	−44	+250	−25
Cox Communications	18.8	21.6	26.7	27.9	14.8	−13	−19	−4	+89	+27
BCE	18.0	14.3	23.0	58.2	17.8	+26	−38	−60	+227	+1
KPN	16.0	12.8	16.6	46.6	14.4	+25	−23	−64	+224	+11
Sprint FON/PCS[h]	14.9	24.1	43.2	96.7	31.0	−38	−46	−55	+212	−52

Yahoo!	14.6	11.0	16.7	110.3	12.7	+33	−34	−85	+769	+15
Alltel	13.9	17.3	21.2	26.0	12.9	−20	−18	−18	+102	+8
Singapore Telecom	13.7	15.4	23.6	33.1	25.0	−11	−35	−29	+32	−45
Ericsson	11.1	34.3	90.9	114.7	37.0	−68	−62	−21	+210	−70
SK Telecom	10.6	19.5	19.8	28.2	2.0	−46	−2	−28	+1310	+430
Alcatel	9.1	17.4	68.3	45.4	17.3	−48	−75	+50	+162	−47
Nortel Networks	8.2	14.2	113.4	136.4	21.4	−42	−87	−17	+537	−62
NTT Data	7.9	12.1	18.7	64.4	10.4	−35	−35	−71	+519	−24
Corning	7.2	7.2	51.3	30.3	6.8	0	−86	+69	+346	+6
Qwest Communication[i]	6.1	13.7	75.9	29.8	10.2	−55	−72	+54	+192	−40
Lucent Technologies[j]	5.9	16.2	52.3	235.0	91.0	−64	−69	−78	+158	−93.5
TDC (Tele Danmark)	5.1	7.0	10.0	16.0	10.5	−27	−30	−38	+52	−51
WorldCom	−	20.0	56.0	150.6	86.2	−	−64	−63	+75	−

Notes: [a]Vodafone bought AirTouch [offered $66.5 billion in January 1999] which at the end of 1999 was ranked 93 with a capital value of $32.7 billion. Mannesmann bought Orange [offered $34.2 billion in October 1999] which at the end of 1998 was ranked 332 with a capital value of $11.4 billion, but Vodafone's purchase of Mannesmann [offered $123 billion including Orange in October 1999], which at the end of 1999 was ranked 39 with a capital value of $116.6 billion, made it necessary to pass Orange on to France Télécom [offered $46.4 billion in May 2000]. A small minority stake has been sold in Orange which was worth $38.8 billion at the end of March 2003, considerably more than its parent! [b]NTT retains a 64 per cent stake in DoCoMo which is worth considerably more than the whole of NTT! [c]SBC Communications bought Ameritech [offered $62 billion in May 1998] which at the end of 1998 was ranked 55 with a capital value of $52.3 billion. [d]Deutsche Telekom bought One-2-One [offered $13.8 billion in August 1999] and VoiceStream Wireless valued at $28.8 billion at the end of 2000. It has floated a small minority stake in T-Online. [e]Telecom Italia retains just over one half of TIM. [f]AT&T bought Tele-Communications (TCI) [offered $48.5 billion in October 1998] which at the end of 1998 was ranked 177 with a capital value of $20.5 billion, and MediaOne [offered $58 billion in April 1999] which at the end of 1999 was ranked 113 with a capital value of $47.5 billion. In-between, it also paid $5.0 billion for the IBM Global Network. At the end of 2000, the partly demerged AT&T Wireless was worth $50.2 billion. Although AT&T Wireless is now independent, their market values are added together here for ease of comparison. AT&T Broadband was sold to Comcast during 2002. AT&T was worth $13.1 billion and AT&T Wireless was worth $18.3 billion at the end of March 2003. [g]Motorola bought General Instruments [offered $11.0 billion in September 1999] which at the end of 1999 was ranked 408 with a capital value of $13.9 billion. [h]Sprint has been split in two. At the end of 1999, Sprint PCS was worth $44.1 billion and Sprint FON was worth $52.6 billion; at the end of 2000, Sprint PCS was worth $22.3 billion and Sprint FON was worth $20.9 billion; at the end of March 2002, Sprint PCS was worth $9.7 billion and Sprint FON was worth $14.4 billion; at the end of March 2003, Sprint PCS was worth $4.2 billion and Sprint FON was worth $10.7 billion. [i]Qwest bought US West but has since subsided into Chapter 11 bankruptcy. [j]Lucent bought Ascend [offered $19 billion in January 1999] which at the end of 1998 was ranked 425 with a capital value of $9.0 billion.

unusual performance of Comcast essentially reflects the acquisition of AT&T Broadband. So, not much sign of the meltdown coming to a grinding halt, but a generally more positive picture than during the (longer) period (C to D). Taking the longer view, represented by the period (A to E) containing both a sharp upturn followed by an equally sharp downturn, the picture is predictably much more mixed. Not only is the number of positives much the same as of negatives, but there are substantial changes in both directions ranging from the 770 per cent increase at Qualcomm to the wipe-out at WorldCom. On the whole, equipment manufacturers had a bad time of it, but as ever there is the exception that proves the rule – in this case Nokia. It must feel strange at a company like Cisco Systems to note that after more than 50 acquisitions the company is worth no more than when it started its acquisition spree. However, it must be said that there has been a fairly sharp improvement in the fortunes of TMT companies since March 2003, suggesting that an end-year 2003 snapshot will prove to be much more positive even if the relative position of the TMT sector will have improved rather less because the stock market gains since March have pretty much been across the board.

Strategic issues

Consolidation

The above data show clearly that, at least in the developed world, the TMT sector increasingly rose to prominence as the dominant industrial sector during the period from mid-1997 to mid-2000. In a simple sense this reflected a faster growth in the capitalization of companies in this industry compared to others. Such a phenomenon can, however, have more than one possible origin and, in particular, reflect either purely internal growth, takeovers or both.

Until fairly recently, the prevailing doctrine was that joint ventures and alliances would provide the means to achieve the kind of one-stop shop demanded by multinationals. To this end, a number of global alliances were formed, all of which have come to grief in some respect or other. For example, the Global One alliance, involving European and US partners, recently collapsed amid acrimony, with the three partners going their separate ways.[2] In addition, the Unisource alliance of European telcos was broken up and its constituent parts sold off, simultaneously severing its transatlantic link with AT&T. Finally, the Concert alliance lost its US-based constituent MCI to a takeover by WorldCom, and, reformed as a joint venture between AT&T and BT, was itself later disbanded. Not surprisingly, financial market analysts have become very wary of joint ventures essentially created to widen geographic spread where there are no substantive cross-shareholdings involved, and they are unlikely to play any significant role for the foreseeable future.

So is independence a viable option? Organizations that choose to remain independent and retain their existing structure are necessarily reliant upon organic growth. Organic growth is, all other things being equal, a 'good thing' because it is relatively easy to manage compared to a joint venture, but it is not necessarily a sensible strategy for survival during a period of unprecedented change. The valuations placed upon companies that, for whatever reason, relied heavily upon organic growth during 1998 and 1999, grew relatively slowly by the standards of industry as a whole. Put crudely, the view taken by the financial markets during 1999 was that if an organization was not taking over some other part of the industry, or hiving off the exciting ('new economy') bits of its operation into separately listed subsidiaries, it was by definition a boring 'old economy' organization – although its share price would still tend to rise modestly simply because rises were the norm across the board in the main equity markets.

As the millennium drew to a close, experience dictated that simply becoming organically larger, when other companies in the industry were growing even more rapidly, was also a dangerous strategy because, eventually, no matter how large a company became, there was an even larger organization somewhere out there looking at any and every potential bid target. Furthermore, to gain market advantage – for example, either the ability to extend an existing footprint or to provide new services to customers – by organic growth was impractical when technical change was as fast as it was during this period because by the time the expertise in some existing technology had been developed in-house, it was no longer the technology of choice. Ultimately, it was much easier simply to buy a 'state-of-the-art' technology via a takeover bid.

But with valuations rising throughout the industry, how could such a strategy be afforded? Cash reserves could provide one possible approach or, more dangerously, borrowings from a variety of financial intermediaries. However, cash reserves are easily run down, and borrowings create an obligation to repay capital and interest. Far better, clearly, to use something that creates no such obligation – a company's own equity.

The model is crude but effective. A company offers to buy another company – which if this method is used does not necessarily have to be smaller than the bidder[3] – via an issuance of new equity. If the financial markets do not approve of the choice of target, the bidder's share price collapses and the target readily rejects the offer. It may be noted that it is commonly the practice nowadays to set upper and lower limits on the bidder's share price such that, if the price falls out of this 'collar', the target can legitimately claim that the offer has become unacceptable irrespective of its merits when originally launched. Interestingly, recent experience indicates that if the bidder is in any way under the control of government, principally because the latter retains a significant shareholding, its plans can expect to meet with little enthusiasm.[4] If, however, the financial markets approve of the logic of the bid, the bidder's share price may even rise despite the larger number of shares that will end up in issue.[5] They are much more likely to approve if the bidder has previously taken over other companies, integrated them successfully and shown a rising trend of earnings per share.[6]

The immediate effect on the bidder's share price admittedly reflects the markets' 'gut instinct' response to the proposed offer, and market sentiment may change over time. One way or another, however, the markets' response will affect the target's perception of whether to accept the offer. If the bidder's share price is not sufficiently resilient, it may struggle to get the bid accepted because shareholders in the target company want to trade their existing shares only for others that they expect to grow more quickly in value than their own. No matter how satisfied they are with the target's performance, that principle will carry the day provided governments do not interfere. Hence, for example, Vodafone was effectively challenged to justify why it believed that its share price would rise faster than that of Mannesmann even though the latter was deemed to be doing very well as an independent company. It met the challenge, ostensibly by persuading the markets that its strategy based exclusively on wireless was preferable to the fixed-mobile convergence strategy of Mannesmann. Subsequently, the markets changed their mind when Vodafone spent huge sums on 3G licences.

There is a further feature of that takeover that needs to be considered, namely the fact that institutionally held monies are increasingly invested in 'index tracker' funds. These funds hold a portfolio that reflects precisely a given share's importance in the relevant index. Thus, if Vodafone is worth, say, 10 per cent of the total value of the FTSE-100, index trackers must hold 10 per cent of their portfolios in that company's shares. As a result, once Vodafone was expected to succeed in buying Mannesmann, index trackers began to buy additional Vodafone shares to build up their holdings on the assumption that the price would rise once the bid was accepted and other tracking funds joined in. But this behaviour served to drive up Vodafone's share price, and hence increased the value of the bid which offered a stated number of Vodafone shares per Mannesmann share, and this in turn made it more certain that the bid would be accepted.[7]

When the mood in the equity markets is very optimistic, as throughout much of 1998 and 1999, the all-paper bid comes into its own and almost every company becomes a potential target – which in turn helps to buoy up valuations throughout the industry. And if a company is not a potential target, then it is probably viewed as a potential bidder – which helps to buoy up valuations. Although it is difficult to come up with a specific number because the relevant industry bounds grow fuzzy at the edges, there were at least 46 relevant takeover bids during 1999 where the target was valued at over $2 billion, many of which are listed in Table 1.3. By no means all of these were all-paper bids, and not all were successful, but the lesson had clearly been learned since of the 18 bids worth over $2 billion recorded during the first three months of 2000 only four, all quite small, were financed with cash.

Table 1.3 Illustrative recent major[+] mergers[++] and acquisitions

Bidder	Target	Date	Value ($billion)
US West	Continental Cablevison	February 1996	10.8
Bell Atlantic	Nynex	April 1996	25.6*[ka]
Southwestern Bell	Pacific Telesis	April 1996	16.5*[kb]
WorldCom	**MFS**	**August 1996**	12.5
AirTouch	**US West cellular**	**April 1997**	2.3+2.3 debt
WorldCom	**MCI**	**September 1997**	37.0*
WorldCom	**Brooks Fiber Properties**	**October 1997**	2.4
AT&T	**Teleport**	**January 1998**	11.3
Qwest	LCI International	January 1998	4.4*
SBC	Southern New England	March 1998	4.4
Alltel	360 Communications	March 1998	4.0
SBC	Ameritech	May 1998	62.0*
Nortel	Bay Networks	June 1998	8.0*
Bell Atlantic	GTE	July 1998	53.0*+14.0 debt
AT&T	**TCI**	**October 1998**	37.5*+11.0 debt
America Online	Netscape	November 1998	4.2*
AT&T	IBM Global Network	December 1998	5.0
Vodafone	AirTouch	January 1999	66.5*
Lucent	Ascend	January 1999	19.0*
Yahoo!	Geocities	January 1999	4.7
@Home	**Excite**	**January 1999**	6.7*
Uniphase	JDS Fitel	January 1999	6.1[++]
Telenor	Telia	January 1999	n/a*[c]
Olivetti	**Telecom Italia**	**February 1999**	58.5[d]
Global Crossing	Frontier	March 1999	11.2*
Comcast	MediaOne	March 1999	53.0*+7.0 debt[e]
Yahoo!	Broadcast.com	April 1999	5.7*
GTE	Ameritech cellular	April 1999	3.3
Deutsche Telekom	**Telecom Italia**	**April 1999**	60.7*[f]
AT&T	**MediaOne**	**April 1999**	58.0
Global Crossing	US West	May 1999	31.3*[g]
Qwest	US West	June 1999	41.3*+10.0 debt [h]
Qwest	Frontier	June 1999	13.6+1.4 debt[h]
NTL	**CWC Consumer**	**July 1999**	9.6 + 3.0 debt
CMGI	AltaVista	July 1999	2.3[i]
Cisco Systems	Cerent	August 1999	6 .9*
Deutsche Telekom	One-2-One	August 1999	11.0+2.8 debt
Viacom	CBS	September 1999	36.0
Motorola	General Instruments	September 1999	11.0*
Earthlink	Mindspring	September 1999	3.3[j]
MCI WorldCom	**Sprint**	**October 1999**	115.0*+14.0 debt[k]
BellSouth	Sprint	October 1999	n.a[l]
Mannesmann	**Orange**	**October 1999**	31.3+3.1 debt
Vodafone AirTouch	**Mannesmann**	**October 1999**	123.0*[m]
Comcast	Lenfest	November 1999	5.1*+1.5 debt
NTL	**Cablecom**	**December 1999**	3.6[n]
UPC	Cablecom	December 1999	3.5[n]
Cisco Systems	Pirelli Optical Systems	December 1999	2.2*
Telewest	**Flextech**	**December 1999**	3.1*
DDI	KDD/IDO	December 1999	n/a[o]

Table 1.3 (Continued)

Bidder	Target	Date	Value ($billion)
America Online	**Time Warner**	**January 2000**	160.0*
BT	**Esat Telecom**	**January 2000**	2.4
JDS Uniphase	E-Tek Dynamics	January 2000	15.0*
Lucent	Ortel	February 2000	3.0*
BCE	Teleglobe	February 2000	6.6*p
SBC	Sterling Commerce	February 2000	3.9
Alcatel	Newbridge Networks	February 2000	7.1*
Global Crossing	IPC Info. Systems/Ixnet	February 2000	3.8*
VeriSign	Network Solutions	March 2000	21.0*
Telefónica	Endemol	March 2000	5.6*
Cisco Systems	ArrowPoint Comm	May 2000	5.7*
Terra Networks	Lycos	May 2000	12.5*
NTT Communications	Verio	May 2000	4.9q
France Télécom	**Orange**	**May 2000**	46.4r
Lucent	Chromatis Networks	May 2000	4.5*
Vivendi	**Seagram**	**June 2000**	34.0*+4.0 debt
Tele Danmark	NetCom ASA	June 2000	1.7s
Telia	NetCom ASA	June 2000	2.6s
Sycamore Networks	Sirocco	June 2000	2.9*
Deutsche Telekom	VoiceStream Wireless	July 2000	50.7*+4.2 debt
JDS Uniphase	SDL	July 2000	41.0*
Lucent	SEC	July 2000	3.1*t
Nortel Networks	Alteon WebSystems	July 2000	7.2*
Deutsche Telekom	Powertel	August 2000	5.8*+1.2 debtu
Global Crossing	Digex	September 2000	5.3
Exodus Comm's	Digex	September 2000	8.0*
WorldCom	**Intermedia**	**September 2000**	3.0*+3.0 debtv
Tiscali	World Online	September 2000	5.2*
Wind	Infostrada	September 2000	9.9
Corning	Pirelli optical interests	September 2000	3.6w
Enel	Infostrada	October 2000	9.6+0.9 debt
France Télécom	Equant	November 2000	3.0*x
Wanadoo	Freeserve	December 2000	2.3*
Ciena	Cyras	December 2000	2.4*+0.2 debt
Vodafone Group	**Eircell**	**December 2000**	4.1*+0.2 debt
Singapore Telecom	**C&W Optus**	**March 2001**	9.0
Seat-Pagine Gialle	Eniro	April 2001	2.7*
Apax/Hicks Muse	**Yell**	**May 2001**	2.1*
Alcatel	Lucent	May 2001	23.0*y
e-Island	Eircom	June 2001	2.6z
Valentia	Eircom	June 2001	2.4z
Comcast	**AT&T Broadband**	**July 2001**	44.5*+13.5 debt
Earth Lease	**BT local loop**	**July 2001**	11.6aa
Furukawa Electric	Lucent fibre-optic	July 2001	2.8bb
Alltel	CenturyTel	July 2001	5.9*+3.1 debt
EchoStar	Hughes	August 2001	30.4*+1.9 debt
WestLB	**BT fixed-wire**	**August 2001**	25.6
AT&T	**TeleCorp**	**October 2001**	2.3*+2.3 debtcc
Telia	Sonera	March 2002	6.5*

Table 1.3 (Continued)

Bidder	Target	Date	Value ($billion)
Carlyle/Welsh Carson	QwestDex Yellow Pages	August 2002	7.1
Cisco Systems	Andiamo	August 2002	2.5[dd]
RH Donnelley	Sprint Yellow Pages	September 2002	2.2
Vodafone	**Cégétel**	**October 2002**	12.9[ee]
Comcast	Walt Disney Corp.	February 2004	49.3*+11.9 debt
Cingular Wireless	**AT&T Wireless**	**February 2004**	41.0
Vodafone	**AT&T Wireless**	**February 2004**	38.0*
KPN	**mmO$_2$**	**February 2004**	14.4*+0.5 debt

Notes: Not all bids have yet received regulatory approval. [+]Valued at over $2 billion. [++]Deals involving US companies frequently took place under 'pooling-of-interests' accounting regulations whereby, if they wished, companies could simply 'merge' their assets and earnings. The 'purchase' method, used elsewhere – and, as in the case of Vodafone's acquisition of AirTouch, occasionally chosen voluntarily in the USA – required one company to 'take over' the other. Anything it paid above the target's net asset value was then deemed to be 'goodwill' and had to be recorded on its balance sheet and written off against earnings in future years, usually without tax offsets. Pooling-of-interests were structured as all-paper offers and were usually tax-free to investors. The US Financial Accounting Standards Board announced in April 1999 that these arrangements were to be terminated before the end of 2000. In practice, it has always been a rarity to find a 'merger' where both parties ended up with exactly half of the combined company. The table lists as the bidder the company that ended up with the majority stake in the combined company. The only known exception was Uniphase and JDS Fitel in January 1999 which became equal partners in JDS Uniphase. *All, or almost all, by way of a stock offer, the value of which varies with the bidder's share price. [a]Called Bell Atlantic. [b]Called SBC Communications. [c]Between two state-owned companies (in Norway and Sweden), valuation of which had to await a partial flotation of the merged entity. However, the merger plans collapsed in acrimony in mid-December 1999. [d]Olivetti initially gained acceptances for just over 50% of the shares bid for at a cost of roughly $33 billion. [e]Comcast withdrew its bid on 5 May 1999, upon payment of a $1.5bn termination fee, in order to leave the way open for the competing offer by AT&T. [f]Dependent upon the Deutsche Telekom share price. The bid was unsuccessful. [g]See counter-bid by Qwest. Global Crossing withdrew its bid on 18 July 1999. [h]Assuming both companies were acquired. The offers were respectively worth $1.1 billion and $0.4 billion less if only the one company was acquired, as proved to be the case when Qwest withdrew its bid for Frontier on 18 July 1999. In March 2000, Deutsche Telekom intervened with an unofficial approach to take over Qwest, with or without US West, but the latter vetoed the deal before it was made public. [i]For an 83 per cent stake. In February 2003, CMGI sold AltaVista to Overture for $60 million in cash plus $80 million in stock. [j]The total value of the merger companies' assets accounted for as a pooling of interests. [k]In June 2000, the bid was vetoed by both the European Commission and the US Department of Justice. [l]The value of the bid was not declared, but was estimated at roughly 5 per cent below that of MCI. [m]Including Orange. [n]The NTL offer was accepted. [o]IDO is not a listed company. [p]BCE already held a 23% stake in the target. [q]For the 90% of the shares not previously owned. [r]Consisting of $20.7 bn in cash, $16.9 bn in France Télécom shares, $2.7 bn of debt and $6.1 bn of future liabilities. [s]Tele Danmark already held a 40% stake. The valuation is for the entire company. In August 2000 Telia acquired Tele Danmark's stake and became sole owner of NetCom. [t]NetCom already owned 17.8% of SEC. [u]If Deutsche Telekom's existing offer for VoiceStream Wireless had broken down, the offer for Powertel would have reverted to VoiceStream, again on an all-paper basis. [v]Intermedia owned 54% of Digex but controlled 97% of the votes. [w]For a 90% stake. The remaining 10% were to be acquired from Cisco in return for shares in Corning. [x]For a 54.3% stake yielding full control of the network. [y]Excluding Lucent's 58% stake in Agere Systems. [z]For the non-mobile assets excluding Eircell. [aa]EarthLease is a consortium led by US-based Babcock & Brown and Chancery Lane Capital together with three banks. [bb]This includes $225 million paid by Corning for Lucent's stake in two Chinese joint ventures. [cc]For the 77% of the shares not already owned. [dd]The exact figure will be determined when the deal closes in early 2004. Cisco already owns convertible debt equivalent to 44% of Andiamo. [ee]For details see Vivendi Universal, Vodafone case studies.

Since April 2000, the equity markets have been highly volatile and frequently moving in a downwards direction. Not surprisingly, therefore, the stream of takeovers has lost momentum. As those where negotiations opened months earlier came to fruition, there was a surge in takeover activity during the third quarter of 2000, but the number of bids subsequently collapsed during the fourth quarter and takeover activity effectively ground to a halt during the first half of 2001. It has yet to recover.

Indebtedness

The main driving force in the telecoms industry is currently the not inconsequential matter of indebtedness. Debts can pile up over time for a variety of reasons – most obviously as a result of trading losses but also, for example, as a consequence of downsizing costs or the use of cash to pay for acquisitions in whole or in part. At an individual enterprise level some of the figures have become frighteningly large, but the key issue must obviously be whether they can be financed, whether they can be reduced within a reasonable time frame and whether there is a real threat of bankruptcy. Unlike BT, neither France Télécom nor Deutsche Telekom, for example, have yet come up with a wholly credible plan for debt reduction, but both retain substantial state shareholdings so there is little concern about bankruptcy as such – the government has even been heard to discuss openly the possibility of renationalizing France Télécom if all else fails. One interesting side effect of high levels of debt is that operators have to tread much more carefully than in the past in relation to taking majority stakes which require the acquired companies' debts to be consolidated by the acquirer. A good example was the agonizing round of negotiations between France Télécom and MobilCom which was resolved by the increasingly popular expedient of 'parking' shares with financial intermediaries for possible repurchase, and hence consolidation, at a later date when overall indebtedness has been reduced.

Initial public offers

A second indicator is the possibility of a resurgence in initial public offer (IPO) activity in the TMT sector. Such evidence as exists can only be construed as negative. Not only has the level of activity been low, but it has taken place entirely outside Europe and the USA and even the apparent successes such as Telkom in South Africa disguise the fact that the IPO was delayed for a year and the price was reduced at the last minute. Of course, the war in Iraq hardly provided a positive environment in the Spring of 2003, but there was very little activity in the pipeline for the rest of the year.

Cleansing of balance sheets

A third factor relates to the cleaning up of balance sheets. During the peak period of M&A activity, enormous premiums were paid to acquire TMT assets which subsequently fell heavily in value. The question as to whether the so-called 'goodwill' involved needs to be written-off on purchasers' balance sheets is very much a function of accounting rules which differ between jurisdictions, although these have generally been tightened up across the board in recent times. What is apposite is that the widespread writing-off of over-valued assets is usually a prelude to a 'new start' – a recognition that mistakes have been made and that they will not be repeated. In practice, the cleansing of balance sheets has now largely taken place and on a truly gargantuan scale in some instances, as illustrated in Table 1.4. Unfortunately, this is only the first step: Moving forward is very difficult if the companies remain unprofitable since, for example, any future acquisitions with a view to consolidation will have largely to be financed with cash rather than the distressed equity of prospective purchasers, and unprofitable companies do not generate sufficient free cash flow. In any event, shareholders remain very nervous about M&A activity – a case of several times bitten, continuing to be shy. These factors clearly provide the main explanation for the slow progress towards consolidation.

Despite the recent write downs, there is a surprising amount of goodwill left on TMT balance sheets, as shown in Table 1.5. It is possible to justify

Table 1.4 Illustrative major write-downs

Company	Date	Amount ($mn)	In respect mainly of
WorldCom	03/03	79,800	Goodwill, property
AOL Time Warner	04/02	54,000	New accounting rules
JDS Uniphase	03/02	50,100	Various acquisitions
AOL Time Warner	01/03	45,500	AOL/cable/films
Qwest Communications	10/02	34,800	Goodwill/networks
Vivendi Universal	03/03	25,000	Seagram/Canal+
Deutsche Telekom	03/03	21,700	VoiceStream Wireless/3G
France Télécom	03/03	19,800	Mobilcom/Equant/NTL
Telefónica	02/03	17,600	3G/Terra Lycos/Argentina
Vivendi Universal	03/02	14,500	Seagram/Canal Plus
DoCoMo	03/02	11,200	E-Plus and others
France Télécom	05/02	10,100	MobilCom, NTL etc
KPN	08/02	9,000	3G/E-Plus
Vodafone	03/02	8,700	Various acquisitions
Vodafone	11/02	7,160	Various acquisitions

Table 1.5 Goodwill on balance sheet, March 2003 ($ million)

Company	$ million
Vodafone	182,000
AOL Time Warner	36,040
Deutsche Telekom	30,730
France Télécom	29,790
Vivendi Universal	21,990

this. Vodafone argues that its prospects have not been materially affected by the events of the past year and hence that there is no need to revalue its assets: Analysts are less than convinced. At the end of the day, the issue boils down to the state of the stock markets. If the Dow Jones and FTSE-100 rise sharply then it will be possible to argue that assets on the balance sheet are now under-valued rather than the opposite, but if these indices either fall further or move sideways then further write downs will become necessary.

Bankruptcy

A final issue relates to bankruptcy. One of the pre-conditions for a new start is the clearing away of dead wood, leaving room for the healthy survivors to grow. The period to March 2002 witnessed a sharp upsurge in the number of TMT bankruptcies, and during the subsequent year the reality was that the tide of bankruptcy continued to flow towards the shore with little sign of ebbing. The situation does now seem to be easing, and the worst is almost certainly over. However, the downside is that under the provisions of Chapter 11 of the US bankruptcy code, many of the companies entering Chapter 11 subsequently emerge after a debt-for-equity swap with their debts largely written off and hence are in a position to put competitive pressure on those companies that had previously avoided bankruptcy. Whatever its virtues, Chapter 11 unquestionably serves to hold back the process of restructuring, and the re-emergence of the likes of WorldCom in its new guise as MCI will continue to destabilize the sector until well into 2004. The list of major bankruptcies, almost all Chapter 11, includes Teligent (May 2001); PSINet (June 2001); 360networks (June 2001); Covad Communications (August 2001); Excite@Home (September 2001); Global Crossing (January 2002); McLeod USA (January 2002); Metromedia Fiber Networks (March 2002); Flag Telecom (April 2002); Williams Communications (April 2002); Teleglobe (May 2002); KPNQwest (May 2002); NTL (May 2002); Adelphia Communications (June 2002); Versatel (June 2002); WorldCom (July 2002); AT&T Canada (October 2002); UPC (January 2003); AT&T Latin America (April 2003); and Leap Wireless (April 2003)

Conclusions

In general, the precipitous decline in the affairs of TMT companies, which was so evident prior to mid-2002, has clearly slowed down, but this has been as much a matter of the mathematics involved as of a sea change in the fortunes of the companies involved. Individual companies have shown considerable resilience and are making good progress – Nextel Communications is an obvious case in point and Nokia and Samsung have done relatively well among the equipment manufacturers – but most remain under considerable pressure to clean up their balance sheets, eliminate debt, improve free cash flow and start paying proper dividends again. While this remains true, it will be more a case of marking time than going forward. It remains hard to raise funds for any purposes, let alone M&A activity, and hence for the time being there is likely to be more shedding of assets by the likes of Vivendi Universal than consolidation. It remains the case, however, that everyone believes that consolidation is a pre-condition for real progress to be made. Time after time the mantra is repeated – six mobile operators in the USA is too many; there are too many 3G licensees in Europe; and so forth – but reciting mantras serves little purpose unless funds are available and shareholders are in a more forgiving frame of mind.

Chapter 2

Strategic models

A tour of the literature

Introduction

The aim of this chapter is to introduce readers to a set of theoretical models that are subsequently to be used to analyse the ten cases that follow. As it is assumed that the reader is already familiar with many of these models, given the probability that the book is being used in conjunction with a course involving the teaching of strategic concepts, it is perhaps more appropriate to say that the aim of this chapter is to re-familiarize the reader with a series of models capable of shedding light on strategies within the technology, media and telecommunications sector. As a result we provide only a relatively brief summary of the models in the following sections, albeit sufficient for one unfamiliar with the textbooks to use the models to analyse the cases.

The key factor determining the choice of theoretical models included in this chapter is their ability to help us understand change within the sector. One consequence of this is that the list is not comprehensive; another is that the reader may disagree with the choices that we have made. On the one hand, the reader can find more comprehensive and detailed lists of strategic management models, or models for understanding change, in one of the plethora of dedicated textbooks that are available. Burnes (2000), Finlay (2000) and Johnson and Scholes (2002) are but three of the many textbooks that are available in this field. On the other hand, the choice has been shaped by our desire to illustrate how these models can be applied to the detailed case studies that follow. Thus, the ability of the models to highlight different dimensions of the strategies enacted in the TMT sector was a key factor determining whether or not they should be included in the chapter.

The first part of the chapter concentrates on the more general models. These are well known and common to strategy textbooks and include SWOT analysis and Porter's Five Forces. In the second part of the chapter, the emphasis is on models that have been applied in the literature to the TMT sector. One such model is the 'flagship firm' model while another is the 'strategic states model'.

SWOT analysis

Burnes (2000, p. 200) summarizes SWOT – Strengths, Weaknesses, Opportunities and Threats – analysis as follows: an assessment of the internal strengths and weaknesses of the organization in the light of the opportunities and threats posed by the environment in which it operates. This summary is illustrative as it draws attention to the two sides of a SWOT analysis. On one side there is the assessment of the internal resources that the company possesses, while on the other side there is the environment in which the company operates. These interact to fashion the company's strengths and weaknesses on the one hand and its opportunities and threats on the other.

What is involved in a SWOT analysis? A SWOT analysis will often begin with the management of the company identifying who their main competitors are, as this will ease their task of identifying the company's strengths and weakness as well as the opportunities and threats that it faces. It is not a straightforward task to identify who these competitors are. Competitors can be found in the same line of business as well as in those that are related through, for example, technological convergence or the development of substitutable products.

Once competitors have been identified, the next task is to identify what the company's strengths are. This can be done through asking a series of questions – for example: What advantages does the company possess? What does it do well? What differentiates it from the competitors? Here a company may identify its strengths as being its brand, cost efficiency or possession of unique content. Regardless of the strengths that are identified, an essential component of the analysis is that these are realistically identified.

The next step is for the process to be repeated for the other three components, with the analysis normally being presented in the form of a grid (as shown below in Figure 2.1). In each case, a series of questions are used to identify the company's weaknesses, opportunities and threats. Weaknesses will range from those activities that the company presently does not perform at all to those that it performs badly or unsatisfactorily.

Both opportunities and threats relate to the environment in which the company finds itself, and sometimes it is hard for the company to determine

Strengths ●	Weaknesses ●
Opportunities ●	Threats ●

Figure 2.1 Pro-forma for a SWOT analysis.

categorically what is an opportunity and what is a threat. Indeed some environmental developments are double-edged: for a mobile operator the emergence of new and popular forms of content represents an opportunity as it opens up a new and potentially lucrative source of revenue. However, the emergence of such content is also a threat in that it may be unique to a competitor so there is no access to it or be subject to strong competitive forces with one company dominating the market.

Two aspects of the external environment are particularly important for companies in the TMT sector. The first is the pace and nature of technological developments. The development of new technologies affects cost structures within the sector as well as encourages product substitution. Technological advances can also reduce the barriers that companies face when wishing to enter the market. However, the increasingly costly nature of technological development may also discourage companies from entering the market.

The second aspect of the environment that companies must consider when identifying the opportunities and threats that they face is the nature of regulation and, particularly within the telecommunications industry, the degree to which markets have been liberalized. Regulation can significantly shape how competitive a market is, and as a consequence shape the opportunities and threats that a company may encounter. Regulatory authorities are wary of vertical integration as it allows products to be bundled and cross subsidization to occur. If the regulatory authorities actively seek to forbid vertical integration and the abuses of market power that result, this will create opportunities in the market. If, on the other hand, they are not as zealous as they could be, the presence of vertical integration will be more threat than opportunity.

The presence of bottleneck assets such as distribution channels or the 'last mile' of the telecommunications network in a market also tends to attract the attention of regulatory bodies. Those companies that control such assets can stifle competition either by not allowing others access to them or, even if they do allow access, by charging excessively high prices so as effectively to force their competitors out of the market. As regulators have progressively forced the owners of bottleneck assets to allow others to access them, this has created opportunities in the market that can be exploited if companies wish to do so. Conversely, the attention that ownership of bottleneck assets brings from regulators is also a threat to the company owning the asset.

While the basic rubric of a SWOT analysis can be applied in virtually all circumstances, Finlay (2000) makes a useful distinction between a SWOT done for the short term and one done for the longer term. Undertaking a SWOT analysis for the longer term involves a change in emphasis: the analysis is more strategic in character. The company will seek to identify those key products, processes and resources that will underpin its strategy over the longer term. The steps inherent to both the short-term and long-term SWOT analyses are shown below in Table 2.1.

Table 2.1 Steps in short- and long-term SWOT analysis

Step	Action
Short-term	
1	Identify the present competitors
2	Identify the present critical offer features
3	Identify the present significant operating factors
4	Identify the present strategic resources
5	Identify the present issues and divide them into opportunities and threats
Long-term	
1	Identify the present situation
2	Identify the future critical offer features
3	Identify the future strategic resources requirement
4	Determine where the organisation's strengths and weakness lie in respect to the future strategic resources requirement
5	Divide the issues into opportunities and threats

Source: Finlay (2000) p. 335.

It should be borne in mind that conducting a SWOT analysis is easier to do if the time horizon involved is relatively short. Quite simply, there will be fewer environmental changes – technological advances, the emergence of new competitors, regulatory advances etc. – to take into account when the analysis is being performed. Moreover, it is also easier to identify and then evaluate these changes in the short term. As the time frame extends, greater uncertainty is introduced into the analysis, and this in turn means that the analysis is less reliable.

By way of a summary we can say that a SWOT analysis provides a model for understanding the relationship between a company's internal resources and its external environment.

Growth share matrix

Companies rarely operate in a single market. More typically, companies operate in several markets that collectively form a portfolio of businesses. The role of management is to actively manage this portfolio of businesses, identifying the businesses in which the company should be active and where in the portfolio to invest resources (capital). However, this is by no means a straightforward task.

The growth share matrix provides management with a framework to assist them in this task. This framework is comprised of a two by two matrix. The vertical axis is the growth rate of the market in which the business unit operates, while the horizontal axis is derived from the relative competitiveness of the business unit in this market. Relative competitiveness is usually expressed in terms of market share. By dividing the two axes into 'high' and 'low', four cells are formed as shown in Figure 2.2:

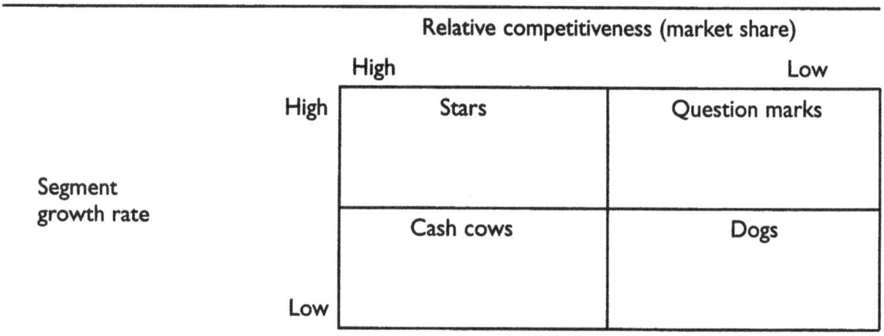

	Relative competitiveness (market share)	
	High	Low
High	Stars	Question marks
Low	Cash cows	Dogs

Figure 2.2 Growth share matrix.

- *Star* businesses have a high market share in a market where the growth rate is also high.
- *Cash cows* have a high market share in a market where the growth rate is low.
- *Question mark* businesses have a low market share in a high growth market.
- *Dogs* command a low market share in a low growth market.

It is self evident that businesses within each of these four categories will differ from one another. 'Cash cow' businesses generate capital that can be invested elsewhere within the company, enabling, for example, other businesses with a brighter future to be supported while they grow. Businesses classed as 'stars' are considered to have a bright future ahead of them and will benefit from additional investment by the company. Although 'star' businesses may receive capital generated elsewhere in the company, this should not be interpreted as indicating that they are incapable of generating capital in their own right but rather as indicating that the company's management believe that only through additional capital will the business be able to reach its full potential.

'Question mark' businesses, as their very name suggests, are more problematic for management to deal with. If the business is to be transformed into a star, substantial investment may be required, and it is the job of the company's management to decide, first, whether this is possible, and, second, whether the return from the necessary investment would justify such an action. If it does not, then either the business can be left as it is or sold off.

The label appended to the fourth and final type of business – 'dogs' – is also very evocative. Those businesses identified as being 'dogs' are unattractive as they have a low market share in a low growth market. These conspire to ensure that their future potential is limited. Consequently, the company should either sell or close any businesses that fall into this category.

What advantages accrue to management from using the matrix? One advantage is that the growth share matrix enables management to build a picture of how well their businesses are performing. A second advantage is that it questions the shape or form that the portfolio of businesses within a company should take. Businesses classed as 'dogs' will be divested, and those considered to be 'cash cows' allowed to decline gently as the cash that they generate is used to support star businesses within the company. Question mark businesses may either be invested in or sold.

Although the matrix is a relatively simple tool for management to use, it should be used with circumspection. Both Johnson and Scholes (2002) and McKiernan (1992) note that the matrix should be used with a certain degree of caution. The task of discerning whether growth rates and market shares are 'high' or 'low' is not straightforward; the resulting dichotomous classification may not accurately reflect the realities of the market. The use of the matrix may also result in companies focusing on larger businesses at the expense of smaller but potentially significant competitive potential or assuming that the growth rates of markets are either high or low when growth rates may actually form a continuum from low to high.

The unit of analysis within the matrix is the business unit, but this assumes first that the business unit can be defined and second that the products within this unit are homogenous in their growth rates and market share. However, in network industries identifying the business unit may be problematic. Not only is it common for several products to be distributed over the same infrastructure, but these products are also frequently bundled together into service packages. It is important to compare like with like.

The language of the matrix may also mislead users and encourage flawed strategies to be adopted. The emotive language of the matrix suggests that 'stars' are to be rewarded and 'dogs' avoided or closed. However, businesses classed as 'dogs' may play an important role in attracting or retaining customers even though they contribute little direct growth to the company. This is likely to be particularly true in industries where companies compete in a range of markets that are complementary to one another. Thus, the classification of business units that the matrix encourages merely offers management a starting point for their strategic thinking and should not be viewed as the end point of strategy determination within the company.

Scenario planning

Scenario planning is a way of conceptualizing the future. More accurately, scenario planning enables companies to conceptualize the future, understand how this future may arise and develop appropriate strategies that will allow them to remain competitive. Scenario planning is particularly useful in those industries with significant environmental uncertainty due, for example, to the rapid pace of technological change or the complexity and instability of relationships between actors in the industry.

Johnson and Scholes (2002, p. 107) define a scenario as 'a detailed and plausible view of how the business environment of an organization might develop in the future based on groupings of key environmental influences and drivers of change about which there is a high level of uncertainty'. This definition is a useful starting place as it draws our attention to several important issues within scenario planning. The first of these is that the scenario must be plausible: in other words, it must be realistic. For example, for a company scenario planning in the TMT sector it would unrealistic to assume that technologies within the media or mobile telecommunication industries would remain constant over the next 15 years or so. A more realistic assumption would be to say that technologies in these industries will at best remain constant over the course of the next two or three years.

Second, the company needs to be able not only to identify the environmental influences and drivers of change but also to identify which of these are critical and which have the greatest degree of uncertainty associated with them. In practice, this is quite a challenge. It is quite conceivable that a company may swiftly identify a plethora of environmental influences and drivers of change only to see the process grind to a halt when it comes to identifying those which are critical. Those constructing the list may not be able to reach agreement amongst themselves as to what is, or what is not, a critical environmental influence or driver of change.

If this disagreement is resolved by discussion amongst those constructing the list, then what is likely to emerge is a shared and more robust understanding of what are the critical environmental influences and drivers of change. If, on the other hand, the deadlock is resolved through a compromise then inevitably not everyone will be pleased. Moreover, the resulting list of influences and drivers may be longer and less robust than would otherwise be the case.

Once a list of critical influences and drivers of changes has been identified, these are then combined into a series of scenarios. This then raises the issue of how many scenarios should be developed. If, for example, just two scenarios are developed it is invariably the case that one will be positive (optimistic) and one negative (pessimistic) in character. If a third scenario is developed this will inevitably fall somewhere in-between these two extremes and, according to Finlay (2000, p. 267), unless great care is taken the focus will tend to fall on this scenario. Hence, four scenarios are normally developed. However, irrespective of the number of scenarios developed, the critical influences and drivers must be combined together plausibly so that different views of the future are described. It is in relation to these that the management of the company should develop appropriate strategies to remain competitive.

Figure 2.3 provides an example of four scenarios developed by a mobile operator. After much discussion, the management of the company decided that the key influences and drivers of change with the greatest degree of uncertainty associated with them are subscriber and ARPU (average revenue

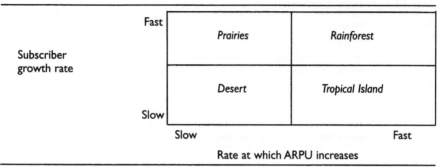

Figure 2.3 Subscriber vs. ARPU growth rate scenarios.

per user) growth rates. The ability of the company to manage its growth in these two areas will be the critical determinants of the success or otherwise of the company. Four scenarios were developed from these two variables, and each appropriately named as follows: Rainforest, Desert, Prairies and Tropical Island.

Within each of these scenarios the market will vary quite considerably. In the most optimistic of the four scenarios, Rainforest, both the number of subscribers and ARPU will increase fairly rapidly, while in the Desert scenario they will both grow slowly, if at all (negative outcomes are possible). In the Prairies scenario, the subscriber growth rate will be fast but the ARPU growth rate will be slow while in the final scenario, Tropical Island, the ARPU growth rate is fast but the number of subscribers added will only slowly increase. Given that the market differs in each of these four scenarios, the strategies developed by the company will also differ. The slow growth in subscriber numbers of the Prairie scenario will lead the company to focus on cost control strategies, whilst the Tropical Island scenario could encourage the company either to develop new packages that broaden its subscriber base or to develop new services so that even more revenue is extracted from each subscriber.

Adopting such an approach to the development of scenarios normally leads to their construction from the bottom up. The steps in an alternative approach – top down – are illustrated below in Table 2.2. A theme is given to each of the scenarios that effectively summaries the end-state. End-state is the term used by Finlay (2000) to refer to the situation after the chosen time frame has run its course. Critical environmental factors are then identified, and after setting the time frame and taking into account those variables whose variation can be predicted, the number of scenarios is reviewed to see if it remains appropriate or not.

Regardless of which approach is adopted, once the scenarios have been developed the next step for the management of a company is to develop appropriate strategies so that, if any one of these alternative futures does occur, the company will not be placed at a competitive disadvantage. In

Table 2.2 Eight steps to end-states

Step	Action
I	Define the purpose
2	Set the 'tone' of the scenario themes
3	Identify the important factors in the environment
4	Determine an appropriate time horizon
5	Identify and give values to the predetermined factors
6	Review the number of end-states
7	Determine plausible range of values for the scenario variables
8	Write down the cause-and-effect relationships

Source: Finlay (2000), pp. 270f.

other words, the scenarios developed act as the starting point for strategy development within the company. Whatever strategies are developed, the value of the process to management is that it forces them to examine the environment in which they operate and to identify the key influences and drivers of change within it. Through doing so, their existing assumptions and understanding of this environment will be challenged as the scenarios are developed and appropriate strategies devised.

Value chain analysis

A value chain is a series of steps that transform inputs into products. A value chain can occur within a company as well as at the level of an industry. As a consequence, the value chain will initially be analysed within a company before broadening the scope of the discussion to examine the notion of a value chain at the industry level.

It is helpful to look initially at what happens within a company before moving on to examining how an individual company fits within an industry's value system. Porter (1985) divides the internal activities of a company into primary activities and support activities. The relationship between these two sets of activities is shown in Figure 2.4. There are five primary activities, namely inbound logistics, operations, outbound logistics, marketing and sales and service. Within a company, inbound logistics is concerned with receiving, storing and then distributing those inputs required by the company to produce its products or services. In contrast, outbound logistics deals with the collection, storage and distribution of the final product to the company's customers. Operations within the company transform its inputs into the final product, while marketing and sales functions advertise and promote the product so that potential consumers are aware of it. The role of the service function is to install the product and then support its use by the customer through such expedients as after-sales care.

There are four supporting activities – procurement, technology development, human resource management and firm infrastructure. The procurement support activity is the process of acquiring those resources that are used by

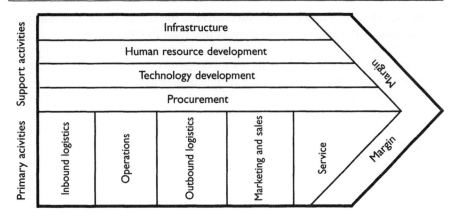

Figure 2.4 The generic value chain.
Source: Porter (1985), p. 37.

the primary activities of the company. Procurement often occurs both centrally as well as across the company. Centralization allows for costs to be minimized, whereas decentralization allows the various operating parts of the company, which may be specialized, to tailor the inputs that they purchase to their own particular needs. The technology development support activity is very broad in its remit, covering all those parts of the business that in some way involve technology. Thus, this not only includes the research and development operations of the company, but also the improvements to the production process that arise from process innovations.

The human resource management support activity recruits, trains and manages the employees of the company. This is clearly an important function, especially as many companies regularly state that their employees are their most important resource. The final support activity, infrastructure, is also broad in its remit. Broadly speaking, this organizes the other activities so that the company can actually achieve its objectives. The infrastructure of the company is not limited just to its management but also includes the information systems that manage the company's inventory or track the location of partially completed products. Also included here are the accounting and finance activities of the company that manage all the financial aspects.

These activities are important to a company for two related reasons. In the first place, the steps add value to the inputs as they are transformed into products. The value added is the difference between the cost of production and the revenue raised through the sale of a product. As we can see from Figure 2.4, value added is sometimes referred to as margin. Second, the steps also underpin the company's competitiveness. This may be due to their tight and unique integration and co-ordination, and may result in a differentiated product that other companies in the market cannot copy or in a product that is cheaper than its competitors. Alternatively, the company may be competitive because it does some of the steps better than its competitors.

Stonehouse *et al.* (2000, p. 53) suggest that certain activities within the company may correspond to its core competences and that these can be termed core activities. They define core activities as those activities that add the greatest value to the product, add more value than the same activity in competitors or are related to and reinforce the core competences of the company. In other words, the core activities are those that are the most valuable to the company.

Until now the focus has been entirely on a single company. Companies, however, are located within an industry and it is often the case that the inputs used by one company are, in fact, the finished products of a company located elsewhere in the same industry. Porter (1985) refers to the resulting inter-company links as a value system (Figure 2.5).

The notion of a value system is useful as it draws attention to two issues. In the first place, because a company can purchase its inputs from other companies, it has the option to specializse in those activities that it does best. If a company decides to specialize this will inevitably affect its scale and scope. Specialization will mean that its scope will be restricted and that its resources will be concentrated on a smaller range of activities than was hitherto the case.

Second, there is a need for the company to manage its relationships within the value system. As the company purchases inputs from other companies it must ensure not only their continued availability but also that they meet its requirements in terms of quality and price so that it remains competitive. At the same time, the company also needs to ensure that it can distribute its products to those who want to purchase them. The company's relationships

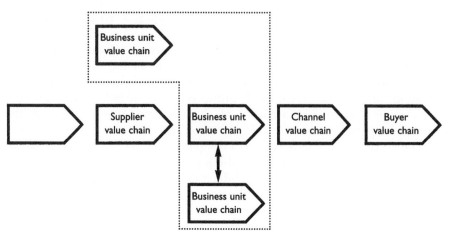

Figure 2.5 The value system.
Source: Porter (1985), p. 35.

with its suppliers illustrate the 'upstream' linkages that are present within a value system, while those with its distributors are examples of the 'downstream' linkages that are present.

Within the TMT sector another consideration that companies need to take into account is the extent to which convergence has occurred. Convergence is the blurring together of previously separate value chains and is driven by technological advances such as digitization, fibre optics and the increasing availability and declining cost of bandwidth. What convergence means in practice is that a single infrastructure can support the delivery of a greater range of products to customers: for instance, broadcasting and telephony services can be offered over a cable-TV network.

The implications of convergence for a company are, however, more than simply facilitating the delivery of a greater array of products over the same infrastructure. Convergences forces companies to reassess which markets they are active in and what products they produce. If the company decides that it needs to expand its product range, it may do so by expanding into markets that are either vertically or horizontally related to its existing markets. Vertical integration occurs when a company expands into markets that provide it with its inputs or which distribute its final products. The former is an example of backward integration while the latter illustrates forward integration.

In contrast, horizontal integration occurs when the company expands into markets related to its existing product range. Such an expansion may be driven by the desire of the company to complement its existing products with new ones. These would reinforce its position in the marketplace. Alternatively, the company could decide to exploit its core competences in an unrelated market.

The value chain model is useful as it draws attention to three areas that a company must understand if it is to remain competitive. The first of these is identifying activities within the company in terms of their value added and contribution to competitiveness. The second is the relationship that a company has with its suppliers and customers, while the third is the importance of co-ordination. Co-ordination is important not only within the company, where the integration of the activities that it does undertake plays a pivotal role in determining its competitiveness, but also with respect to how it interacts with its suppliers and customers.

Naturally, the task of understanding each of these three areas is complicated by the fact that all three interact with one another. If a company decides to specialize on the handful of activities that it does best, then this in turn will elevate in importance its relationships with its suppliers on whom it will become ever more reliant for inputs. Conversely, if the company's relationships with its suppliers are fraught with difficulties, it may decide to expand into these markets so that supplies of key inputs are assured. As the company undertakes more activities, its ability to co-ordinate its activities becomes ever more important. The inability of a company to co-ordinate what it does and how it relates to other companies will obviously undermine its competitiveness.

Porter's Five Forces

This model provides a way for companies to understand their environment and through this to determine their strategy. The Five Forces that companies need to understand are respectively the bargaining power of buyers, the bargaining power of suppliers, new entrants, the threat of substitutes and industry rivalry.

The interplay between the Five Forces is shown in Figure 2.6. Although what follows will describe what is meant by each of the forces in turn, it is important to remember from the onset that they interact with one another. The number and size of suppliers shapes their bargaining power in an industry, as does whether there is a diversity of supply of a product or whether substitutes are available. These collectively determine whether suppliers are able to turn a transaction to their advantage. If a product or service is supplied by only a handful of companies, then buyers will find it difficult to reduce the price that they pay. This is also true if the product is highly differentiated, as buyers will not be easily able to replace one supplier with another.

In many respects, the bargaining power of suppliers is the reverse of the bargaining power of buyers (consumers). Suppliers are most powerful when they are few in number or provide products that are either sought after or essential to an industry. Suppliers are also powerful when individual customers do not represent a significant proportion of their sales: quite simply, they can walk away from buyers who are not prepared to pay the prices that they want if most others are prepared to do so.

Substitution means that new products replace existing products. This is possible because they perform the same function, or a very similar function, in the eyes of the buyer to the product that is being replaced. Substitution

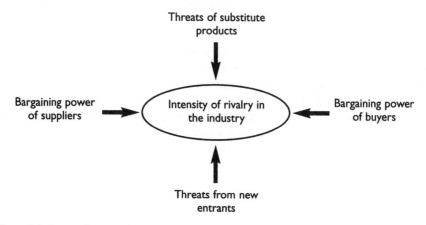

Figure 2.6 Forces driving industry competition.
Source: Porter (1980), p. 4.

plays an important role in determining the competitiveness of the market. If products can be freely substituted for one another, the market will be more competitive than if this is not the case. Companies, however, seek to implement strategies that prevent substitution. One such strategy is branding, while another is the bundling of related products together into a single offering. The aim of both strategies is to heighten the differentiation that is present between products in the market, and thereby to limit the opportunity for substitution.

The fourth force identified is the threat of new entrants. The easier it is for a company to enter a market, the greater the degree of competition is likely to be. Within any market, a range of entry barriers are present. Sometimes these barriers are legal. For example, if a company wishes to participate in the mobile communications market through the building of a network, it requires a licence to do so and these are limited in number. If a company is unsuccessful in the awarding auction, it will not be able to participate in the market. Naturally, this does not prevent the company from entering the market through other means such as becoming a 'virtual' operator – one that sells its services using another company's network to reach the customer.

More usually, the entry barriers relate to the characteristics of the market in question. The large size of existing companies may provide them with economies of scale (whereby average cost per unit falls as output rises due, for example, to the spreading of overheads) or economies of scope (whereby savings in, for example, marketing expenses can be made by bringing together related products or services). At worst, these could deter companies from entering the market at all, while at best could provide the existing companies with a cost advantage over any new entrant. The market may also require the entrant to develop competences that it does not already have. If these are substantial, then the barriers to entering the market are high and this may dissuade the company from attempting entry. A company might also be reluctant to enter a new market if it is not able to distribute its products or if it has to establish commercial relationships with suppliers for the first time.

The final force shaping change within an industry is the intensity of rivalry between companies in the market. Within a specific market, rivalry can take several forms: companies may compete on the basis of price, branding or the range, design and functionality of the products offered. However, the intensity of the rivalry is conditioned by the number and size of the companies in the market and whether their products are substitutable. The existence of a large number of companies of roughly equal size is likely to lead to a more competitive market than if there are only a handful of companies present and one of them is substantially larger than the others.

How quickly the market is growing also contributes to the degree of industry rivalry. In a rapidly growing market, all companies should be able to expand regardless of their underlying competitiveness. However, as growth begins to slow and a market matures, they will have to compete against one another for market share and, as this occurs, industry rivalry will increase. At this point it is important to remember that the other four forces will help to shape this rivalry.

The Five Forces model can be used in two ways: it can be used to identify change within the market or, alternatively, it can be used by a company to identify those areas of its business where it faces some form of competitive threat. Regardless of how the model is used, its strength is that through providing an overview of the challenges that companies face in the market, it enables them to develop an appropriate strategic response.

The flagship firm

What is a flagship firm? It is a multinational enterprise that co-ordinates the investment and operational activities of other companies within its business network. The business network that surrounds the flagship firm is illustrated in Figure 2.7 and is comprised of four elements: suppliers, customers, non-business infrastructure and selected competitors.

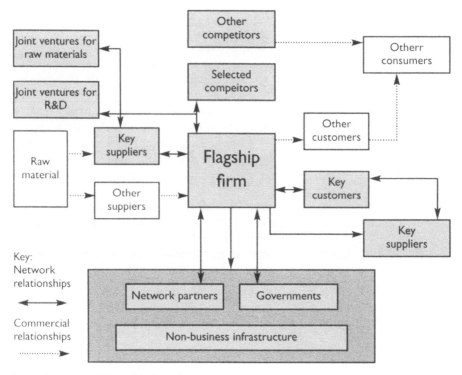

Source: Rugman and D'Cruz (2000), p. 84.

Suppliers provide the business network with resources. According to Rugman and D'Cruz (2000, p. 19), the role of suppliers has been affected by two contradictory trends. First, many companies have reduced the number of suppliers with which they deal. Where a company may previously have dealt with a dozen or so suppliers, not least to ensure that it did not become dependent on any one of these, it now deals only with a handful of suppliers. Second, suppliers are increasingly providing a larger proportion of a product's value added. Suppliers have been asked to undertake research and development and partially to assemble products before shipping them to their customers so that the pace of final assembly can be quickened.

To all intents and purposes, customers are intermediaries that align the flagship firm with the end consumer. The flagship firm views the inter-mediaries, and not the end consumers, as being its customers. If the flagship firm is to improve its relations with its customers then it must move from treating each transaction on an individual basis to viewing it as part of a stream where the value of the relationship to both parties is maximized (Rugman and D'Cruz, 2000, p. 20). This involves more than simply the sharing of information and procedures, as without the aligning of strategies both parties will remain suspicious of one another.

However, within the business network not all suppliers and customers are of equal importance as some are termed 'key' by the flagship firm. Key suppliers are those companies which provide resources that contribute to the develop-ment of competitive advantage (Rugman and D'Cruz, 2000, p. 9). This entails close co-operation with the flagship firm: strategies, information, resources etc are all shared. One consequence of this alignment is that key suppliers are likely to experience increased sales, whilst another is that the relationship will become more stable compared to where the company was merely one among many suppliers to the flagship firm.

Key customers are both a market for the flagship firm in their own right as well as a source of information on market conditions. They are able to collect such information, as they are intermediaries that link the flagship firm with the ultimate consumer.

The non-business infrastructure is comprised of educational institutions, trade associations, unions and government agencies that collectively provide the flagship firm and its business network with human and technological capital. This capital contributes to the competitiveness of the business net-work through, for example, educating and training the labour force as well as providing facilities and equipment for the business network to use.

On occasion the flagship firm enters into co-operative arrangements with selected competitors. Many of these co-operative arrangements are motivated by the desire of the flagship firm to gain access to resources – technology, content, etc. – that it does not possess. Co-operative behaviour may also be motivated by the desire to establish market sharing arrangements that allow the flagship firm and its competitors to market their products and services in one another's markets. Joint research and product development provides a third motivation for co-operation, namely to offset the cost and risk inherent in such activity.

The business network is bound together through what D'Cruz and Rugman (1994, p. 60) describe as 'network relationships' that entail close co-operation and the sharing of resources. Within this network the flagship firm 'provides strategic leadership and direction for a vertically integrated chain of business that operates as a co-ordinated system or network, frequently in competition with similar networks that address the same end markets' (Rugman and D'Cruz, 2000, p. 84). In other words, the flagship firm sets the strategy, co-ordinates the network to ensure its achievement and competes against similar business networks.

The flagship firm is able to co-ordinate activities because its relationships with other parts of the business network are asymmetric. 'Strategic asymmetries' occur between the flagship firm and the other parts of the business network where the flagship firm has control over the strategy of its partners but the partners do not have the same reciprocal influence over the flagship firm (ibid.). Strategic asymmetry enables the flagship firm, inter alia, to direct the capital expenditure programme of its partners and delimit the markets in which they operate. In return, partners gain access to the flagship's business network with the promise of 'significant sales volumes, access to advanced technology, and participation in the benefits of the brand image of the flagship' (ibid.).

By exerting influence over the other components of the business network, the flagship firm can change the location of production within the business network. The flagship firm undergoes 'de-integration' and retreats to concentrate on its core competences (ibid., pp. 55–61). While this is happening, suppliers within the business network take on those production activities previously undertaken by the flagship firm whilst customers become an increasingly important source of information to the business network.

Thus, the key role played by the flagship firm within the business network is one of co-ordination. This co-ordination can manifest itself in several ways. The flagship firm might co-ordinate the activities of the companies within the business network so that they all target the same set of end consumers in a similar fashion. Not only could this entail a similar set of products, but it could also involve common branding and pricing strategies. The flagship firm might also co-ordinate investment strategies across the business network. One benefit of this would be to minimize the degree of investment duplication that occurs across the business network, while another would be to encourage specialization. Specialization would, in turn, lead to increased revenues for the specializing companies as companies across the business network become reliant on it for a particular good or service. Increased sales should also lead to reduced costs as scale economies take effect, and quality should improve.

From the perspective of understanding developments within the TMT sector, the flagship firm model is useful as it highlights three related issues.

The first of these is co-ordination. Co-ordination takes place across the business network, and as the flagship firm focuses on its core competences this assumes a critical role in determining its competitiveness. Second, specialization occurs. Not only does the flagship firm specialize on its core competences but other companies, especially key suppliers and customers, specialize as well. Third, co-ordination acts to bind together the business network so that the strategic priorities and interests of the constituent elements are aligned.

Strategic states model

This model proposes that, through an understanding of the characteristics of the company and the environment in which it operates, it is possible to identify four optimum strategies that a company may follow. These four strategies are, according to Pehrsson (2001b, p. 441), 'the most effective way to reach high performance'.

There are two dimensions to the model: segment penetration and segment adaptation. The first of these dimensions enables the environment within which the company operates to be understood, while the second focuses on shedding light on the company. Segment penetration is the number of markets in which a company is present. If a company decides to increase the number of markets in which it is present, it is following a 'divergence' strategy that will diminish its reliance on any one specific market. In contrast, if the company decides to decrease the number of markets in which it is present, it will become more dependent on a reduced number of markets. Pehrsson (2001b, p. 442) terms this strategy 'concentration'.

Segment adaptation is how far the product meets the specific needs of a market. Again, there are two alternative strategies that a company may utilize. If a company decides on 'adaptation' then the product will be adapted to meet the needs of a specific market, whereas if the company opts for 'standardization' the reverse will occur. The relationship between the two dimensions and the four alternative strategies is shown in Figure 2.8.

As we can see from the figure, there are four extreme states within the model. In State A, products are standardized and the company is present in only a handful of markets. As customers do not perceive those products in the market to be differentiated, the primary way in which companies compete against one another is price competition. As a consequence, cost control and rationalization are particularly important to a company as these enable it to compete on price. Price competition also implies that maximizing the volume of products sold is the only way that the company can maximize its profitability.

In State B the company continues to produce a relatively standardized range of products, but does so across more markets than was previously the case. Absent from all of these markets is the presence of a dominant company, and this, more than anything else, ensures that price remains the

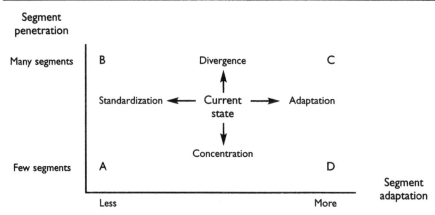

Figure 2.8 Strategic states model: dimensions and strategies.
Source: Pehrsson (2001a), p. 15.

principal way through which the company competes in these markets. However, that the company is present in multiple markets raises in importance how it manages its relationships with distributors. Distributor relationships are important as they have access to the final customer. Quite simply, without distributors the company will not be able to sell its products in the market. Although the company may want to develop lasting relationships with customers it will find this hard, if not impossible, to achieve. Competing mainly on the basis of price does not allow the company much room to develop strategies such as product differentiation that encourage customer loyalty.

The products in State C are, in contrast to States A and B, more adapted to the customers' needs. At the same time, the company is present in a limited number of market segments. This combination of increased product adaptation and limited market presence ensures that the risks faced by the company increase. One factor contributing to the increased risks faced by the company is the need to command a higher price for its adapted products than for standardized products, while another is that the company is present in a limited number of markets. By producing an adapted product for a limited number of markets, the company will inevitably encounter difficulties when expanding into new markets since the product is not adapted to the particular requirements of these new markets.

State D is the fourth extreme state identified by the model. In this state, not only is the product adapted to the needs of the market, but the company is also present in many different market segments as well. According to Pehrsson (2001a: p. 74), 'this state is quite demanding'. The reasons for this are threefold. In the first place, the company has to distribute more products to more markets than was hitherto the case. Second, the company must decentralizse so that it is able to adapt its product to the needs of specific markets. Third, adaptation across multiple markets inhibits the extent to which such matters as scale economies in production are possible.

Strategies within each of these four states will differ. Companies that find themselves in both States A and B will compete on the basis of price, but those in State A will combine price competition with relations based competition, whereas those in State B will combine price competition with competition in respect of distribution instead. In contrast, responsiveness is common to the strategies of companies in States C and D. However, those companies in State C will combine responsiveness with relations whereas those in State D will combine responsiveness with distribution. Pehrsson conceptualizes these four strategies – price, distribution, relations and responsiveness – as forming the four sides of a box and refers to each as a 'competitive edge'. As a competitive edge is the main way a company competes in the market, these edges can be viewed as being the source of the company's competitive advantage. The different combinations of competitive edges are shown in Figure 2.9.

How can the model be used? One way is as a tool for the company to identify its optimum strategy. If so, then Pehrsson (2001b, p. 446) suggests that a stepwise process is followed. After determining which of the four states applies to the company, the second step is to assess how sensitive the company is to the four competitive edges. More specifically, this involves exploring how changes in price, relations, distribution and responsiveness will affect the company's competitiveness. Once this has been undertaken, the third step involves identifying which of the four optimum strategies is the most appropriate. It is unlikely that the company will adopt any one of the four alternatives in its pure form, with the consequence that some form of combination, as shown in Figure 2.9, will result. This in turn will dictate how the company will compete in the market.

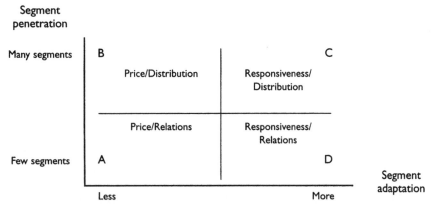

Figure 2.9 Crucial competitive edges within the strategic states model.
Source: Pehrsson (2001b), p. 444.

A company can also apply the model to identify the strategies being enacted by its competitors. This requires that the process outlined above is repeated for each of its competitors, enabling not only their strategies to be identified but also for companies to be grouped together according to whether their strategies are similar or not. This will provide the company with an overview of the market and competition therein, allowing it to formulate its own strategies in response. This is, however, a static analysis of competition in the market that will not reflect the changing nature of competition. This can be overcome by repeating the analysis for a company at two points in time. One of these points is the present, while the other is in the past. By comparing the strategies of the company at these two points in time, any changes in the company's strategy will be illuminated. Figure 2.10 provides an example of this in practice.

The diagram clearly draws attention to how the strategies of companies in the UK and Swedish telecommunications markets have changed over the years. For example, in Sweden Tele2 has increased the number of markets in which it is present. In 1990, Tele2 initially focused its activities on the provision of communication services to corporate customers, but by 1996 had broadened its scope to include consumers as well. In other words, the number of markets that Tele2 competed in broadened between 1990 and 1996. Such a strategy in the language of Pehrsson would be described as divergent, as the reliance of Tele2 on any one market was diminished. However, because the company continued to adapt its products to the needs of its customers a more accurate description of the strategy is divergence/adaptation. This would also describe Mercury's strategy in 1996. However, in contrast to Tele2, Mercury moved from providing relatively

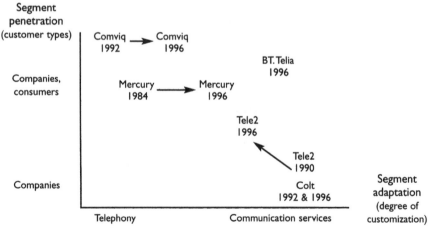

Figure 2.10 Business strategy development of companies operating telecommunications networks in the UK and Sweden.

Source: Pehrsson (2001a), p. 219.

standardized products to its customers in 1984 to offering them adapted products so that it no longer competed solely on the basis of price.

Leadership and culture

Although our primary focus is on understanding company strategies within the TMT sector, the cases that follow highlight, sometimes quite dramatically, the important role that key managers such as the managing director/CEO play in shaping and executing company strategy. The aim of this section is to draw attention to the leadership role that senior managers play within the company since it needs to be borne in mind as the cases are being read and analysed.

Managers come in all shapes and sizes, adopting quite different managerial roles and styles. Table 2.3 identifies five different approaches to strategic leadership that managers may adopt: strategy, human assets, expertise, control

Table 2.3 Strategic leadership approaches

	Strategy	Human assets	Expertise	Control	Change
Focus of attention	Strategic Strategic strategy formulation	Developing people	Disseminating expertise as source of competitive advantage	Setting procedures and measures of control	Continual change
Indicative behaviour	Scanning markets, technological changes, etc.	Getting the right people, creating a coherent culture	Cultivating and improving area of expertise through systems and procedures	Monitoring performance against controls to ensure uniform, predictable performance	Communicating and motivating through speeches, meetings, etc.
Role of other managers	Day-to-day operations	Strategy development devolved	Immersion in and management of expertise area	Ensure uniform performance against control measures	Change agents, openness to change
Implications for managing change	Delegated	Recruiting/ developing people capable of managing strategy locally	Change in line with expertise approach	Change carefully monitored and controlled	Change central to the approach

Source: Adapted from Farkas and Wetlaufer (1996) by Johnson and Scholes (2002, p. 551).

and change. In the first of these approaches, senior management develop the company's strategy, while in the second approach the emphasis is on identifying employees to whom responsibility for strategy development at the market or divisional level can be delegated. In the third approach, the focus is on a particular area that will provide the company with its competitive advantage, whereas in the control approach the emphasis is on ensuring that all parts of the company behave in a similar fashion. The fifth approach recognizes that the company must change if it is to remain competitive.

To a greater or lesser extent, all of these approaches to strategic leadership can be witnessed in the TMT sector. For example, the strategy approach would seem to describe events in those companies led by a visionary or charismatic CEO who sets ambitious goals for the company to achieve. These goals are often espoused in terms of market leadership. The CEO then develops and implements a far-reaching strategy, and in the process becomes intertwined in the popular perception with the company that he or she leads. One example here is Jean-Paul Messier at Vivendi Universal, while another is Bernie Ebbers at WorldCom.

Another approach that is informative is that of human assets as it sheds light on two areas. First, the approach draws attention to the development of a cadre of managers who are capable of managing strategy development at the divisional/national level, while, second, a common organizational culture is also highlighted. In other words, this approach draws attention to where within the company strategy is developed as well as the bonds that bind the company together. If these bonds are missing, then it is likely that the interests of the different divisions will increasingly diverge from one another. The difficulties that AOL Time Warner experienced between its formation in 2002 and its recent reversion to the name Time Warner illustrate not only the difficulties of creating a single common culture in a company that is formed through a merger, but also how this can adversely affect a company's performance.

A cruder categorization of the style of management adopted by senior managers is offered by Johnson and Scholes (2002, p. 550), who argue that senior managers are sometimes categorized as being either charismatic or instrumental/transactional in character. Charismatic managers develop a vision of the company and then organize and motivate the company's employees to achieve this. In contrast, those managers characterized as being instrumental/ transactional focus on developing systems and controlling the activities in which the company engages. Thus, charismatic managers focus on the big picture and how to achieve it whereas instrumental/transactional managers concentrate on the operational details of the company.

A cautionary note is needed here. If the senior management of the company focus solely on one of these areas to the detriment of the other, then they are highly likely to come unstuck because the vision and operations of the company are, in practice, closely related to one another. The company's operations provide the resources that are used to achieve the vision, and if the operations cannot deliver the products sought at reasonable cost then the vision will not be achieved. It is for this reason that Johnson and Scholes note (2002, p. 550) that the most successful managers appear to have a good grasp of both areas.

Whatever some managers may like to believe, they are only human and are subject to a myriad of influences. One particularly important influence is the behaviour of the rest of the TMT sector. On the one hand, the management of a company may be left wondering if they are doing something wrong if the rest of the industry is investing in a specific market or product and they are not. Fear of being left out of 'the next big thing' could motivate the senior management of a company to change their strategy and enter those markets they had previously avoided. Such investments, however, are unlikely to form an integral part of the company's strategy and are effectively a way of monitoring the environment. On the other hand, if the company's strategy is increasingly at odds with that of the rest of the sector then its senior management will come under increasing pressure to justify and defend such a stance.

The financial markets will also influence the senior managers of companies in the TMT sector through pressurizing them to enact strategies that will be rewarded by the markets. The heady valuations placed on Internet-related companies at the beginning of the century encouraged many companies to devise and enact strategies that they hoped would result in their being valued as an Internet stock. In addition, the messages sent to company managers by the financial markets can change quite rapidly, and it is sometimes the case that strategies favoured one week are criticized the next. For example, in the run up to the licensing of 3G in Europe, many analysts drew attention to the great potential of the services that this new technology would make possible. It was also widely suggested that if an incumbent 2G operator failed to gain a 3G licence it would be placed at a significant competitive disadvantage. This encouraged companies to acquire a licence.

However, when it become apparent that the cost of 3G would be more than previously thought, and that the underlying technology was not as robust as many had suspected, analysts began to question both the wisdom of participating in 3G and how companies would repay the large debts that had amassed from this participation. Many analysts are now arguing that the potential of 3G to deliver innovative services is not as great as was first thought, that the new services will not be as profitable as envisaged and that the 'killer application' will be voice telephony – an 'old economy' service. As a consequence, those companies that have continued to view 3G positively have been criticized for doing so. They have, in effect, been criticized for enacting a strategy that many financial analysts had previously encouraged them to enter into. Moreover, if the senior management of the company had listened to the messages emanating from the financial community, then not only would the company's strategy have undergone a substantial strategic change but it is also highly likely that the management would be criticized for not developing a strategic vision of their own.

Within the numerous messages emanating from the financial community, the senior management of a company may be prone to pay particular attention to the advice of star analysts like Jack Grubman of Saloman Smith Barney. While seeking to explain the boom and bust of the telecommunications industry between 1996 and 2002, Fransman (2002) suggests three different hypotheses to explain how managers select and handle the information available to them; these are biased incentive hypothesis, information processing/bounded rationality hypothesis and guru hypothesis. It is argued that the views of 'gurus' disproportionately influence senior management who are prepared to listen to them because they lack the time to understand the issues for themselves. One of the key advantages of gurus for managers is that they provide a certainty in their analysis, while another is that they legitimize the strategies that management in turn adopt.

But how does the senior management of a company choose its gurus? The (perhaps) surprising answer of Fransman (2002, pp. 15f) is that gurus are chosen on the basis of a 'leap of faith', with managers feeling confident that their guru is providing them with relevant information. However, these managers do not know whether this information is biased in any way, nor do they know whether the guru is wrong until it is too late.

Accounting issues

Although this final section is not strictly 'strategic', its relevance is enhanced by the increasing tendency to treat a company's finance director/chief financial officer as a major player in devising its strategy rather than simply as an accountant and controller. Furthermore, it is necessary because there is a tendency in case studies to include (often quite a lot of) accounting data which it is claimed will be very helpful in the interpretation of a company's strategic thinking. Unhappily, this proposition is dubious at the best of times unless there is a lengthy accompanying statement about the accounting methodology involved, and a glance at a company's annual report and accounts will quickly disabuse the reader of the belief that (a) this does not need to be lengthy and (b) it does not matter. Furthermore, accounts are by their very nature retrospective and hence cannot be used readily to interpret recent events.

These problems are particularly acute in the TMT sector for the reasons set out below. As readers will discover, certain cases include no accounts at all, either because secretive private companies are involved (such as the KirchGruppe) or the accounts are deemed to be so unreliable as to serve to confuse rather than illuminate the case (such as WorldCom). In addition, so many TMT companies have undergone substantial restructuring that it is very difficult to compare like with like over a period of years, in which case the accounts include overlapping periods to ensure a reasonable degree of consistency.

It is salutary to begin by clarifying the link with the previous section on leadership. As many of the case studies show (and it has been much the same story in other industries), deregulation, liberalization and privatization have combined with greed and a self-serving managerial class to corrupt the capital structure of the TMT sector. Historically, the managerial class accepted a good salary (defined in terms of an acceptable multiple of a shop floor worker's wage) while using investor funds to build the business. While bonuses might also be paid, especially in the USA, these were linked to performance as generally measured by conventional profitability. During the late 1990s boom, however, managerial reward systems became detached from the reported accounts and raced ahead of any conventional measure of company performance. These reward systems were generally devised by investment bankers anxious to be offered astonishing levels of fees for helping the companies 'evolve' into new areas of business. As a result, management reward systems became increasingly regarded as 'corrupt', although this tended to be a moral judgement since it was only rarely that company law was broken in the process. For reasons best known to themselves, institutional shareholders rarely used their legal powers to intervene, although there are signs that that is now beginning to change.

The classic conundrum arose in the TMT sector because so much activity related to the provision of new, or upgraded, products and services which could only generate revenues after huge up-front outlays on providing the needed infrastructure. Hence, while money would consistently flow out, it would not generate any offsetting incoming cash flow for years to come, and if there were no real revenues there could be no profits as conventionally understood. For this reason, it became the custom to use a concept called 'ebitda' – earnings before interest, tax, depreciation (loss of value through use) and amortization (the difference between the value of an asset on the company's books and its value if sold in the market). Needless to say, it is a lot easier to produce positive ebitda than positive profitability and companies and their backers were at pains to proclaim their ebitda achievements while often making no visible progress towards break-even let alone profitability.

Although this was problematic, it was nevertheless above board in the sense that almost everyone knew that accounting games were being played but chose to connive at the practices. However, things did not stop there. In the first place, it must be borne in mind that few ideas are wholly original, and that in the TMT sector it was often the case that several start-ups would be approaching different lenders with precisely the same game plan – for example, to build a fibre-optic network linking the major cities of Europe. The plan itself was superficially sound since there clearly was money to be made by providing tailored services to high-data-usage companies. Unfortunately, there was unlikely to be any profits made if several competing networks set up in business at roughly the same time, and even less if the technological capability of each network was improving in leaps and bounds such that any single one of them would end up capable of supplying the entire market by itself.

Needless to say, the companies concerned were less than anxious to keep investors informed, and in many cases continued to draw down additional funds while proclaiming that their prospects were undiminished. Unfortunately, once a problem of this kind emerges, the temptation to engage in underhand practices becomes severe. Thus it was that, in the above example, operators which had not yet completed their networks decided to swap completed sections so that they could each claim to be providing a complete dedicated network for their customers. Company A would accordingly 'swap' section X with company B's section Y and then – and this was the nub of the issue – both would claim to be leasing out the relevant section and would record a cash inflow arising from the lease even though absolutely no cash payment was involved. Alternatively, to boost revenues, companies would sell long-term (indefeasible) rights to use capacity, either to one another at inflated prices or, in the case of customers, would book the entire sum involved immediately even though the revenue stream would take place over 20 years and the customers might go bankrupt in the interim.

In such circumstances it is arguable that fraudulent behaviour is involved, although much depends upon the precise wording of the relevant accounting principles which is often in practice too vague to determine whether it is 'bending the rules' to their utmost or fraud that is involved. This has been particularly problematic in respect of amortization. This involves the concept of 'goodwill', especially in the context where one company takes over another, and although it may be deemed a fairly straightforward exercise to determine the difference between the value of a machine on a company's books and what it would fetch if sold, it is far less so where 'intangibles' such as an employee's skills or customer loyalty is concerned.

Normal practice is to conduct an impairment test which involves estimating the future cash flows from an asset and making a comparison with predictions made at the time of acquisition. If the cash flow is lower than expected, goodwill must be reduced on the balance sheet by way of a charge in the profit and loss account. For obvious reasons this is open to manipulation. For example, an existing board of directors is likely to be very reluctant to write off goodwill because of the likely effects upon matters such as the share price and credit ratings. On the other hand, if the board is replaced then the first thing the new board will want to do is to write off everything in sight and blame it on its predecessor. Equally, where cash is unlikely to flow in for years, it is possible for companies in identical positions to treat goodwill in wholly contradictory ways – hence, for example, Vodafone's insistence on keeping its 3G licences on its books at cost at a time when its competitors were writing off the associated goodwill, sometimes down to zero.

Without wishing to labour the point, one further example will suffice (but see Howell, 2002, for others). A practice often employed by cable companies is to treat the provision of set-top boxes to subscribers as a capital cost rather than an operating expense that is incurred as soon as the service is switched on. This latter practice would serve to depress ebitda, thereby affecting the achievement of targets linked to bank covenants, credit ratings and management bonus schemes. Nevertheless, it is not a clear-cut issue of right or wrong practice. Most cable operators, for example, effectively lease their boxes to subscribers and reclaim them when a subscription is terminated (although the box may not be re-useable). In contrast, a satellite operator may treat the box as a free good to subscribers, using it as an inducement to get them to sign up in the first place.

What is particularly fascinating about the above is the difficulty of pinning down the guilty parties. According to company executives, they cannot do anything without the agreement of the company's auditors so the latter must ultimately be responsible in respect of their inadequate auditing. Equally, if their institutional investors demand that a record of rising earnings is needed to warrant holding on to the company's shares, executives can hardly be blamed for meeting their expectations one way or another – and so forth. So, in conclusion, readers are advised to treat a company's published accounts with a slightly jaundiced eye when considering their role in guiding strategy.

Part I

Illustrative application of strategic modelling I

The following three chapters chart the trials and tribulations of AT&T, BT and Telecom Italia. While all three companies have retained their primary status as incumbent operators with their origins in the fixed-wire market, the exact nature of the challenges that the companies had to address reflected – as it still does – the variety of markets in which they operated. As a consequence, the strategies that management adopted also demonstrated some important differences as well as many commonalities.

Several issues are common to AT&T, BT and Telecom Italia, and it is helpful to outline these before illustrating how the strategies adopted specifically by AT&T can be analysed using one of the strategic models outlined in Chapter 2. The first of these common issues is that of restructuring, with all three companies engaged in what appears to be a seemingly continuous bout of reorganization. However, the motives for such restructuring differed between AT&T and BT on the one hand and Telecom Italia on the other. The restructuring of AT&T and BT was driven by the need of both companies to react to market-driven developments such as increased competition in their core markets and the need to increase the value attributed to the different parts of the business by the stock market. In contrast, the restructuring of Telecom Italia was driven to a significant degree by the peculiar nature of Italian capitalism with its tendency to use cascading holding companies, with a lesser emphasis upon the need to address competitive issues.

Closely related to the issue of restructuring is that of debt. For both BT and Telecom Italia, debt played a significant role in shaping their strategies although, not surprisingly given the above, debt affected BT and Telecom Italia quite differently. The dramatic increase in the level of its debts initially encouraged BT to shed non-strategic assets, but as these failed substantially to reduce the debt burden it was forced into a much more comprehensive restructuring that saw it divest businesses and exit markets that it had hitherto considered to be strategically important – often referred to as 'core'. Almost all of the international businesses were eventually sold, and the company even exited the mobile market (which it is currently seeking to re-enter).

In the case of Telecom Italia, the need to manage debt arose after the company was subjected to two takeovers by entrepreneurial Italian holding companies that combined family capitalism with big business. In both cases, the use of cascading holding companies resulted in debt and managerial control residing at the top of the pyramid whilst the revenues and profits resided at the bottom. Thus, the restructuring in this case was motivated by the need to reduce the gap between the top and bottom of the pyramid so that the debt could be repaid while ensuring that the acquirers retained control of Telecom Italia.

A third issue is the changing strategic focus of all three companies. This is true both operationally and geographically. AT&T, BT and Telecom Italia have shifted their operational focus, though this is perhaps more noticeable in the cases of AT&T and BT than it is for Telecom Italia. Not only have new markets been entered, only to be exited several years later, but some of the 'traditional' businesses of incumbent operators have also been sold as the companies have struggled to come to terms with increasingly competitive markets and rising levels of debt. For example, BT sold Yell, its directory publishing business, as it sought to reduce its debt burden. Another example of shifting strategic priorities is provided by Telecom Italia's involvement in the directory publishing market. In 2001, Telecom Italia decided to merge Tin.it, its Internet subsidiary, with its partially owned directory publishing business, Seat Pagine Gialle. Although acquisitions were made to bolster its position in the market, Telecom Italia subsequently opted to break the company up. In doing so, it also exited the directory publishing market.

Common to all three companies was their geographical expansion and subsequent retrenchment to predominantly their home markets. Perhaps the most drastic geographical retrenchment of the three was that of BT. For many years, a core component of BT's strategy was its international expansion through the acquisition of equity stakes around the globe, often in relatively new entrants, and through establishing Concert, its alliance with AT&T. However, its debt-induced retrenchment saw it exit the majority of its international markets in the space of just a few years as well as the closure of Concert, so that, once again, its geographical focus is predominantly on the United Kingdom.

A more systematic understanding of the strategies of AT&T, BT and Telecom Italia is possible if several of the strategic models outlined in Chapter 2 are applied to the cases that follow. The benefits of so doing can be seen if, for purposes of illustration, the Five Forces model is applied to AT&T. As readers will recall, the Five Forces identified by Michael Porter are, respectively, the bargaining power of buyers, the bargaining power of suppliers, the threat from new entrants, the threat of substitute products and the intensity of industry rivalry. Each of the Five Forces illuminates a different dimension of the strategic challenge that AT&T faced in 1998.

If we begin with the threat of substitute products, then the use of the model draws attention to mobile and cable-TV. Both of these products can replace the local telephone network as the means through which the final consumer is reached, albeit in somewhat different ways. Mobile substitution starts out, in essence, as voice telephony substitution. In contrast, cable-TV substitution involves substituting one network for another, but, significantly, this new network can support the delivery of a 'bundle' of products including voice telephony. Like fixed-wire networks, both are capable of development to utilize the full potential of digital communications.

Although the long-distance telecommunications market in the USA had been competitive for several years, the Telecommunications Act of 1996 proposed to change the nature of competition in a radical way through allowing the RBOCs (the local/regional operators) to enter the long distance market once they could demonstrate that their local markets were competitive. Unlike many other companies in the long distance market, these new entrants would be well resourced and would have recognized brand names and access to a substantial customer base through their existing local and mobile businesses. In other words, they would be potentially formidable competitors. Furthermore, their position would be strengthened by the increasing tendency of subscribers to 'churn' from one network operator to another to take advantage of ever more enticing bundles of services.

A possibly more worrying aspect for AT&T was that it would be forced simultaneously to compete and collaborate with the RBOCs. The RBOCs would compete with AT&T in the long-distance market while continuing to act as the main conduit through which customers would access its long-distance network. Clearly, collaborating and competing at the same time would place AT&T in an uncomfortable, even subordinate, position to the RBOCs.

The entry of the RBOCs into the long-distance market would widen consumer choice. As the primary product in this market is much the same irrespective of the company providing it, the entry of more companies into the market would inevitably result in price competition. Even prior to the RBOCs gaining regulatory approval to enter the long-distance market the average price per minute charged by AT&T, and consequently its overall revenues from long-distance traffic (which was no longer a growth area), were declining. The entry of the RBOCs would simply serve to exacerbate this decline.

So how did AT&T react to the challenges it was facing? In 1998, AT&T acquired two cable-TV companies, TCI and MediaOne, at a total cost of $106.5 billion. On the one hand, these acquisitions would allow AT&T to re-enter the local market for the first time since 1984 and, in so doing, AT&T would no longer be totally reliant on the RBOCs to reach its domestic customers. On the other hand, the acquisitions broadened the product portfolio of AT&T. Being able to offer a broader range of products would enable AT&T to compete on the basis of differentiation as well as, and in preference to, price. AT&T also sought to bolster its position in the mobile market through acquiring Vanguard Cellular for $1.5 billion.

By using the Five Forces to structure the analysis, the nature of the challenge facing AT&T in 1998 can be mapped out. However, as Chapter 4 demonstrates, this is not the end of the story. If we fast-forward a few years, then repeating the process draws attention to the changing nature of the challenge faced by AT&T. The decline in the average price per minute charged and long-distance revenues has accelerated, and attempts to broaden the product portfolio have failed. Upgrading the cable-TV networks via digitization so that they could carry a broader range of products proved to be a more costly and protracted process than initially envisaged and led ultimately to the sale of the cable interests to Comcast. In the mobile market, competitive pressures from carriers such as Verizon Wireless and Cingular Wireless increased, and the company was forced to switch the technology used from TDMA to GSM/GPRS to ensure its compatibility with the networks of other operators, while at the same time arranging for its wireless arm, AT&T Wireless to be hived off as a stand-alone company. On this occasion, the strategy developed by AT&T was accordingly to retreat from the mobile and cable-TV markets so that its primary focus would be, once again, on the long-distance market in the USA where it retained a (steadily weakening) competitive advantage via its incumbency and brand name.

Nevertheless, because of its vastly reduced circumstances and reliance upon a declining market, it is now possible to think of the rump of AT&T as a potential takeover target rather than as the swaggering telecoms giant of much of the twentieth century. As the Five Forces model demonstrates, declining customer loyalty, increased competition in staple markets and a comparative disadvantage in new service provision can lay low even the mightiest corporation.

Chapter 3

British Telecommunications (BT)

Back to the future

Introduction

British Telecommunications (hereafter BT) provides an interesting case study because it was the first European incumbent to be wholly privatized, commencing almost two decades ago. Like all European operators of any size, BT was historically a domestic service provider with virtually no links into other, mostly closed, European markets. Fortunately, one result of privatization was that it enabled BT to slim itself down and to improve productivity – although it had been reluctant to do so until pressure exerted by competition and the regulator forced its hand – so by the mid-1990s it was financially very sound with a low debt to equity ratio.

Despite some acquisitions made during the initial decade post-privatization, BT's global reach was by no means complete and it remained relatively weak outside the European Union. During the 1990s, BT came to the conclusion that there were enormous opportunities in the global marketplace for carriers willing to take risks and, from humble beginnings in the form of an office in Japan, set about creating a global alliance which evolved into Concert Communications. Its main foray into Europe took the form of an agreement to pay \$1.7 billion[1] for a 25 per cent stake in Cégétel, joining with Vivendi, SBC and Mannesmann, but it was noteworthy that BT did not acquire a majority stake in its other significant European joint ventures until April 2000. Given that C&W's weakness was long held to be its widely dispersed minority holdings, it was surprising that BT chose to follow the same route.

However, all of BT's foreign forays were small scale in relation to the announcement on 3 November 1996 of the biggest transatlantic merger in history between BT and MCI. Strictly a takeover by BT at a cost of \$21 billion at the then value of BT/MCI shares, the new company – to be known as Concert Communications – would have had a 1996 capitalization of at least \$60 billion, revenues of \$38 billion, pre-tax profits of \$6 billion and a 20 per cent share of the US long-distance market. However, after many regulatory delays both in the USA and EU, the BT offer, now worth \$24 billion due to BT's higher share price, seemed to have been to no avail when WorldCom tabled a \$30 billion bid on 1 October 1997. BT rapidly decided to take the money and run and although BT's global ambitions could clearly be said to have been thwarted for the time being, it was set to gain financially. Once the takeover was approved in September 1998, it was able to sell its MCI holding for total proceeds of $6.3 billion, on which it made a $1.75 billion exceptional pre-tax capital gain after taking into account goodwill originally written off when acquiring the stake.[2] Furthermore, since the markets were unenthusiastic about its relationship with MCI, its share price promptly rose. BT repurchased from MCI its stake in Concert for $980 million, and embarked on a $250 million project to ensure total separation between the two companies' systems. WorldCom agreed to distribute the services of Concert on a non-exclusive basis in North America for a further two years, and BT was left free to pursue other alliances.[3]

Accumulating debts and restructuring

Seeking partners

Clearly, BT needed to search for new partners if it truly wished to be a global operator, and final regulatory approvals for a joint venture with AT&T came in November 1999. Subsequently, the link between BT and AT&T – also known as Concert – was widened to link their wireless networks via a strategic alliance trading as Advance, although this had no legal form and hence was organized to function separately from the fixed-wire agreement. It was widely believed that a merger of some kind between AT&T and BT was inevitable, although both were so highly valued that the financing of a takeover by either party would be highly problematic. Outside Europe and the USA, BT was busy setting up ventures in the Far East such as the purchase of a 39.5 per cent stake in Bharti Cellular (BCL), India's largest mobile operator, in January 1997. It also acquired a half share of a joint venture, BT Bharti. To this was added a 33.3 per cent stake, costing $430 million, in Binariang of Malaysia – a fixed-wire and wireless operator trading as Maxis – completed in October 1998. This was followed in the same month by the purchase of a 23.49 per cent stake in LG Telecom, a South Korean mobile operator, for $360 million. In Singapore, BT acquired a 20 per cent stake in StarHub, a joint venture also involving NTT. BT also took steps to consolidate its early modest foothold in the Japanese market. In April 1997, BT.NIS obtained a Type 2 licence, followed in May 1998 by the obtaining of a Type 1 licence for BTCS, a joint venture with Marubeni trading as Harmonix. However, the key move was the purchase of a 15 per cent stake in Japan Telecom, acting in co-operation with its new partner AT&T.

BT felt obliged to justify its minority stakes in European joint ventures by claiming that it was generally the key telecoms provider among the venture partners and that it had to strike a balance between taking a sufficiently large stake and having as a consequence to provide the capital to cover the inevitable early losses. Furthermore, its pre-emption rights would allow it to increase its stakes progressively as opportunities arose. Unfortunately, when it came to the crunch, and it sought to increase its stake in Airtel in Spain, Vodafone AirTouch decided to do the same and emerged victorious.[4]

Even its successful takeover bid for Esat Telecom in Ireland in March 2000 was promptly trumped by the AOL bid for Time Warner,[5] generating fears that BT had neglected the Internet to its peril. It reminded analysts that, after conducting trials in Colchester many years previously, BT had ripped out equipment that would have potentially allowed it to be the market leader in Internet connectivity. When it reported its 1999Q3 results, the message was ominous. BT was losing revenue on its basic voice business because interconnection charges were very low; it was able to charge much less for calls to mobile handsets due to regulatory pressure; Concert was struggling; and BT was no longer market leader in mobile telephony or Internet connectivity. From a peak of £15, BT's share price fell below £10 although it subsequently recovered somewhat.

Proposed reorganization

On a more positive note, BT began to embark on the creation of a global franchise in the classified directory business. To this end, in August 1999, it spent $665 million in cash to acquire Yellow Book USA, the largest independent publisher of telephone directories in the USA with 300 directories to its name. In January 2000, it acquired a further 55 directories covering the Chicago area from Sprint Publishing for $45 million. It also announced the creation of a new unit to offer global mobile Internet services, signing strategic partnerships with over 30 content, software and equipment providers including Microsoft, BSkyB, Ericsson and Motorola. The core of the unit was the BT Cellnet Genie Internet product combined with the WAP-enabled handsets launched in January 2000.

The financial markets remained unimpressed. An examination of the net debt position demonstrates why.[6] As of 1 April 1997, net debt stood at £176 million, down from £948 million the previous year. By 1 April 1998 it had risen sharply to £3,977 million but, assisted by profits of over £1 billion on disposals, the figure was back down to £953 million by 1 April 1999. However, cash outflows soared during the ensuing year – for example, it cost £3.15 billion to buy out Securicor's stake in UK mobile operator Cellnet in November 1999 and further large sums were spent on Esat Telecom and Yellow Book USA – causing net debt to balloon to £8.7 billion by 1 April 2000. As a result, and anticipating the auctions of 3G licences which were set to commence in April 2000, a number of strategic responses, as set out in Table 3.1, came under discussion. Clearly, the 'do as little as possible' option was a non-starter:[7] something more meaningful was needed and, in April 2000, BT attempted to deliver it. It announced a reorganization which would replace a geographic with a market segment structure as follows:

Table 3.1 BT's strategic choices to reduce debt

Strategy	Drawbacks
Do as little as possible	Debt rerating increases servicing costs
Float BT Wireless	Depressed market. Orange float a failure
Sell non-core assets	Depressed market
Emergency rights issue	Dilutes holdings of those refusing offer
Scrap final dividend	Induces sales by disaffected shareholders
Cut capital investment	Reduces longer-term prospects

- A fixed-wire unit divided into wholesale and retail sections to provide transparency and facilitate regulation.
- An international data-centric broadband IP business focused on corporate and wholesale markets called Ignite.
- An international mass-market Internet business focused increasingly on broadband called BT Openworld.
- An international mobile telephony business called BT Wireless.
- An international directories and e-commerce business based on Yellow Pages, The Business Database and Yell.com, called Yell. This would be floated towards the end of 2000 with a likely valuation of $10–12 billion.
- Concert Communications.

The purpose of the exercise was to demonstrate that BT was badly under-valued in relation to the sum of its parts. For analysts, the hardest part of the equation was putting a value on the fixed-wire network in the UK. In part, this reflected the general valuation problem that some analysts favoured value per connected line while others modelled cash flows. In particular, however, uncertainty arose from the value to be placed on the ongoing roll-out of broadband, and hence valuations fell in the $58–70 billion range.

The international operations consisted of Concert, valued at $13 billion, and the collection of European assets valued at roughly $27 billion. To these could be added BT Cellnet which was worth roughly $32 billion, the Genie portal worth perhaps $6–7 billion, Yellow Pages worth some $4–8 billion, and BT Internet/BT Click/Line One worth $10–14 billion. However, if these interests were combined and valued as an e-commerce platform, they were potentially worth more than the sum of the parts. The residual interests such as Syntegra, Syncordia and the share of Open were worth in the region of $4–5 billion.

Against these sums had to be set debt of $10 billion, leaving a total value in the range of $144–166 billion.[8] Expressed as a price per share, and eliminating the extreme values, one would have expected BT shares to trade in the £14–16 price range. In the light of subsequent experience it is necessary, perhaps, to remember that not only was this a valuation as BT stood in March 2000, but also that it was considerably below what would have to be paid to take it over at the time which would have been much nearer

$200 billion. This accounts for why rumours of a takeover by AT&T were so readily dismissed.

Unfortunately, such calculations were fast becoming somewhat hypothetical because, by mid-November 2000, BT's debts were approaching $45 billion. In addition to the existing debts and expenditures mentioned previously, the most significant element bumping up debt during the financial year to 31 March 2001 related to UMTS licensing, and in particular the cost of the licences in the UK ($6.1 billion in April 2000) and Germany ($7.7 billion in August 2000), together with the associated acquisition of the outstanding 55 per cent stake in Viag Interkom in Germany and 50 per cent of Telfort in the Netherlands ($1.8 billion in June 2000).[9] A further $15 billion or so was accounted for by the need to invest heavily to upgrade BT's networks to cope with such matters as broadband. The sale of BT's 34 per cent stake in Sunrise of Switzerland made only a modest offsetting contribution of roughly $700 million to the cash pile.

BT accordingly put forward what purported to be a much more radical restructuring proposal of its own, although this appeared little different from its predecessor in practice. What was being added was a new name – NetCo – for the network division providing wholesale services; a proposal to float not only roughly 25 per cent of Yell but the same proportion of BT Wireless, BT Ignite and, eventually, NetCo; and an admission that the corporate culture should concentrate more upon customers and less on engineering excellence. Given that NetCo controlled the vast majority of fixed-wire infrastructure in the UK, it would necessarily be subjected to tight regulation,[10] but by separating it from retail services it was hoped that the latter would no longer need such regulation. The decision not to attempt a full demerger of any division reflected the expectation that this would damage BT's already severely dented credit rating. However, it was argued that partial demergers would be costly and leave managers just as subject to head office control as previously. Furthermore, it would take up to two years to put the series of IPOs into effect. As a consequence, the share price dropped sharply.[11]

A quarter of BT Wireless was expected to fetch between $8 and $15 billion and a quarter of Yell roughly $1.5 billion. In addition, if real inroads were to be made into its debt mountain, BT would need to sell some minority European interests such as in Airtel (Spain), SFR (France) and possibly Blu (Italy), as well as most of the minority stakes acquired opportunistically in Asia – although these were worth comparatively little if Japan Telecom was excluded – plus Rogers Wireless in Canada. To these was added in January 2001 the potential disposal of $3 billion of real estate in the UK.

Early in 2001, it was rumoured that BT would merge together BT Openworld with Yell. Although this would represent yet another strategic reversal, it was argued that it would permit BT to compete more effectively with France Télécom subsidiary Wanadoo. Meanwhile, the deadline for an IPO of Yell, which had yet to break out from the south-east of England, began to recede as an ongoing investigation by the UK Office of Fair Trading into controls imposed on Yell in 1996 failed to reach a resolution, and it was rumoured that BT would now proceed with a full demerger of Yell. This was confirmed by the new finance director, Philip Hampton, in March.

The somewhat disastrous IPO of Orange in February 2001 – its share price dropped after the IPO despite several reductions prior to its listing – sent a clear signal that further wireless IPOs would be ill-received. Furthermore, there was insufficient time to forge a link with another mobile operator. BT accordingly turned its thoughts to an IPO involving preferential allocations or entitlements for existing shareholders, although these would require both Inland Revenue and regulatory clearances. In essence, the argument was that if assets needed to be sold at a discount, this should go to loyal shareholders rather than outsiders. In principle, there was no objection to a massive rights issue, perhaps worth $7.5 billion. However, it was immediately made clear by major shareholding institutions that such an eventuality would have to be accompanied by the resignation of BT's chairman and/or chief executive.

It was also argued that if BT largely eliminated its next final dividend it could save over $1 billion. Meanwhile, the price tag for Line One was falling by the day so other saleable assets were placed on the table. These included BT's stakes in Japan Telecom, StarHub and Maxis Communications. To these could be added its stakes in LG Telecom of South Korea, its three investments in India, Impsat Fiber Networks of Argentina and Rogers Wireless.

On a more positive note, BT arranged a sale and leaseback operation for its 7,500 sites which would produce cash inflows of up to $3 billion by the summer, and announced a similar deal, worth perhaps $1.5 billion, covering its fleet of 58,000 vehicles – it subsequently added the sale of its corporate headquarters to the list. However, it should be noted that sale and leaseback deals are treated by credit rating agencies as a form of borrowing rather than as a reduction in debt. In March 2001, it was rumoured that two offers had been made for wholly owned New Zealand subsidiary Clear Communications, valued at roughly $400 million. BT sold its stakes in an Indian Internet group and a satellite network builder to its partner, Bharti Enterprises, for $175 million. There were also signs of progress in relation to Yell with an anticipated offer in the $4.5 billion range.

BT was hardly in a position to go on a spending spree but it nevertheless took the opportunity to pay $1.25 billion for the residual stake in Esat Digifone in April 2001. Furthermore, BT faced something of a dilemma when, in April 2001, it was offered options to take stakes of almost 5 per cent in the three operating companies of J-Phone at any time prior to September. J-Phone was apparently motivated by the desire to prevent Vodafone from becoming overly dominant as a shareholder, but although the options were attractively priced at $560 million, taking them up would add to BT's debt mountain. The replacement of BT's much criticized chairman, Iain Vallance – but not that of CEO Peter Bonfield – suggested that strategic issues would be addressed with more firmness than previously, and this was partly borne out by the decision to dispose of all of BT's interests in Japan

Telecom and its subsidiaries, as well as its stake in Airtel. All of these were sold to Vodafone early in May, with the Japanese assets yielding $5.3 billion and the Airtel stake $1.6 billion. At this point, BT Wireless was left comprising BT Cellnet, Viag Interkom, Telfort Mobiel, Esat Digifone and mobile portal Genie. With roughly 45 per cent of its debt reduction plan achieved in one fell swoop, a further 30 per cent expected from the sale of Yell and $503 million in cash from the sale of the stake in Maxis, the outlook for BT seemed to be so much improved, as shown in Table 3.2, that talk of a rights issue began to die down.

The rights issue is launched

In the event, however, BT proved to be committed to the rights issue which, on a 3-for-10 basis, was announced on 10 May 2001 and comprised 1.98 billion shares priced at £3. This represented a 47 per cent discount relative to the £5.69 share price ruling on the previous day. The share price promptly dropped to £5.28, but compared to a theoretical ex-rights price of £5.06, this augured well for the take-up. However, when the shares first traded ex-rights on 21 May, they opened close to their then theoretical ex-rights price of £4.83, only to fall to £4.58 by the end of the day. Despite this, the final tally was a commendable take-up of 89.5 per cent. The final step was to issue to institutional shareholders the 207 million shares not taken up by investors at £4.30, the market price at the time. In total, the rights issue raised roughly £5.9 billion ($9 billion) net of expenses.

The rights issue prospectus was accompanied by further information on restructuring plans. BT Wireless (Cellnet, Digifone, Telfort Mobiel, Viag Interkom, Manx Telecom and Genie) was to be spun off with roughly $3 billion of debt, with what remained to be called BT Group and no longer saddled with the limitation on an individual shareholding of 15 per cent. BT Group's non-core constituents would comprise Yell, Concert and BT Ignite, but only while they remained unsold. The core elements would be divided into BT Retail, BT Wholesale and BT Openworld, with the former two each turning over roughly $15 billion a year. However, Wholesale would provide two-thirds of the operating profits and BT Openworld only $300 million. In effect, BT Group would be a European-centric cash-generative but low growth voice and data business. BT also stated that it was forgoing the outstanding dividend and would make no promises concerning the level of dividends to be paid beyond February 2002.

As is shown in Table 3.2, various other measures were adopted to reduce the debt burden in addition to matters discussed previously:

• At the end of May 2001, BT agreed the sale of Yell to a joint venture between private equity groups Apax Partners and Hicks, Muse, Tate and Furst. The price, $3.04 billion, was a third less than had been mooted earlier in the year.

Table 3.2 Contributions to debt reduction, 2001–2002 ($ million)

Contribution	$ million		
Current (effected or agreed end-June 2001)			
Debt outstanding	−39,600		
Rights issue		+8,600	
Assets sold			
Airtel		+1,600	
Bharti Cellular		+175	
Japan Telecom/J-Phone		+5,300	
Maxis Communications		+500	
Rogers Wireless		+380	
Yell		+3,050	
Telenordia		+15	
stake in BSkyB		+180	
Sale and leaseback[a]			
Property[b]			+3,500
Sites			+3,000
Vehicles			+1,500
Pension shortfall (annual)	−400		
Total	**−40,000**	**+19,715**	**+8,000**
Future			
Disposals			
Clear Communications		+180	
Savings (2001–02)			
Dividend reduction		+1,600	
Capital spending reduction		+730	
Cost base		+850	
Credit rating downgrade	−50		
Additional charges (2001–02)			
Pension costs	−900		
Asset write-downs[c]			
Impsat/SmarTone/StarHub	−1,000		
Concert/AT&T Canada	−1,500		
Additional stake in Blu	−95		
Potential sales/revenue raising			
Syntegra	offered then withdrawn June 2001		
Cégétel (26%)	worth, at best, $4 billion		
LG Telecom (22%)	under negotiation		
SmarTone	under negotiation		
Eutelsat (18%)	under discussion for perhaps $350 million		
Fraud protection department	possible spin-off into independent company		
Further shares in BSkyB	acquired in May 2001 and November 2002		

Source: Compiled by authors.

Notes:
[a]Not counted as part of debt reduction process by credit rating agencies. [b]Delayed to November 2001 due to legal problems. The property transactions are discussed in detail in the BT Group Annual Report and Form 20–F 2002, pp. 37–8. [c]Of which $750 million was announced in September 2001 to include Impsat in Argentina, plus $1 billion potentially arising against AT&T Canada depending upon the outcome of the Concert break-up, plus possible write-offs against SmarTone in Hong Kong and StarHub in Singapore. The actual write-offs resulting from the closure of Concert are separately itemized.

- BT announced that it would be withdrawing from Telenordia, its Swedish fixed-wire/Internet joint venture with Telenor.
- In mid-June, BT announced the agreed sale of its UK property portfolio – excluding 'operational buildings' – for $3.2 billion to property developer Land Securities Trillium and the William Pears Group, subject to their joint venture, Telereal Holdings, raising funds on the bond market. BT agreed to lease back the properties.
- In early July, AT&T bought BT's stake in Rogers Wireless for $379 million in cash with BT making a net loss on the venture.
- BT was alleged to have received approaches to buy Syntegra, valued at approximately $1.5 billion. However, almost immediately after sending potential bidders information packs, BT withdrew Syntegra, claiming that it had raised sufficient money to make its sale unnecessary.
- BT opened talks with Telefónica Móviles in June 2001 with a view to a potential merger of the latter with BT Wireless.
- In July 2001, BT sold half of the 19 million shares in BSkyB it had received in exchange for its stake in British Interactive Broadcasting (BiB).

Taken overall, the picture painted by Table 3.2 was fairly positive. On a strict accounting view, roughly half of the outstanding debt had been written down and what remained was manageable for a company the size of BT. Future outgoings had been limited via reductions in dividends and capital spending, and sale and leaseback operations had introduced greater flexibility. Further sales were still on the cards, with that of Clear Communications at an advanced stage of negotiations with Jump Capital/Todd Corporation/ Berkshire Partners for $206 million.

The main remaining priority of the new chairman, (Sir) Christopher Bland, was to deal with the Concert issue. During May, 400 staff at Concert were laid off, leaving roughly 6,000. However, losses continued to mount up and at the beginning of July 2001 the fate of Concert seemed finally to have been determined – or possibly not. With AT&T engrossed in its own restructuring, the European Commission unlikely to approve a merger of any of BT's and AT&T's assets without a long inquiry and BT reluctant to cede control of Ignite, the logical option seemed to be the break-up of Concert which by that time was losing up to $30 million a week. With Concert's assets divided up among them, most customers would hopefully continue to choose to be serviced by either BT or AT&T. Though clearly proposed as a 'least worst' option, it was sufficient to cause a sharp, albeit brief, upturn in BT's share price. BT also sought to address the issue of subscriber losses to cable operators offering combined cable TV/telephony packages by announcing alliances with ITV and BSkyB whereby BT customers would get discounted subscriptions to their pay-TV services.

At the end of July, BT announced its first quarter figures to the end of June. Although the core utility business remained profitable, all of the 'high growth' businesses, including wireless, had traded at a loss. BT Wireless, in particular, had been dragged down by problems at Viag Interkom, which did not bode well for the prospects of BT Wireless if floated as an independent company. Interest charges had been a heavy drain, but would fall in parallel with debt. More positively, the overall level of indebtedness had fallen to roughly $23 billion, implying gearing of 79 per cent, with more to come (see Table 3.2) compared to the $51 billion declared by France Télécom at the same time – although the latter, unlike BT, was growing rapidly. BT stated that it hoped to receive permission to separate BT Wholesale from BT Retail by September. Overall, the view expressed by analysts was that BT had once again become 'dull and boring'.

If so, the subsequent announcement that a financial consortium trading as Earth Lease, led by Babcock & Brown, a US asset finance house, and Chancery Lane Capital, a merchant bank, had offered $11.7 billion for BT's local loop infrastructure, including 5,500 telephone exchanges and 28 million lines, introduced some new excitement. It was estimated that BT was earning a return of only 0.5 per cent on these assets, and that disposing of them would hugely reduce regulatory scrutiny, but BT nevertheless rejected the offer, for which it was widely criticized. In effect, the issue appeared to boil down to whether BT's core asset was its infrastructure or its customers, and BT remained in a strategic limbo, unwilling to make a choice between the two.

Shortly afterwards WestLB, a German investment bank leading a consortium of unspecified partners, offered to buy the entire fixed-wire network for $25.6 billion. BT would retain its customers and pay for use of the network. The irony was that these two proposals would have made more sense when BT's debts were at their height, but, having reduced them to manageable proportions, and with the network independently valued at $35 billion, BT now preferred to plunge ahead with the IPO for BT Wireless and asked banks to tender for a $5.7 billion loan to achieve this. Nevertheless, justifying this decision was less than straightforward, and, in essence, the argument appeared to be that ownership of the network conferred 'strategic value' over and above book value.

Hiving off wireless

The initial intention was to start BT Wireless off with roughly £2 billion ($2.8 billion) of debt and an equal sum in working capital. However, early in September, it was announced not merely that the amount of debt to be transferred would only be £500 million ($723 million) – equivalent to roughly 5 per cent gearing, intended to be comparable to that of Vodafone and to leave room for heavy expenditure on 3G networks – but that the new company would trade as mmO_2 in the UK and eventually wherever the former BT Wireless operated. It would use the brand name O_2. In the process, the existing mobile Internet brand Genie, which was incurring substantial losses, would be killed off. Each existing share in BT would entitle the owner to receive one share in mmO_2 – where the 'mm' was an abbreviation for Mobile Media and 'O_2' for oxygen – and one in the rump BT Group (comprising BT Retail, BT Wholesale, BT Ignite and BT Openworld) in mid-November. No cash would be raised. The reaction of the financial markets was to slash the BT share price, which had reached almost £5 in mid-August, to well below £4 on the grounds that mmO_2 would be worth no more than $15 billion compared to earlier estimates of up to $25 billion. It was widely assumed that mmO_2 would be rapidly swallowed up by the likes of Telefónica Móviles or TIM.

There was also an announcement to the effect that a number of 'operational buildings' in which BT had retained the freehold when selling most of its properties to Telereal would be partly developed for domestic occupancy, commencing with the Marylebone exchange. The Telereal contract was finally signed in November.

In August, BT ended talks with TIW in relation to the 22 per cent stake in LG Telecom of Korea. It had been hoped to sell this prior to LG Telecom making a bid for the third 3G licence in South Korea as BT was not interested in becoming involved, but the successful bid for the licence now complicated the sale. The market volatility that followed the attack on the World Trade Center in September saw BT's share price fall as low as £3.50 and its total value to less than $50 billion. An unsecured loan facility was obtained by mmO_2, but was rated just above junk status at BBB- by Standard & Poor's which also rated mmO_2's long-term debt at the same level, with Moody's assigning Baa2. It was also announced that BT Openworld would concentrate on basic Internet access services and forgo the provision of content, and that Concert's assets would be divided up between BT and AT&T. AT&T was not particularly keen on this strategy because of its lack of an international network to replace Concert.

In September 2001, BT announced that it would be taking a $750 million charge against assets including Impsat in Argentina and AT&T Canada. The latter had not been mentioned at the time of the rights issue, so there was widespread dismay when it was revealed that if Concert was held together for a further two years, BT would be obliged to take an additional stake in the worthless AT&T Canada at a cost of $1 billion, whereas if Concert were to be disbanded previously then AT&T would have to buy out BT's stake for $370 million. BT would also have to meet $900 million in additional pension charges due to lay-offs resulting from the attack on the World Trade Center, and further write-offs would arise in relation to other overseas assets and, possibly, to Concert. All told, the net debt position at the end of March 2001 was expected to lie between $23 and $26 billion.

The first real sign that BT no longer considered itself to be under severe pressure came in early October when it announced that it had shelved proposals to separate its wholesale and retail businesses. This meant that it would be very difficult for there to be a takeover bid for BT's network infrastructure, and both Earth Lease and WestLB effectively withdrew anything other than an expression of interest to proceed should BT be so inclined in the future.

In October, BT formally announced that it would no longer be pursuing its break-up strategy involving the creation of NetCo, although it still expected to execute a managerial and operational separation of its wholesale and retail arms. This was generally well received by the financial markets, but they were disappointed by the third-quarter subscriber figures for mmO$_2$ that saw the growth of 643,000 new customers to an overall total of 16.8 million comprise largely of pre-paid contracts. Nevertheless, shareholders voted through the demerger of mmO$_2$ with trading to commence on 19 November 2001 – see Figure 3.1. At the end of October the situation in relation to Concert was finally unravelled: Concert would be broken up into its constituent parts, with BT reclaiming its managed services network infrastructure in Europe, Africa, the Middle East and the Americas, and AT&T reclaiming it in the Asia-Pacific. The submarine assets would be reclaimed as originally contributed. The Canadian joint venture would be wound up. BT would take an immediate $1.2 billion charge to include the elimination of a $500 million interest in AT&T Canada, a $300 million write-off of BT's share in Concert's goodwill and an $850 million write-down of fixed assets transferred back to BT, partly offset by a $400 million payment by AT&T for BT's stake in AT&T Canada. Subsequently, BT would take a further $300 million exceptional restructuring charge to take account for redundancies at Concert.

At the end of September, pending the divestment of mmO$_2$, BT Group's net debt stood at roughly £16 billion ($24 billion). BT Retail continued to provide over half of its turnover, with BT Ignite, BT Openworld and mmO$_2$

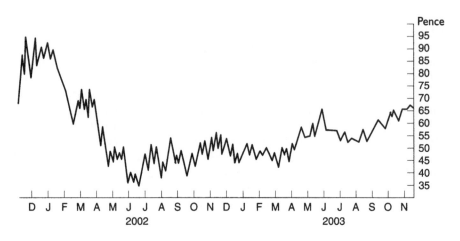

Figure 3.1 mmO$_2$ share price, 2002–2003 (pence).
Source: Daily share prices in the *Financial Times*.

showing operating losses. It was anticipated that BT Group would be obliged to acquire an additional 9 per cent stake in Blu under a shareholding agreement with Mediaset even though it also wanted to dispose of its own stake, and the transaction duly took place in December 2001. Trading in the grey market for mmO$_2$ commenced on 9 November with 437 million shares of the total of 8.7 billion changing hands and the price easing up to finish at £0.74. In the event, when trading began officially on 19 November, mmO$_2$ opened at £0.83, valuing the company at just under £7 billion ($10 billion), with the BT Group trading at £2.86 and accounting for 77.5 per cent of the total value. Three days later mmO$_2$ – with its Cellnet subsidiary renamed O$_2$ UK and Digifone renamed O$_2$ Communications (Ireland) – peaked at £0.93.

Meanwhile, BT announced the disposal of its stake in Maxis for $510 million. It also disposed of Clear Communications of New Zealand for $165 million to the TelstraSaturn joint venture, and opened negotiations to sell its stakes in SmarTone and LG Telecom.

The BT Group[12] stands alone[13]

In early December 2001, the BT Group – with its board restructured yet again – see Table 3.3 – announced that it would be cutting its labour force by 13,000

Table 3.3 Directors' merry-go-round – BT and BT Group

Alexander, Helen	Non-executive – appointed 01/06/98 – retired 14/01/02
Anderson, Iain	Non-executive – appointed 1995 – retired 30/09/01
Bland, Sir Christopher	Chairman (part-time) – appointed 01/05/01
Bonfield, Sir Peter	CEO BT – appointed 01/01/96 – resigned 31/01/02
Brace, Robert	Executive – retired 31/12/00
Brendish, Clayton	Non-executive – appointed 01/09/02
Cockburn, Bill	Executive – appointed 01/04/98 – retired 31/03/01
Danon, Pierre	CEO BT Retail – appointed 19/11/01
De Moller, June	Non-executive – appointed 01/09/99 – retired 14/01/02
Fergusson, Sir Ewen	Non-executive – retired 31/03/99
Green, Andy	CEO BT Global – appointed 19/11/01
Greener, Sir Anthony	Appointed 01/11/00 – Deputy Chairman from 01/01/01
Hampton, Philip	Former CFO – appointed 01/11/00 – resigned 08/04/02
Hughes, Louis	Non-executive – appointed 01/01/00
Isdell, Nevill	Non-executive – appointed 01/07/98 – retired 14/01/02
Jay, Baroness	Non-executive – appointed 14/01/02
Livingston, Ian	CFO BT Group – appointed 08/04/02
Marshall, Lord	Former Deputy Chairman – retired 18/07/01
Nelson, John	Non-executive – appointed 14/01/02
Oates, Keith	Non-executive – retired 31/12/00
Reynolds, Paul	CEO BT Wholesale – appointed 19/11/01
Symon, Carl	Non-executive – appointed 14/01/02
Vallance, Sir Iain	Former Chairman – resigned 01/05/01. President Emeritus
van den Bergh, Maarten	Non-executive – appointed 01/09/00
Verwaayan, Ben	CEO BT Group – appointed 01/02/02
Weston, Sir John	Non-executive – appointed 01/10/98 – retired 14/01/02

over a three-year period, primarily in BT Retail, in part fulfilment of the promise made by BT at the beginning of 2001 that it would be reducing numbers by 5–6,000 a year. It also announced plans to convert BT Retail into a more 'bundled' business, in part by re-entering the mobile market, probably via an arrangement with Virgin Mobile to supply the consumer market.

The demise of Excite@Home, although largely an issue for AT&T, also affected BT Group in that BT Openworld owned 42 per cent of Excite UK. In light of the failure to attract a strategic partner, the portal was shut down in December 2001. The financial markets were not over-impressed either when BT Group appointed the relatively unknown Ben Verwaayen to be its new CEO on 1 February 2002, especially given his previous experience with struggling KPN and Lucent. He declared that there would henceforth be three principal parts to BT Group's strategy: a relentless and passionate concern for its customers; the pursuit of growth; and the delivery of broadband Britain.[14] However, it was Chairman Sir Christopher Bland who made waves in the New Year by suggesting that BT Group would probably use its network to distribute TV within two years in competition with the cable companies which were posing a threat because of their ability to offer a 'bundle' of voice telephony, TV and Internet access. He also suggested that BT Group would either make its own content or invest in existing TV businesses, developing a business similar to BSkyB although it had yet to hear whether its November 2001 application for a TV broadcasting licence had been granted. After some large shareholders expressed disquiet at this scenario, Sir Christopher Bland promptly denied that BT Group intended to emulate BSkyB, given the lack of available investment funds, and reiterated that it would concentrate instead upon developing a high-speed Internet business and defending its traditional voice telephony services. BT Group also announced its intention to invest in developing its call centre business in conjunction with Siebel Systems, further announcing a consolidation into 150 more automated centres, involving 1,000 job losses, in February 2002 and the closure of 53 centres over a two-year period in March 2002.

Faced with a barrage of criticism, especially from the government, over its alleged stalling in relation to the roll-out of broadband lines – there were fewer than 150,000 subscribers at the time – BT Group responded by cutting the connection charge paid by ISPs from roughly £135 to £45 and the monthly fee from roughly £28 to £25 in January 2002. The reductions would coincide with the distribution of self-install kits. At the end of February, the wholesale monthly fee was reduced to £14.75 ($21), roughly the norm across the rest of Europe, although it was observed that BT now had the retail ADSL market more or less to itself even if it faced fairly strong competition from broadband cable. The retail price then stabilized at £29.99, although BT Group introduced a 'no frills' service in late April 2003 which undercut the BT Openworld ISP offering by £3.[15]

Early 2002 saw further boardroom changes as shown in Table 3.4. Setting aside the non-executives, the crucial appointments were, first, that of the new

CEO and, second, that of the proposed new CFO, Ian Livingston, who was to move across from retailer Dixons in April. The new CEO bought one million shares at £2.50 and his Chairman bought shares worth £1 million to demonstrate their faith in the company – which has so far proved to be misplaced. Although Ben Verwaayen was holding back on the publication of his strategic plan for the company, he took the first step in dismantling his predecessor's structure when he announced that Affinitis, set up in October 2000 to operate a number of services businesses such as the property portfolio and vehicles, would be dissolved with the loss of 6,000 jobs. He also announced the creation of an operating committee of division heads to tackle issues such as customer services and financial performance on a speedier basis than previously. February also witnessed the first disposal under his control, that of the 50 per cent stake in e-peopleserve to partner Accenture for £70 million ($105 million) with additional sums over five years based on e-peopleserves' revenues.

In early April, loss-making BT Ignite changed its strategy in the face of a disappointing take-up of broadband from one of servicing businesses of all kinds to a concentration upon roughly 10,000 large businesses in Europe. At the time, the network covered 55,000 km and 290 cities. As part of his three-year strategy announced on 8 April, Ben Verwaayen stated that unless BT Ignite's businesses in Germany, the Netherlands and Spain were restored to ebitda[16] break-even by March 2003 they would be shut down, as would the former Concert operations merged with BT Ignite if they failed to reach ebitda break-even by December 2003. Other parts of the strategy included the reaffirmation of existing cost-reduction and revenue targets for BT Retail and BT Wholesale, the decision not to branch out into the creation of media content nor to provide mobile infrastructure, and the provision of 'communication tooling' services for PC users such as access to video via the home PC. Positive free cash flow was anticipated during the financial year to 31 March 2003 at which point a dividend would again become payable. The response in the financial markets was broadly neutral and the share price, which as shown in Figure 3.2 had performed very respectably during the previous three months, held stable at £2.75.

Although BT Group had already agreed to be a reseller of mobile services provided by mmO_2, it decided to go one better in April by purchasing a block of mmO_2 spectrum for resale to its corporate customers with a view to offering a bundled package of fixed-wire, mobile and Internet access. It also unveiled plans to set up wireless local area networks (W-LANs or Wi-Fi) across the UK, to comprise 4,000 'hotspots' in airports, railway stations, hotels and cafés by June 2005, of which the first 400 would be installed by June 2003.[17]

The annual results for the year to 31 March 2002, published in mid-May, were generally well received as shown in Figure 3.1. Turnover on continuing activities had risen and a more than halving of net debt had been achieved through a combination of the rights issue, the mmO_2 demerger, sales of

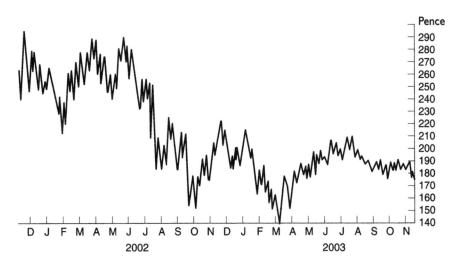

Figure 3.2 BT Group share price, 2002–2003 (pence).
Source: Daily share prices in the *Financial Times*.

investments and the Yell business and the property sale and leaseback transaction. BT Retail appeared to have stemmed subscriber churn through initiatives such as the BT Together tariff. Even BT Ignite's performance was better than expected, reflecting sharp reductions in costs. A final dividend of 2p was proposed.[18] Figures for the fourth quarter were also seen in a positive light, if only because they had mostly been so bad elsewhere in Europe. According to Lex,[19] BT Group was 'rebuilding its credibility' and the share price held at £2.75 – see Figure 3.1.

Naturally, it was too good to last and that price has yet to be seen again. One contributory factor has been the ongoing 'black hole' in the BT Group pension fund which was estimated to be as large as £1.8 billion in early June when calculated in accordance with the new FRS17 accounting standard. Figures for the first quarter of financial year 2003 did not help either as they revealed almost no growth in turnover, year on year, and a very modest reduction in net debt although interest charges were much reduced.[20]

At the end of June, BT Group agreed to buy Scoot.com – once valued at £2.5 billion but now on offer for £8.2 million – as part of a strategy to re-enter the directory enquiries business now the agreement not to compete with its former subsidiary Yell had expired.[21] In July, the regulator rejected a parliamentary report calling for a break-up of BT Group on the grounds that it was inhibiting the roll out of broadband. However, it subsequently proposed that BT Group should halve the wholesale price of partial private circuits (PPCs) used by ISPs for Internet access and cut line rental costs by 30 per cent.[22]

In October 2002, BT Group finally walked away from its investment in Blu, selling its 29 per cent stake to TIM for $5 million and writing off the rest of its investment of roughly $450 million. Fortunately, the sale of a further 20 million shares in BSkyB for £122 million ($185 million) on 10 November was less damaging to the balance sheet.

The BT Group tries to deliver

In early November 2002, Ben Verwaayen's honeymoon with investors came to an abrupt end. Six months previously he had promised to achieve 'tough but achievable' revenue growth of 6 to 8 per cent annually over the following three years and an incremental £2.4 billion of 'new wave' revenues essentially through broadband initiatives. Analysts were sceptical, and rightly so, as was shown when the results for the second quarter were published. These revealed only a 2 per cent increase in turnover although pre-tax profit rose by one-half, partly due to a better performance at BT Ignite. Net debt fell by £285 million with a further £2.6 billion in cash (equivalent to a £1.6 billion net profit) pencilled in from the anticipated sale of Cégétel. An interim dividend of 2.25p was declared.[23] On the whole, the financial markets were relieved and the share price peaked at over 60p above the low of early October, but it was rapidly depressed by a warning from the regulator that if it pushed through plans to allow alternative operators to provide a single bill incorporating charges for both calls and line rental – the latter billed separately by BT Group at that time – then BT Group could lose up to two million customers.

In mid-November, Sun Hung Kai Properties offered to buy for cash all the shares in SmarTone it did not already own[24] and BT Wholesale announced its intention to slice one billion pounds from its operating expenditure by March 2007, primarily by outsourcing equipment maintenance. However, no amount of such positive news could offset the reappearance of the pension 'black hole' which it was alleged had exploded from £1.8 billion at the end of March 2002 to £8.8 billion at the year-end, equivalent to over half the market value of BT Group. BT Group responded that its own actuaries estimated the pensions deficit at a mere £1.5 billion – using the SSAP24 accounting standard rather than FRS17 as used by analysts – and that it would not be necessary to increase the planned top-up of £220 million during the financial year (as well as the following four) now that it had closed its final salary scheme.[25]

Third quarter results revealed turnover up by a meagre 1 per cent and net debt down by £200 million. Faced by increasing numbers of new entrants such as retailers into its core market for telephony, BT Group responded with a new Together tariff setting a maximum of 6p for off-peak calls lasting up to an hour. It also reduced the wholesale price for broadband supplied over BT's network to £13 in the hope that retail prices would fall to roughly the £25 level charged by cable operators.[26]

In early April 2003, BT Group decided to shed its prancing piper logo – introduced in 1991 – and replace it with that used by BT Openworld – six differently coloured spheres revolving to form the shape of a globe – to signify that it was no longer a mere fixed-wire operator. However, the process would be gradual and cost only £5 million. It also decided to re-brand BT Ignite as BT Global Services and cancel any plans for an IPO.

Plans were revealed to more than double the size of the US network to fill gaps created by the closure of Concert. The decision to cut the monthly DataStream charge of £9.25 by 70p, plus a further 17p for bulk orders from broadband resellers which wanted to provide a service over their own lines, was, however, forced upon BT by the regulator, although potential competitors continued to complain that BT would retain a stranglehold over the market. A further 50p reduction was imposed in September 2003.

In May, JP Morgan calculated that under FRS17 the pension fund deficit, adjusted to take account of the projected return on the fund's investments, amounted to a net £2.8 billion although the position would be ameliorated by the facility to recover part of the total each year due to BT's ability to include pension charges within its regulated cost base and, hence, retail and interconnect charges. Meanwhile, BT's profitability would be underpinned by much reduced interest charges. However, BT subsequently reported that its own revaluation based on FRS17 indicated a £6.3 billion deficit overall and a net shortfall of £2.1 billion, and it pledged to put an additional £3.5 billion into its fund over the ensuing 15 years – much less than predicted by analysts.[27]

The annual results (see Table 3.4) were generally well received, encompassing as they did a substantial pre-tax profit, restoration of a respectable dividend and a reduction of the net debt below £10 billion. However, worries remained over the size of the aggregate pension fund deficit, the threat posed to BT's core markets posed by the entry of the likes of Tesco and Carphone Warehouse, the provision of a cheaper DataStream product and the imminent liberalisation of directory enquiries. Analysts took the view that BT was once again little more than a dull domestic utility – 94 per cent of revenues were generated in the UK – and should accordingly refrain from expansionary activities while raising its dividend. However, BT had somewhat different ideas, with the CEO of BT Retail lauding a string of 'new wave' measures centred around the re-entry into the mobile market – it negotiated an MVNO arrangement with T-Mobile in July with a view to launching BT Mobile Home Plan in October via high street outlets – and the rolling out of broadband.[28] In turn, analysts queried whether these would simply serve to cannibalise existing sources of revenue.[29]

mmO₂'s less than glorious year

A few comments are in order concerning the progress of mmO₂ since the demerger bearing in mind that BT's shareholders were given one share in

Table 3.4 BT Group, five-year financial summary, year ending 31 March (£ million)

	2003	2002	2001	2000	1999
Group turnover	18,727	20,559	20,427	18,715	16,953
of which:					
continuing activities	*18,727*	*18,447*	*17,141*	*16,125*	*15,197*
discontinued activities	–	*2,112*	*3,286*	*2,590*	*1,756*
Other operating income[a]	215	362	359	216	157
Operating costs[b,c]	(16,370)	(21,400)	(20,759)	(15,359)	(13,305)
Group operating profit (loss)	2,572	(479)	27	3,572	3,805
of which:					
goodwill amortization/exceptionals	*(218)*	*(3,059)*[g]	*(3,230)*[k]	*(200)*	*(69)*
Profit (loss) from associates/joint					
ventures[d]	329	(1,381)	(397)	(400)	(342)
Total operating profit (loss)	2,901	(1,860)	(370)	3,172	3,463
Profit on sale of:					
fixed asset investments/group					
undertakings[e]	1,691	4,389[h]	619	126	1,107
property fixed assets	11	1,089	34	26	11
Amounts written off investments	(7)	(535)	–	–	–
Net interest payable[f]	(1,439)	(1,622)	(1,314)	(382)	(286)
Profit (loss) pre-tax	3,157	1,461	(1,031)	(2,942)	4,295
Profit (loss) post-tax	2,698	1,018	(1,743)	1,985	2,972
Average number of shares (million)	8,616	8,307[i]	7,276	7,235	7,183
Basic earnings (loss) per share	31.2p	12.0p	(25.7p)	27.6p	41.1p
Dividends per share	6.5p	2.0p	7.8p	19.6p	18.3p
Return on capital employed (%)	15.5[j]	6.6[j]	14.9	18.2	19.2
Net cash flow from operating activities	6,023	5,257	5,887	5,849	6,035
Capital expenditure/financial investment	(2,381)	(1,354)	(8,442)	(3,752)	1,046
Acquisitions and disposals	2,842	5,785	(13,754)	(6,405)	(1,967)
Decrease (increase) in net debt	4,128	14,241	(19,242)	(7,747)	3,146
Net debt outstanding	9,573	13,701	27,942	8,700	953
Intangible fixed assets	218	252	18,380	5,777	742
Total assets	28,217	27,673	54,799	37,588	27,962

Source: BT Group Annual Report and Form 20–F 2002, pp. 26–7; 2003, pp. 26–7.

Notes:
[a] Including MCI merger break-up fee net of expenses. [b] Operating costs include net exceptional costs.
[c] Includes redundancy and early leaver costs. [d] Includes exceptional costs. [e] Including gain on MCI shares sold in 1999. The total for 2001 was mostly accounted for by Sunrise. [f] Includes exceptional costs (credits). [g] Mainly £3 billion of goodwill impairment in respect of Viag Interkom. [h] Comprising (a) gross sum raised £mn (b) profit (loss) pre-tax £mn:

Japan Telecom/J-Phone	(a) 3,709	(b) 2,358	BiB	(a)	241	(b)	120
Yell	(a) 1,960	(b) 1,128	Clear Communications	(a)	119	(b)	(126)
Airtel	(a) 1,084	(b) 844	e-peopleserve	(a)	70	(b)	61
Maxis Communications	(a) 350	(b) (4)	Other	(a)	173	(b)	31
Rogers Wireless	(a) 267	(b) (23)	TOTAL	(a)	7,973	(b)	4,389

[i] The increase resulting from the rights issue in May 2001. On 21 November 2001, each share was reduced in value from 115p per ordinary share to 5p per ordinary share. The surplus of £9,537 million arising from this capital reduction was credited to the Group profit and loss reserve. [j] Based on continuing activities. [k] Mainly £2.2 billion of goodwill and fixed asset impairment in respect of BT Ignite's European activities.

each company. As shown in Figure 3.2, the initial response was extremely positive, only to turn sharply negative in early January 2003 such that, only a month or so later, the share price had fallen by a massive 50 per cent to 60p. The problem was that, irrespective of the general prospects for wireless, mmO₂'s subscriber numbers for 2G were only growing slowly and it faced heavy expenditure to roll out its 3G networks. Furthermore, the situation in Germany, where Viag Interkom was struggling to compete against two dominant operators in the form of Vodafone and T-Mobile, suggested that mmO₂ would probably continue to make substantial losses for the foreseeable future. CEO Peter Erskine stated that if the German operation could not be turned around then it would be sold. Meanwhile, the UK operation would shed 1,400 employees and shut 133 of its 320 retail outlets.

In April 2003, mmO₂ announced plans to build out a pan-European broadband mobile data highway to support multimedia services. To achieve this, existing supply contracts would be consolidated and replaced with strategic partnerships with Nokia and Nortel Networks. A seamless core GPRS network would be developed together with a common, group-wide network management system. All told, the equipment would cost £1.3 billion, and equipment costs for the five years after the demerger would amount to £6.5 billion – much less than the £8 billion estimated in the demerger document. The share price responded with a temporary burst above 70p. However, by late April, analysts were already beginning to express the view that if the problems in Germany were not addressed quickly, mmO₂ might even be worthless.[30] What was clear was that the financial markets were ascribing negative value to the operations in Germany and the Netherlands.

On the last day of April the O₂ brand was launched in the five European markets served by mmO₂. The results for the financial year ending 31 March were published at the end of May. Total revenue had risen to £4,276 million of which 64 per cent came from the UK where turnover was static; the pre-tax loss had been reduced to £873 million, and there were also reductions in the operating loss and capital expenditure (see Table 3.5). Net debt, at £617 million, was somewhat higher than at the time of the demerger. The number of employees was to be reduced from 7,500 to 6,100 over the coming year. Altogether a reasonable performance but, to the surprise of Peter Erskine,

Table 3.5 mmO₂ financial summary, year ending 31 March (£ million)

Summary	2003	2002
Turnover	4,874	4,276
Ebitda before exceptionals	859	433
Operating loss before goodwill and exceptionals	(104)	(337)
Exceptionals	(9,664)	(150)
Loss pre-tax	(10,203)	(873)
Year-end net debt	549	617

Source: www.mmo2.com/docs/investor.

the share price continued to fall as investors concentrated on the failure to grow turnover in the UK which they believed would limit the amount of cash generated to subsidize operations in Germany and the Netherlands.[31]

The first half results published in November were much better, especially in respect of the German subsidiary, although KPN had declared that it was no longer interested in a merger. Net debt was slightly lower and cash flow much improved, but set against that was the expectation that the UK Competition Commission would significantly reduce the price of calls from fixed-wire to wireless handsets.[32] In April 2003, announcement of the sale of O_2 Netherlands (the former Telfort Mobiel) to private equity group, Greenfield Capital Partners, for £17 million in cash, caused the share price to surge, even though the sale necessitated a £1.4 billion write-off, on the grounds that further losses would no longer appear on the balance sheet.

However, it was not to last, since mmO_2's full-year accounts in May revealed the decision to write off £2.4 billion in goodwill, plus £5.9 billion (£2.1 billion in the UK, £3.8 billion in Germany) in respect of licences and other intangible assets and investments at continuing operations and a further £1.4 billion to cover shutting down the operations in the Netherlands – representing in total roughly half of its net assets. This was reflected in a pre-tax loss of £10.2 billion on revenues of £4.9 billion, but cash flow was strong and debt only £549 million. Further, the company re-iterated its confidence that the German operations would become profitable, kept £4 billion of 3G assets on its balance sheet and more than doubled the anticipated investment in 3G for the year ahead. Interestingly, the share price barely budged since investors chose to treat the write-down as a non-cash loss for the company which previously had assets (£18.8 billion) well in excess of its market valuation (£7.3 billion at flotation) and which would now avoid paying UK tax for several years. Analysts nevertheless continued to argue for the closure of the German operations. Later in May, mmO_2 unveiled its rival to Vodafone live!, branded as O_2 Active, initially available on 15 handsets.

Conclusions

The central issue in understanding the present structure of the telecommunications industry is that liberalization, increased competition and rapidly changing technology combined to make ever larger inroads into the cash cows of former incumbents – their circuit-switched voice telephony services. The almost universal response was to seek new, faster-growing markets linked to data networks based on IP technology and mobility. Unfortunately, the immediate need created by such a strategy was to spend vast sums of money on new or upgraded networks without any guarantees either that sufficient customers would emerge or that fierce competition would leave adequate profit margins.

Looked at from the perspective of incumbents, the one apparent protection that they had relative to nimble, focused new entrants was sheer scale and the ability to supply a full array of services. Hence, 'bundling' had immense attractions as a strategic response to adversity. With anything remotely to do with telecommunications prospering during 1999, it was possible to imagine that this was indeed the 'killer strategy' but, as noted, this did not stand up to scrutiny if relative changes in share prices were examined, and there was an ongoing tendency to value holding companies at much less than the sum of their parts other than, perhaps, at the peak of the market in the spring of 1999. Those operators that committed themselves heavily to bundling as a strategy were accordingly the worst sufferers once confidence in the sector took a turn for the worse in 2000. BT's bundling strategy was flawed, not so much because it lacked coherence as such, but because the risks were arguably excessive. It was acquiring opportunistic minority holdings which lacked a clear geographic focus. In addition, the timing also proved to be totally wrong, and hence when the financial markets turned against it there was a mountain of debt to climb. Furthermore, when it decided to implement what in effect amounted to a complete reversal of its strategy, not only had it missed the narrow aperture of opportunity to dispose of stakes in subsidiaries at 'top dollar' prices but it was forced to divert its attention away from the Concert alliance on which so much expectation had previously been placed.[33]

It is ironic that BT, with its long history of private ownership and relatively large size, was expected to be one, and possibly the greatest, of the success stories of European telecommunications, yet in early 2001 its strategy was in tatters – unless, of course, selling everything that moves could be considered as a strategy rather than emergency action – and it had yet to address the full implications of unbundling the local loop. Its alliance with AT&T had ended in tears, but at least it recognized that it had to concentrate its efforts geographically on Europe, the USA and Japan where most of the money was to be made. Unfortunately, its high level of indebtedness meant that it could not even pursue the latter strategy and it was forced to sell off its Japanese and many of its European interests, leaving itself as little more than the national fixed-wire and wireless operator it had been prior to its privatiz-ation. By choosing to separate itself into two parts it ran the risk that the rump, shorn of the mobile interests, would be acquired by an opportunistic buyer, but in the event BT was sufficiently strong to brush away the approaches when they duly transpired.

Naturally, what remained may have lacked excitement, but it did generate cash flow which is what the markets wanted above all else, and hence consolidation within the rump BT Group was the order of the day until the debt was brought down to manageable proportions. That done, BT Group set out to replace some of the bits it had previously shed while concentrating upon broadband. As things stand, that strategy is viewed fairly neutrally by the financial markets. Although the share price has risen off the floor reached in March 2003, this reflects a general trend in equity markets rather than an out-performance by the company. Furthermore, the introduction of carrier pre-selection in the UK, which obliges BT to connect calls to cheaper providers automatically, has already led over one million customers to turn to the likes of Carphone Warehouse and the main utilities and supermarket groups. Although BT has responded with its Together tariff,[34] a rapid expansion of broadband, a foray into Wi-Fi and its post-mmO$_2$ reincarnation as a virtual mobile operator, these have yet to provide sufficient revenue, let alone profits, to satisfy sceptical analysts that the dominant aspect of BT's future operations will be the steady decline of its fixed-wire business.

Chapter 4

AT&T

Tattered & torn

Introduction

In January 2003, Lex in the *Financial Times*[1] commented that 'AT&T should be renamed AT&Troubled. The capacity of the telecommunications giant to disappoint already modest expectations is a marvel to behold.' As we know from fairy stories and the Bible, giants can be cut down to size readily enough, but when it comes to telecoms, especially in the USA, the possibility that AT&T might actually be broken up and its various pieces taken over by much less well-known brands would come as a considerable surprise to the general public. The purpose of this case study is to analyse how this possibility has come about.

Background

Prior to 1998, American Telegraph & Telephone (AT&T) had a significant history of divestment. In 1984, it had been forced to spin-off the Regional Bell Operating Companies (RBOCs), and during 1996–97 both NCR and Lucent Technologies had been demerged. However, these were in most respects fairly straightforward affairs involving distinct areas of existing business. Subsequently, in recognition of an inevitable 'commoditization' of AT&T's traditional basic long-distance voice business, a plan was hatched by chairman Michael Armstrong to concentrate upon the then in-vogue strategy of 'bundling' together local and long-distance voice telephony, broadband Internet access, digital TV services and wireless.

Commencing in January 1998, AT&T accordingly launched itself into a programme of expensive acquisitions, the primary purpose of which was to overcome its lack of copper-pair fixed-wire access to local telephony subscribers despite the best intentions of the 1996 Telecommunications Act. At the heart of the plan, accordingly, lay the need to build up a national cable network – although cable businesses at the time were largely analogue and hence needed costly upgrades to cope with broadband digital services. However, a further factor was AT&T's desire to establish itself as a global operator which led to the creation of the Concert link – discussed in detail below – which also spanned this period. The major acquisitions were Teleport ($11.3

billion in January 1998); Tele-Communications Inc (TCI) ($48.5 billion in October 1998); Vanguard Cellular ($1.5 billion in October 1998); IBM Global Network ($5.0 billion in December 1998); and MediaOne ($58.0 billion in April 1999 after defeating a counter-bid by Comcast).

As shown in Figure 4.1, the AT&T share price manifested little volatility between 1993 and 1997, much as had been the case during the 1970s and early 1980s prior to the divestment of the RBOCs. Commencing from a low point in spring 1997, AT&T enjoyed a re-rating based upon the expectation that it would be able to transform itself from a dull but dependable 'old economy' company into something with expanded horizons in the aftermath of the 1996 Telecommunications Act. At the end of 1998 it was the seventeenth largest company in the world, valued at $102 billion, and although by the end of 1999 its ranking had fallen to eighteenth, it was now worth $162 billion – due, in good part to the value placed upon the acquisitions listed above. Nevertheless, despite the 60 per cent improvement, this represented a proportionate increase that was relatively modest by the standards of the TMT sector as a whole.

Unfortunately, the strategy proved to be flawed in at least two major respects. First, while the long-distance business declined as expected, as shown in Table 4.1, the cable business failed to boom – in good part because the acquired networks needed much more time and money to realize a broadband capability than had been expected. Second, 'bundling' went

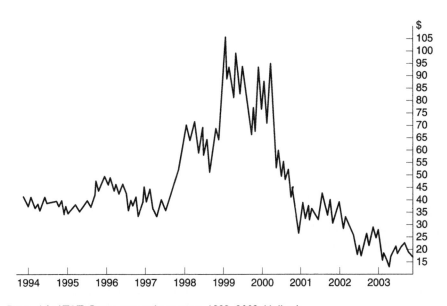

Figure 4.1 AT&T Corporation share price, 1993–2003 (dollars).

Source: Daily share prices in the *Financial Times*.

Table 4.1 Long-distance traffic, year-over-year change (%)

Traffic	1997	1998	1999	2000	2001
Average long-distance price per minute	–	−9.6%	−12.6%	−14.1%	−16.7%
Long-distance call volumes	–	+5.1%	+7.2%	+1.7%	−2.5%
Long-distance voice revenue	–	−3.1%	−3.0%	−12.0%	−17.2%
Total revenue	$41 bn				$27 bn

Source: AT&T Annual Report 2001.

progressively out of fashion, with market sentiment switching to favour the divestment of focused subsidiaries and 'pure plays' such as bandwidth wholesalers and wireless operators. As for holding companies such as AT&T, these became valued at much less than their 'sum-of-parts' value. Although this did not seem particularly obvious during 1999, given AT&T's substantial increase in value, it was quite evident when account was taken of the fact that Vodafone AirTouch came from nowhere to achieve the same overall value as AT&T by the year-end and that a 'focused' TMT company such as Yahoo! grew in value by 770 per cent during the year.

The Concert episode

The history of 'old' Concert need not concern us here. For our purposes, the story begins with the announcement at the end of July 1998 that BT had reached an agreement with AT&T which, although stopping short of an exchange of equity, would position AT&T as the main distributor of Concert services in the USA via a joint venture to be called 'new' Concert. 'New' Concert was subject to regulatory approvals in the usual way, which proved to be long-winded – for example, a full four-month investigation was initiated by the European Commission in December 1998,[2] with clearance coming in March 1999 subject to undertakings. Final approvals for 'new' Concert from the US regulatory authorities came in November 1999. It was potentially a major realignment of power in the global marketplace, and although the two companies never chose to exchange equity interests it was intended to be a fully committed relationship and hence, unusually, no 'pre-nuptial' agreement was signed indicating how assets would be divided up in the event of a 'divorce'. Indeed, this decision was a specific recognition of the fact that both parties had previously had to withdraw from joint ventures where 'pre-nuptial' agreements existed, so this time around they did not even make provisions for arbitration.

The joint venture combined the trans-border assets and operations of the two companies 'including their existing international networks, all of their international traffic, all of their international products for business customers – including an expanding set of Concert services – and BT and AT&T's

multinational accounts in selected industry sectors'.[3] Further, the two companies intended to develop the world's largest IP-based global network, in conjunction with their partners, to support services such as 'global electronic commerce, global call centres and new Intranet based solutions to support global organizations and executives on the move'. The new global platform supporting the network would operate at 200 Gbps, and would initially link 100 cities.

The venture would be divided into three key profit-generating businesses: a global voice and data business (Global Products); a global sales and services business (Global Accounts); and an international carrier services business (ICS). A crucial aspect of the venture was that BT would cede its ownership interest in 'old' Concert as part of its contribution. AT&T's acquisition of IBM's global data network, announced in December 1998, was intended to facilitate the rapid deployment of Concert services because it already covered 93 of the 100 international cities earmarked by BT and AT&T for the initial phase of their joint venture. Once fully operational, 'new' Concert's 21 joint ventures stretched across 237 countries and territories with its managed network incorporating 6,000 nodes in 52 countries covering nearly 1,000 cities. It also had investments in 115 undersea cables. Subsequently, the link between BT and AT&T was widened to link their wireless networks via a strategic alliance trading as Advance, although this had no legal form and hence was organized to function separately from the fixed-wire agreement. In effect, what was proposed was a form of marketing pact, termed a 'strategic alliance', which would use the Advance brand name, that was sufficiently loose to avoid any need for regulatory approvals, although the possibility of a pooling of interests at a later date was not ruled out. One of the immediate difficulties was that BT used GSM while AT&T used TDMA on three different analogue and digital frequencies. Hence, a common device would need to be capable of handling calls across four networks. This was not all that problematic from a technical viewpoint, but handsets would need to be no larger than those used for other networks if they were to be widely adopted. The full benefits of Advance were only likely to appear with the introduction of third-generation W-CDMA since BT and AT&T would then be able to operate on a common standard. Meanwhile, the two companies intended to develop billing and other systems that would enable them to offer cheaper international wireless calls to their global corporate customers.

However, despite the show of unity and apparent progress, the seeds had already been sown which would lead to the dismemberment of 'new' Concert. Neither party appeared to be keen to treat Concert as a business in its own right, with each seeing it rather as a means to generate traffic for its own existing network. Big corporate clients were instructed to sign contracts with the parent companies, and Concert was not permitted to develop its own strategy. In the USA, such clients were simultaneously courted by Concert, AT&T and AT&T Solutions, while, in Europe, BT sought to develop its Ignite division in direct competition with Concert. Furthermore, AT&T had expected BT to take increased, majority stakes in other European operators, and appeared not to realize that BT's partners such as Vodafone and Vivendi would not tolerate such an outcome. At the end of the day, however, the crucial factor was that Concert's management was ineffectual – in part because of the 50:50 ownership structure – and its strategy of competing in international telephony where there was an increasing glut of bandwidth was increasingly dubious.

In September 2000, it emerged that BT and AT&T were holding talks with a view to merging their business services divisions and, separately, their wireless operations, leaving both free to pursue independently their domestic retail markets, a move tantamount to splitting both companies into three parts (business, consumer, wireless). In principle, a combination of the AT&T business operations – accounting for nearly half its overall revenue – with Ignite and Concert would create a very powerful international provider of business data services, while the combined wireless operation would be able to develop into a major international provider of third-generation mobile services. Nevertheless, all was not entirely well. For example, AT&T had become disenchanted with the scale of BT's European network that was AT&T's route into Europe via Concert, in part because of the plethora of minority holdings, whereas BT was suspicious that AT&T was not sharing all of its customers in the USA. In the event, as discussed below, these pressures were to drive the would-be partners into dissolving the alliance in October 2001.

The new millennium brings restructuring

In line with other TMT stocks, AT&T's share price rose back to near its peak value in the Spring of 2000. It took the opportunity at the end of April to launch an initial public offer (IPO) for roughly 15 per cent of AT&T Wireless (AWE) – launched as a 'tracking' stock[4] – in the process raising $10.6 billion on the back of optimistic projections for the first quarter and full year. Almost immediately afterwards, AT&T released much less favourable first quarter figures for the company as a whole, causing the share price to suffer its worst one-day fall for 13 years and lawsuits to be launched by disgruntled AWE investors.

With its share price trading at a discount of more than one-third to the notional sum-of-parts value, Mr Armstrong was besieged with demands that AT&T be split up, a policy especially favoured by John Malone who had become the largest individual shareholder via the all-paper purchase of MediaOne.[5] The proposed deeper links with BT discussed above were the first apparent response, but they had rapidly become overtaken by events. The eventual restructuring plan was published in late October with a view to its implementation by the end of 2001 – provided shareholder, Internal Revenue Service (IRS) and regulatory approvals were forthcoming.

The first proposal was to offer AT&T shareholders the opportunity to exchange roughly $10 billion of AT&T shares for shares in AWE. AWE's share price was trading below that at the time of the IPO because, being a tracking stock, AT&T remained the legal owner of the whole of AWE and also held a majority stake. By increasing the publicly held stake via the share swap, and following on with a distribution of the rest of AWE to AT&T shareholders in mid-2001 – thereby creating an independently quoted stock – those taking up this opportunity to exchange shares were likely to do extremely well. Furthermore, AWE would ultimately be able to raise additional capital and make acquisitions in its own right.

A second division, Broadband, would bring together the cable television interests and broadband ISP Excite@Home with a view to the initial creation of a tracking stock followed by an eventual IPO. However, this was complicated by ongoing regulatory issues arising from the purchase of MediaOne (see below). The rest of AT&T would then be split into respective Consumer and Business Services divisions. Services to be included in the Consumer division – essentially residential long-distance – were in decline, and regulators had previously prevented WorldCom from spinning-off its own consumer services on the grounds that this would lead to insufficient investment, so the only answer was to create another tracking stock which would include the existing WorldNet ISP. Meanwhile the AT&T Business division – effectively the part previously due to be merged with BT's Ignite – would inherit the brand name, the stock market listing, the fixed-wire network and the research laboratories. It would therefore become the technical parent of AT&T Consumer.

The four divisions would trade among themselves at market prices, but only the Consumer and Business Services divisions would attract a dividend and the issue of how to allocate the $60 billion of debt was left unresolved. The ultimate justification for the exercise was to divest the fast-growing parts of AT&T from the declining Consumer division and to eliminate cross-subsidization, thereby adding focus and transparency. Unfortunately, the response of the financial markets was to note the complexity of the proposal, the overall level of debt involved, the lengthy period over which it would come to fruition – if at all – and the unresolved issue of the relationship with BT/Concert, and promptly marked down the AT&T share price. By the end of 2000, AT&T's total debts stood at roughly $65 billion and it was in urgent need of additional cash. But how to raise it?

Subsequent upon its acquisition of MediaOne, AT&T had been given three options by the Federal Communications Commission (FCC) with a view to reducing its market share of US cable networks – capped under FCC regulations at 30 per cent overall with AT&T claimed to hold 42 per cent. AT&T now declared that its preferred option was to float Liberty Media, its TV programming arm, which was already trading as a separate tracking stock with full managerial autonomy. However, this option was dependent upon an IRS ruling that no tax liability would arise, and such a ruling would anyway take months to appear. If it proved to be unfavourable, then AT&T proposed to sell its 25 per cent holding in Time Warner Entertainment

(TWE) to Time Warner.[6] This stake was notionally worth $10 billion, but Time Warner, now wholly in control of TWE, was using the fact that it did not need to buy in order to obtain control as a lever to hold out for a much lower price. In principle, the issue had to be settled by the FCC deadline of May 2001, but what appeared to be a reasonably clear-cut choice was thrown into confusion when the Appeals Court for the District of Columbia ruled that the 30 per cent cap was unconstitutional and arbitrary. This effectively meant that the FCC would struggle to impose its original divestment ruling without a return to the courts – and certainly not before May.

On a more positive note, NTT DoCoMo agreed to pay $9.8 billion for a 16 per cent stake in AT&T Wireless.[7] This surprisingly high price reflected DoCoMo's anxiety to raise its international profile, and was to be succeeded by a listing for DoCoMo on Wall Street in January 2001 to help pay for the investment. However, any expectations that DoCoMo would move to take over AT&T Wireless were clearly premature given that this would require an all-paper bid using shares that would for some time remain unfamiliar to US investors. Furthermore, AT&T would itself retain only $3.6 billion of the payment with the rest having to be put on the books of AT&T Wireless when it was floated in mid-2001.

Another sensible disposal would therefore be AT&T's 15 per cent stake in DoCoMo's rival, Japan Telecom – much prized by fellow shareholder BT not to mention Vodafone. However, even if BT bought the stake, AT&T's withdrawal from the main Asian base for Concert would raise further questions about the ongoing relationship between AT&T and BT. There was also AT&T's 25 per cent stake in Cablevision, worth roughly $3.5 billion, which would anyway have to be sold as part of the Liberty Media spin-off package to satisfy the FCC.

Just prior to Christmas 2000, AT&T cut its revenue and earnings forecasts for the fourth quarter for a second time, admitting that the switch to mobile telephony and e-mail was eating into its long-distance fixed-wire business at an unprecedented rate even though the RBOCs had struggled to get long-distance licences. However, it was also forced to admit that its outsourcing arm, AT&T Solutions, was obtaining fewer contracts than forecast as recessionary conditions began to bite in the USA. AT&T accordingly proposed to slash its dividend from 88c to 15c a share. The market's response was to knock its share price down to 30 per cent of the 2000 peak value achieved in March (see Figure 4.1), and the value of the entire company to $63 billion at its lowest point. AT&T's debts were accordingly roughly as large as its market valuation.

However, unlike many other cash-strapped carriers, AT&T did at least have a plan in place to reduce its $64 billion of debts. As noted above, $9.8 billion would initially be paid to AT&T by DoCoMo, to which would be added the roughly $1.4 billion paid in cash by Vodafone for AT&T's stake in Japan Telecom in May 2001 and the $2.2 billion offered for a collection of mostly small-city cable networks by Mediacom Communications in February

2001. By the latter part of 2001, the sale of AT&T's stake in TWE would hopefully be negotiated for perhaps $9 billion, plus roughly 60 per cent of its Cablevision stake for perhaps $2 billion. When AT&T Wireless was spun off, AT&T would hold back a stake worth $3 billion to be sold off later in the open market. Market conditions permitting, an IPO of AT&T Broadband would subsequently bring in $5–10 billion, and additional non-metropolitan cable stakes could be sold off without much problem. Naturally, the latter arrangements were subject to varying degrees of uncertainty, but an optimistic scenario would see almost half of AT&T's end-2000 debts repaid by the end of 2001.

The sale of AT&T Wireless bonds, completed at the beginning of March 2001, was a success, with the total on offer raised from $4 billion to $5. However, an attempt by AT&T to alter its charter so as to permit an event such as a major restructuring to proceed with the support of 51 per cent rather than the existing 67.7 per cent of shareholders led to legal action being initiated by several large pension funds. The action was subsequently dropped when AT&T agreed to improve union workers' access to new jobs during any restructuring.

In March, AT&T took advantage of the bankruptcies beginning to strike down a variety of operators by acquiring, subject to regulatory approvals, the assets of broadband ISP NorthPoint Communications for the knockdown price of roughly $135 million. In April, AT&T announced that, following on from an IRS ruling that no tax liability would thereby arise, tracking stock Liberty Media would be spun off in August. Subsequently, AT&T sold its 12.7 per cent stake in Maxis Communications of Malaysia – acquired as part of the MediaOne purchase – to Usagha Tegas for $179 million in cash.

As a preliminary step towards the flotation of AT&T Wireless, AT&T exchanged 372 million of its own shares (roughly 10 per cent of those in issue) for 438 million shares in AT&T Wireless in a May transaction worth $7.8 billion.[8] It then traded cable systems to Charter Communications in exchange for $1.04 billion in cash, $500 million of Charter stock and two small Florida cable networks.

The plan to split AT&T, with the Consumer and Broadband business trading as tracking stocks and the bulk of the debt (based on the end-2000 amount) allocated to the Broadband ($28.4 billion) and Business Services ($27.1 billion) divisions, was filed with regulators in mid-May. Shareholders were expected to vote on the proposals around September time, by which point the debt reductions already achieved by May (roughly $17.5 billion) plus the receipts from the TWE disposal and other cable interests would leave all four divisions, but especially Broadband and Business Services, in much better financial shape.

However, things did not run smoothly in respect of plans to launch interactive TV services. A development programme had been initiated with Microsoft in 1999, with Microsoft investing $5 billion in AT&T to secure the use of its software in the set-top boxes. In the interim, AT&T had also been testing equipment made by Liberate Technologies, but in June 2001 AT&T announced that it did not believe the potential demand would justify launching anything other than a much simpler device than originally planned, and would not clarify who would make it although, in practice, the existing DCT-2000 box was supplied by Liberate while the proposed DCT-5000 boxes would have contained a Microsoft operating system.

The dangers of making deals in a highly volatile environment for telecoms was brought home to AT&T in May 2001, when it was obliged to renegotiate an agreement made with Cox Communications and Comcast in May 2000 to buy their shares in Excite@Home, paying $48 a share in either cash or AT&T shares. Both Cox and Comcast opted for AT&T paper, in principle becoming entitled to 134 million shares worth $2.9 billion in a tax-free exchange. However, the Excite@Home shares, worth $34 apiece at the time of the deal and $94 at their peak, were now worth a mere $4, valuing the 60.4 million shares which AT&T was getting in return at only $138 million. What was agreed was that Cox and Comcast would keep these shares *plus* receive 155 million AT&T shares (to allow for taxes arising from the deal) – in principle an astonishing act of generosity but, in practice, not so since AT&T could now record the transaction as a loss to be set against tax, thereby saving $1.2 billion. In consequence, AT&T's stake in Excite@Home remained at 23 per cent but with roughly a 74 per cent share of voting control.

AT&T Wireless launches

In mid-June, a specific date for the flotation of AT&T Wireless was fixed at 9 July 2001. Prior to that date, all outstanding AT&T Wireless tracking stock would be redeemed for shares in AT&T, including the stakes held by those who had subscribed to the April 2000 IPO and by DoCoMo (for the subsequent history of the share price, see Figure 4.2). The newly created ordinary shares in AT&T Wireless would then be distributed to all AT&T shareholders of record on 22 June by way of a special stock dividend comprising roughly 1.16 billion shares, with AT&T holding on to shares worth $3 billion as expected. This would leave AT&T shareholders with roughly 63 per cent of AT&T Wireless shares. Meanwhile, AT&T made an arrangement with two investment banks to swap AWE's debt for AT&T Wireless shares which would then be sold on. This would account for roughly the first half of the $3 billion of shares held back, and would be highly beneficial to AT&T because no tax liability would be incurred. The final tranche of 91 million shares was duly sold off in December. All told, the divestment of AT&T Wireless generated a tax-free gain of $13.5 billion representing the difference between the fair value of the tracking stock on 9 July and the book value in AT&T's accounts.

However, the prospects for the new company were clouded by two major issues. First, it had decided to move to a W-CDMA version of 3G which meant that it had first to roll out a GSM network overlaid on top of the

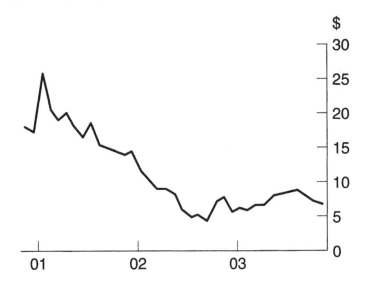

Figure 4.2 AT&T Wireless Services share price, 2001–2003 (dollars).
Source: Daily share prices in the *Financial Times*.

existing TDMA network. The first section was due to be launched in Seattle during the summer, with 40 per cent of its markets covered by the end of 2001. Just how much this would cost, and how long it would take to transfer subscribers (15.7 million in total at that time) over from the older networks remained unclear. Second, AT&T Wireless would be short of spectrum, especially when it came to rolling out W-CDMA. It thought that it had partially overcome this difficulty when it bid $2.9 billion, via affiliate Alaska Native Wireless, for 44 'C' and 'F' block licences, including one in New York, as part of an FCC auction in December 2000. However, NextWave, from whom many of the licences had been reclaimed, overturned the auction outcome in the courts, thereby depriving AT&T Wireless of its new licences, and leaving it able to reach only 70 of the 100 largest US markets. This suggested to analysts that a merger proposal would soon be forthcoming for AT&T Wireless, although DoCoMo had the right to veto any investment falling between the limits of 15 and 50 per cent of the total company.

While AT&T Broadband backtracks

As noted previously, AT&T Broadband was also destined in principle for a tracking stock IPO later in the year, but it came as little surprise when Comcast, a much smaller but financially strong company, announced in July that it had tabled a hostile bid for the business after failing to reach agreement with AT&T. The offer constituted 1,052,500 Comcast non-voting shares, at the time worth $44.5 billion plus $13.5 billion of AT&T debt taken on,[9] or roughly $4,000 per subscriber compared to the norm for cable companies of $4,500. Comcast also indicated its willingness to take over other AT&T holdings in cable operators such as Time Warner Entertainment, Cablevision Systems and Rainbow Media. The AT&T share price promptly rose by over 20 per cent while that of Comcast fell, reducing the all-share offer to $40.8 billion, a figure that AT&T considered far too low: deducting the assets that had either already been sold or were on the block, the cost of the cable systems acquired as part of TCI and MediaOne amounted to $65 billion, to which further investments of roughly $4 billion needed to be added. There was the additional downside that there was neither cash nor protection against a fall in the Comcast share price while the deal was going through. The bid was promptly rejected, although AT&T simultaneously postponed the Broadband IPO. Immediately afterwards, AT&T commenced talks with AOL Time Warner with a view to merging their respective cable operations. The plan would involve AT&T Broadband being spun off prior to a merger with Time Warner Cable leaving AT&T shareholders with a minimum 50 per cent stake in the merged company and AOLTW with 45 per cent together with full ownership of Warner Bros. film studio and Home Box Office. An attraction was that such a restructuring would incur no tax liabilities. Comcast's response was to sweeten its bid by offering to acquire AT&T's stake in Time Warner Entertainment.

Valuing AT&T

But what was AT&T really worth? For the moment, AT&T Broadband could be valued at the offer price of $40.8 billion, to which could be added anything between $20 and $40 billion for the other cable interests. The other assets such as the residual stake in AT&T Wireless, the Canadian holdings and Concert, were worth roughly $8 billion. As for AT&T Consumer and AT&T Business, these were best valued as multiples of ebitda[10] – but at two and a half times for the former as against five for the latter given their relative prospects – yielding respectively $12 billion and $43 billion. All told therefore, if a mid-figure was taken for the cable interests, AT&T had an enterprise value of $138.8 billion.

AT&T's total debts stood at the time at roughly $46 billion, but $8.6 billion of this represented the securitisation of stakes in Comcast, Microsoft and Vodafone, so $37.4 billion needed to be deducted from the enterprise value, leaving $81.4 billion. Given 3.6 billion shares in issue, this was equivalent to a figure modestly higher than the actual market price, but well within the bounds of error given the uncertainties inherent in the calculation. In other words, unless Comcast could be persuaded to raise its offer considerably, AT&T was worth almost exactly the sum of its parts.

Meanwhile, there was some progress on the overseas front. At the end of June, Birla-AT&T-Tata agreed to merge with BPL Communications, thereby forming India's largest cellular operator with one million subscribers. AT&T would end up with 16.9 per cent of the enlarged group plus an indirect stake via its 49 per cent holding in one of the two BPL operating companies, BPL Cellular. AT&T also agreed to buy BT's stake in Rogers Wireless in Canada for $379 million in cash, thereby raising its stake to 33.3 per cent. At the end of July, AT&T and Verizon Communications agreed in principle to sell their combined 49 per cent stake plus management control in Czech mobile operator EuroTel Praha to Ceský Telecom for roughly $1.5 billion in cash.

There was a further piece of good news on the cable front when an appeals court ruled that AT&T did not have to provide access to its cable networks to rival ISPs.[11] However, second quarter results posted in May demonstrated only too clearly that whereas AT&T Wireless was trading profitably as a separate company, the residual parts of AT&T were actually making a loss albeit in part because of the need to write off $1.1 billion (before tax) of investment in Net2Phone (partly offset by the gain on the disposal of the Japan Telecom stake[12]). It also needed to write off heavy losses at Excite@Home. The prospects for AT&T Wireless were enhanced by the fact that it was about to launch the first-ever GPRS service in the USA, in Seattle, with national roll-out by the end of 2002. Following the pattern established in Japan by shareholder DoCoMo, prices would reflect the amount of data downloaded at 100 kbps with a $50 per month fee entitling users to a free allocation of 400 minutes of regular voice calls and one megabyte of data transfer.

On 10 August the spin-off of Liberty Media was completed and was rapidly followed by the announcement that Excite@Home, saddled with $1 billion of debt, would probably declare bankruptcy. Subsequently, by way of details revealed in the flotation document for BT's mmO2, it emerged that AT&T was a major shareholder in AT&T Canada which had outstanding debts of $2.5 billion. AT&T Canada was therefore effectively worthless, and AT&T was potentially liable for its own plus BT's commitments which would be passed on to AT&T unless it kept Concert together for a further two years, in which case BT would itself be obliged to acquire a much bigger stake in AT&T Canada.

By the end of September the markets were swirling with rumours relating to one kind of restructuring or another. One suggested that AT&T and Comcast were again negotiating the transfer of AT&T Broadband; another that AT&T had approached Qwest with a merger proposal (which, interestingly, caused Qwest's share price to plummet); and yet another that AT&T had approached BellSouth. Meanwhile, Excite@Home finally filed for Chapter 11 bankruptcy protection – a potentially costly exercise for AT&T[13] but one that had a potential golden lining if AT&T's offer to buy its broadband ISP business with its 3.6 million customers worldwide for a meagre $307 million was accepted. At the same time, AT&T announced that it intended to dispose of its stake in Cablevision Systems, left over from its purchase of TCI, followed by its stake in Cablevision subsidiary Rainbow

Media. This was completed on 23 October.[14] However, this did not imply a policy of simple retrenchment, as evidenced by the announcement in early October of the purchase by AT&T Wireless of the outstanding 77 per cent of the shares in TeleCorp for $2.3 billion plus $2.3 billion of debt and preferred stock taken on. This all-share purchase, justified by the low price at which TeleCorp's shares were trading, brought a further 32 million potential customers in the mid-West and South into the fold of AT&T Wireless and extended the direct reach of AT&T Wireless to 75 per cent of the US population. Because of the share swap, DoCoMo's stake in AT&T Wireless was diluted to 15.2 per cent, and it immediately acquired a further 26.6 million shares to take its stake back to 16 per cent.

It subsequently emerged that AT&T had indeed been engaged in discussions with BellSouth about a possible merger. However, BellSouth did not wish to take on AT&T's cable interests, and the tax position should the cable interests and voice networks be sold separately was potentially adverse. AT&T's response was to sell most of its stake in Cablevision Systems for $1.3 billion.

In late October, AT&T announced that it no longer considered it worthwhile to sink any additional investment into its fixed wireless business to gain the requisite scale, and would be taking a $1.3 billion charge prior to exiting. Further costs would arise due to the disbanding of Concert, announced on 16 October, which would involve AT&T reclaiming its Asia-Pacific and submarine assets as originally contributed. Write-downs of these assets would become necessary as well as provisions against the cost of redundancies. AT&T would acquire BT's 9 per cent stake in AT&T Canada and move to take complete control over the company in order to protect its ability to service business customers throughout North America.[15] All told, roughly $7 billion would need to be set aside to resolve the outstanding issues. The repurchase of assets in Concert was approved by the European Commission in December 2001.

Not surprisingly, the reported financial data for the third quarter indicated that long-distance telephony revenues were suffering at the hands of mobile telephony and e-mail – a situation that was expected to deteriorate even faster during 2002. The net loss for the quarter, adjusted for the closure of Concert, came to $2.2 billion. The trading situation at AT&T Broadband was more positive, but it would be necessary to take a charge against the stake in Excite@Home. With its overall indebtedness at $36.5 billion, and the sale of its stake in Time Warner Entertainment and the Comcast bid on hold, AT&T announced that it would sell or rent out its huge headquarters at Basking Ridge and raise a further $5–7 billion via a global bond offering. Its senior unsecured debt ratings were promptly downgraded to A- by S&P and to A3 by Moody's, but, despite the need to pay a substantial premium over the rate for government bonds, AT&T felt comfortable because of the historically low level of interest rates at the time. In the event, AT&T was able to raise the global offering to a total of $10.09 billion – all providing a

2.5–3.0 per cent yield over and above that on government bonds – making it the second-largest bond issue by a US company and the fourth-largest ever.

The situation with respect to AT&T Broadband became confused in November when bids were indicated by Comcast, Cox Communications and AOLTW, with Microsoft discussing the possibility of a major investment if AT&T Broadband remained independent or, alternatively, participation in a successful bid by either Comcast or Cox. Revised bids by all three were submitted in December, and in the event it was Comcast that won the day with an offer of Comcast stock worth $47 billion, plus $21 billion of debt taken on, to include the 25 per cent stake in TWE. As a consequence, AT&T shareholders would in principle end up with a 56 per cent economic stake and a 66 per cent voting interest, with the Roberts family obtaining a 33 per cent voting interest, in what would be known as AT&T Comcast when the deal was closed towards the end of 2002. In addition, Microsoft agreed to convert $5 billion of AT&T subsidiary trust convertible preferred securities into shares in Comcast. It was calculated that the residual AT&T long-distance businesses would carry $15 billion of debt.

The situation with respect to Excite@Home also moved to resolution. Although AT&T had been the only bidder for Excite@Home's assets, the latter's creditors/bondholders rejected its offer, hoping to force up the price. This proved to be a miscalculation since AT&T promptly began to switch customers onto its own network with Cox and Comcast preparing to follow suit, in the process cutting Excite@Home subscribers by half to two million. Excite@Home was accordingly left with no option but to announce that it would be ceasing operations at the end of February 2002.

In mid-November, AT&T announced that it would probably be cutting a further 4,000 jobs in addition to the 9,000 that had already been shed – representing a reduction of over one-tenth of the 125,000 workforce in jobs at the beginning of the year – and as a result taking a $1 billion restructuring charge. For his part, CEO Michael Armstrong declared that he would be the new Chairman of AT&T Comcast in due course with a large salary and bonuses even though he was approaching the retirement age of 65, but would remain at AT&T until it came into being. As two of the three legs of the AT&T edifice – wireless and cable – were to disappear, many critics took the view that he was being rewarded for having failed rather than the reverse. He would be replaced by AT&T President David Dorman.

Taking stock

In the Annual Report for 2001, CEO Michael Armstrong admitted (p. 6) that every strategic move 'wasn't choreographed from the beginning. Nor did I anticipate everything . . . I certainly didn't expect the dot.com bubble to burst . . . foresee the worldwide downturn in telecom stocks . . . or the US recession.' He added that he had been naive to believe that the 1996 Act would lead to AT&T being able to provide real competition in the RBOCs' local markets. Nevertheless, he concluded that he was 'proud of what we accomplished'. He did not, however, comment on whether his shareholders felt the same way.

At the beginning of 2002, shareholders in AT&T faced the prospect of holding multiple shareholdings by the year-end, namely:

- in AT&T
- in AT&T Consumer, by way of a tracking stock
- in AT&T Wireless
- in AT&T Comcast.

But was this really the right way to proceed?

In the USA, the RBOCs had already completed a good deal of consolidation, and were finally beginning to win long-distance licences, although it scarcely bore repeating that five years had passed since the Act of 1996 'liberalized' markets. However, even the slow progress in what was the forming of horizontal linkages between local and long-distance markets was making life increasingly difficult for AT&T. Furthermore, the languishing share price effectively eliminated the possibility for all-paper bids. The experience of WorldCom/Sprint indicated that consolidation was anyway going to run up against all kinds of regulatory restraints within the USA unless, as in the case of the cable rules, successful legal challenges could be mounted. Given these uncertainties, the AT&T break-up plan certainly made a good deal of sense – but only for a while. The first stage – the flotation of AT&T Wireless – was duly achieved, but the opportunistic bid by Comcast for AT&T Broadband suggested that continuation of the process would be far from smooth and take rather longer than intended. Furthermore, it became evident that, with AT&T Wireless spun off and AT&T Broadband in the process of being acquired by Comcast, the rest of AT&T could potentially be mopped up by other operators with AT&T disappearing in its entirety. One way out of this dilemma – a merger with a RBOC – ceased to look feasible when BellSouth declined to proceed, and the experience of WorldCom did not augur well for further flotations of the other pieces of AT&T identified in the break-up plan. Furthermore, the depressed state of the US economy, especially in the aftermath of the attack on the World Trade Center in September 2001, did not indicate that it was an opportune time for IPOs. The alternative strategy was accordingly to reverse the break-up process and consolidate even if it represented a rather extraordinary reversal of strategy.

To some extent such a reversal was more logical than it had been previously given the possibility that the US economy was sliding into recession, since sheer size is generally seen as providing some protection against adversity in such circumstances. Furthermore, although AT&T's share price had tracked sideways during 2001, this was no longer seen as a bad performance compared to the collapses seen in the share prices of many, if not most, other companies in the TMT sector, and it also meant that floating off other parts of the company would be unlikely to boost AT&T's share price significantly. However, as noted in many of the other case studies, boards of directors are reluctant to change course for fear that they are deemed to have got their strategy wrong with the attendant possibility of losing their positions.[16]

2002 in practice

At the beginning of 2002, the prevailing view, expressed by *Fortune* magazine, was that AT&T was 'dying'. However, as *The Economist* noted, the only party not to have noticed was AT&T itself.[17] It went on to argue that this was not an entirely unreasonable view since, although AT&T would eventually shrink back to essentially the long-distance operator it had been up to 1997, its sheer size in relation to its competitors, and the value attached to its nationally-known brand, would permit it to maintain its favoured position with the biggest blue-chip companies. Furthermore, up to $25 billion of its debts would pass along with AT&T Comcast, leaving it in relatively good shape financially – and this, of course, before WorldCom, its biggest rival, imploded later in the year. Even the collapse of Concert still left AT&T with its original, extensive, global network which competitors could not match. But did the events of 2002 prove that AT&T was right to be so sanguine?

In January 2002, AT&T Wireless agreed to sell its fixed wireless assets for $45 million in cash and shares to Netro Corp., leaving AT&T Wireless with a 13.5 per cent stake in Netro. These assets, once a significant part of AT&T's strategy to bypass the Baby Bells, had attracted a mere 47,000 subscribers.

On 1 April, Concert was officially unwound.[18] One day later, AT&T announced that it was set to quit Indonesia where AriaWest International, 35 per cent owned by AT&T, had agreed to sell its joint operating partnership back to incumbent PT Telkom for roughly $320 million. It subsequently announced that it would be making a further $200 million from the sale of its Basking Ridge HQ to Pharmacia Corp. in July. On 29 May, Moody's lowered its rating on AT&T's long-term debt from A3 to Baa2 – two notches above 'junk' – while Fitch followed with a downgrade from A– to BBB+, the same as Standard & Poor's which had remained unchanged. By the standards of operators at the time, these represented average ratings, albeit ones under review pending completion of the AT&T Comcast transaction.

On 10 July 2002, AT&T shareholders approved a one-for-five reverse stock split with a view to restoring a 'respectable' share price and to avoid any possibility of being de-listed from the New York Stock exchange.[19] On the same day, the creation of the Consumer Services Group tracking stock was also approved as was, in conjunction with Comcast shareholders, the creation of AT&T Comcast. Although, under SFAS 142, AT&T had decided to calculate impairment charges during the final quarter of the financial year, this event was treated as a 'trigger event' necessitating a calculation for impairment in respect of AT&T Broadband in the second quarter, and this resulted in a $12.3 billion franchise cost impairment charge and a $4.2 billion goodwill impairment charge as shown in Table 4.2.[20] Once AT&T Broadband was spun off and simultaneously merged, together with Comcast, into subsidiaries of the newly formed AT&T Comcast, AT&T shareholders would receive approximately 0.3235 of a Comcast share for each existing AT&T share.[21] On 21 August, AT&T and Comcast entered into an agreement with AOL Time Warner for the restructuring of TWE whereby AT&T Broadband would receive $2.1 billion in cash, $1.5 billion of common stock in AOLTW and an effective 21 per cent passive interest in a new cable company to be named Time Warner Cable which would consist of all of AOLTW's cable properties including those already in TWE.[22] The creation of AT&T Comcast was cleared by the Justice Department in mid-September; received a favourable tax ruling permitting the sale of AT&T Broadband to be tax-free to AT&T shareholders in mid-October; and was backed by the Federal Communications Commission in mid-November. The bond exchange was also concluded in mid-November and on 18 November the deal was finally concluded via the issuing to AT&T shareholders of 1.2 billion new Comcast shares worth $31.1 billion to create a cable group with 21.4 million subscribers and 59,000 employees in 41 states, making it, it claimed, the world's leading provider of broadband video, voice and data services. Altogether, AT&T Comcast assumed $24 billion in debt from AT&T and was valued at roughly $60 billion.

In March, the situation at loss-making AT&T Canada was fast reaching crisis point with debts of C$4.7 billion that had been downgraded to 'junk' in February but only C$500 million in cash. AT&T claimed that the debt was entirely a matter for AT&T Canada even though it would theoretically be obliged to buy up the outstanding shares by mid-2003 under existing arrangements. In practice, on 30 September, AT&T still held roughly 31 per cent of AT&T Canada but on 8 October, Tricap Investments Corp., a wholly-owned subsidiary of Brascan Financial Corporation, purchased roughly 63 per cent of AT&T Canada and CIBC Capital Partners purchased the outstanding 6 per cent or so. Both purchases were funded by AT&T, partly with the $2.5 billion net proceeds arising from the sale of 230 million AT&T common shares on 11 June. AT&T continued to hold its 31 per cent stake which was limited by Canada's foreign ownership rules.[23] Meanwhile, AT&T Canada's debt had been cut to 'default' status in September, and on 15 October it announced that it had won bankruptcy protection from a Canadian court after striking a provisional restructuring deal with bondholders that would wipe out its debt in return for the receipt by bondholders of C$200 million plus the entire equity. AT&T's response was to request that AT&T Canada remove AT&T from its brand name by the end of 2003 with certain exceptions.[24]

Problems also arose during the year in relation to Mexican operator Alestra in which AT&T held a 49 per cent economic interest. Alestra announced that it would be unable to make a $35 million bond payment due on 15 November

Table 4.2 AT&T consolidated accounts, year ending 31 December ($ million)[a]

	2002 restated[b]	2001 restated[b]	2000 restated[b]	2001	2000	1999
Revenue (A)	37,827	42,197	46,850	52,550	55,533	54,973
of which:						
AT&T Business Services	26,558	27,705	28,559	27,056	27,972	28,070
AT&T Consumer Services	11,527	14,843	18,643	15,079	18,894	21,753
AT&T Broadband	–	–	–	9,785	8,212	5,069
Corporate and Other	(258)	(351)	(352)	–	–	–
Operating expenses (B)	33,466	34,365	34,057	48,796	51,305	43,515
of which:						
amortization of goodwill, etc.	4,888	4,559	4,538	2,473	2,665	1,057
net restructuring and other charges	1,437	1,036	758	2,530[c]	7,029[d]	975
Operating income (A)–(B)	4,361	7,832	12,793	3,754	4,228	11,458
(Loss) income from continuing operations	963	(2,640)	9,532	(6,842)	4,133	10,781
Gain on disposition: discontinued operations	1,324[f]	13,503	–	13,503[e]	–	–
Net (loss) income	(13,082)	7,715	4,669	7,715	4,669	3,428
of which:						
accounting change	(856)	(652)	–	904	–	–
Total assets	55,272	165,481	242,802	165,282	234,360	163,457
of which:						
cash	8,014	10,680	–	10,592	64	–
Total liabilities	42,960	105,778	–	105,322	121,611	–
of which:						
long-term debt[g]	18,812	24,025	13,572	40,527	33,089	23,214
total debt	22,574	34,159	42,338	–	–	–
Employees, continuing operations	71,000	77,700	84,800	–	–	–

Source: AT&T Financial Report 2001 and Annual Report 2002; www.att.com

Notes:
[a] Effective 1 January 2002, AT&T adopted SFAS 142 which required that goodwill and indefinite-lived intangible assets no longer be amortized but instead be tested for impairment at least annually. As of 1 January the fair value of the reporting units' goodwill exceeded their carrying value and therefore no impairment loss was recognized – see Financial Report 2001, p.7. [b] When the results for 2002 were published they were restated to reflect the one-for-five reverse stock split and the discontinuation of AT&T Broadband within the accounts. The table accordingly contains two sets of three-year periods of which two are overlapping to indicate the effect of the restatement. The Annual Report 2002 contains (p. 6) the restated accounts covering a seven-year period commencing 1996. [c] $1.3 billion attributable to headcount reductions, $1.2 billion asset impairment largely attributable to Excite@Home. [d] $6.2 billion asset impairment attributable to Excite@Home, $0.75 billion attributable to restructuring. [e] These consolidated accounts reflect the disposition of AT&T Wireless on 9 July 2001 such that the revenues and costs of that company are excluded as from 30 June 2001 and a non-cash tax-free gain on disposition recorded in 2001. [f] This represented the difference between the fair value of the AT&T Broadband business at the date of the spin-off and AT&T's value in AT&T Broadband. [g] The structure of the debt is set out in the Financial Report 2001, p. 66.

and set in motion a restructuring of its debt. AT&T declared that, if this proved successful, it would consider further investment in Alestra,[25] but it was nevertheless something of a surprise when, in January 2003, AT&T joined Alfa Group and Bancomer, co-owners of Alestra, in a provisional agreement to invest $80 million in Alestra.

Meanwhile, AT&T Latin America (ALA), in which AT&T held a 65 per cent economic interest and a 95 per cent voting interest, announced in April 2002 that it had restructured its debts and was confident of remaining fully funded for years to come. Despite this, it announced in October 2002 that it anticipated a liquidity shortfall in the coming months due to the deteriorating economic climate, and AT&T pulled the plug on further financing and announced the possibility of a $1.2 billion charge.[26] On 6 January 2003, AT&T agreed to sell its holding to Southern Cross group for $1,000 and took an asset impairment charge of $1.1 billion in 2002Q4.[27]

On 5 November 2002, AT&T was served with a shareholder lawsuit in Delaware which named AT&T and every board director of AT&T Latin America as defendants, asserting, *inter alia*, that they variously breached their fiduciary duties to ALA. On 7 November, certain creditors of @Home Corp. filed a class action against AT&T in California in connection with @Home's declaration of bankruptcy and subsequent efforts to dispose of some of its businesses or assets.

2003 dawns

On 6 January 2003, the new CEO, David Dorman, announced that a further 3,500, mostly managerial, jobs would go during the first half of the year. Although publication of results for the fourth quarter of 2002 was accompanied by a one-off gain relating to the disposal of AT&T Broadband, and the tenor of the commentary was broadly positive, analysts were concerned that this optimism was of the 'rate of decline in revenue is slowing' variety and that the company would no longer issue forward forecasts, and the share price promptly dropped 20 per cent as shown in Figure 4.1.[28] However, AT&T subsequently claimed that it was winning substantial new contracts as customers deserted its distressed rivals such as WorldCom. With $8.5 billion in cash in the bank, AT&T separately announced that it would reduce its $22.6 billion debt by buying back $4.33 billion of bonds for cash, and redeemed $3.75 billion of these in early February.

In mid-April, AT&T announced that it would be eliminating layers of management and combining corporate functions such as billing and customer service in order to speed up decision making and improve service. First-quarter results, published at the end of April, were generally better than predicted – essentially because expectations were so low. Although revenues at the consumer division showed the predicted decline because of falling long-distance prices, margins were better than expected at 24.9 per cent and subscriptions appeared to be holding up. However, operating profits were down sharply on the year previously as the business division struggled to cope with fall-out from the financial services and travel industries. Since the latter was seen as the growth sector, the 23 per cent rise in the share price seemed somewhat over-done.

In mid-June, the AT&T share price, which had risen by 50 per cent since the announcement of its first quarter results, suffered its first real setback due to a downgrading by Merrill Lynch even though it had forecast a reduction in its net debt to under $10 billion by the year-end. However, AT&T remained resolutely upbeat, stating that it would be forging several non-exclusive agreements to resell services from other companies or to offer co-branded products. Analysts were divided, the more sceptical among them pointing out that 'co-option' implied loss of control and a heavy dependence on potentially unreliable partners. The possibility of a merger was of more interest in some quarters because the six-month moratorium on merger discussions dating from the sale of AT&T Broadband had expired on 25 May 2003.

With the Baby Bells securing an ever-larger number of permissions to offer long-distance service outside their territories, AT&T hit back by arranging via a partnership with Covad Communications to start the provision of broadband Internet connections as part of a package also containing its own local and long-distance services. AT&T had roughly three million local subscribers at the time, but with the price of phone calls on a downward trend it needed to find a means to improve customer loyalty. It had also arranged to resell the services of AT&T Wireless. AT&T also set out to repurchase additional debt. Its cash holdings had dwindled from $8.0 billion at the end of 2002 to $5.3 billion at the end of June 2003, but it determined to use another $1.5 billion to reduce its interest costs and strengthen its balance sheet, relying upon its strong cash flow to renew the cash cushion.

The results for 2003Q3 revealed that revenue had dropped for the fifteenth successive quarter. This was not unexpected given the steady drain of customers, but what was much less welcome was the revelation that two employees had circumvented internal accounting controls such that certain expenses in 2001 and 2002 had been understated by $125 million.

Meanwhile, AT&T Wireless was progressing satisfactorily on its own, with the time spent on the phone on average per subscriber up by 18 per cent year-on-year to 508 minutes per month and the company showing a net profit of five cents a share compared to a net loss of seven cents a share a year earlier. The switch from TDMA to GSM/GPRS/EDGE was moving rapidly forward and roaming agreements had been signed with T-Mobile USA and Cincinnati Bell. However, up to 1,000 jobs were to be shed during 2003 to be added to the 2,000 shed the previous year. In June 2003, AT&T Wireless agreed to sell its 24.5 per cent stake in Czech mobile operator EuroTel Praha to Ceský Telecom for $525 million plus a dividend of $100 million. It also obtained $511 million by way of a tax refund relating to 2002. In late July, it was able to report that it was on target to introduce the W-CDMA variant of

3G, operating in the 1900 MHz band, in four markets by the end of the year, as agreed with DoCoMo in December 2002. Also in July, it reported that its net profitability had soared during the second quarter compared to a year previously, with expenses and churn under tight control; while in August it reported the sale of its 35 per cent stake in AriaWest International of Indonesia to PT Telkom for an undisclosed sum. It followed up with the sale of its 22.74 per cent stake in Taiwan's Far EasTone for $330 million.

Conclusions

At the end of January 2003, Lex commented that 'diversification has failed' and that AT&T's strategy 'looks like the thrashings of a dinosaur'. It added that 'at some price a company with $37 billion in revenues ... must offer fair value', but as Figure 4.1 shows, although this was the day when the share price fell to $20.50, having been $26.50 only one week earlier, there was worse to come.

The main criticism of AT&T is that it paid far too much for its acquisitions and too much per cable subscriber. Its response is to argue that it paid largely with its own paper[29] and that the cable networks were worth more to AT&T than to others since it intended to use them for communications as against simply for video transmission. In the event, AT&T failed to sell sufficient telephony and Internet services over its cables after investing billions in the attempt, but was that a failure of vision or execution or both? Given the implosion of WorldCom – whose vision and execution show up AT&T in a relatively favourable light – and ongoing cut-throat competition in the fixed-wire market as the RBOCs obtain licences in an increasing number of states, it is hard to see what AT&T can do in the near future to arrest the decline in this business short of cutting costs to the bone, including trimming the interest charges on its still considerable debt. But the bottom line question is whether, shorn of its Broadband and Wireless interests, there is any point in having AT&T as a stand-alone company. The BT case study may have something to contribute on that score as there are clear parallels between the two companies' experiences, but incumbency has greater clout in Europe than in America and the prospects for survival are accordingly healthier. But who would want to buy AT&T, especially as a share price premium would be required? Logically, only a RBOC, but they have problems of their own. Unless the new CEO comes up with some smart ideas, and quickly, it seems possible that AT&T will trundle on, consuming itself from within, until it becomes so cheap that a takeover becomes irresistible. For a company with such an illustrious history, that would indeed be an ignominious ending.

Needless to say, the new AT&T management dismiss such an outcome out of hand. They point out that AT&T will end 2003 with 64,000 employees yet be generating 35 per cent more revenue per employee than MCI, and that much of its failure to respond nimbly to a rapidly changing environment could be ascribed to its 14 layers of management which had now been significantly whittled down. Furthermore, it would be offering bundled long-distance and local services in 35 states by the end of 2003, and eventually on a national basis. Hence, MCI or Sprint FON were more likely to fall prey to a takeover bid. Given that much of the improvement in its financial health can be put down to cost cutting, which is necessarily a finite activity, such optimism may prove to be excessive, but the odds on AT&T surviving as a stand-alone company have certainly improved in recent months.[30]

Chapter 5

Telecom Italia

Ascending Mt Olimpia

Background

Until the mid-1980s, all European countries had an incumbent monopolist as the national provider of telecoms services. The situation in Italy was particularly complex. Telecom Italia started out as a company majority owned by Stet, which was itself majority owned by the state holding company IRI. In 1995, Telecom Italia Mobile (TIM) was split off from its parent and partially sold off, with Telecom Italia retaining a 60 per cent stake. The plan was to privatize the entire IRI holding in Stet during that year, but the government had failed to set up an independent national regulatory authority by that point in time so the plan was postponed.

In November 1996, the government authorized the immediate transfer to the Treasury of the IRI stake in Stet, at a cost of roughly $8 billion, and put back the privatization to the autumn of 1997 to leave time for the regulatory issues to be resolved. The chosen method to prepare for the sale was to merge Telecom Italia into Stet since the latter was already quoted on Wall Street. The share exchange was announced in March 1997 as ten Stet ordinary shares for 18 Telecom Italia ordinary shares and ten Stet savings shares for 17.2 Telecom Italia savings shares. Completion of the share exchange in July 1997 left the government owning 44.71 per cent of the ordinary shares and 0.62 per cent of the savings shares in the new company, which was renamed Telecom Italia, in addition to a 'golden share' giving the government the right to veto certain arrangements such as a change of ownership.

The government preceded the offer of shares to the general public by offering a 15 per cent stake to a 'hard core' of industrial companies and financial intermediaries. Fourteen bids were tabled for a total stake of 9 per cent. Among these bidders, both AT&T and Unisource, an alliance of European operators, agreed to take 1.2 per cent stakes. Other participants assembled themselves into four groups: Assicurazioni Generali, Alleanza Assicurazioni and Comit agreed to take 1.2 per cent, as did Ifil and Fondazione Sao Paolo di Torino, while Credito Italiano and Rolo Banca took 1 per cent, as did Istituto Mobiliare Italiano and INA.

Overall, Olivetti appeared to pose the most significant potential threat to Telecom Italia because it not only owned a stake in fixed-wire operator

Infostrada but had also acquired a 30 per cent stake in Omnitel Pronto Italia (OPI), holder of the second GSM cellular licence in competition with TIM. OPI consisted of two parts: Omnitel Sistemi Radiocellulari (OSR), dominated by Olivetti and Bell Atlantic, and Pronto Italia which included AirTouch and Mannesmann among its main owners. However, Olivetti then developed serious financial problems, and, in December 1997, Mannesmann stepped in with an initial injection of $620 million in return for a 25 per cent stake in Olivetti's telecoms activities, to be followed by the acquisition of a further 24.9 per cent prior to March 2000. These activities were regrouped into a new company known as Oliman, and Mannesmann subsequently took a further 12.5 per cent stake in September 1998 for $383 million, followed with the move to 49.9 per cent in February 1999. Mannesmann also took a 2.26 per cent direct stake in Olivetti and formed a joint venture called Euro.map in which it would be the majority shareholder with a view to producing and managing a portfolio of advanced telecoms products.

The first contest for Telecom Italia

The need to prepare for privatization brought to the surface internal dissent about the future strategic direction for Telecom Italia, as well as disputes over how best to reduce inefficiency and over-manning. An element of needed stability was introduced with the appointment of Franco Bernabe as managing director towards the end of 1998. Crucially, however, the impression remained of a company which would find it difficult to explain its vision for the future and hence why it should retain its independence.

Olivetti makes an offer

In February 1999, it became apparent that Olivetti was holding discussions with the government about the possibility of making an audacious takeover bid for Telecom Italia, a company many times its own size, and that the government was not opposed in principle. The government's permission to proceed needed to be sought because of the existence of the 'golden share', but in any event this was the first time in Italy that any privatized concern had attracted the attention of a predator and the government's attitude to such an event needed to be clarified. Furthermore, anti-trust issues needed to be resolved since Olivetti was a major competitor of Telecom Italia.

The financial markets' response can best be described as sceptical. Under the leadership of its new chief executive, Roberto Colaninno, Olivetti had shed assets, refocused upon its telecoms activities and formed a strategic alliance with Mannesmann. Nevertheless, it was very short of cash and any bid would need to be highly leveraged. Furthermore, it was one thing to turn itself around, quite another to tackle the difficulties faced by an inefficient monolith emerging from public ownership into an increasingly competitive environment.

The bid was announced on 21 February 1999. At the time, Olivetti was worth $9.4 billion whereas, in its entirety including its stake in TIM, Telecom Italia was valued at roughly ten times as much. In order to make the bid credible, Olivetti accordingly needed to resort to a time-honoured feature of Italian capitalism generally known as 'Chinese boxes' or 'capitalism without the capital'. In effect, a chain of holding companies is created, with each company in the chain owning a part – often a minority part – of the next company in the chain. Through this structure, a person or organization owning a controlling stake in the first company in the chain can exercise an influence upon subsequent companies in the chain wholly disproportionate to the actual number of shares that is owned.

At one end of the chain in this case stood Roberto Colaninno who, with his family, owned roughly 16 per cent of Fingruppo, which, in turn, was the largest shareholder in Bell with roughly a 40 per cent stake. In November 1998, Bell had become much the largest single shareholder in Olivetti, eventually accumulating a 15 per cent stake. Thus, in practice, Mr Colaninno exercised control despite owning only approximately 1 per cent of Olivetti's capital largely because, in the absence of pension funds and other institutional investors, the shareholder base of Italian companies tends to be highly fragmented.

However, an added complexity arose from the fact that Olivetti did not make an offer for the whole of Telecom Italia, since it excluded the non-voting savings shares that made up a good part of the total capital, nor was the majority of its offer in the form of cash. Altogether, given an offer price of €10 per ordinary share, Olivetti needed to raise €52.6 billion (to which €1.6 billion had subsequently to be added to pay the expenses incurred by the bid). Of this, little was available in cash, so €7.6 billion would be raised by selling off its existing telecoms interests to Mannesmann, and €2.6 billion via a rights offer. A further €20.7 billion would be borrowed by an Olivetti subsidiary, Tecnost, a manufacturer of lottery and football pools electronic ticket distributors, which was to be used as the vehicle for the takeover. What was still needed would be paid for in Tecnost shares.

The effect of the latter part of the offer would be to leave Olivetti with 59 per cent of Tecnost shares as the fifth element in the chain, and Tecnost with 71 per cent of Telecom Italia. However, the seventh, and final element would comprise Telecom Italia's interests in TIM, comprising 60 per cent of the voting shares and 20 per cent of the savings shares, or 53 per cent overall.

While the lengthy chain had the virtue, from the perspective of Colaninno, that he would be able to exercise much greater control over Telecom Italia than his indirect shareholding of well under 1 per cent would otherwise merit, the financial engineering involved appeared to be questionable. As was noted, revenue would flow in to Telecom Italia and TIM, and these would be obliged to pay dividends on any ensuing profits to the holders of savings shares in Telecom Italia and to the holders of the 40 per cent minority of TIM. What was left would percolate up to Tecnost, but Tecnost would be faced with the need to service bank borrowings of €20.7 billion and €7.4 billion of bonds. Furthermore, because under Italian law Tecnost would not be able to consolidate Telecom Italia's accounts with its own, the latter would end up paying huge amounts of corporation tax but Tecnost would be unable to utilise tax deductions on its interest charges.[1]

Competing strategies are set out

The strategic options tabled by the protagonists are set out in Table 5.1. Telecom Italia's board rejected the bid outright on 25 February and mandated Mr Bernabe to study a possible merger with TIM. For its part, Olivetti signed the contract to sell its telecoms interests to Mannesmann for €7.6 billion. On 26 March, Olivetti was able to announce that it had secured the biggest ever syndicated loan to the value of €22.5 billion, with half falling due for repayment after one year and 80 per cent after 18 months. The eventual package amounted to a loan facility of €28 billion.

Foreign intervention is rebuffed

Denied approval for its strategy to fend off Olivetti, Telecom Italia turned its thoughts towards attracting a foreign 'white knight' to save it from the clutches of Olivetti. It was revealed that talks were already going on to merge

Table 5.1 Competing strategies

Telecom Italia	Olivetti
Merge with TIM	Integrate, but not merge, Telecom Italia and TIM
Sell property assets in Italy	Sell property assets in Italy
Sell international assets outside Latin America	Sell Latin American assets
Sell stakes in Italtel, Finsiel and Sirti	Sell stake in Italtel, but not immediately; possibly sell Sirti; keep Finsiel
Cut long-distance and international charges by 50% by 2002	Cut long-distance and international charges by 70% by 2002
Overall, reduce workforce by 40,000	Reduce fixed-wire workforce by 13,000
Reduce cost base by L1,000 billion by 2002 and produce synergies worth L1,250 billion	Reduce cost base by L4,500 billion by 2002
Expand Internet, electronic trading and data	Expand Internet, electronic trading and data
Invest L42,000 billion by 2003	Invest L26,500 billion by 2003
Convert Telecom Italia savings shares into ordinary voting shares	
Buy in up to 10% of outstanding shares	Buy in up to 25% of outstanding savings shares

Telecom Italia with Deutsche Telekom. This was somewhat surprising since the government was clearly going to disapprove of, and possibly use its 'golden share' to veto, a non-Italian bidder, although the European Commission could be expected to take issue with the government were the latter tactic to be employed. A merger – as against a joint venture – between these companies presented several major difficulties. In particular, Deutsche Telekom remained majority-owned by the German government, so the merger would not merely look remarkably like a form of re-nationalisation but one conducted by a foreign state. In addition, Italian national sentiment would clearly not be satisfied with anything other than a merger of equals even though the companies were manifestly unequal in size.

Discussions faltered when the German Finance Ministry made it clear that it would neither dispose of, nor waive, its voting rights in Deutsche Telekom. The European Commission, in its turn, indicated that, while it was unlikely to veto the merger, it would undertake an in-depth investigation and probably impose conditions. The situation deteriorated further when Deutsche Telekom stated that it would expect to take a 56 per cent stake in the merged company

On 4 May, Olivetti moved to bring proceedings to a close, issuing its formal offer document and allowing shareholders only two weeks to accept or reject its offer. When the offer officially closed, Olivetti was able to claim acceptances equal to 51.02 per cent of the voting capital. It had pulled off arguably the most audacious takeover bid in European history. Significantly, it had managed this in part because all of the 'hard core' companies bar Credit Suisse, which had been acting as an adviser to Telecom Italia, chose to accept the offer even though the whole point of the 'hard core' was in theory to ensure loyal support for Telcom Italia. Olivetti was committed to a payment of €30.8 billion for its stake in Telecom Italia, comprising €18.5 billion in cash, €4.5 billion in Tecnost shares and €7.8 billion in Tecnost debt. There was widespread concern that Olivetti was obliged to meet a stringent timetable to repay the €6.9 billion borrowed from banks at a time when Telecom Italia's workforce was badly demoralised, and its victory was widely seen as bordering on the Pyrrhic.

Post-merger restructuring

The takeover was widely viewed as an historic turning point for Italy's corporate and political culture. However, this view had to be treated with caution. On the positive side was firstly the fact that an inefficient and over-manned company not long out of public ownership had been acquired by a predator that intended to improve its efficiency and reduce its manning. A further positive outcome was the potential demise of the system of 'Chinese boxes' and of 'hard cores', since these institutional arrangements had helped to engender a climate in which corruption (tangentopoli) and cronyism was able to thrive.

In effect, a small number of what in Italy were often powerful family groupings were accustomed to protecting those within their sphere of influence from the unwanted attentions of 'outsiders'. The 'hard core' formed at the time of Telecom Italia's privatization was expected to continue this practice given a context in which most of the shares were dispersed among a huge number of individually powerless private shareholders. However, the subsequent steady accumulation of these holdings in the hands of financial intermediaries with an interest in achieving a good rate of return on their investment, together with the willingness of most of the 'hard core' to accept the best offer on the table as viewed from their own, rather than the bid target's, perspective, was taken to be an indication that the 'hard core' could no longer be relied on to provide full protection.

The Italian government formally approved the takeover of Telecom Italia on 9 June 1999. Meanwhile, in the traditional manner, Olivetti had put together its own 'hard core' of hopefully loyal stakeholders including Mediobanca, Banca Monte dei Paschi di Siena, Banca Commerciale Italiana, Banca di Roma and Assicurazioni Generali.

In September 1999, Mr Colaninno announced that Tecnost – in which Olivetti now held a 70 per cent stake – would be transformed into the group's main holding company and would be buying Telecom Italia's 53 per cent stake in TIM in return for shares in Tecnost at the rate of 1.50–1.65 Tecnost shares per Telecom Italia ordinary share or savings share. As a consequence of the issue of additional Tecnost shares, Olivetti's stake in Tecnost would be reduced to 42 per cent, but this was considered sufficient to guarantee continued control. It was also agreed by the boards of the various companies concerned that Telecom Italia would buy back a maximum of 34 per cent of its savings shares, accounting for 10 per cent of the company's total share capital, at €6 a share – a 12 per cent premium to the ruling price. This would be financed by disposals.

Unfortunately, this was insufficient to save the day for Mr Colaninno. Infuriated Telecom Italia shareholders demanded a significantly improved offer. At the exchange rate proposed by independent advisers, Olivetti's stake in Tecnost, which had been raised from 70.03 per cent to 72.9 per cent in the open market at the end of October, would have fallen to 38 per cent, thereby threatening its control, and hence no agreement on an acceptable exchange rate could be reached. Mr Colaninno was obliged to beat an embarrassing retreat, and was left with a major headache concerning the means to finance Tecnost's $15 billion debt – made greater by the increase in Tecnost's stake in Telecom Italia via purchases in the open market from 52.12 per cent to 55.02 per cent in late October. He tried to cover this by announcing his intention to spin off Telecom Italia's Tin.it Internet operations into a separate company.

In mid-January 2000, the offer price for the non-voting shares was raised to €6.5, potentially raising the total cost of the buy-back to €4.4 billion. Telecom Italia agreed to offer this price for up to nine months or until one-third of the shares had been tendered.

The Bell stake in Olivetti began to be raised from the initial 15 per cent at the end of 1999 to reduce the possibility of a hostile takeover. In February 2000, the Bell holding was raised to 22.5 per cent, and a target was set of 28–30 per cent. At the end of June, Telecom Italia sold an 81 per cent stake in Italtel for €800 million in cash. An offer for the whole of Sirti worth $300 million was eventually tabled by Interbanca, Techint and others in July 2000, and in Telecom Italia's report on the first half of 2000 it was noted that the sale of stakes in Meie, Italtel and others had generated a net gain of €465 million.

In May 2000, the issue of Tecnost's debts was finally close to resolution when shareholders in Olivetti and Tecnost were asked to approve a merger between the companies (with combined debts of €19 billion). The enlarged Olivetti would be left with the 55 per cent stake in Telecom Italia. At an exchange price of 1.06 Olivettti shares per one Tecnost share, Bell would be left with a stake of roughly 20 per cent in the enlarged Olivetti, but would subsequently purchase additional shares. The various shareholders gave their approval at the end of May.[2]

In July, a further reorganization was launched. All of the fixed-wire and mixed subsidiaries were to be transferred to Stet International Netherlands (SIN), a wholly-owned Telecom Italia subsidiary. Meanwhile, all pure wireless activities were to be transferred to TIM through its taking complete control of Stet Mobile Holding (SMH), the vehicle used for most foreign wireless acquisitions. In order to bring this about, TIM would issue new shares to Telecom Italia, thereby raising the latter's stake from 60.97 per cent to 62.97 per cent.

In a second phase, all TIM savings shares would become convertible into voting shares, with owners receiving one voting share in return for each savings share plus the payment of a cash sum of between €3.7 and €5.1, equal to 38 per cent of the mean price of the voting shares during the 15 days prior to shareholder approval of the plan. Should all 1.56 billion savings shares be converted, roughly €8 billion would be raised and Telecom Italia would once again end up with a 55 per cent stake in TIM; Telecom Italia, owner of 20.3 per cent of the savings shares, would definitely convert its own holding. In early December, it was announced that with the cash element set at €3.7, some 91.56 per cent of the savings shares had been converted, raising €5.2 billion in total.

However, by mid-December Telecom Italia had only bought back less than 10 per cent of its own savings shares compared to the 34 per cent agreed in January – and this despite the fact that between March and December some 850 million such shares had been traded at prices below €6.5 with the price still below that level at the year-end. Telecom Italia claimed that few shares had been tendered during the period to March, and tried to blame regulatory restrictions, but the regulator promptly claimed that these did not apply to the buy-back and a US hedge fund threatened to sue. In principle, with the savings shares trading at a 50 per cent discount to the ordinary share price, there were obvious attractions to a policy of buying back all available shares, but Olivetti did not want Telecom Italia to rack up a further €4 billion of debt since this would reduce the dividend flow to Olivetti.

In January 2001, Telecom Italia announced that it had bought back 5.22 per cent of its savings shares for roughly €711 million, and subsequently placed a completely new proposal on the table, to be voted on by shareholders in March. This provided, first, for savings shares to be converted into ordinary shares at 48 per cent of the ruling market price, thereby raising €10 billion which would then be used to repurchase up to 10 per cent of outstanding Telecom Italia shares at a 15 per cent premium to the ruling market price at the time of the offer, and at no less than €17.50. Olivetti's stake in Telecom Italia would potentially fall from 55 per cent to 44 per cent. In addition, debt would be reduced by a further €5.1 billion. However, the process would be dependent upon a minimum of 80 per cent of savings shares being converted. The response in practice was entirely negative, and a significant number of savings shareholders decided to hold out for conversion at 40 per cent of the market price.

Early in April, Telecom Italia gave way and offered to convert at between 38 per cent and 42 per cent of the market price, but only provided that price rose above €12.5 before the end of 2001 (compared to the then price of €11.4). It simultaneously reduced the voting percentage needed for approval of this proposal from 80 to 60 per cent. Indebtedness would fall by roughly €4 billion, but Telecom Italia and TIM would subsequently reduce dividend payouts to conserve cash. The conversion of savings shares was approved by shareholders in May under rules that permitted approval unless a majority of ordinary shareholders other than Olivetti voted against the proposal.

Seat-Tin.it

As previously noted, Telecom Italia's first thoughts in relation to its Internet subsidiary, Tin.it, were inclined towards an initial public offer. However, it subsequently changed its mind and announced its intention to create Italy's largest e-commerce group by combining Tin.it, which had 2.4 million subscribers at the time, with the 'yellow pages' directory publisher, Seat Pagine Gialle (Seat PG). Seat PG had been demerged from Telecom Italia prior to its privatisation and bought by a consortium led by Banca Commerciale Italiana for €2.05 billion. Telecom Italia retained a 20 per cent overall stake including 10 per cent of the voting shares.

As an initial step, Telecom Italia intended to raise its stake in Seat to 29.9 per cent at a price of €4.5 a share. Subsequently, by reversing Tin.it into Seat, this stake would rise to roughly 64 per cent of the combined entity which, in early March 2000, was valued at a hypothetical €70 billion (but only €50 billion by May). Telecom Italia would be legally obliged to make a public offer for all outstanding Seat shares at that point, and intended to offer €4.2 per ordinary voting share and €2.94 per non-voting savings share. At the end of January 2001, Telecom Italia had a controlling stake of roughly 61 per cent in Seat-Tin.it, although the latter was by now worth only €25 billion.

The antitrust authorities authorized the Seat-Tin.it merger in July 2000 subject to conditions. Seat PG subsequently set out to acquire Italy's third-largest, but loss-making, TV network – Tele Monte Carlo (TMC) plus TMC2 – from the Cecchi Gori media group for €557 million. Seat wanted initially to take a 25 per cent stake together with operational control. At the end of 2000, it would raise its stake to 75 per cent and take out a put option on the residual stake exercisable in 2001. Technically, Telecom Italia was forbidden under the 'legge Maccanico' from buying into free-to-air terrestrial TV, so it appeared that the law would have to be changed for the TMC purchase to become compatible with the enlarged Seat PG. Although the antitrust authorities cleared the takeover in January 2001 subject to conditions, the telecoms regulator ruled that it was illegal. An appeal to a Rome court elicited a demand that the authorities should justify blocking the deal.

An audit of the Colaninno reign

If one was to conduct a brief audit of the Colaninno reign at the helm of Telecom Italia then it would show several pluses as well as minuses. On the plus side, he was prepared to tackle the trade unions in order to bring staffing levels down towards best practice in Europe. He also invested heavily in Tin-it in order to make it a major force in the Italian Internet market, and acquired Seat Pagine Gialle and Tele Monte Carlo. Although he could do little about the decline in fixed-wire telephony, he maintained its financial health reasonably well by attacking costs and concentrating on the business sector. In turn, mobile subsidiary TIM was placed under sound management and performed well by the standards of its peers.

On the minus side was, first, the fact that Telecom Italia was still weighed down with $15.5 billion of debts in July 2001, in part because of the need to pay high dividends to Olivetti. It was held that this ruled out sufficient investment in Telecom Italia's operations. Second, there were the various issues relating to quarrels with shareholders discussed previously. Although these could largely be brushed aside as quibbles by minorities, and the institutional support for his strategy was broadly demonstrated by the popularity of the April 2001 bond issue that raised almost $6 billion, his tendency to arrogance and intemperance made him many enemies. Furthermore, the extraordinary circumstances of his own bid for Telecom Italia helped to expose the strengths and weaknesses of corporate takeover rules in Italy, and inevitably gave other parties pause to wonder whether the very means by which Olivetti had acquired Telecom Italia could be used to acquire Olivetti, especially since Telecom Italia had lost one-third of its value and TIM one-half of its value compared to their highs for the year.

The tables are turned

Whereas most were content to wonder, this was not true of everyone. At the end of July 2001, Italian tyre and cable company, Pirelli, announced that it had set up a joint venture, split 60:40 with the Benetton family's financial vehicle Edizione Holding, and that this had bought from Bell, Olivetti's largest shareholder, a 23 per cent stake in Olivetti. The offer price was €4.17 compared to the ruling market price of €2.3, and the total cost of the stake came to $6.14 billion in cash. Together with its existing stake in Olivetti, Pirelli accordingly had control of the joint venture which had a 27 per cent stake in Olivetti, which in turn owned over half of Telecom Italia. Curiously, the share price of both companies promptly fell. This was understandable in the case of Pirelli since the purchase would erase its net cash holdings and leave it with debts of $2.7 billion, and many doubted the strategic value of combining telecoms services with telecoms cables, tyres and real estate assets – although Pirelli declared its intention to dispose of its tyre interests to concentrate upon telecoms. The effect on Olivetti reflected the fact that Pirelli did not intend to launch a full takeover bid, effectively sidelining minority shareholders. Since Olivetti had been trading at a premium of roughly 20 per cent to net asset value on the possibility of a favourable take-over bid, this could no longer be justified. Furthermore, no other potential predator would now be able to launch such a bid. To no one's surprise, the Italian government welcomed the move by Pirelli, secure in the knowledge that there would be no further embarrassments with foreign predators.

One obvious consequence of the Bell purchase was that the core problem of the old structure – namely the need for the cash-rich companies at the bottom of the chain to sustain the debts of those at the top – did not appear to have gone away. Given the premium paid for the Bell stake, Pirelli's shareholders would be unlikely to want it otherwise in the future unless a tax-efficient way to restructure the company could be devised that would recoup the share price premium. This implied that Olivetti's debts, which would be boosted to $34 billion by the takeover, would have to be reduced, probably via either a capital increase at Olivetti – which would have the virtue of increasing Pirelli's stake in Olivetti – or a merger between Pirelli and Olivetti and/or Telecom Italia, or between Pirelli and Telecom Italia, with Olivetti disappearing in all eventualities. The wider share ownership would, however, be wary about such arrangements since Marco Tronchetti Provera would control all three companies. Table 5.2 shows the evolving structures for controlling Telecom Italia.

It is notable that Mr Provera's 'Chinese boxes' were more than a match for those of Mr Colaninno and his allies, since the operating company Pirelli SpA was controlled by Pirelli & Cie which, in turn, was controlled by Camfin in which Pirelli's chairman, Mr Provera, had an interest. At the time of the bid Mr Provera had only an 0.5 per cent stake in Telecom Italia, or, adjusting for debt at all levels in the chain, a mere 0.1 per cent. In that respect, one set of conflicts of interest had merely been exchanged for another.

Table 5.2 Chinese boxes

Structure

Structure after Olivetti takeover August 1999

    Mr Colaninno>
    16% Fingruppo>
    40% Bell>
    15% Olivetti>
    59% Tecnost>
    71% Telecom Italia>
    53% TIM

Restructured August 2000

    Hopa /Fingruppo (Mr Colaninno) >
    55% Bell >
    23% Olivetti >
    55% Telecom Italia >
    56% TIM+61% Seat Pagine Gialle

New structure August 2001

    Camfin (Mr Provera)>Pirelli & Cie>Pirelli

    Pirelli (60%)+Edizione Holding (Benetton) (40%)>
    100% Olimpia >
    100% Bell >
    27% Olivetti >
    55% Telecom Italia >
    56% TIM+61% Seat Pagine Gialle

Proposed structure Spring 2003

    Camfin (Mr Provera)>Pirelli & Cie>Pirelli [the latter to be merged]

    Pirelli (50.4%)+Edizione Finance (16.8%)+Hopa (Mr Gnutti) (16.%)[a]+UniCredito
    (8.4%)+IntesaBCI (8.4%) >
    100% Olimpia >
    100% Bell >
    28.7% Olivetti >55% Telecom Italia [to be merged][b]>
    56% TIM+61.5% Seat PG[c]/Telecom Italia Media

Notes:
[a] Hopa also had a 4.42 per cent direct stake in Olivetti, so its total stake would be 9 per cent. In turn, Olimpia/Hopa's combined direct stake would amount to 33 per cent. [b] Leaving Olimpia with 11.5 per cent of the merged company (called Telecom Italia). This was raised to 14.2 per cent in October 2003 and is to be raised again to 17 per cent subject to a capital increase. [c] Subsequently sold.

Italy's second-largest bank, UniCredito Italiano, subsequently took a 10 per cent stake in the Pirelli/Benetton holding company Olimpia, paying $467 million, equivalent to €3.91 per Olivetti share – somewhat less than the original offer price but over twice the €1.90 market price for Olivetti. This was followed by IntesaBCI, Italy's largest bank, also taking a 10 per cent stake for $479 million – leaving Pirelli with 60 per cent and Edizione

Holding with 20 per cent. The banks were granted special dispensations to sell their holdings at favourable prices should, for example, Pirelli & Cie be subject to a change in its controlling ownership.

As things stood, therefore, Pirelli's stake in Telecom Italia amounted to roughly 9 per cent (60 per cent x 27 per cent x 55 per cent), but the existence of non-voting shares meant that Olivetti had only 39 per cent of the economic interest in Telecom Italia as against 55 per cent of the votes, so Pirelli's economic interest in Telecom Italia was only 6.3 per cent.

The European Commission appeared content to let the takeover proceed subject to the Benetton family shedding its direct and indirect stakes in Telecom Italia's small competitor, Blu, and the transfer of control of Auto-strade Telecomunicazioni to an independent operator in mid-September. Nevertheless, the Olivetti share price had fallen by then to under €1, less than one-quarter of the offer price. In part, this reflected the poor first-half figures released at this time which included a heavy loss at Seat PG and the need to write-off the better part of €1 billion relating to the purchase of Globo.com, a Brazilian ISP. The price fall induced Pirelli to ask Bell to renegotiate the terms of the offer which could not be signed and sealed until the Commission had sanctioned it. Although Bell would not renegotiate the price, it agreed to buy a $955 million bond carrying a fixed 1.5 per cent yield and convertible into Olivetti shares in order to ease Pirelli's difficulties in financing the deal. Further, two Bell investors granted Olimpia up to the same amount in six-year non-recourse loans.

The proposed strategy

The future strategy for Telecom Italia, as set out in September 2001, was roughly as follows:

- Olivetti would launch a rights issue at the end of October 2001 priced at €1 a share. All Olivetti shareholders and convertible bondholders would be entitled to subscribe at the rate of one new per two held – and Olimpia would subscribe to €1.2 billion of the total rights. It was hoped that this would reduce Olivetti's debts from €17.8 billion to €13.5 billion.
- Telecom Italia would divest its non-core assets and concentrate its efforts on Italy and Latin America. Disposals were expected to include stakes – some held by TIM – in Telekom Austria (29.8 per cent), its subsidiary Mobilkom (25 per cent), Auna in Spain (27.5 per cent), Bouygues Décaux Télécom (BDT) in France and possibly Aria in Turkey, gener-ating up to €5 billion over a two-year period.
- Olivetti would also make non-core disposals worth roughly €1 billion. These would include a 15.82 per cent stake in lottery operator Lottomatica in which Telecom Italia also had a 19.12 per cent stake to be sold off. Olivetti's 2.15 per cent stake in Mebiobanca might follow.

Announcement of these plans reduced the share price of Pirelli to €1.42, of
Telecom Italia to €7.61 and of Olivetti to €0.89 (see Figures 5.1–5.3) and
TIM's share price also suffered (see Figure 5.4). According to the Lex column
in the Financial Times, this represented an unmitigated disaster for Mr
Provera since Pirellli's investment in Olivetti had probably lost its entire value
after taking account of the put options written into the banks' agreements to
take stakes in Olimpia. This situation would only be salvaged in the longer
term via the rights issue and merging together most, if not all, of the
companies involved in the 'Chinese boxes'. In a subsequent comment, Lex

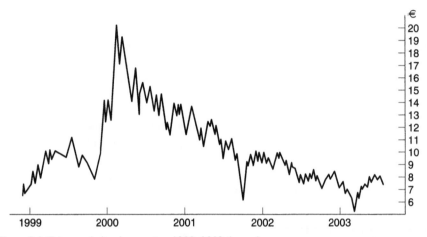

Figure 5.1 Telecom Italia share price, 1999–2003 (euros).
Source: Daily share prices in the *Financial Times.*

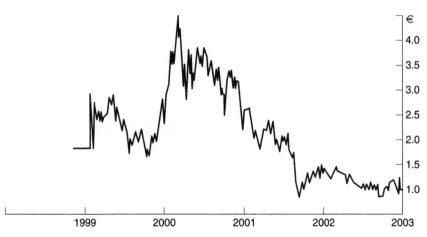

Figure 5.2 Olivetti share price, January 1999–January 2003 (euros).
Source: Daily share prices in the *Financial Times.*

also noted that it would be possible to pick up a sizeable stake in Olivetti – which was now worth almost exactly the value of its shareholding in Telecom Italia and was appropriately viewed as a leveraged bundle of shares rather than as a business – fairly cheaply in the marketplace and contest control with Pirelli. By mid-October, Lex was slightly more sanguine, but summarized the problem as the need to cut Olivetti's debt, merge Olivetti and Olimpia into an operating company and eliminate Telecom Italia's savings shares.[3]

In late October it was proposed that the chain of control would be shortened, possibly via a merger between Olivetti and Telecom Italia, but

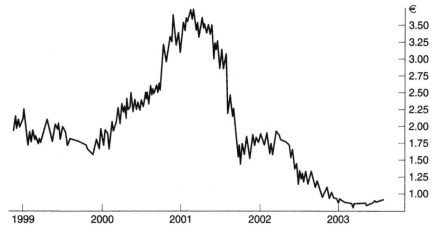

Figure 5.3 Pirelli share price, 1999–2003 (euros).

Source: Daily share prices in the *Financial Times*.

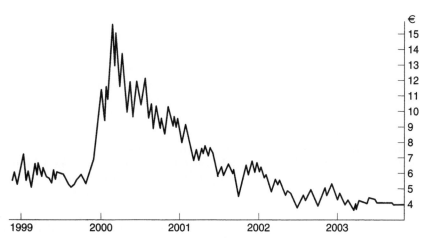

Figure 5.4 TIM share price, 1999–2003 (euros).

Source: Daily share prices in the *Financial Times*.

only provided the share price of Olivetti, now somewhat improved at €1.25, had risen to €3. Meanwhile, a €3.9 billion convertible bond would be launched expiring in 2010 and offering the opportunity to convert between 22 January 2002 and 15 December 2009 at an 18.38 per cent premium to the ruling Olivetti share price. The bond proceeds would be used to repurchase a variable-rate Olivetti bond due to expire in 2004. However, the stock market regulator ordered Pirelli to include in the issue prospectus a warning that it might have to consolidate losses at Olimpia into its accounts – a step it was trying to avoid by claiming that its 60 per cent stake still meant that it did not have exclusive control. In the event, the rights/convertible bonds issue was 99 per cent subscribed, and of the total 3.9 billion shares subscribed overall, 38 per cent consisted of shares and 62 per cent of convertible bonds. Pirelli subsequently launched a successful appeal against the consolidation ruling.[4]

In December 2001, a new holding company was created to which Telecom Italia sold its stakes in Eutelsat, Intelsat, Inmarsat and New Skies Satellites, valued at $500 million. It then took a 30 per cent stake in the new company – Mirror International Holding – for itself, with the rest owned by Lehman Brothers Merchant Banking Partners, IntesaBCI and Interbanca. It also announced the provisional sale of its 27 per cent stake in Spanish operator Auna for €2 billion to other stakeholders, and entered into negotiations to sell its Telespazio subsidiary to Finmeccanica for $400 million. Meanwhile, Olivetti bought back expensive floating-rate bonds with a face value of $2.35 billion, originally issued to finance the purchase of Telecom Italia, for an unspecified sum, leaving €5 billion outstanding, and in December agreed to sell off its Lottomatica stake to Tyche together with that held by Finsiel – 34 per cent in total – for €750 million.

Subsequent events

Telecom Italia caught the markets by surprise when it announced in November that it would be writing-off $1.6 billion of the $12.5 billion invested outside Italy during the two years while in Mr Colaninno's care.[5] This did not bode well for when the various companies reported their 2001 results in February and March 2002. Perhaps most crucially, although Pirelli, which was not itself directly involved in the provision of telecommunications services, reported a modest net debt of €1.1 billion, that of Olivetti amounted to €16.4 billion and of Telecom Italia to €21.9 billion,[6] hence resulting in a consolidated net debt on Olivetti's books of €38.4 billion.[7] TIM's net debt was recorded as €1.5 billion and that of Seat PG as €922 million. Telecom Italia announced that its stake in Brazilian Internet portal Globo.com, bought for $810 million in 2000, was effectively worthless and might be sold: the write-off would amount to €900 million and the total write-off to €4.6 billion.[8] On a more positive note, the 19.6 per cent stake held in BDT would be sold to parent Bouygues for €750 million, resulting in a net profit of €450 million credited to TIM's balance sheet. The 85 per cent stake in its real estate subsidiary Telemaco could also be sold with ease.

It was widely recognized that the ownership structure shown in Table 5.2 was overly complicated, and meant, for example, that Telecom Italia was saddled with the need to pay high dividends to help Olivetti with paying off its debts. For its part, Telecom Italia made it clear that it was embarking on a low-risk, slow-growth strategy designed to ensure that it did not end up like its French and German counterparts, saddled with unsustainable levels of debt. This was clearly not going to be the case for TIM which managed to reduce its net debt to €223 million during the first quarter of 2002. Seat PG also announced excellent results for the quarter, once again restoring itself to profit as a result of job cuts.

In May 2002, the European Commission announced that it was minded to revoke its clearance of the takeover unless Pirelli honoured its agreement to dispose of its stake in Blu. This was causing problems since the Commission did not want Blu to be broken up, which was the preferred option of its various stakeholders. However, TIM signed a provisional contract on 7 August to purchase the equity of Blu for €18 million which was duly approved by the Italian antitrust authorities, and the European Commission was forced to concede in September.[9] Blu was merged with TIM in December 2002.

The possibility of a slightly simplified structure emerged in June 2002 when Pirelli & Cie launched an IPO for its real estate division valued at roughly €1.3 billion. Mr Provera was the main shareholder in Pirelli & Cie, and if the latter used the money from the sale to buy more shares in Pirelli it would become possible to merge Pirelli with Pirelli & Cie without diluting Mr Provera's existing stake in Pirelli, which would simply become direct rather than indirect.

In June, agreement was reached in respect of the Austrian holdings of Telecom Italia/TIM. First, Telekom Austria would repurchase from TIM the 25 per cent stake in Mobilkom for the low price of €690 million, and, second, Telecom Italia would be authorized to dispose of half of its 29.8 per cent stake in Telekom Austria over the ensuing 18-month period.[10] On 4 November, a private placement was executed for a 13 per cent stake which was raised to 15 per cent after the subsequent exercise of a 'greenshoe' option. The price was €7.45 a share and the total raised was €559 million.[11] Agreement was, however, harder to achieve in relation to Stream, the pay-TV venture co-owned by Telecom Italia and News Corp. where the latter was taking over rival Telepiù from Vivendi Universal. News Corp. wanted Telecom Italia to raise its stake in the merged entity to 19.9 per cent which ran contrary to its strategy of disposing of minority interests without control, but News Corp. threatened to shut down Stream if Telecom Italia did not comply, which would leave it with up to €1 billion of long-term contracts to honour that it had signed when it was sole owner of Stream.[12] Telecom Italia duly signed the agreement to raise its stake, subject to regulatory authorization, on 1 October. Authorization was duly forthcoming on 30 March 2003, thereby creating Sky Italia.

The situation in South America was also under review, and in August steps were taken to refocus entirely upon the increasingly competitive mobile sector. As a result, Telecom Italia reduced its stake in fixed-wire operator Brasil Telecom from 37.3 to 19 per cent, thereby ceasing to have a controlling stake and losing its seat on the board. In turn, this meant that TIM was now free to utilize the GSM licences that it had bought for $1 billion earlier in the year. Although rival Telemar already provided a GSM service, TIM would be the only operator able to go national.[13] Although the disposal raised very little cash, the other, previous sales meant that when Telecom Italia reported its first-half results in September it was able to set extra-ordinary gains of €753 million against charges of €355 million relating to staff lay-offs and €367 million in write-offs in relation to 9Télécom. All told, net debt was down by €2.3 billion to €18.8 billion.[14] For its part, TIM was mostly thriving, both domestically and in Greece, Peru and Brazil, but most obviously in Greece where it negotiated the purchase of a 17.45 per cent stake in Stet Hellas from Verizon Communications to add to its existing 63.95 per cent holding. Nevertheless, its third-quarter results revealed a write-down of €1.26 billion in respect of its 49 per cent stake in Turkish operator Is TIM and €75 million in respect of Venezuelan operator TIM Digitel.[15]

On 11 September, Telecom Italia agreed to purchase the Pagine Utili directories business unit from Pagine Italia in exchange for 214 million shares in Seat PG, representing 1.9 per cent of its capital, subject to regulatory authorization. Pagine Utili would subsequently be merged with Seat PG. When the regulators launched a probe, the agreement was withdrawn and resubmitted in a modified form in January 2003.[16] As it happened, Seat PG was unlikely to belong to Telecom Italia for much longer as it was being auctioned among several private equity firms with a view to a purchase later in 2003. Meanwhile, in May 2003, the Seat PG board approved the split of the directories, directory assistance and business information units from the rest of the group. Seat PG shareholders would exchange 40 existing shares for 29 shares in a new Seat PG plus 11 shares in Telecom Italia Media (comprising an ISP, office products retailer and a TV business).

On 29 October, a framework agreement drawn up between Pirelli, Olivetti-Telecom Italia and The Morgan Stanley Real Estate Funds was executed, thereby completing the transfer of the real estate assets of the companies involved and of the entities that provide real estate services within these companies.[17] Olivetti retained an 8.84 per cent interest in the first tranche known as Tiglio I. Altogether, €1.6 billion of assets were transferred in the course of Tiglio I and II.

In total during the period 1 October 2002 to 6 November 2002, as approved by the shareholders' meeting of 7 November 2001, Telecom Italia purchased 4,448,000 of its savings shares at an average price of €5.10 and a total outlay of €23 million, together with 301,000 of its ordinary shares at an average price of €7.32 and a total outlay of €2 million. This brought the total repurchases since 1 January 2002 to 27,488,000 savings shares at an average price of €5.47 and 4,748,000 ordinary shares at an average price of €8.24. The total outlay amounted to €190 million. Despite these ongoing repurchases, the net debt position had improved further by December 2002, with Olivetti reporting a consolidated €33.4 billion, of which €18.1 billion was booked to Telecom Italia. This is shown in Table 5.3, where other financial data for 2002 are also listed as well as comparative Olivetti Group data for 2001.

On 18 December 2002, a further provisional restructuring took place, involving many-times prime minister Silvio Berlusconi – a regular attendee in court on corruption charges – and Emilio Gnutti – a financier recently convicted of insider dealing and barred from sitting on the board of publicly-traded companies. In October, Mr Berlusconi – via Fininvest, his family holding – had agreed to take a 5.4 per cent stake in ·Hopa, a cash-rich investment group managed by Mr Gnutti.[18] Subsequently, Hopa agreed to buy a 16 per cent stake in Olimpia. This had the effect of reducing Pirelli's stake in Olimpia to 50.4 per cent, but as Hopa already owned a direct 4.4 per cent stake in Olivetti, it now owned over 30 per cent of Olivetti as a 'concert party' together with Olimpia. Since a 30 per cent stake would trigger a takeover bid for Olimpia under Italian law, Hopa needed to reduce its direct stake in Olivetti to bring the concert party below the 30 per cent threshold. The entire set of transactions was due to be completed by June 2003.[19] How much the cost would be remained unclear, but Mr Gnutti agreed to cancel €1 billion of Pirelli's debt by handing over an investment vehicle called Holly which had a net worth of €960 million.[20] Olimpia's debt would fall by €476 million to €3.1 billion.

Table 5.3 Consolidated accounts of Olivetti Group, year to December 2002 (€ million)

	Olivetti	Telecom Italia	Olivetti Tecnost	Olivetti Multi-services	Total Group 2002[a]	Total Group 2001
Net revenues	–	30,400	914	119	31,408	32,016
Amortization	(1,386)	(2,054)	(11)	0	(3,462)	(3,561)
EBIT[b]	(1,419)	1,850	(63)	20	520	1,983
Result before taxes	(2,150)	(313)	(80)	18	(2,516)	(3,097)
Net post-tax income	(548)	(97)	(87)	11	(773)	(3,090)
Total assets	26,376	52,862	761	204	83,384[c]	94,227
Total liabilities	17,345	40,526	700	155	62,760[d]	67,874
Net debt	(15,195)	(18,118)	(60)	(54)	(33,399)	(38,362)

Source: www.Olivetti.com

Notes:
[a] Individual entries do not total to the figure given for the Group as generally small adjustments need to be made for the Webegg Group, finance companies and consolidation. [b] Earnings before interest and taxes. [c] In this case, the finance companies contributed €16,720 and the consolidation adjustment represented €(13,539). [d] In this case, the finance companies contributed €16,346 and the consolidation adjustment represented €(12,312).

A further event of late 2002 was the decision by the Italian government to sell off its remaining 3.5 per cent stake in Telecom Italia ordinary shares at €7.5, a 5.7 per cent discount to the ruling price, together with the residual 0.7 per cent of its savings shares,[21] but the government still retained its 'golden share'. However, the final event was the agreed sale by Telecom Italia of a 29 per cent stake in Telekom Srbija for €195 million plus taking on €100 million of debt – the majority to be paid in four instalments commencing in January 2003.[22] The incomes and capital gains associated with this and other transactions are set out in Table 5.4.

At the beginning of 2003, Olivetti successfully sold €3 billion of 5/10/30 year debt, indicating that it would be able to reduce its interest costs over the coming year. However, the crucial news was Mr Provera's revised restructuring plan announced in early March, the purpose of which was to shorten the chain of command by merging together Pirelli with Pirelli & Cie and Olivetti with Telecom Italia. It was proposed that Pirelli & Cie would swap four new shares for three Pirelli ordinary shares and ten new savings shares for seven Pirelli savings shares. Pirelli & Cie would also undergo a capital increase of roughly $1 billion including free warrants worth one-quarter of that sum. The main proposal was that seven Olivetti shares would be exchanged for each Telecom Italia ordinary share. During the previous three years the ratio had fluctuated between four and nine, so the offer appeared to be superficially reasonable. However, many minority share-

Table 5.4 Main equity investment acquisitions and disposals 2002, Telecom Italia/TIM (€ million)

Date	Asset	Income (outgoing)	Capital gain (loss)
Feb 2002	Lottomatica	212	73
Mar 2002	Bouygues Décaux Télécom (19.6%)	750	266
Jun 2002	Mobilkom Austria (25%)	756	64
July 2002	Sogei	n/a	176
Aug 2002	Auna	1,998	1,033
Aug 2002	Telemaco Immobiliare	192	64
Aug 2002	EPIClink (86%)	(60)	–
Aug 2002	9Télécom/LDCom	n/a	(267)
Aug 2002	Solpart Participações (18.3%)	–	–
Aug 2002	Stet Hellas (17.5%)	(108)	n/a
Aug 2002	Netesi (69.1%)	(11)	n/a
Sep 2002	Pagine Utili	–	–
Oct 2002	Blu	(83)	n/a
Oct 2002	Tiglio I & II	234	150
Nov 2002	Telespazio	239	36
Nov 2002	Telekom Austria (15%)	559	(135)
Nov 2002	IMMSI	69	41
Dec 2002	Mediocredito Centrale (3%)	(36)	n/a
Dec 2002	Telekom Srbija (29%)	195	–

holders in Telecom Italia claimed that the true ratio lay between ten and 20, and hence that the offer was wholly unacceptable. In order to sweeten the deal, Olivetti offered to pay Olivetti shareholders between €1.01 and €1.12 a share should they wish to sell out, and to that end had raised financing worth almost $10 billion from JP Morgan and other banks. Anything left over would potentially be used to buy out Telecom Italia shareholders at between €7 and €8.40 a share. The merged Telecom Italia would absorb the existing Olivetti net debt of $16 billion plus the financing used for the share buy-backs, but Mr Provera promised to wipe out the latter within two years on the back of improved cash flow resulting from the shorter chain of command. Debt would also be reduced via asset sales worth up to $4.5 billion, largely arising from disposal of the yellow pages unit of Seat PG. The remaining holders of Telecom Italia savings shares would be entitled to savings shares in the new entity.[23]

The effect of the announcement was an 11 per cent drop in the Telecom Italia share price while that of Olivetti rose by 4 per cent – allegedly because Telecom Italia shareholders were switching into Olivetti in order to vote down the proposal. At least two-thirds of both companies' shareholders would need to authorize the proposal when it fell due to be considered in May, so the issue was whether the 30 per cent held by Olimpia would be sufficient to underpin a 'yes' vote at Olivetti. Not surprisingly, thoughts turned to Mr Colaninno's failed attempt to mollify minority shareholders that had partly led to his downfall, although Mr Provera remained confident. According to Lex, the offer was superficially fair and transparent, and it would result in Olimpia owning between 14 and 16 per cent of the merged company – sufficiently low to raise the possibility of the merged Telecom Italia behaving like a normal company. However, this figure could rise as high as 25 per cent if there was a purchase of Olivetti and Telecom Italia minorities that used up all the available financing.

It was noted that because Olivetti was the acquirer, but did not hold any telephony licences, it would have to alter its so-called 'purpose of corporation' which would in turn oblige it to make a cash offer to all those who wished to sell off their investments. Some rebels argued that it would anyway be much better for Telecom Italia to buy Olivetti since that would remove the need for the monies set aside to buy out minority shareholders, but this was said to be impractical because Telecom Italia would be obliged to buy back 55 per cent of its own shares. On the whole, despite the strong feelings against the proposal, few believed that it would fail to transpire and it was approved as expected by the Telecom Italia board on 14 April. Subsequently, holders of Telecom Italia savings shares also gave their approval and Pirelli shareholders approved the merger with Pirelli & Cie with completion in August.

In early May, Telecom Italia reported a reduction in revenue for the first quarter of 2003, but a rise in both operating and net profit (up 32 per cent due to increased cash flow and reduced investment). Net debt fell by roughly

€2 billion during the quarter. The results reflected a very strong performance at TIM, which recorded an operating profit of €897 million. Telecom Italia subsequently announced that it would be investing €2.5 billion during 2002/2005 to extend its broadband service via ADSL, which was available at the time to 78 per cent of the population, concentrating in particular on improving access speeds and the introduction of a pre-paid service. The entire population was expected to have access by mid-2003.

Telecom Italia's dominant position within the Olivetti Group is most obviously seen in terms of employment since it accounted for 100,765 of the total 104,379 employees at the end of March 2003. Although at this point net indebtedness had fallen to €31.9 billion from €33.4 billion at the end of 2002, this represented a smaller reduction than at Telecom Italia alone. Furthermore, the 2 per cent reduction in quarterly revenues at Telecom Italia appeared to be a very satisfactory result compared to the 34.5 per cent reduction at Olivetti Tecnost and 41.6 per cent reduction at Olivetti Multiservices.

By mid-June, the structural issues began to resolve themselves. During the previous weeks, the attractiveness of the cash offer for Olivetti shares had declined to nothing due to a rise in the share price in line with general market trends. This meant that all but €11 million of the €9 billion available could be used to purchase Telecom Italia ordinary and savings shares at €8.01 and €4.82, respectively. However, it was distinctly possible that the share prices would rise above the offer prices which would have the effect of diluting Olimpia's stake in the post-merger Telecom Italia.

The sale via a 'sudden-death' auction of the 61.5 per cent stake in Seat PG directories to a private equity consortium led by BC Partners, for €3.03 billion plus €708 million of debt taken on, produced a valuation of €5.65 billion for the whole of Seat PG directories – the consortium was offering to buy out the minority stakes as well at the same €0.598 per share paid to Telecom Italia – and €1.9 billion for the part being demerged as Telecom Italia Media at the beginning of August. This was generally regarded as excessive: Lex, for example, placed its value at only €1 billion.[24] Telecom Italia would start with a 61.5 per cent stake but was expected to offer to buy out the minorities, sell off the office products retailer and bring the rest back in-house.

At the end of June, the antitrust authorities opened a probe to determine whether Telecom Italia had abused its dominant position in respect of its interconnection charges. On a more positive note, the company agreed to sell property assets to Lastra Holding for €355 million and to buy German broadband operator Hansen.net (for €250 million) and Italian news agency AP.Biscom from e.Biscom, in the latter case for a symbolic €1.

The buy-back offer for Telecom Italia shares was completed on 18 July. At this point in time the offer price was almost identical to the market price, providing little incentive to sell. However, €5.2 billion of stock was tendered, representing 55.1 per cent of the applicable ordinary shares and 9.52 per cent of Telecom Italia's ordinary share capital, together with 70.4 per cent of the applicable savings shares and 12.2 per cent of the savings share capital. As a consequence Olivetti ended up with 64.5 per cent of Telecom Italia and Olimpia was set to end up with an 11.5 per cent direct stake in the enlarged Telecom Italia, which it increased to 14.2 per cent in October. Subject to approval of a €800 million capital increase in mid-November, that figure will rise to 17 per cent.

Telecom Italia expressed outrage when Moody's downgraded its long-term credit rating from Baa2 to Baa1 in August, despite the fact that Standard & Poor's had left its rating at BBB+. However, Moody's took the view that it had to include the debt of Olimpia in making its assessment of the implications of the takeover of Olivetti, as well as the loss for Telecom Italia bondholders of their priority claim over the company's cash flows now shared equally by the previously subordinated bondholders of Olivetti. Further bad news came in the form of a decision by the regulator to introduce price caps on calls made from fixed lines to mobile handsets, commencing on 1 January 2004 for at least two years. However, this was more than compensated by news that the European Court of Justice had ruled in favour of Telecom Italia in a dispute with the government concerning the legality of €2 billion of charges that it had imposed between 1999 and 2003 on the basis of Telecom Italia's turnover.

Conclusions

The history of Telecom Italia is highly unusual in a number of respects. Most obviously, it is the only major European incumbent to have been taken over[25] – and not merely once but twice. Second, the circumstances surrounding both takeovers illustrate the way in which business deals often continue to be done behind closed doors in Italy,[26] although there was a clear move towards more international 'Anglo Saxon' codes of behaviour on the second occasion. Third, the continued involvement of politicians – not only in terms of the government retaining a 'golden share' in the national incumbent operator conferring the right to veto the acquisition of more than 3 per cent of Telecom Italia, which is in defiance of a ruling by the European Commission, but in terms of having personal stakes, albeit indirect – is wholly contrary to accepted practice in, for example, the USA and UK.

Interestingly, the obvious manifestation of a more open, 'Anglo-Saxon' approach is the willingness of governments to countenance privatization, and the Italian government was at least superficially willing to accept that this was a process that should be pursued fairly wholeheartedly – unlike its French and German counterparts who still have shown no real interest in ceding control of their respective incumbents. However, coming over a decade after privatization in the UK, that in Italy was fairly late in the day and, significantly, a 'golden share' was retained. The more interesting issue is whether any of this has made any real difference since the government plainly interferes in the activities of private business in Italy and there is a degree of xenophobia about letting foreigners gain control of 'national champions' – compare this with the situation in the UK where the nationality of bidders is generally irrelevant. However, it may indeed be argued that the Italian government held the moral high ground when Deutsche Telkom bid for Telecom Italia, since it is hard to imagine the German government welcoming an Italian, or indeed any foreign takeover bid for Deutsche Telekom.

There are a number of respects in which this case study echoes others in this book. For example, Pirelli seemingly ignored the views of the financial markets – so tellingly expressed in their hammering of Marconi earlier in 2001 and more recently in relation to AOL Time Warner – that 'old economy' assets should not be traded for 'new economy' assets; it traded cash for debt; and it paid a substantial premium for the Bell stake. Furthermore, Pirelli intended to sell its profitable energy cable business to finance the deal. Second, insofar that Pirelli intended to bring in new, highly regarded management, it gave Telecom Italia shareholders something to cheer about. On the other hand, Mr Provera was initially unable to explain how he intended to revive Telecom Italia – he claimed not to have inspected the books – and there were few obvious synergies. On balance, the markets' response was understandably negative, and the Pirelli share price was hammered as a result.

From the viewpoint of corporate governance, the fact remains that Pirelli was able to gain control without making a bid for a majority of the Olivetti shares, a practice that would not be countenanced in an Anglo-Saxon regulatory system. A cash pile of €7 billion sufficed to secure a company with a market value of €110 billion. What this suggests is that despite the election of a new centre-right government claiming to favour transparency and competition – but headed by a media tycoon and politician, Silvio Berlusconi, with deep roots in the old system of patronage – the preference for family dynasties controlling Italian financial and economic life has yet to die away. Benetton may be a relative 'new kid on the Italian industrial block', but the same can hardly be said of partner, Pirelli. As Mr Provera is wont to remark, the Anglo Saxon financial markets may be highly efficient, but de-industrialization is occurring less rapidly in Italy where family businesses remain the dominant force. One key change may, however, be detected in the willingness of 'hard cores' to stay loyal through thick and thin. Mr Colaninno failed to deliver and was shown the door as a result – although there are recent signs of a comeback – so the new owners of Telecom Italia might need to deliver improved performance if they wish to avoid a similar fate. Fortunately for them, however, the list of other Italian companies in a position to bid for the post-merger Telecom Italia is rather thin. In any event, Mr Provera's grip on Pirelli is tight and a predator cannot hope to acquire Telecom Italia via a takeover of Pirelli.

As elsewhere in the telecommunications sector, debt is the key issue to be addressed. Because of the 'Chinese boxes' it was always difficult to associate the indebtedness of each element in the chain of control with its operational performance. Clearly, something needed to be done to reduce the length of the chain, but as soon as the pressure on management at the top layer began to ease it curiously seemed to lose interest in matters of good corporate governance. Mr Provera has finally bitten at least part of the bullet in this respect. The two mergers have now shortened the chain significantly, but the pressures have certainly not gone away – Telecom Italia's consolidated debt is no trifling matter. Fortunately, it enjoys the benefit of being compared to its French and German counterparts where net debt is considerably higher, and both Telecom Italia and TIM are trading well under the prevailing circumstances.

Part II

Illustrative application of strategic modelling II

Over the course of the next two chapters, two quite different companies are analysed. The first of these is the Vodafone Group (hereafter Vodafone), while the other is WorldCom. These companies operate in contrasting markets: Vodafone is to be found almost exclusively in the mobile telecommunication market, having recently sold off its fixed-wire subsidiary in Japan, whereas WorldCom operates fixed-wire and data networks and has no mobile operations of any consequence. A further, significant contrast is that Vodafone is one of the most admired companies in the telecommunications industry, whereas the bankruptcy of WorldCom has resulted in it becoming a byword for (financial) mismanagement.

Having said this, there are also some intriguing similarities between the companies. As can be seen in the chapters which follow, both companies grew primarily through acquisitions. In the case of Vodafone, two acquisitions in particular – of AirTouch in the USA and Mannesmann in Germany – greatly increased its operational footprint, as well as strengthened its grip on subsidiaries across Europe and the Far East. WorldCom made many more acquisitions than Vodafone overall, but while many of these were relatively small, WorldCom came to prominence through its hugely costly September 1997 acquisition of MCI from under the nose of BT. Ironically, however, its attempt to achieve a further quantum leap in size via the acquisition of Sprint in October 1999 for $115 billion, which was primarily designed to achieve national mobile connectivity in the USA in one fell swoop (through Sprint PCS) proved to be one mega-deal too far and ultimately led to WorldCom's fall from grace.

Another similarity was that in both cases individuals came to personify their respective companies. In the case of Vodafone, Sir Christopher Gent came to the fore during the hostile takeover of Mannesmann and, as Chapter 7 shows, the stories of WorldCom and its exuberant CEO, Bernie Ebbers, are inextricably interwoven. But there the similarity ends. Sir Christopher handed over a healthy company to his successor, Arun Sarin: Bernie Ebbers did not. Significant irregularities were found in WorldCom's accounting which led to the accounts being re-stated and the company filing for Chapter 11 bankruptcy.

The models described in Chapter 2 can all be used to shed light on the strategies of both companies, though they will naturally highlight different aspects of the strategies that have been adopted. If we use the Flagship Firm model of Rugman and D'Cruz to look at the strategies of Vodafone, then three areas of its strategy are illuminated. The first of these is co-ordination, while the second is specialization. The third is alignment of strategic priorities within the business network that surrounds the flagship firm.

When Vodafone first ventured overseas from the UK, its preferred method of expansion was through joint ventures. In these, Vodafone was a minority investor, with the rest being spread across a wide variety of other companies such as financial investors, utilities and, on occasion, other telecommunications companies. Such an approach to international expansion was in keeping with the company's broader strategic approach, and was motivated by a desire to minimize risk while investing in as broad a range of countries as possible. Through its merger with AirTouch, Vodafone expanded into new countries (not simply the USA since AirTouch had several overseas subsidiaries of its own) and consolidated its position as a shareholder in some of its international ventures where ownership overlapped.

However, the merger still mostly left Vodafone as a minority stakeholder in its international ventures and these were as a consequence effectively separated from one another for operational and strategic purposes. The ability of Vodafone, or for that matter any other shareholder, to co-ordinate these international businesses to its advantage was severely restricted by the presence of the other shareholders. The international businesses were, therefore, managed for the benefit of all shareowners and not just Vodafone. If the interests of all shareholders had been the same this would at least have enabled the businesses to be managed effectively, but given that certain shareholders tended to have contrasting strategic imperatives – it was generally the case, for example, that one substantial one was domestic while the others were foreign, as in the case of SFR in France – there were bound to be disagreements and difficulties were inevitably encountered. The bid for Mannesmann by Vodafone was in part triggered by Mannesmann's decision to enter the UK market by acquiring Orange. If successful, this acquisition would have resulted in Mannesmann competing with Vodafone in the UK and German mobile markets while collaborating with it elsewhere.

Although the hostile acquisition of Mannesmann did further strengthen the position of Vodafone, it still did not provide majority control in most of its markets. Vodafone sought to resolve this in one of two ways. In the first place it acquired additional equity from other large shareholders while, as opportunities presented themselves, it also bought shares in the open market from private investors. Vodafone was able to fund these purchases from its own ever-growing free cash flow as well as from the sums raised through disposing of non-core businesses inherited from Mannesmann and selling bonds. As Chapter 6 shows, these purchases enabled Vodafone to take control – initially majority and subsequently outright – of most of its international businesses.

In parallel with its purchase of additional equity, Vodafone also began to re-brand its international businesses. Initially, each of these operated its own brand. In Sweden, for example, Vodafone was an investor in Europolitan Holdings which used the Europolitan brand in the marketplace. In a two-stage process, the various national brands were replaced. The first stage involved Vodafone adding its name to the national brand while in the second the latter was subsequently dropped. Thus, if we return to our Swedish example, Europolitan became successively Vodafone Europolitan and then simply Vodafone.

Re-branding is a clear and visible demonstration of the control that Vodafone was able to exert over its various international businesses. Vodafone was only able to exercise such control because it was a large, and generally the majority, shareholder in these businesses. Interestingly, even where it was a minority shareholder, as in the case of Proximus in Belgium, the other shareholders subsequently came to realize in most cases the advantages of at least partially using the Vodafone brand in preference to their own. The launch across Europe of common services such as Vodafone live! served to accentuate the ability of Vodafone to control and co-ordinate its businesses.

Nevertheless, even today Vodafone still does not control all of its international businesses. Within Europe, the most glaring example of Vodafone's lack of control is in France where it owns 43.9 per cent of SFR – a large minority stake but one that carries with it no control since the rest of the shares are held by a single operator, Vivendi Universal, at least for now. The same is true in the USA, where Vodafone owns 44.3 per cent of Verizon Wireless but has to defer to majority shareholder Verizon Communications on matters such as the technology of choice (CDMA rather than the GSM standard used elsewhere by Vodafone). The lack of control in France means that common services and brands cannot be readily adopted although Vivendi has recently come to see the virtues of Vodafone's live! portal. Resolving the control issues in France and the USA are among the key strategic challenges that the new CEO, Arun Sarin, faces. One obvious option in France would be to acquire Vivendi Universal and then sell off all of the businesses except for SFR, but given the need to pay a potentially large premium on the market price this option is unlikely to be well received by financial analysts, even though it would leave Vodafone with control over the last major gap in its European coverage.

Cost will also play a significant role in resolving the strategic challenge in the USA. Even if Verizon Communications were to become a willing seller, which is extremely unlikely given that the bundling up of fixed-wire, Internet and mobile services is very much the strategic 'in thing' in the USA, the premium that Vodafone would have to pay on the market price would undoubtedly attract the adverse comments of the financial community. Vodafone superficially has much to gain by opting instead to acquire one of the national GSM operators, AT&T Wireless, Cingular Wireless or T-Mobile USA, but even to attempt to do so would seriously antagonize Verizon

Communications – it could not afford to sell its stake in Verizon Wireless before making such a bid for fear of being left without any kind of network – yet even if it proved to be successful, the financial community would almost certainly be up in arms about what it would regard as over-payment.

Another area that the use of the Five Forces model highlights is specialization. Vodafone has not diversified into other (telecommunications) markets. In the aftermath of its takeover of Mannesmann, Vodafone has divested its inherited portfolio of industrial holdings as well as its fixed telecommunication businesses. Vodafone was able to sell the industrial portfolio relatively swiftly, though as market sentiment turned against the telecommunications sector the sale of the fixed telecommunications businesses took longer than anticipated and raised less than initially expected. Hence, after a few stumbles along the way, Vodafone was able to restore its status as a mobile pure play with international linkages that far outweighed its competitors.

There is, however, another dimension to specialization. After its unhappy early experiences with its portal Vizzavi, the ambitions of Vodafone in the area of content became much more modest than had previously been the case. When coupled with the fact that no other investments were made in content companies, Vodafone remained a mobile operator with only a passing interest in content.

Thus, the use of the Five Forces model draws attention both to key dimensions of the strategy adopted by Vodafone as well as the issues that it needs to address at some point in the future. As noted above, the preferred solution to these issues may well not be popular in certain quarters, so it is hardly surprising that Vodafone's current strategy is merely to suggest what it would like to do one day rather than to lay down any kind of specific timetable. There is no desperate need to act. Through specialization and the effecting of control over most of its international businesses, Vodafone has been able to co-ordinate their operations and align their strategic focus. No doubt WorldCom wishes that it could say the same.

Chapter 6

Vodafone

The quest for worldwide mobility

Background

Prior to the takeover of AirTouch of the USA, Vodafone, somewhat unusually, was a fully listed UK-based company – that is, its shares had been floated on the stock market – and, interestingly, no other telecoms operator had acquired a significant stake. It had started out as a subsidiary of Racal in 1984, with an analogue licence dating from 1982, at which time it was the only private sector competitor to the then publicly-owned incumbent, British Telecommunications (BT).

Vodafone's initial success had a lot to do with the marketing skills of Chris Gent and his boss until 1997, Gerry Whent. The parent company knew about technology but not how to sell its products. Once Vodafone had generated considerable success in locking up the business market for mobile handsets, an initial public offer became both feasible and desirable as a means of generating cash for Racal. An IPO of 20 per cent of the capital duly took place at the end of the 1980s, and released Vodafone from the admittedly modest restrictions imposed by its parent. The company, renamed the Vodafone Group, was fully demerged from Racal in September 1991.

The first digital mobile operator in the UK market with a licence granted in 1991, Vodafone became and remained the market leader, although it eventually faced competition from three other digital networks – Cellnet (60 per cent owned by BT and licensed in July 1994), Orange (licensed in April 1994) and One-2-One (licensed in September 1993). BT bought out the minority shareholder in Cellnet, Securicor, in October 1999. The controlling shareholder in Orange was Hutchison Whampoa, based in Hong Kong. One-2-One was owned by MediaOne of the USA and Cable & Wireless of the UK. It was put up for sale in March 1999 and bought by Deutsche Telekom in August.

Vodafone was much the most internationally minded of the four UK mobile operators. By the end of 1998, it had acquired fairly extensive interests in Europe, some wholly owned but usually in the form of minority stakes taken in consortia bidding for new licences. Elsewhere in the world it had, for example, acquired stakes in Australia, Fiji, Malta and South Africa. Nevertheless, it lacked a base in the two most significant markets outside Europe –

the USA and Japan. In considering its international strategy, Vodafone was able to take advantage of its unusual situation in that, unlike other UK operators and, indeed, most operators elsewhere, it was a pure mobile operation, whereas the norm was a greater or lesser degree of fixed-mobile convergence. The crucial issue was that either Vodafone would have to expand so as to gather together a coherent worldwide network and gain economies of scale or it could expect to be taken over by one of the European or American incumbents. Not surprisingly, it preferred the first option, and it was in a position to deliver because its rapidly rising share price meant that it could make all-paper takeover bids.

Growth via acquisition

Vodafone/AirTouch

The various telecoms markets in the USA were undergoing massive structural changes in the aftermath of the Telecommunications Act of 1996. In January 1999, one of the Baby Bells, Bell Atlantic, made an all-paper takeover bid worth $45 billion for cellular operator, AirTouch. AirTouch was already Bell Atlantic's co-partner in PrimeCo of the USA and in Omnitel of Italy. Vodafone, long considered as a potential partner for AirTouch and itself involved with it in joint ventures in Sweden (Europolitan) and Egypt, immediately made a counter-bid worth roughly $55 billion, consisting largely of its shares together with a small amount of cash. This much higher offer was facilitated by the fact that Vodafone's own share price had soared during 1998 (see Figure 6.1), with the result that it was worth $35.5 billion at the year-end. The offer was proposed as a merger of equals, but structured as an acquisition with a 50.1 per cent stake allocated to Vodafone's shareholders.

Aside from their existing collaborations, AirTouch also operated European joint ventures in Belgium, Germany, Italy, Poland, Portugal, Romania and Spain, whereas Vodafone operated in the UK, France, Germany, Greece, Malta and the Netherlands. Germany was, therefore, the only European country in which they competed at the time, and Vodafone was perfectly happy to dispose of its interest in E-Plus while taking on AirTouch's interest in Mannesmann Mobilfunk's D2 network. There was no overlap elsewhere in the world. This indicated that there would be few obvious cost savings, but collaboration in selling and technology was expected to produce savings. Certainly, the two companies would together form the first more-or-less global mobile carrier, to be known as Vodafone AirTouch, operating on five continents albeit biased towards Europe. However, AirTouch was a regional operator in the USA and would have to take steps to acquire a national footprint to compete with the likes of AT&T Wireless and Sprint PCS. Vodafone's offer was subsequently raised to $62 billion, comprising $85 in Vodafone stock per AirTouch share plus $7 in cash, at which point Bell Atlantic withdrew. By the end of June, the takeover had been ratified by both

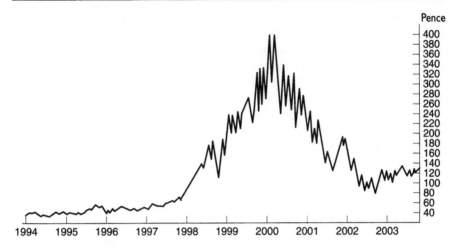

Figure 6.1 Vodafone Group share price, 1994–2003 (pence).
Source: Daily share prices in the *Financial Times*.

sets of shareholders, the FCC and the European Commission – the latter making it conditional upon the disposal of Vodafone's interest in E-Plus. The company was renamed Vodafone AirTouch.

In a fit of pique, reacting to the disappointment of a lost opportunity to stitch together a coast-to-coast network in the USA, Bell Atlantic had dissolved the PrimeCo arrangement with AirTouch in April. However, the synergies implicit in combining AirTouch's licences in 25 western states with Bell Atlantic's licences in 24 eastern states were potentially too good to miss out on, and in September 1999 it was announced that the two companies were negotiating to merge their US cellular interests into a separate company. The result was an arrangement whereby Bell Atlantic would end up with a 55 per cent controlling stake and the majority of board members. However, to compensate for its loss of control – regarded as worthwhile given that the alternative was to construct its own network from scratch at huge expense – and also by way of compensation for the premium that Vodafone had paid when bidding for the assets held by AirTouch, Vodafone AirTouch's 45 per cent stake would be larger than its contribution of 40 per cent of the overall number of subscribers in the new venture. In addition, Vodafone AirTouch would transfer $4.5 billion of debt to the venture. Finally, because Vodafone AirTouch was concerned that its minority interest would leave it in a vulnerable position should the relationship turn sour, it insisted that the venture should be partially floated after three years to provide it with an exit route. Once its own merger with GTE to form Verizon Communications was given regulatory clearance, Bell Atlantic was able to add GTE's mobile assets to the new venture on 10 July 2000. This made it possible to proceed with the previous agreement between Bell Atlantic and Vodafone AirTouch to create Verizon Wireless, with Verizon Communications as majority shareholder with a controlling interest. It was announced that Verizon Wireless, now with 24 million subscribers, would seek a stock market listing which would value it at in excess of $100 billion. However, adverse market conditions delayed the listing. It was widely believed that Vodafone would try to take control of Verizon Wireless, if only because it wanted to use the W-CDMA version of 3G to which it was committed elsewhere, whereas Verizon Communications preferred the incompatible cdma2000, but so far this has been resisted.

Mannesmann/Orange

Mannesmann had its origins in several industrial sectors – engineering, automotive and tubes. It had diversified into telecoms and was known to be actively seeking to expand its telecoms interests in Europe. It had become involved in the ultimately successful bid by Olivetti for a majority stake in Telecom Italia, and was widely believed to have been the main beneficiary of that bid in that it had acquired stakes in mobile operator Omnitel and fixed-wire operator Infostrada at the very cheap price of $8.2 billion. It had also acquired the fixed-wire business of o-tel-o in Germany.

The Mannesmann chairman, Klaus Esser, who had been appointed in May 1999, was understandably keen to separate the company into two parts, each to be given its own listing. This process was instigated in September 1999. In mid-October, it was revealed that Mannesmann was in talks with Hutchison concerning the future of Orange. What was proposed was for Hutchison to swap its large stake in Orange for a much smaller stake in Mannesmann. When the cash plus paper deal was announced, it valued Orange at $31 billion, in addition to which Mannesmann agreed to take on Orange's debt of roughly $4 billion. For its part, Hutchison agreed to exchange its 44.8 per cent controlling stake in Orange for a 10.2 per cent stake in Mannesmann and to hold on to a minimum 8.5 per cent stake for 18 months. The move on Orange, which was approved by the European Commission in December 1999, sent a fairly explicit message to Vodafone AirTouch: You are the minority partner in D2 and Omnitel, and if we consider our interests to be best served through alliances with other potential partners then we will go ahead irrespective of your wishes.

Vodafone AirTouch/Mannesmann

This was not the message Vodafone wanted to hear. The European mobile operations of itself and Mannesmann presented an excellent strategic fit, but if Mannesmann acquired Orange then Vodafone AirTouch would be participating in several major joint ventures with a co-partner that appeared to be as much of a competitor as an ally. It did not take very long for the financial markets to conclude that the only rational response for Vodafone AirTouch would be to make a takeover bid for the whole of Mannesmann. Indeed, France Télécom immediately informed Vodafone AirTouch that it would be happy to take Orange off its hands were such a bid to succeed. What was certain was that Vodafone AirTouch would not be able to forestall the Mannesmann offer for Orange since Mannesmann did not need to seek shareholders' permission to issue the requisite number of additional shares and Hutchison had given an irrevocable acceptance in response to Mannesmann's offer.

Before launching such a bid, Vodafone AirTouch had to take account of a long list of complicating factors. For example, Mannesmann had a core of loyal shareholders and no hostile takeover had ever been successful in Germany. These were by no means trivial problems, so why was Vodafone AirTouch so keen to proceed? In the first place, its existing network in Europe consisted of too many minority stakes, and the addition of the stakes held by Mannesmann would greatly strengthen its hand, especially in the major economies. Second, there was the lure of sheer size. On a proportionate basis, the merged company would have roughly 42 million subscribers. Not only would this reduce the need for roaming agreements with other carriers, but more of the latter would have to pay for Vodafone AirTouch to deliver their calls. Finally, the investment in developing a platform for mobile data and Internet services would be much easier to justify if the resultant technology was to be adopted on a much larger scale.

Hence, despite these difficulties, Vodafone AirTouch decided to press ahead with a 'friendly' bid valued at 43.7 of its own shares for each Mannesmann share – equivalent to roughly €203 per share or just over €100 billion (roughly $90 billion – one euro was typically worth $0.9 at the time[1]) for the entire company. This offer was dismissed by Klaus Esser as 'wholly inadequate'. The reply by Vodafone AirTouch was to 'go hostile' on 15 November. Klaus Esser responded with a vigorous defence, emphasizing the virtues of an approach based upon the integration of fixed-wire and mobile networks, rather than the pure mobile approach advocated by Vodafone AirTouch. Chris Gent, now the latter's CEO, responded that he did not intend to dispose of any fixed-wire assets acquired as part of a takeover of Mannesmann. He also stated that he would be retaining the whole of the Mannesmann workforce and that any existing plans to hive-off non-telecoms assets would be allowed to proceed.

At the end of November, Mr Esser claimed that he believed in shareholder democracy and that he would concede defeat if Vodafone AirTouch secured over 50 per cent of Mannesmann shares. However, he indicated that a fair take-out price would be at least €300, effectively leaving Mannesmann shareholders with a majority stake in the merged company. The formal offer was tabled on Christmas Eve. The closing date of the offer was set at 7 February 2000.

On 19 January, Chris Gent appeared to make some concessions. He stated that he was prepared to consider an increase in the offer price, albeit in

Vodafone AirTouch shares rather than in cash, but only a very modest one and that under no circumstances would it result in lifting Mannesmann's share of the merged company to more than 48.9 per cent as against the original 47.2 per cent. This, he claimed, was the best offer his own share-holders would tolerate. He also stated that he would consider holding on to Mannesmann's fixed-wire operations.

There was no sign of a 'white knight' riding to the rescue since, at the end of the day, the cost was simply too high for rival bidders to pay. The biggest potential problem therefore seemed to be the attitude of the European Commission, which confirmed that it had begun its first-stage inquiry with a deadline of 17 February. At the very end of January, Vivendi Universal of France created despondency in the German camp by announcing that, far from wishing to form an alliance with Mannesmann, it had agreed to join forces with Vodafone AirTouch. This 50:50 alliance between VivendiNet, a joint venture between Vivendi and Canal Plus, and Vodafone AirTouch was temporarily named Multi Access Portal (MAP). In return for its support, Vivendi secured an assurance that Vodafone AirTouch would sell it half of Mannesmann's stake in Cégétel in France, thereby raising its own stake to 51.5 per cent. On the face of it, this was a poor deal for Vodafone AirTouch, especially since there was no certainty that Vivendi would have struck a deal with Mannesmann, but it did not ultimately appear to be too big a sacrifice in the greater scheme of things. As in respect of the arrangement with Bell Atlantic noted above, Chris Gent appeared unusually ready to make pragmatic concessions in the pursuit of longer-term objectives.

The financial markets now took the view that the bid would succeed, boost-ing Vodafone AirTouch's share price on successive days to end 2 February at £3.85. This meant that each Mannesmann share was valued at €344 and the overall bid at €178 billion. The following morning it was confirmed that Mannesmann had accepted the bid on the basis of 58.96 Vodafone AirTouch shares per Mannesmann share, worth €353 at that time, giving Mannesmann shareholders 49.5 per cent of the new company. In June, the European Commission cleared the takeover subject to the commitment to sell off Orange and the provision of access to other operators of roaming facilities and wholesale services for a period of three years.

Orange

The future of Orange was finally resolved at the end of May 2000 when an offer was accepted from France Télécom which consisted of €21.4 billion (roughly $19 billion) in cash together with 9.87 per cent of its shares worth roughly $15 billion and the assumption of debts of $2.4 billion and of future liabilities of $6.3 billion relating to the UMTS licence in the UK.[2] In order to avoid the Vodafone Group ending up with an undesirably large stake in the French operator, a $2 billion replacement loan note was issued, together with a complex set of call and put options which would serve to reduce the stake gradually over time. The European Commission cleared the deal in mid-August subject to the disposal of the Orange stake in KPN Orange in the Netherlands. Orange was thereafter Vodafone's main competitor.

E-Plus

As noted above, Vodafone AirTouch already knew that it would be obliged by the European Commission to dispose of its 17.24 per cent holding in E-Plus, the third-largest mobile operator in Germany, because it was acquiring Mannesmann's interest in the larger D2 network. Since they were themselves going through a restructuring, and wished to sell off peripheral interests, Veba and RWE of Germany – trading as VR Telecommunications – also decided to dispose of their own interests in E-Plus at the same time. As a result, 77.5 per cent of E-Plus became available in early December. France Télécom was extremely anxious to acquire the Vodafone AirTouch stake in E-Plus, and negotiated a deal to buy the available shares for €9.1 billion. However, it had not bargained for the fact that BellSouth of the USA, the owner of the residual 22.5 per cent stake, would exercise its pre-emption right to buy the stake at the same price, and the deal went through on 4 February 2000, realizing a profit for Vodafone of roughly $1.4 billion.

Re-branding

Mobile service users in developed markets are a fairly fickle group, seemingly willing to switch brands without much concern as to whether the new service is likely to be much different to that currently consumed – which in general it isn't. It is as yet unclear whether the mobile market can ever develop strong brand loyalty, but operators understandably prefer to believe in the possibility. For this reason, it was announced on 28 July 2000 that, in order to establish a global brand name, Vodafone AirTouch would henceforth become the Vodafone Group and trade, wherever possible, simply as Vodafone. This name will be used for convenience in what follows.

One obvious disadvantage for Vodafone compared to Orange was that the latter had a compelling set of brand values and a resonant advertising image that had helped to generate rapid subscriber growth combined with relatively low churn. Not surprisingly, therefore, France Télécom was moving rapidly to make Orange its universal mobile brand. By comparison, the Vodafone brand could be said to lack any kind of 'personality'. It could be argued that Vodafone was much the largest and most successful mobile operator, so this was unlikely to hold it back overmuch. Nevertheless, having collected a set of assets that were being marketed under a variety of brands in different markets, Vodafone was in need of a global brand image, although there was clearly a downside to replacing a recognized and successful brand name in certain of its markets.

The intention is currently that the Vodafone brand will eventually become universal, but the initial stage was to combine it with an existing brand, with the latter dominant – for example, the ex-Mannesmann brand D2 in Germany became D2 Vodafone, in Italy it traded as Omnitel Vodafone and in Portugal as Vodafone Telecel. Similar rebranding also occurred in Greece, the Netherlands, Spain and Sweden, but not in Belgium and France because Vodafone was not the controlling shareholder in the relevant operator (see footnotes to Table 6.1). Vodafone already traded under its own name in Malta and Hungary, but could not re-brand in Poland and Romania for the same reason. More recently, Vodafone has signed a number of partner agreements whereby, despite the absence of an equity stake, a company such as Mobilkom adopts the Vodafone brand name in its marketing.

Tidying up the structure

Mannesmann

There were quite a few matters left over from the Mannesmann takeover to tidy up. In February 2000, for example, Vodafone offered to buy all outstanding Mannesmann convertible bonds at the rate of 1,440 new Vodafone shares per convertible bond. Further, it had been expected that the sale of Atecs, the engineering and automotive unit of Mannesmann, would be pushed through by the Mannesmann supervisory board before Chris Gent obtained the all-clear from the Commission and officially took over. Thyssen Krupp had tabled a €8.75 billion bid, but this was trumped by a €9.1 billion joint bid from Siemens and Robert Bosch (which was subsequently increased to €9.6 billion consisting of €3.1 billion payable by September 2000, €3.7 billion payable by the end of December and €2.8 billion of assumed pension liabilities). In the event, the offer was accepted shortly after Vodafone took over.[3] In August, the European Commission authorized, first, the sale of Mannesmann subsidiary Demag to Siemens and Bosch, and, second, the sale of three engineering subsidiaries, Dematic, VDO and Sachs, to Siemens. However, it opened an investigation into the sale of Rexroth to Bosch, which was eventually authorized in December subject to Bosch selling its existing piston pump business. In December, Vodafone sold its ex-Mannesmann watches business to Richemont of Switzerland for €1.8 billion in cash. This left as a non-telecoms interest only the 8.2 per cent stake in Ruhrgas which was finally sold on to E.ON on 8 July 2002 for roughly €90 million in cash.

On the telecoms side, a Mannesmann-related disposal took place in November 2000 when Warburg Pincus acquired Mannesmann iPulsys, the Dutch-managed IP service, for an undisclosed sum. However, the main issue was the fate of Mannesmann Arcor. Arcor was the only fixed-wire operator in Germany other than Deutsche Telekom to serve both business and residential customers with a local loop. In late March 2000, Vodafone announced that the need to raise funds to bid for UMTS licences was proving problematic,

Table 6.1 Vodafone Group operations in Western Europe, 30 June 2003

Country	Operator	Holding (%)	Subscribers (000s)	Pre-paid (%)
Austria	a	–	–	–
Belgium	Proximus*	25.0	1,047	–
Denmark	a	–	–	–
France	SFR*b	43.9	6,012	–
Germany	Vodafone*c	100.0	23,261	53
Greece	Vodafone*d	74.8	2,724	71
Ireland	Vodafone*e	100.0	1,765	71
Italy	Vodafone*f	76.8	15,044	92
Netherlands	Vodafone*g,k	99.8	3,312	58
Portugal	Vodafone*h,k	100.0	3,129	73
Spain	Vodafone*i	100.0	9,184	57
Sweden	Vodafone*j,k	99.1	1,331	30
Switzerland	Mobile Com*	25.0	895	–
UK	Vodafone*	100.0	13,313	59

Source: Compiled by authors, partly from Vodafone Annual Report and Accounts for the years ending 31 March 2002 and 31 March 2003 and www.vodafone.com

Notes:
Subscriber numbers are the latest available on the web site – currently June 2003. They represent Vodafone's proportion, based upon its percentage holding, of the network's total subscribers.
* UMTS licence holders, sometimes as part of a consortium. a Vodafone has a partner agreement with Mobilkom Austria in Austria, TDC Mobile in Denmark, Radiolinja in Finland and Og fjarskipti in Iceland whereby Vodafone roaming services are marketed under the joint names. It also has an agreement with Swisscom covering Liechtenstein. These Agreements cover co-operation in roaming products as well as joint product development, marketing and global account management. b Including the stake bought from SBC in January 2003. Vodafone owns 20 per cent directly, and a further 23.9 per cent via its stake in SFR parent Cégétel. SFR and Cégétel are being merged under the SFR brand. c Listed as Vodafone D2, it was rebranded from D2 Vodafone to Vodafone in March 2002. d Listed as Vodafone-Panafon, it was rebranded as Vodafone in January 2002. In November 2003, Vodafone agreed to buy a 9.4 per cent stake from Intracom, and this enlarged stake is that listed in the table. Vodafone is currently offering to buy out the other minority interests, and had reached 80.8 per cent in early December. e In December 2000, Vodafone made a successful all-paper bid worth €4.5 billion, including €250 million debt taken over, for Eircom of Ireland's mobile subsidiary Eircell. f Listed as Omnitel Pronto Italia, it was rebranded as Vodafone Omnitel in June 2002 and as Vodafone in May 2003. g Formerly Libertel and now listed as Vodafone Libertel, it was rebranded as Vodafone in January 2002. h Formerly Telecel and now listed as Vodafone Telecel, it was rebranded as Vodafone in October 2001. i Formerly Airtel Móvil and now listed as Vodafone Spain, it was rebranded as Vodafone in October 2001. j Formerly Europolitan and listed as Europolitan Holdings, it was rebranded as Vodafone in April 2002. k In January 2003, Vodafone offered to buy out all of the minority holdings in these three subsidiaries. Once it owned between 90 per cent and 95 per cent, depending on the particular shares, it was able to use 'squeeze out rights' to forcibly acquire the rest. Europolitan was delisted in Sweden in March 2003. Vodafone has also delisted the former Libertel in which it now has a 99.7 per cent stake and Telecel (in May 2003).

and that it accordingly intended to float a 25 per cent stake in Arcor which was worth roughly €4 billion at the time despite being loss-making. However, although this had been pencilled in for March 2001, it was indefinitely postponed in December 2000.

The central problem lay with Deutsche Bahn, the railway company, which held an 18.8 per cent stake in Arcor – but also a blocking 25 per cent plus one share of the voting rights – with the other shares divided between

Vodafone with 73.2 per cent and Deutsche Bank with 8 per cent. Arcor DB Telematik was created at the beginning of 2002, 50.1 per cent owned by Arcor and 49.9 per cent by Deutsche Bahn, to take over Arcor's role of telematics provider to the railways, comprising roughly 25 per cent of its turnover. Deutsche Bahn was given the option to take full control of the new company from 1 July 2002 – which it duly exercised at a cost of €1.15 billion (just over $1 billion). Arcor also transferred all of its rail-related tangible assets to Deutsche Bahn in return for roughly $1 billion in cash, with the latter retaining an 18 per cent stake in Arcor.

Vodafone's one move which seemed to conflict with its overall strategy was with respect to tele-ring in Austria, a fixed-wire and PCN operator previously majority owned by Mannesmann. In November 2000, it acquired an UMTS 3G licence in Austria trading as Mannesmann 3G Mobilfunk, subsequent to which Vodafone bought out the other stakeholders. Despite this, it sold its entire holding to Western Wireless International of the USA for an undisclosed sum in May 2001. Interestingly, it subsequently signed a partner agreement with Mobilkom Austria whereby the latter will trade using the Vodafone name.

Other European interests

Post-Mannesmann, Vodafone's European interests were somewhat patchy and it was keen to consolidate. This meant, in particular, taking action in France (see under Vizzavi, below) and Spain where, in April 1999, Grupo Endesa and Unión Fenosa, opting to concentrate their interests in Retevisión and needing to avoid conflicts of interest as required by the regulator, had announced that each would put its 8.14 per cent stake in competitor Airtel up for sale. Banco Santander Central Hispano (BSCH) decided to exercise its right of first option to buy the shares, thereby raising its stake to 30.45 per cent, but it also announced its intention to sell the shares on to the other shareholders when the price had risen sufficiently.

Airtel remained one of the few European mobile operators without a controlling shareholder. Hence, in December 1999, seeking to take advantage of the opportunity thus presented, the now enlarged Vodafone offered to exchange the BSCH stake for roughly 5.5 per cent of its own shares, worth €7.2 billion on the day of the offer, seeking thereby to gain majority control. However, just as the deal was about to be signed, BT not only stepped in with a higher paper bid, equivalent, on the day of the offer, to roughly a 5 per cent stake in BT, but also invoked a shareholder agreement binding the companies, including Vodafone, which specified that any additional acquisition of Airtel equity by any of them would, if the others so wished, have to be shared out equally among them.

In January 2000, Vodafone signed an agreement with the three minority partners in the shareholding pact by way of a 'put' option giving it the exclusive right to buy their combined 16.9 per cent stake should they decide to sell, but the ownership issue still required final resolution. The compromise eventually reached left both Vodafone and BT as shareholders, but with the former firmly in control with a majority stake. Initially, BSCH sold its stake to Vodafone, receiving in return a stake of over 3 per cent in the latter and becoming its largest shareholder. Vodafone then built up its stake to 73.8 per cent overall by further purchases from other shareholders. The residual shareholding was divided between BT (17.8 per cent), Acciona (5.4 per cent) and Torreal (3 per cent). Vodafone then paid $1.6 billion in cash for the BT stake in May 2001 and dropped plans for a flotation. Airtel was rebranded as Vodafone in October 2001. Vodafone bought a further 2.2 per cent stake from Torreal for $576 million in April 2002.[4]

The position in Italy was that Vodafone wanted to concentrate upon its successful mobile network and to dispose of its stake in fixed-wire operator Infostrada. In October 2000, Infostrada was provisionally sold to Enel of Italy, but the antitrust authorities stipulated that Enel could proceed only if it sold 5,500 megawatts of generating capacity representing a profit reduction of over $1 billion a year. As a result, the initially agreed sale price was renegotiated, with the offer falling in value by 34 per cent to €7.4 billion plus €0.8 billion of debt, but payable in full in cash rather than partly in Enel bonds on 29 March 2001.

Vodafone seemed generally disinterested in the smaller markets of Scandinavia other than Sweden,[5] as shown in Table 6.1, although it subsequently signed a partner agreement with TDC and was active in other smaller European markets. In November 2000, for example, it was announced that Vodafone would be buying a 25 per cent stake in Swisscom Mobile in March 2001 assuming that the latter had been partly floated off from its parent and had been successful in acquiring a 3G licence in November 2000 – which it was. The purchase from Swisscom would form part of a strategic partnership with Vodafone paying in cash, shares or both at its discretion, with the price of the equity element to be fixed as an average of the price ruling during the final few days before closing.[6] In addition, an enhanced service provider agreement would be signed between Vodafone subsidiary Mannesmann Mobilfunk and Swisscom's German subsidiary Debitel, authorizing Debitel to resell Mannesmann's UMTS services. In March 2001, Swisscom shareholders authorized the sale at a price of $2.64 billion – approximately half on closing the deal and the rest plus interest no more than one year later with $1.4 billion paid in cash at the end of September. Not long after, Vodafone moved to acquire Eircell, the mobile subsidiary of Irish incumbent Eircom, when the latter was split up.[7]

Elsewhere in the world

As shown in Table 6.2, Vodafone has a wide spread of interests outside Western Europe, but two among them are individually more important than the others, as can be judged by the number of proportionate subscribers

Table 6.2 Other Vodafone Group holdings,[a] 30 June 2003

Country	Holding (%)	Main partners	Proportionate customers[h]
Albania (Vodafone)	83.0	Vodafone Greece	364,000
Australia (Vodafone)*	100.0	n/a	2,593,000
China (CMHK)	3.3	n/a	4,800,000
Egypt (Vodafone)	67.0[f]	EFG Hermes	1,609,000
Fiji (Vodafone)	49.0	Telecom Fiji	56,000
Hungary (Vodafone)	87.9	Antenna Hungaria	952,000
India (RPG Cellular)[b]	20.6	RPG Cellular	[37,000]
Japan (Vodafone KK)*[c]	69.7	Japan Telecom	10,035,000
Kenya (Safaricom)	30.0	Telkom Kenya	320,000
Malta (Vodafone)	100.0	n/a	126,000
Mexico (Iusacell)[b]	34.5	n/a	[675,000]
New Zealand (Vodafone)*	100.0	n/a	1,349,000
Poland (Polkomtel)*	19.6	TDK, KGHM, PKN, PSE	1,100,000
Romania (Mobifon)	20.1	TIW, ROM GSM	580,000
South Africa (Vodacom)[d]	35.0	Telkom, Rembrandt Group	2,970,000
USA (Verizon Wireless)[e]	44.3	Verizon Communications	15,332,000
Vizzavi Europe[g]	100.0		

Source: Adapted from www.vodafone.com/worldwide

Notes:
* 3G licensee. [a] Vodafone also has partner agreements with Radiolinja Eesti in Estonia, Mobilkom Austria in Croatia (VIP-Net) and Slovenia (Si.mobil), Bité GSM in Lithuania (a subsidiary of TDC) and MTC in Kuwait whereby services are marketed under the joint names. MTC-Vodafone Kuwait owns 60 per cent of MTC-Vodafone Bahrain. The latest partner is MobileOne (M1) in Singapore, signed up in November 2003. [b] On 6 June 2003, Vodafone announced that it was selling its stake in RPG Cellular with closure expected in July, and in July 2003, Vodafone announced that it was selling its stake in Grupo Iusacell to América Móvil with closure expected in August. [c] In December 2001, J-Phone adopted the J-Phone Vodafone dual logo. In late March 2003, J-Phone shops began to be converted to Vodafone shops, and in May, the decision was taken to re-brand solely as Vodafone KK as of 1 October. The J-Sky wireless Internet service was re-branded as Vodafone live! at the same time. [d] Vodacom also has networks in the Democratic Republic of Congo, Lesotho, Mozambique, Tanzania and Zambia. [e] Verizon Wireless is the trading name – the joint venture is called the Cellco Partnership. Vodafone has a 'put' option enabling it to force Verizon Communications to buy back $10 billion of its stake during a 60-day window commencing 10 June 2003 or 10 June 2004, and a further $10 billion in 2005, 2006 or 2007. [f] A 16 per cent stake is to be sold to Telecom Egypt. [g] Trading as Vodafone live! This service was launched in Egypt in October 2003 at which point it was available in 13 countries. By the year end the total was 16. [h] Some figures are extrapolated from those reported in March 2003.

contributed in Table 6.2. The first of these is Verizon Wireless in the USA, the formation of which has already been discussed. A further link is that, in April 2001, Vodafone paid $973 million in cash for a 34.5 per cent stake in the second-largest mobile operator in Mexico, Grupo Iusacell, in which Verizon Communications already held a 37.5 per cent stake (but one which has now been disposed of by both parties – see below).

The second is in Japan where Vodafone needed to establish a foothold in order to provide the third major link in its proposed worldwide network. As of the beginning of December 2000, Japan Telecom, one of the main rivals to NTT, was partly owned by AT&T and BT via a holding company, whereby the former held a 10 per cent stake and the latter 20 per cent. In turn,

Japan Telecom held a 54 per cent stake in J-Phone Communications (JPC), a holding company for its mobile interests, which, with nine million subscribers, was a major rival to NTT DoCoMo – both had been awarded free 3G licences by the government, with a third going to KDDI. Vodafone also held a 26 per cent stake in JPC, with the remaining 20 per cent owned by BT. In turn, J-Phone Communications controlled the three operating companies, J-Phone East (JPE), J-Phone West (JPW) and J-Phone Tokai (JPT). Japan Telecom also operated the J-Sky service providing Internet access for four million subscribers. This complicated situation meant that BT and Vodafone would be keen to battle it out for control of the real jewel in the crown – JPC. During December, Vodafone bought a 15 per cent stake in Japan Telecom from two of its founding railway companies for $2.2 billion in cash. Also in December, responding to a planned 16 per cent stake in AT&T Wireless to be taken by DoCoMo, AT&T put its Japan Telecom stake up for sale. In late February 2001, Vodafone offered to buy the shares for $1.35 billion in cash, a 37 per cent premium to the ruling market price, provided AT&T could deliver them by the end of April. With this purchase, Vodafone ended up with a combined 39.5 per cent direct and indirect stake in JPC. This grew further in May 2001, when cash-strapped BT agreed to sell its various interests in Japan Telecom for $5.3 billion. Vodafone now owned a 45 per cent direct stake in Japan Telecom, a 46 per cent direct stake in J-Phone, and enlarged minority stakes in the three J-Phone operating subsidiaries. It also inherited from BT options to buy a further 5 per cent stake in the J-Phone subsidiaries.

Vodafone arranged for J-Phone's operating subsidiaries to be merged under the J-Phone Co banner in November. As a result, Vodafone ended up with a 39.67 per cent stake in J-Phone while Japan Telecom ended up with 45.1 per cent, but Vodafone's stake in Japan Telecom meant that its economic interest in J-Phone would rise to almost 60 per cent. In October this became larger again, at 69.7 per cent, when Vodafone bought from East Japan Railway Co roughly an 8 per cent stake in Japan Telecom for cash as part of a successful tender offer to buy 21.7 per cent overall for $2.6 billion and thereby gained control of Japan Telecom with a 66.7 per cent stake.[8] Vodafone stated that it did not intend to sell off the loss-making fixed-wire business for the time being nor to list J-Phone. However, it implemented a restructuring plan in February 2002 called 'Project V' which recognized that the JT brand was weak, especially now that its links with BT and AT&T had gone.[9]

Obtaining a foothold in China, the fastest-growing market in the world, was never going to be as simple, but the situation was eased by the IPO of China Mobile (Hong Kong). In October 2000, Vodafone accordingly signed an MoU to buy a 2.18 per cent stake in China Mobile (HK) for $2.5 billion in cash, and formalized the contract in mid-January 2001. It had first refusal to increase its stake should the opportunity arise and, in May 2002, it increased its stake to 3.27 per cent by subscribing for new shares worth $750 million.[10]

Although the second batch of shares was much cheaper – CMHK's share price having fallen heavily during the interim period – the downside was that Vodafone was obliged to write down its original investment of $2.5 billion to $1.34 billion in March 2002. By way of contrast, Vodafone withdrew completely from the South Korean market, probably the most advanced in terms of mobile developments, when on 24 August 2001 it sold its 11.68 per cent stake in Shinsegi Telecom to SK Telecom for an estimated $150 million.

Vizzavi and SFR

In June 2000, MAP was launched under the renamed Vizzavi banner to provide e-mail, search facilities, information, entertainment and e-commerce. It was intended to be the default home page for the three companies involved and to utilize mobile phone, PC, TV and personal digital assistant platforms. Content would primarily be provided by VivendiNet (Canal Plus, Havas and Havas Interactive). It would operate initially in France, Germany, Italy and the UK with the existing Vodafone and Vivendi operating companies being rolled up into Vizzavi and offered a 20 per cent stake in the national subsidiaries. Vizzavi was cleared by the European Commission in July subject to the requirement that customers should be able to access third-party portals, change the default portal for themselves or authorize a third-party portal to alter the default portal on their behalf.

Despite the authorization, Vizzavi became mired in a dispute with BT which took Vizzavi's owners to court in France alleging that Vivendi and Vodafone should have involved their partners in Cégétel under the terms of the latter's shareholding pact. The claim was dismissed, but the door was left open for further action relating to Cégétel mobile subsidiary SFR, owned 80 per cent by Cégétel and 20 per cent by Vodafone. As it happened, the court also gave Vodafone permission to transfer half of its 15 per cent stake in SFR to Vivendi, leaving the latter with a 51.5 per cent controlling stake although it would not be able to take direct control until the shareholding pact expired on 24 September 2002. By the spring of 2001 it was widely believed that both BT and SBC would welcome the sale of their stakes, and Vivendi moved to prevent these falling into Vodafone's hands by claiming a pre-emption right should the shares become available. Nevertheless, with Vivendi increasingly interested in resolving the fall-out from its acquisition of Canal Plus and Seagram and the formation of Vivendi Universal, it seemed probable that Vodafone would eventually emerge with control of Cégétel and SFR. As a first step, Vodafone agreed in June to swap its 15 per cent stake in Cégétel for 12 per cent of Vivendi's stake in SFR – on the face of it a technicality but in line with Vodafone's desire to withdraw from stakes in fixed-wire operators.

In April 2001, Vizzavi announced that it had acquired 700,000 registered users and that it would seek a separate listing by the end of 2003. In addition to the existing Vizzavi services in the Netherlands and the UK, Vivendi Universal would transfer its online operations in France in May 2001 and set up Vizzavi sites in Italy and Germany by the year-end. By December, the number of customers had risen to six million, but revenue remained modest with $45 million predicted for 2002 – a poor return on an investment of roughly $1.5 billion. A new model of operation was accordingly introduced. Rather than Vizzavi sharing revenues on a 50:50 basis with its backers, it would henceforth take 80 per cent of the money earned. In addition, it would take a 5 per cent share of the call revenues generated.[11] However, in August 2002, faced with its own mounting debts, Vivendi ceased all further new investment in Vizzavi leaving Vodafone to foot the entire $600 million required to reach break-even in March 2004. Understandably, Vodafone's response in September was to buy Vivendi's half share (other than Vizzavi France which was passed over to Vivendi) for a superficially trifling $140 million, although it had been necessary to downgrade Vizzavi's ambitions to be merely a provider of news, information and games to Vodafone's subscribers, re-branded as Vodafone live![12] A multimedia messaging service was launched in October 2002.

Share price woes

After the bid for Mannesmann was successfully concluded in February 2000 the share price suffered a reversal, but soon recovered to reach a peak of almost £4 in March. Subsequently, it began to fall inexorably, eventually bottoming-out at £2.40 at the end of May – a drop of 40 per cent from its peak. This reflected a general loss of faith in the prospects of telcos, but in particular serious reservations about the cost of acquiring UMTS/W-CDMA licences, especially in Germany and the UK (see Tables 6.1 and 6.2 for countries where licences have been won). Between March and October the share price broadly fluctuated between £2.60 and £3.20, but mid-October saw another severe dose of bearish sentiment about the prospects of all telcos, driving the Vodafone share price to a new low of £2.35. It traded in the £2.40–2.60 range during most of the ensuing three months, but the beginning of 2001 saw the share price under pressure once again, reflecting the share overhangs (discussed below) (see Figure 6.1).

The financial difficulties were compounded by other factors. In Germany, for example, the purchase of Mannesmann stimulated Deutsche Telekom subsidiary T-Mobile to cut tariffs and raise handset subsidies. Vodafone responded in kind, with the result that customer acquisition costs rose to $60 a head, with repeat costs whenever replacement handsets were purchased. Subscriber numbers duly soared, improving the longer-term outlook but simultaneously damaging short-term profitability.

A further issue affecting the share price was the stake held by Hutchison Whampoa, which it acquired when Mannesmann was bought by Vodafone. In March 2000, roughly 1.5 per cent was sold for $5 billion via the world's largest share placing at a 7 per cent discount to the market price, and a further 0.9 per cent was sold via a convertible bond in September at £2.80.

Hutchison was left with a 3.47 per cent stake, and was not keen to hold on to it once the lock-up period agreed as part of the Mannesmann takeover had expired because it had a controlling stake in an UMTS competitor to Vodafone in the UK. It promised not to make further sales without consulting Vodafone, and needed to take account of the fact that the market price was unattractive at the beginning of 2001. What transpired in January 2001 was an announcement that it would issue a $2.5 billion convertible three-year bond equivalent to roughly a 1.1 per cent stake in Vodafone, in the process depressing Vodafone's share price to a 12-month low of £2.15 compared to the bond's strike price of £3.10. This was not, however, the only potential source of overhang, since over 5.5 per cent of Vodafone was transferred during the purchase of its enlarged stake in Airtel and more was transferred to purchase its stakes in Swisscom, Eircell and Japan Telecom (see above).

A final consideration was that the purchase of Orange by France Télécom, agreed when the latter's share price stood at €143, involved a put option (right to sell) linked to a floor value for the share price which the agreed formula delivered at €106. In practice, having repurchased 15.4 million shares at the original issue price in return for the loan note, France Télécom was committed to repurchasing the remaining 113.8 million of its shares held by Vodafone in three instalments during 2001/2002, commencing with 58.2 million at €104.2 in early March 2001 and followed by 5.92 million at €99.66 at the end of March and 49.73 million at a minimum of €100 at the end of March 2002. In practice, the final instalment was cashed in for €4.7 billion ($4.4 billion) in April 2001 and Vodafone ceased to hold any France Télécom shares.[13]

Vodafone seemed happy to leave investors somewhat in the dark about its finances. In mid-November 2000, for example, it emphasized the surplus cash flow of roughly $5 billion for the first half of 2000. In contrast, the conventional accounts revealed a pre-tax loss of roughly $6 billion because Vodafone had paid much more than net asset value when buying AirTouch and Mannesmann and needed to write this off as goodwill. It was true that such a write-off did not involve a cash outflow as such, but the accumulated debts of roughly $20 billion in September needed to be serviced, and the Mannesmann purchase meant that earnings per share would fall sharply in the short term.

In late-February 2001, with its share price trading at £1.85 because of the delay to the Infostrada sale discussed previously, Vodafone's capitalization fell below that of BP Amoco (and to not much more than it paid for Mannesmann) and it ceased to be the largest company in Europe. However, on a more optimistic note, Vodafone was able to announce in March 2001 that it had reduced its borrowings to $10 billion following the sale of Infostrada. By comparison with almost all other telcos at the time this was an extremely modest figure, but it was insufficient to restore Vodafone's share price above the £2 mark. Curiously, Vodafone also sought to boost its share price by no longer counting inactive customers who had not made a call during the previous three months – almost 10 per cent of the 83 million worldwide total. The benefit arose from the fact that average revenue per user (ARPU), which was apparently in decline because of the trend towards pre-pay packages, was thereby enhanced. Vodafone went on to calm market fears about indebtedness by promising to concentrate upon customer retention rather than acquisition; not to go on an acquisition spree; and to introduce GPRS[14] as part of a more gradual roll-out than originally expected of its third-generation networks.

The agreement to buy BT's stakes in Japan Telecom, J-Phone and its operating companies in early May caused a reappraisal of Vodafone's prospects to take place. On the face of it, Vodafone's net debts at the time stood at not much more than $10 billion allowing for the cash paid for the AT&T stake in Japan Telecom. However, the BT stakes were set to add roughly $5.3 billion directly to this total, and there were two additional factors which potentially arose because Vodafone would end up with a combined direct plus indirect stake of over 50 per cent in J-Phone. First, Vodafone would have to find the majority of the remaining cash – perhaps $6 billion – needed to finance J-Phone's new 3G network. Second, as majority owner, Vodafone could be obliged to consolidate J-Phone's existing debts of $10 billion onto its own balance sheet, although Vodafone argued that this would not be necessary because it did not have a 'dominant influence' over J-Phone. The simultaneous purchase of the 17.8 per cent BT stake in Airtel initially added a further $1.6 billion to Vodafone's debts, but Vodafone moved immediately to place a block of new shares at £1.94, the total value of which was raised from $4.3 billion to $5 billion (representing 2.8 per cent of the issued share capital) thereby covering the bulk of its immediate outgoings for the various purchases. The fact that the new shares could be issued at a very small discount (10 per cent) to the ruling market price was a positive sign, although little immediate upturn could be anticipated given the pre-existing share overhang and, indeed, those subscribing to the issue very soon had cause to regret their behaviour as the share price began to plummet once again.

A need to reconsider the strategy

In May 2001, Vodafone reported better than expected results for the year ending 31 March 2001. Turnover and pre-tax profit rose sharply due to the various purchases during the year, although write-offs relating to Mannesmann meant that a large, but fairly meaningless overall loss was reported. Net debt stood at £6.7 billion (roughly $10 billion), a mere 5.4 per cent of market value. The $15 billion anticipated cost of rolling out 3G networks was budgeted to come from its own resources. The main worry was that Vodafone was not consolidating its share of the debts of associated companies such as J-Phone and Verizon Wireless, leading analysts to estimate true indebtedness at roughly $23 billion – hence the need for the share placing discussed above

– but broadly the overall picture was much healthier than that of its rivals despite Vodafone's admission that roughly 10 per cent of its subscribers were inactive (in which respect it was probably quite typical).

Nevertheless, by mid-June the Vodafone share price had fallen to £1.70 as the share overhangs began to weigh heavily on the market. KPN and Telia were now entitled to sell 370 million shares acquired via the sale of stakes in Eircell and Airtel shareholders were about to become entitled to dispose of up to $5 billion of Vodafone shares.[15] Further, Vodafone moved to mop up the holdings of 7,400 small shareholders left over from the Mannesmann purchase with an offer worth $500 million in total.

As viewed by analysts, Vodafone needed to address three central, inter-related issues: to integrate its recent acquisitions; to switch from a strategy involving the pursuit of all-out growth in subscriber numbers and market share to one emphasizing the improvement in profit margins and cash flow growth; and to bring 3G to profitable fruition. Central to this would be the withdrawal of handset subsidies, the creation of common products and services (for example, a pan-European roaming tariff for both contract and pre-pay subscribers including both voice and text messaging), and the creation of a common brand. It would also be possible to squeeze suppliers' margins given Vodafone's enhanced buying power, but the introduction of GPRS and 3G would probably require additional, hopefully short-term, handset subsidies. Any growth would occur via exploiting existing geographic concentrations, especially with a view to increasing average revenue per user (ARPU) which had tended to move inversely to subscriber numbers; although opportunities to increase potentially strategic stakes, especially in the likes of China Mobile (HK), would be taken up.

According to analysts' discounted cash flow models in May 2001, Vodafone shares should have been trading at roughly £2.70, indicating significant upside potential once the share overhangs were cleared, and, if 3G did prove to be a success, Vodafone was expected to be the major beneficiary. The first of the overhangs were duly cleared in June when Telia sold 80 million shares and KPN disposed of 220 million at £1.56, in the process setting off a further decline to almost £1.40. The apparent decision by BSCH to hold on to its 1.84 billion shares then set off a modest upturn in the share price, but it subsequently announced that it had cut its Vodafone stake from 2.71 per cent to 1.62 per cent, stopping the share price in its tracks. In any event, analysts had by then largely given up on TMT stocks for the year and were talking in terms of stabilization around the £1.50 mark, representing a monumental loss of value since the Mannesmann takeover.

During the three months to the end of June 2001, Vodafone's proportion-ate subscriber numbers grew by over three million and a further 7.1 million were added due to acquisitions, raising the total to 93.1 million. However, the share price stayed down and, indeed, fell below £1.40 during July when Vodafone announced that it was struggling to obtain GPRS handsets and hence the introduction of its services in Europe would be delayed, albeit hopefully not until Christmas; that 3G handsets would be slow to arrive in bulk, and hence that it would be delaying the full launch of 3G services until 2003 in the UK, while saving money in the interim by reducing the number of base stations to be built during 2001 from 1,250 to 750; that ARPU had fallen in both the UK and Germany; and that it had heavily written down the number of active users in the UK to 10.5 million, leaving it in third place behind Orange and BT Cellnet.

In late September, Vodafone paid $1.4 billion in cash as the second tranche of its payment for its 25 per cent stake in Swisscom Mobile, but recovered roughly half this sum the following month by selling off its stake in Ruhrgas inherited with Mannesmann. Figures for the third quarter indicated pre-paid subscriptions running at 88 per cent across the entire company with some signs that markets were stabilizing. However, this was insufficient to forestall the announcement of 600 redundancies among UK-based staff in mid-October.

In November, Vodafone announced its half-year results which were dominated by a write-down of roughly $10 billion on three investments, most notably $7 billion relating to Arcor. Significantly, Vodafone refused to write down any of its investments in mobile telephony including 3G licences. Net debt was up at $13.5 billion. However, its turnover and operating profit were up significantly, and its worldwide customer base was declared at 95.6 million of whom 90 per cent were active. At this point Hutchison Whampoa sold its stake down to 2.95 per cent by disposing of 135 million shares.

As shown in Figure 6.1, shareholders were happy for a while to invest in Vodafone's prospects for growth, especially via GPRS and 3G, but it was not to last as analysts persistently argued that with saturated markets and increasing competition, together with delays in 3G, Vodafone should no longer be viewed as a growth stock.[16] To make matters worse, regulators, especially in the UK, were looking to impose limits on such matters as termination charges levied on calls to mobile handsets. Even the fact that Vodafone passed the 100 million proportionate subscriber mark failed to inspire as numbers were growing slowly and China Mobile (HK) had overtaken it. Chris Gent preferred to argue that the company was in sound shape and was simply suffering from 'bear raids'.[17]

In May, rumours began to spread that Vivendi Universal's problems would force it to offer for sale its stake in French mobile operator SFR. Since France was the only major country in Europe where Vodafone did not have a controlling stake (see Table 6.1) – at the time it held a 20 per cent direct stake plus a 12 per cent indirect stake via its holding in parent Cégétel – this would present too good an opportunity to miss, although Vodafone already had the option of bidding for the stakes held by BT and SBC. The financial markets made it clear that they were unenthused about any action that would add around $10 billion to Vodafone's net debt – although Vodafone's credit ratings of 'A' from Standard & Poor's and 'A2' from Moody's would not be threatened and more than sufficient existing credit lines were available – and when Vodafone published somewhat reduced forecasts within the context of a generally bullish long-term outlook, many analysts treated it as a profits warning and the share price fell below £1.[18] However, the accounts for the year ending 31 March 2001 (see Table 6.3) were greeted with relief, despite recording the largest loss in UK corporate history. In particular, the goodwill write-down, albeit heavy, was less than expected and the level of net debt and gearing (at under 10 per cent) relatively low compared to competitors.[19]

The popular distaste for excessive pay packages for executives, especially those in companies whose shareholders had lost a lot of money, did not pass Vodafone by, and in June there was an entire page in the *Financial Times* devoted primarily to Chris Gent's pay.[20] He was unrepentant, and spent a bit more of his shareholders' money on increasing Vodafone's stake in China Mobile (HK) to 3.27 per cent, even though half of the original investment had been written off. The implosion of WorldCom caused the Vodafone share price to fall once again to a mere 85p, partly because Vodafone's accounts were complex and relied too much on ebitda, and hence just might be hiding something nasty.[21]

Things moved slowly on the restructuring front. In Japan, moves were afoot to divide up Japan Telecom so as to put the fixed-wire business on a stand-alone basis, but although that seemed to be a preparatory move before a disposal of that business, an offer from Tokyo Electric Power (Tepco) was turned down in August. For its part, mobile operator J-Phone continued to make good progress, acquiring its one-millionth subscriber to its Movie Sha-mail service, launched in March 2002, after only nine months. Altogether, there were nearly eight million subscribers to various Sha-mail services – the standard photo-messaging service introduced in June 2001 – by the end of 2002.

In Europe, Vodafone set out gradually to increase its holdings with a view to being able eventually to force out the residual shareholders and take full control.[22] Meanwhile, with the 'standstill' rights about to expire, Vodafone indicated that it was willing to acquire the entire outstanding shareholding in Cégétel for roughly £12 billion. It was initially thought that Vivendi Universal would be happy to sell out given its own debts, but the opposite proved to be the case, with Vivendi seeking to increase its stake to in excess of 50 per cent. Vodafone accordingly tabled two separate cash offers; $6.2 billion for the stakes held by BT (26 per cent) and SBC (15 per cent), and $6.7 billion for that held by Vivendi (44 per cent). The latter was later withdrawn, then reinstated. However, Vivendi was in a position, due to pre-emption rights, to match the offers for BT and SBC, and in December Vivendi agreed to buy the BT stake for $2.7 billion in cash, while Vodafone agreed to buy the SBC stake for $2.2 billion. This meant that Vivendi would have a 56.1 per cent direct plus indirect stake in SFR with Vodafone holding the rest.[23]

In September, a class action lawsuit was tabled in the USA claiming that Vodafone had misled the financial markets between 7 March 2001 and 28 May 2002, artificially inflating Vodafone's share price. Separately, Stern

Table 6.3 Five-year summary of consolidated results,[a] year ending 31 March (£ million)

	2003	2002[b]	2001	2000[c]	1999
Total Group[d] turnover	39,152	33,541	23,993	11,521	–
Group turnover	30,375	22,845	15,004	7,783	3,360
in respect of:					
continuing operations	*30,375*	*17,940*	*6,637*	*4,498*	*3,302*
acquisitions	–	*4,905*	*8,367*	*3,375*	*58*
Total Group[d] operating (loss)/profit	(5,451)	(11,834)	(6,989)	798	963
before (A) and (B)	9,181	7,044	5,204	2,538	–
(A) goodwill amortization	(14,056)	(13,470)[f]	(11,873)	(1,710)	–
(B) exceptionals	(576)	(5,408)[g]	(320)	(30)	–
(Loss)/profit for financial year	(9,819)	(16,155)	(9,885)	542	594
(Loss)/earnings per ordinary share £	(0.14)	(0.24)	(0.16)	0.02	0.04
Total assets	163,280	162,900	172,390	153,546	3,681
Long-term obligations	13,757	13,118	11,235	6,374	1,179
Shareholders' funds	128,671	130,573	145,007	140,594	512
Operating cash flow	11,142	8,102	4,587	2,510	1,045
Net cash outflow for investment[e]	(5,373)	(4,447)	(19,011)	(756)	–
Net cash (outflow)/inflow: acquisitions and disposals	(4,880)	(7,691)	30,653	(4,756)	–
Free cash flow	5,171	2,365	(13,278)	256	22
Closing net debt	(13,839)	(12,034)	(6,722)	(6,643)	(1,508)

Source: Vodafone Group Annual Report and Accounts for the year ending 31 March 2002, pp. 26, 33, 74–5 and for the year ending 31 March 2003, pp. 22, 31, 74.

Notes:
[a] Prepared according to UK GAAP which differs in certain significant respects from US GAAP. Certain prior period comparative information has been restated following the adoption of FRS during the period. Dollar equivalents are roughly one and a half times pounds sterling. [b] The Group's interest in Verizon Wireless is accounted for as an associated undertaking and the results of Verizon Wireless have been included in the consolidated profit and loss account on the equity basis of accounting from 12 April 2000. The results of Mannesmann have been included in the consolidated profit and loss account from 12 April 2000. The results of Airtel, now operating as Vodafone, have been fully consolidated with effect from 29 December 2000 under UK GAAP. The results of Eircell and Japan Telecom and the J-Phone group have been fully consolidated with effect from 14 May 2001 and 12 October 2001 respectively. [c] The consolidated financial results for the year ended 31 March 2000 include the results of AirTouch from 30 June 1999. [d] The Total Group figures include joint ventures and associated undertakings, of which the latter comprises almost the whole. As can be seen, the associated undertakings – particularly Verizon Wireless – have formed a significant proportion of turnover in recent years. [e] Capital expenditure and financial investment. [f] As in 2001, a full year's amortization is recorded for Mannesmann on top of which there is a charge in 2002 for Eircell, Japan Telecom and J-Phone. The value of takeover bids invariably exceeds the estimated value of the assets acquired, sometimes by a substantial margin. It may eventually need to be 'written down' in the accounts with damaging effects upon profitability. The way in which goodwill has to be accounted for varies by country. [g] Impairment charges of £5,100 million relate to the carrying cost of goodwill for (mainly) Arcor, Cégétel, Grupo Iusacell and Japan Telecom. Only the latter at £408 million was significant in 2003.

Stewart's Wealth Added Index calculated that Vodafone had destroyed value for shareholders to the tune of $200 billion over the five-year period ending in October 2002.[24]

The half-year results to the end of September 2002 were greeted with enthusiasm as they revealed respectable rises in revenue, partly due to the consolidation of Japan Telecom and J-Phone and partly to healthy trading in Germany and Japan, and big improvements in margins reflecting tightened cost controls and delays in building out 3G networks. However, the prognosis for the second half was less favourable because of the need to invest heavily in 3G and Vodafone live![25] The share price recovered somewhat but this was insufficient to prevent Chris Gent – one of the few CEOs of major operators not to have been sacked as yet – to express his intention to retire in July 2003. His chosen replacement was Arun Sarin, formerly chief operating officer of AirTouch before its acquisition by Vodafone.[26]

The first half of 2003 witnessed extensive activity in respect of non-UK holdings, following on from the purchase of a 3.5 per cent indirect stake in Vodacom of South Africa for $125 million at the end of 2002. In January 2003, Vodafone offered to acquire all of the outstanding shares in the former Europolitan, Libertel and Telecel, although the prices offered were thought to be somewhat unattractive, having previously upped its stake in the former Panafon by 10.85 per cent via a cash payment of $346 million to France Télécom. It subsequently paid $10 million to raise its holding in Safaricom by 5 per cent, mopped up the remaining stake in the former Airtel at a cost of $2.1 billion, completed the purchase of the SBC stake in Cégétel for $2.27 billion and bought a 15.57 per cent stake in Vodafone Hungary from RWE for an undisclosed sum. In February, the stake in Vodafone Sweden was raised to 99.1 per cent at a cost of $625 million. In the period to end April, the stake in Vodafone Netherlands was steadily increased to 99.7 per cent at a total cost of $954 million and in Vodafone Portugal to 94.4 per cent at a total cost of $832 million. In all cases, the residual shares will be compulsorily acquired. A further 1.27 per cent of Vodafone Greece was bought in the open market and, in early May, the outstanding 4.5 per cent of Vodafone Australia was acquired for $69 million.[27] By way of contrast, Vodafone agreed in June to sell its 20.76 per cent indirect stake in RPG Cellular of India and its 34.5 per cent holding in CDMA operator Grupo Iusacell of Mexico (at a huge loss), as well as a 16 per cent stake in Vodafone Egypt (which will leave it with 51 per cent). In mid-June, Vodafone declared that it was now generally happy with 'the places . . . we are already at', that it was 'happily married' with Verizon Wireless and that no further major acquisitions were in the pipeline. However, as Vodafone is well aware, its coverage is poor in Central and South America where CDMA has so far been the dominant technology. As for the relationship with Verizon Communications, it is true that Vodafone is apparently not availing itself of the opportunity to exercise its put option in Verizon Wireless this year, but it must surely be considering the virtues of exchanging part of the latter for Verizon Communication's stake in the former Omnitel in Italy.

As of 31 March, Vodafone live! had reached its target of one million subscribers, of whom 375,000 were in Germany, 220,000 in the UK and 190,000
in Italy. A further 420,000 customers in these markets owned an MMS-
enabled device. By the end of June, sales of live! camera-phones had risen to
1.75 million with availability in 13 countries and by October there were one
million subscribers in Germany, 700,000 in the UK and 450,000 in Italy.
However, these numbers paled compared to the 12.5 million subscriptions to
J-Sky in Japan which was to be re-branded as Vodafone live! in October.

The annual results for the year to 31 March 2003 attracted a variety of
responses. Vodafone naturally preferred to look on the bright side, emphasizing the growth in Group revenues which mainly arose through consolidation
of J-Phone Vodafone and Japan Telecom, the improvement in the operating
profit before adjusting for goodwill amortization and exceptionals and the
substantial free cash flow (see Table 6.3). However, it was pointed out that,
despite according with accounting conventions, these measures meant almost
nothing without adequate information on the capital used to generate them,
and that Vodafone had allegedly failed to cover its cost of capital since
2000.[28] On the issue of goodwill, Vodafone continued to insist that it needed
to write off very little and nothing in relation to its 3G licences despite the
contradictory behaviour of the likes of mmO$_2$.

The situation in Japan is about to be resolved. In mid-July, US investment
fund Ripplewood Holdings agreed to buy Japan Telecom for $2.2 billion. In
turn, Vodafone is retaining the redeemable preferred equity in order to
maintain a connection with Japan Telecom. Vodafone also had good news to
report about sales of own-branded handsets made by Sharp.[29] Although
Nokia remained responsible for 40 per cent of all Vodafone handset sales,
the Sharp handsets were selling at a faster rate.

The agreement with Vivendi Universal not to acquire any more of its
shares potentially expires in January 2004. In August 2003, Vodafone served
notice that it would be terminating the agreement. This was seen in some
quarters as a declaration that it would be seeking control over SFR by acquiring Vivendi, which Vodafone was quick to deny. Meanwhile, Vodafone was
acquiring two UK resellers, Singlepoint and Project Telecom, for just over
£500 million in order to gain direct control over more of its subscribers.

In an interesting development in late September, given the previous antipathy between the companies, the CEO of Vivendi announced that 'Our
strategy is clear. We are part of the Vodafone family.' By this he appeared to
mean that Vivendi Universal would be tapping into the purchasing and
marketing clout of partner, Vodafone, and introducing an equivalent to the
popular Vodafone live! portal. This sparked rumours that this was the initial
step along the path leading to a takeover of SFR by Vodafone. In mid-
October, substance was added to the rumours when Vivendi and Vodafone
announced that they had agreed in principle to merge Cégétel's various
units including SFR, Cofira and Transtel into the Cégétel Group and rename
it SFR. As a result, Vodafone would hold 43.9 per cent of SFR and Vivendi

would hold 55.8 per cent, with the remainder held by some minority shareholders of Cofira. In addition, Cégétel and French railway operator SNCF would merge the two units of their fixed-wire businesses, with Cégétel taking a 65 per cent stake in the merged entity. These arrangements were expected to release tax credits leading to a €400 million improvement in cash flow.[30] Ironically, these arrangements also meant that the more Vodafone contributed to the prospects for SFR, the more it would be obliged to pay should it have the opportunity for a takeover.

Conclusions

This case study raises a number of interesting points in seeking to understand how the enormous scale of the reduction in the value of Vodafone transpired. Vodafone's strategy of expansion via acquisition is hard to fault overall in the light of the circumstances of the time, and this explains why, ultimately, the reputation of the Vodafone management has been but little damaged by the sniping of critics blessed with hindsight. During his term as CEO, Chris Gent had seen Vodafone's market value rise by a factor of ten, and even though he had spent roughly $200 billion, very little had been in cash so the company was still financially sound despite the heavy write-downs. One has only to see how debt piled up at the likes of BT and Deutsche Telekom to appreciate how easily things could have gone awry. However, there were risks involved because a massive share overhang was created and these shares, if released into the market on a large scale, and in close proximity, would obviously depress Vodafone's share price significantly and for some time, as indeed transpired from mid-2001 onwards. The point was nevertheless that most of the shares were not initially expected to be released because investing in Vodafone was seen as a better bet than investing in the companies that Vodafone had taken over, and it was hardly Vodafone's fault that TMT stocks in general suffered such a catastrophic collapse during the first half of 2001.

Reasonable risk is one thing, but it is possible to argue that the Vodafone strategy was nevertheless flawed in certain respects for which management could reasonably be held responsible. For example, mobile penetration cannot rise exponentially, and although saturation is seemingly not reached until much higher penetration levels are achieved than was thought to be the case even a few years ago, simply buying new networks was never going to enable Vodafone's revenues to grow rapidly for ever. Clearly, Vodafone was not unaware of this awkward fact of mobile life, and this realization underpinned the move into 3G and a reliance upon mobile data to pick up where mobile voice could not continue to go. Again, this was strategically sound at the time, but what about the licence fees? The problem here is that although in the case of auctions it was left to bidders to calculate how much to bid, and hence they had to rely upon their commercial judgement for better or worse, they also had in many cases (as did Vodafone in nearly every case) to bear in mind their 2G incumbency and the consequences of failing to get a 3G licence. The fact that they sometimes overbid, especially in the UK and Germany, could therefore be said to be more a case of force of circumstance than of managerial miscalculation. Vodafone certainly did nothing that the other major telcos were unprepared to do and, significantly, of which the financial markets were unsupportive at the time. When the financial markets withdrew their support, Vodafone, like other carriers, generally bid much less. Significantly, however, Vodafone participated in France, the one market where the licence fee was manifestly over-priced, an action that could only be partly excused by the desire to protect SFR's 2G incumbency.

The recent technological glitches that have held back the introduction of both GPRS and 3G are less to do with carriers than with equipment manufacturers, but there can be no question that a widespread air of pessimism has begun to pervade analysts' reports assessing the prospects for mobile data. Vodafone, unsurprisingly, continues to have faith in its projections, and points out that it is the analysts who are unable to agree what anything is worth while Vodafone's business model has remained unchanged through good times and bad. Given the explosion of demand for mobile voice and subsequently the SMS, Vodafone may be right to carry on regardless of what analysts believe, and its Vodafone live! service is certainly beginning to gather pace and show signs of developing a market-leading brand. Nevertheless, with so many other carriers writing off the goodwill from purchases, Vodafone's massive amount of goodwill in its accounts does appear difficult to justify. Vodafone resolutely claims that if assets are valued via a discounted cash flow model, then nothing fundamental has happened to alter the numbers and the goodwill figure should stand. In this respect it is increasingly isolated because critics can readily point to the upsurge in competition, the tendency for ARPU to decline and for subscriber acquisition costs (SACs) to rise, regulatory moves against allegedly excessive roaming and fixed-to-mobile call termination charges and delays in the roll-out of new services, and hence it must remain for now a case of 'only time will tell'.

Chapter 7

WorldCom

Veni, vidi, vici, I got caught

Introduction

Over the past two years a number of companies in the telecommunications sector have justly earned the sobriquet 'infamous', but, despite the fierce competition, WorldCom must be considered the most infamous of all. What is particularly interesting about this is that WorldCom was for many years held up as a shining star in the telecommunications firmament – the proverbial 'new kid on the block' who successfully set out to show old-fashioned incumbents such as AT&T how to do business in a fast-moving, data-centric world. Ordinarily, we would be able to trace the story through the financial data, but in this case we have a problem: on 25 June 2002, WorldCom announced that it would be restating its 2001 and first-quarter 2002 financial statements and that previous versions could not be relied upon.[1] To put the matter bluntly, executives at WorldCom had been fiddling the books and the company was bankrupt. Precisely who the perpetrators were, and the true extent of their involvement, is now a matter for the courts, and may not be fully unravelled before this book is published. However, this in no way detracts from a fascinating story that, were it not entirely true, might have won awards as fiction.

Background

The story of WorldCom cannot be separated from that of the now discredited Bernie Ebbers. A Canadian by birth, he settled in Mississippi as a student and subsequently managed a garment factory warehouse, coached high-school basketball and began to invest in businesses including a chain of hotels. In 1983, he and two friends sketched out on the back of the pro-verbial envelope – in this case a napkin – a plan to buy long-distance minutes at wholesale rates from the likes of AT&T and sell them on to local retail customers. Their waitress suggested the name Long Distance Discount Services (LDDS). Although he knew nothing about telecoms except how to use the phone, Bernie Ebbers had become CEO of LDDS within two years. LDDS went public in 1989 when it engineered a reverse takeover of Advantage Companies, and in 1992 it expanded via an all-stock merger with a similar reseller, Advanced Telecommunications. In 1993, a three-way stock and cash transaction brought together LDDS, Resurgens Communications Group and Metromedia Communications to form the fourth-largest long-distance carrier in the USA.[2] One year later LDDS acquired domestic and international carrier IDB Communications Group in an all-stock deal worth $936 million, to be followed in early 1995 with the purchase for $2.5 billion in cash of voice and data transmission company WilTel Networks. At this point LDDS evolved into WorldCom Inc. which promptly grew much larger via the $12.4 billion takeover in August 1996 of MFS Communications Company – owner of local network access facilities via fibre-optic cables in and around 50 major American and European cities – which had itself recently acquired UUNet Technologies, a business Internet access provider, for $2 billion. MFS WorldCom thereby became the world's largest Internet access provider and the first carrier in the USA capable of combining long-distance, local and Internet services.[3]

Ordinarily, a spending spree on this scale should have had a depressive impact upon WorldCom's share price, partly because of the additional shares in circulation where the takeovers were financed with WorldCom's own shares, partly because a premium needed to be paid for acquisitions thereby creating a lot of goodwill to be written off, and partly because integrating the various businesses would take time and might run into a whole variety of problems such as clashing cultures. However, as is shown in Figure 7.1, WorldCom's share price was extremely resilient. In good part, this could be ascribed to Bernie Ebbers who, as the plain-speaking front-man,[4] promised to strip unnecessary costs from acquisitions while freeing them from bureaucracy. However, he was ably supported by his chief financial officer (CFO), Scott Sullivan, who gained a reputation on Wall Street for his astute management of the various transactions, and the now infamous Jack Grubman, the 'visionary' telecoms analyst at Salomon Smith Barney who supplied the intellectual justification for the deals and constantly recommended the shares to his clients.

The crucial point was that because the financial markets and private investors were prepared to swallow the 'growth is good' story more or less wholesale, and the WorldCom share price remained resilient, WorldCom was able to continue making ever more grandiose bids using exclusively its own stock at a time when rivals were restricted either by their lack of cash or less-sought-after stock. In retrospect, of course, it is easy to see how WorldCom set out to disguise the true nature of its finances in the aftermath of its takeovers, but at the time few cavilled with the practice of taking substantial one-off write-offs against profits immediately after an acquisition, thereby removing the need to do so in stages in future years and, in the process, deflating reported profitability. Equally, few objected at the time to the now discredited pro forma accounting which, by restating earnings after each acquisition, made it very difficult to make valid comparisons over time.[5]

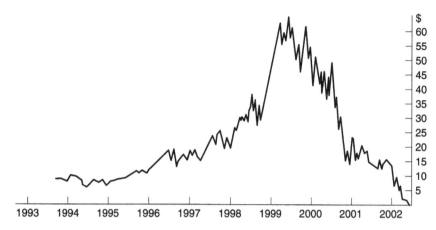

Figure 7.1 WorldCom Inc. GA New share price, 1993–2002 (dollars).
Source: Daily share prices in the *Financial Times*.

During the late 1990s WorldCom appeared to be an unstoppable force. In September 1997, BT of the UK moved to acquire its American partner, long-distance carrier MCI Communications, only to have the prize snatched from under its nose by a bid by WorldCom eventually worth $40 billion – with BT's existing 20 per cent stake bought for cash. Some idea of the awe in which WorldCom was held in the financial markets can be gleaned from its issuance, in August 1998, of $6.1 billion of new bonds – the then world's largest-ever corporate bond issuance. Even the most expensive tranche of the issue, the 30-year bond, was launched at a mere 1.38 per cent above the Treasury bond rate at the time. One month later, WorldCom snatched up Brooks Fiber Properties, to be followed up with the acquisition of CompuServe Corp. and ANS Communications at a total cost of $1.4 billion. As shown in Figure 7.1, WorldCom's share price soared during 1998, reaching a peak of $61.90 on 21 June 1999. At the end of 1998, WorldCom was valued at $86.2 billion, making it the twenty-fourth most valuable company in the world. One year later, having seen some retreat from the mid-year peak value of $180 billion, and now only the world's twenty-sixth most valuable company, WorldCom was nevertheless still worth a staggering $150.6 billion. But the boom period for the TMT sector was over, and like many of its peers WorldCom was set on the slippery downwards slope. However, no one imagined at the time just how slippery it would be, and the now renamed MCI WorldCom itself remained sufficiently confident to launch, in October 1999, an all-stock bid for rival, Sprint, worth $115 billion plus $14 billion of debt taken on.[6] The bid was audacious but, in truth, seemed to have only a minimal chance of gaining the approval of regulators given the potential combined strength of MCI and Sprint in the US long-distance market and the fact that WorldCom had been advised to pursue no more mega-bids after the MCI deal achieved regulatory approval. However, MCI WorldCom had belatedly realized that it had a weakness it had previously not thought to be worthy of much consideration, namely the lack of a mobile arm. In bidding for Sprint, its real target was Sprint PCS. On 1 October, MCI WorldCom guaranteed itself at least some wireless assets by acquiring SkyTel Communications for $1.8 billion.

A strategic U-turn is needed

Seen in retrospect, 2000 was the year when the rot began visibly to set in at WorldCom, although it could be argued that – and is elsewhere in this book – this was a general truism for the TMT sector as a whole. As Figure 7.1 shows, the irony was that the only relief was afforded in mid-year when, as expected, both the US Department of Justice and the European Commission vetoed the bid for Sprint.[7] The issue in Europe was ostensibly the anti-competitive effects of combining the Internet backbones of WorldCom and Sprint, but some felt that the Commission had it in for WorldCom.[8] For its part, WorldCom was simply unwilling to make the wide-ranging concessions required by the regulators to permit the deal to proceed. In retrospect, the failure of the deal was the crucial turning point in the story because, with its share price in free-fall, WorldCom could no longer scale new heights via ever more grandiose acquisitions. But the unanswered question was whether there was any alternative.

One possibility would have been to acquire a major pure wireless operator, thereby avoiding regulatory problems arising from overlaps, but the obvious candidate, Nextel, was too expensive. Another would have been to switch away from the consumer long-distance operations towards the more profitable business sector, and yet another to offer itself up as a target – the downside being that there were no obvious candidates to take it over.[9] Up to this point in time Bernie Ebbers had never really had to justify WorldCom's strategy. Whenever pressed on the matter, he simply flashed up a picture of WorldCom's share price and replied 'there's the answer to your question'. Unhappily, this no longer worked, so in late July he suggested that the consumer telephony business might be split off, triggering a further sharp fall in the share price in response to shareholder concerns about the complexity of separating the switched voice operations from the Internet, international and data services.

Recognizing that revenue growth would in future come from data services, especially those provided to high-end businesses,[10] WorldCom returned to the acquisition trail in September 2000, successfully offering $3.0 billion plus $3.0 billion of debt taken over for competitive local exchange carrier (CLEC) Intermedia although the real target was Intermedia's 55 per cent majority stake (carrying 94 per cent of the votes) in Web-hosting company Digex.[11]

In November, WorldCom confirmed that it would be issuing two separate tracking stocks at some point during 2001. The first, WorldCom Group, would mirror the performance of the core Internet, Web-hosting and international businesses, while MCI Group would reflect the consumer, small business and wholesale long-distance voice and dial-up Internet access operations. WorldCom would have revenues of $23 billion, of which $6 billion would come from overseas operations in 65 countries, while MCI would have revenues of $16 billion. Shareholders would receive, tax-free, one share of MCI stock for every 25 shares of WorldCom common stock. Roughly $6 billion of debt would be allocated to MCI with $17 billion being carried on the books of WorldCom. Bernie Ebbers would remain president and CEO of both companies. The preference for a tracking stock rather than a spin-off – expressly rejected only in June as 'financial engineering' – was justified by the speed of execution, desire to continue to serve all existing customers, avoidance of regulatory problems and the tax consolidation benefits of doing business as a single company.[12] At the same time, WorldCom was forced to admit that the outlook for 2001 was less than rosy, with increased competition, pressure on prices and increased spending to build up the Web-hosting business and Internet-based virtual private networks[13] all likely to have an adverse effect on the bottom line.[14]

WorldCom also ran into problems with its purchase of Intermedia since, although the deal received court approval in December, the value of WorldCom shares being offered had fallen to $1.2 billion and minority shareholders of Digex appeared to have a case for damages on the grounds that their interests had been ignored by the company's directors.[15] Furthermore, WorldCom was forced to agree to shed all the non-Digex assets as a condition for approval by the Department of Justice. Nevertheless, Digex was seen as an integral part of WorldCom's strategy to shuffle low-growth MCI off to one side and concentrate the markets' attention on its data centres and dedication to IP services.[16] The sharp upturn in the share price at the beginning of 2001 suggested that the message was getting through, but sceptics pointed out that this meant little in the context of the huge drop during 2000, and, in the event, it was not to last.

By late January rumours were circulating that between 10 per cent and 15 per cent of WorldCom's 77,000 US employees would be laid off, the majority at MCI. In the event some 6,000 lost their jobs, equivalent to 7 per cent of the global workforce of 90,000, with redundancies right across the board. The decision was also taken to terminate the UUNet brand name in favour of using that of WorldCom across the full range of activities. The lack of provision for wireless services continued to niggle away in the background, but the company remained sanguine, claiming that it could address wireless issues as a virtual operator and that the foundations of the company remained strong.

In mid-February, the issues surrounding the Digex takeover appeared to have been resolved. WorldCom would need to pay only one of its shares per Intermedia share instead of 1.2 as previously agreed, but, in return, it would make a cash payment of $165 million to Digex shareholders and take on

Digex's funding needs for the part of 2001 remaining after the deal was closed plus the whole of 2002 – up to $900 million in total.[17] Given the fact that Intermedia itself was close to bankruptcy by this point in time, WorldCom's own shareholders were less than amused. They could not understand how Bernie Ebbers could justify paying out $880 million for Intermedia, plus taking on $2.5 billion of its debt in addition to swapping $1.1 billion of Intermedia preferred stock for WorldCom preferred stock – not to mention the additional payments to Digex shareholders. Since the sale of Intermedia's CLEC operations would recoup less than $1 billion of these outlays, the inferred price per Digex share appeared to be in the region of $90 yet the market price at the time was only $14.[18] In essence, the answer was that without Digex, WorldCom's revised strategy would be in tatters and Bernie Ebbers desperately needed to shore up his reputation for prescient deal making and the ability to sustain a growth strategy.

On the whole, spring 2001 was a period of relative stability if judged by the standards of the previous year, with WorldCom standing by its projections for revenue growth, ably supported by optimistic noises emanating from Jack Grubman. WorldCom stated firmly that its depressed share price precluded the possibility of new takeovers, but was also obliged to deny that it had received an approach from SBC Communications – or, indeed, anyone else. Although Standard & Poor's had downgraded WorldCom's senior unsecured debt to BBB+ in February, Moody's had maintained the higher rating of A3 and these were at least as satisfactory as those of competitors. Hence, it was possible for WorldCom to launch a successful tender for $11.9 billion of bonds on 9 May, the largest-ever by a US company although France Télécom had succeeded with a larger tender not long beforehand. WorldCom also had little difficulty raising a total of $8 billion of bank credit. Clearly, at this juncture the prevailing view in the markets was that WorldCom was down but by no means out.

On 7 June, shareholders gave permission for the tracking stocks to be created, and these were launched two days later, only for both share prices to fall by several per cent on the day. At the beginning of July, the Intermedia purchase was finally completed, with the minority Digex shareholders being offered shares in both WorldCom and MCI as part of the litigation settlement. Both second- and third-quarter earnings met expectations and cash flow was more than satisfactory. So had WorldCom finally turned the corner and put its troubles behind it for a while?

Smoke and mirrors

As we have mentioned previously, none of the financial data being put out at this time were, in truth, reliable, and hence the answer to the above question depends upon whether it is viewed in prospect or retrospect. Taken in prospect, the situation appeared for now to be under control even if, like all of its competitors, WorldCom was suffering from recessionary conditions.

Analysts' expectations were mostly being met, consolidated net debt was just about manageable at $28.6 billion and WorldCom even took the opportunity to acquire some of the assets of bankrupt high-speed ISP Rhythms NetConnections in late September 2001 in return for $32 million debtor-in-possession financing including a $10 million advance. At the beginning of 2002 the Internet assets of Intermedia were sold off for an undisclosed amount, and the share price continued to trade in the narrow band in which it had remained for roughly half a year.

However, as shown in Figure 7.1, a further collapse in the share price was imminent, The first sign that all was not well was an ever-growing rumour that Bernie Ebbers was in financial difficulties. On 6 February, he announced that he had $198.7 million in debt obligations but that he would be able to cover his debts without selling WorldCom stock as the company was loaning him up to $155 million at a subsidized interest rate. A day later, the results for the fourth-quarter 2001 were published which revealed a reduction in profits at the WorldCom Group compared to a year earlier from $585 million to $384 million excluding one-off items and investment in Embratel of Brazil. For its part, MCI Group reported a loss of $89 million compared to a profit of $125 million. Consolidated revenues were down from $9.6 billion to $8.5 billion, ascribable to MCI rather than WorldCom. These results were below expectations, but what worried the markets rather more were reduced revenue and earnings forecasts for 2002, the expectation of a goodwill write-off amounting to $15–20 billion, the bankruptcy filings by Global Crossing and McLeod USA and the fear that WorldCom was about to suffer a debt downgrade.[19] The only good news was that WorldCom was able to reassure investors that there were no nasty surprises lurking either on or off its balance sheet!

In early April it was rumoured that WorldCom was about to slash 10 per cent of its workforce. This did not include Bernie Ebbers himself, although he was now the subject of a Securities and Exchange Commission (SEC) investigation into funds loaned to him by WorldCom – $366 million in total – which, it appeared, had mostly gone towards the purchase of pine trees. On the face of it, such solid assets provided rather better collateral than any borrowed money sunk into WorldCom stock – Bernie Ebbers' 27 million shares were down in value from $567 million to $135 million – but the size of the loan, the cheap rate of interest and the omission of any repayment date were the cause of deep unease. His other major assets, the Douglas Lake Ranch – the largest working ranch in North America – bought in 1988 for $47 million, a minor league hockey team and the Hampton Inn in Jackson would all show a loss if part of a forced sale.[20]

To general surprise, Jack Grubman suddenly published his first negative research note on WorldCom on 22 April 2002. 'Clearly, we have been wrong on the stock,' he stated, admitting that his change of heart would attract 'inevitable and justified slings from various parties'. Given that he had persistently issued 'buy' ratings during a period when the WorldCom share price was falling from over $60 to $6, he was scarcely exaggerating, and the share price promptly fell to below $4. In fact, Jack Grubman did not advise investors even then to sell, but other analysts had few qualms in so doing.[21] WorldCom Group promptly lowered its earnings and revenue guidance for full-year 2002 for a second time (although MCI Group did not follow suit), but analysts remained concerned that a cash crunch was on the way which would force the two tracking stocks to be reunited in order that cash flows from MCI could be used to pay off debt at WorldCom.

With its consolidated debt load standing at $27.9 billion at the end of April, WorldCom announced that it would be willing to consider asset sales worth up to $2 billion such as Embratel, but did not feel the need to do so at fire sale prices. The more pressing need was to retain staff who had been awarded retention bonuses in the form of stock options by Bernie Ebbers personally during May and June 2000. These options were now worthless and after July 2002 there would no longer be an obligation to stay with the company in order to avoid having to repay the bonuses plus tax. On the other hand, an incentive to stay put existed in the fact that the original options could be traded in for new ones based on the share price in August 2002, potentially opening up an opportunity to make huge gains in the future. But just how low could the share price fall? On 29 April it hit $2.35, but some analysts still thought this to be too high because if WorldCom's debt lost its investment grade status it would face the prospect of being driven into bankruptcy. Clearly, something had to be done to try and restore confidence, so on 28 April the non-executive directors forced Bernie Ebbers to resign, to be replaced by the former chief operating officer and vice-chairman, John Sidgmore.[22]

Chapter 11 beckons

At the end of a career with WorldCom spanning over 75 acquisitions, it seemed that Bernie Ebbers was no longer the solution but the problem, as evidenced by the rise in the share price that followed upon his resignation. Probably no other single person more clearly epitomized the takeover mania that had hit Wall Street and, in truth, the $60 billion loss in value at Enron which had achieved an extraordinary notoriety in recent months paled into insignificance compared to the $170 billion wiped off the value of WorldCom. But how could WorldCom avoid following Enron (and so many others) into Chapter 11 bankruptcy? The simplest short-term answer appeared to lie in massive asset sell-offs including, if necessary, the entire international operations. Given that a $2.65 billion loan was falling due on 8 June, it was evident that WorldCom's bankers now held the upper hand in any negotiations over WorldCom's future, and private equity houses lost no time in queuing up for a share of the spoils were WorldCom to be broken up.[23] The problem, as ever, was that a fire sale would fail to realize more than a fraction of the true longer-term value of the 100,000 miles of terrestrial and undersea cables. On the other hand, while it made better sense to hang on until the international operations became cash-flow positive, there would need to be additional investment in the short term to achieve that goal, and it was hard to see where the funds would come from.

Although WorldCom's senior unsecured debt was still rated BBB by Standard & Poor's (S&P) and Baa2 by Moody's, it was trading at only 50 cents in the dollar by the beginning of May and the markets increasingly took the view that a company now worth $5 billion could not sustain a net debt of $28 billion for much longer. Superficially at least, the existing cash on hand and that flowing in from ongoing services was sufficient to see the company through until the end of the year, but if, as expected, the debt was downgraded to 'junk' and interest costs accordingly rose sharply, it seemed unlikely that WorldCom could trade its way out of trouble. The downgrade by Moody's and Fitch duly arrived on 8 May, and by S&P a week later, but the markets remained fairly sanguine about the prospects for WorldCom to renegotiate its credit facilities.

However, on 25 June, the bombshell struck. WorldCom announced that in the course of an internal audit it had uncovered improper accounting for almost $4 billion in expenses and that it had responded by firing Scott Sullivan.[24] The SEC would be investigating the irregularities which it claimed were the largest it had ever seen, requiring the results for 2001 and the first quarter of 2002 to be restated to show net losses. The Department of Justice also began a criminal investigation and the House of Representatives Financial Services Committee issued subpoenas to Messrs Ebbers, Sidgmore, Sullivan and Grubman. WorldCom announced that it would be cutting 17,000 jobs in a bid to save $900 million a year, but few analysts expected the company to avoid bankruptcy for more than a few months. The share price of WorldCom Group plunged to 20 cents. WorldCom's auditors, Andersen, already mired in the Enron debacle, promptly claimed that WorldCom had withheld key information and failed to consult it about the accounting treatment of its expenses, although $4 billion did seem a rather large sum to misallocate without the auditors noticing. Andersen were replaced by KPMG.

It transpired that the accounting irregularities, which failed to conform to US GAAP,[25] involved treating expenses as capital expenditures, thereby inflating profitability. More precisely, the issue was that line costs – payments to other carriers for use of their networks – had been 'transferred' to capital accounts.[26] A total of $3.06 billion in 2001 and $798 million during the first quarter of 2002 was initially identified. Accounting professionals and academics remained divided about whether it was reasonable for the auditors to have missed the evidence of improper practice, and whether there had been simply a breaking of rules or outright fraud.[27]

On 26 June, WorldCom bonds were trading at 14 cents to the dollar. The bottom-line issue was that in admitting that its accounts were false, WorldCom had violated several covenants attached to its credit facilities. For the moment, its bankers were prepared to hold off from driving WorldCom into bankruptcy, but could do so at any time simply by declaring WorldCom to be in default in respect of the $2.7 billion unsecured bank lending forming part of its $31.5 billion of outstanding bonds – now 'junk' rated CCC− by S&P and Ca by Moody's – and bank debt. What the bankers wanted was to swap the unsecured for secured credit facilities in order to have first claim on WorldCom's assets in the event of bankruptcy, but no one really knew any longer what figures could be trusted and what WorldCom's assets, on its books at over $100 billion, were really worth other than much less than stated. The one positive aspect of the affair was that the fraud had not done too much damage to net cash flows[28] and these might not be too adversely affected in the future: after all, WorldCom would remain operational even in Chapter 11 bankruptcy[29] and the alternative carriers such as AT&T were themselves hardly the picture of health.

For the most part, investment funds had been dumping their WorldCom shares even at knock-down prices, but one fund, Alliance Capital, was busy accumulating a 7 per cent holding, making it WorldCom's largest shareholder.[30] What agitated analysts rather more was that at least one WorldCom director, Francesco Galesi,[31] had sold shares worth tens of millions of dollars since the beginning of 2002, suggesting that WorldCom's difficulties had come as less of a surprise to some than to others, especially if they sat on WorldCom's audit committee.

In the quest to avoid imminent bankruptcy WorldCom hired Goldman Sachs to dispose of its stakes in Embratel in Brazil and Avantel in Mexico. It also put Australia's second-largest ISP, OzEmail, on the block. Unfortunately, the fate of such 'non-core' assets was fairly irrelevant to the future of WorldCom. Its most desirable assets were the local city networks that it had acquired via the MFS and similar takeovers, and IDT – the most aggressive acquirer of bankrupt telecoms assets – made an offer both for these and MCI, only to be firmly repulsed.[32] In any event, it seemed clear to everyone outside WorldCom that a Chapter 11 filing would be highly advantageous: new lenders would be keen to provide 'debtor-in-possession' financing; a debt-for-equity swap could be arranged, saving up to $3 billion a year in interest payments; and it would forestall lawsuits from aggrieved shareholders and others. The main downside would be the risk of widespread defections by its biggest customers such as the US Navy, EDS, Nasdaq and Toyota.

As now became increasingly clear, there was going to be a repeat of the situation at Enron in relation to employees' 401(k) pension plans. At the end of 2000, roughly 32 per cent of all such pension plan assets were in the form of WorldCom shares – compared to a conventional maximum of 20 per cent – because employees were encouraged, if not positively pressurized, to invest in this way even at a time when the books were allegedly being cooked. In more recent times employees had started to bail out, but had been forced to do so at very poor prices as a consequence of which the value of most pensions had plummeted. WorldCom's response was to claim that there had been no coercion to invest in its shares and that employees were free to trade their investments at any time, unlike at Enron where its shares held in pension plans could not be sold even at times when its top executives were offloading them.

But precisely how much cooking of the books had been going on? In early July WorldCom announced that it was investigating its accounts for 1999 and 2000 in the aftermath of the takeover of MCI. The SEC had forced WorldCom to reduce the immediate write-off of goodwill in MCI (see note [5]), but WorldCom's acquisition accounting was now a matter of more widespread concern. This was not good news for CEO Sidgmore because he had been working closely with Bernie Ebbers at that time, even if he had subsequently taken more of a back seat. It also transpired that Andersen had been warned by two whistleblowers as far back as April 2000 that expenses were being misallocated. This led politicians such as Billy Tauzin to declare that what had been going on went well beyond aggressive accounting and was, in fact, fraud, pure and simple, and a date for a fraud trial to commence was fixed at March 2003. Not surprisingly, Messrs Ebbers and Sullivan pleaded the Fifth Amendment against self-incrimination. The general view was that it would be difficult to pin much blame upon Bernie Ebbers unless he was directly implicated by Scott Sullivan, yet Sullivan could scarcely be exonerated in return for acting as a prosecution witness against his former boss.

In mid-July, WorldCom's bankers took it to court for fraud on the grounds that it had drawn down a $2.65 billion credit facility only weeks before the accounting scandal was announced. Although their main purpose was to force WorldCom to provide security for their loans, this was heavily opposed by bondholders,[33] leaving WorldCom somewhere between a rock and a hard place. Its inevitable response was to put its US assets into Chapter 11 on 21 July 2002 – the largest bankruptcy in US history – but WorldCom was at pains to make clear that it was still operating as normal and that no major clients had defected (so far). Altogether, the Chapter 11 filing listed $107 billion in assets and $41 billion in liabilities, mostly the bonds discussed above, with $2 billion of debtor-in-possession financing forthcoming subject to fairly onerous conditions from Citibank, GE Capital and JP Morgan Chase Bank.

In Chapter 11

WorldCom's first action in Chapter 11 was to quit the wireless reselling business – it was the largest reseller in the USA – transferring its two million customers mainly to AT&T Wireless, Verizon Wireless and Alltel for a token payment in the hope of saving $700 million a year. However, this positive news was rapidly overshadowed by an announcement that WorldCom had uncovered a further $3.3 billion of improperly accounted earnings during 1999–2002, of which $2.9 billion was in respect of 2000 requiring pre-tax profit for 2000 to be reduced from $4.97 billion to $1.70 billion. Evidently, certain reserves – including provisions for bad debt and legal fees – had been reversed into income, although nothing could be said with certainty until KPMG had completed its re-audit of the previous three years. A write-off of up to $50 billion would follow publication of the restated accounts.[34] Scott Sullivan and David Myers were duly arrested for conspiracy to commit securities fraud – carrying up to 15 years in prison – as well as five counts of false filings with the SEC – to which, in Sullivan's case, charges of lying in financial statements to secure credit lines and bank fraud were added in April 2003 – but for now Bernie Ebbers remained relatively unscathed. As for John Sidgmore, although no one questioned that he had taken too much of a back-seat role in 2000 to be implicated in what happened subsequently, introducing revisions relating to 2000, and possibly to 1999, now left him much more exposed. At the end of August, Scott Sullivan and Buford Yates, the director of general accounting, were indicted, but not David Myers, suggesting that he was seeking a plea bargain. Betty Vinson and Troy Normand, Mr Yates' assistants, were also cited in the indictment but not initially charged.

The future of WorldCom International, excluded from the Chapter 11 proceedings, remained unclear. Although still consuming cash and losing customers, it was claimed that the unit would be free cash flow positive by early 2003 and that it remained a core operation. There was accordingly no reason to fear a massive wave of redundancies in the near future either within or outside the USA.[35] Nevertheless, several high-ranking executives such as the head of US sales and global accounts and the chief marketing officer took the opportunity to head for the door, painting a picture of bad blood at the top of the organization. With a good part of their pension plans wiped out, and with their jobs still thought to be on the line, employees in general were becoming increasingly demoralized. Although strategically it made sense to concentrate on customer retention rather than growth, it meant, for example, much less potential for commissions for the sales force. In order to retain customers, WorldCom introduced new incentives such as 180 days to cancel contracts and additional bill credits if service fell below an acceptable standard.[36]

It was increasingly felt that UUNet would determine WorldCom's survival as it carried, according to disputed calculations, almost half of all Internet backbone traffic and was concerned with data rather than voice transmission. Ironically, it used to be headed by John Sidgmore and there were those who argued that if he and others like him had not been prone to hyperbolic claims about traffic growth, the over-capacity that subsequently drove down prices and brought down many carriers, including WorldCom, would never have happened.[37] Partly for this reason, it was widely held that neither the current management nor the new restructuring team it had set up to sort out the mess contained the kind of experience now needed of devising and selling profitable telecommunications services. Unfortunately, events were taking on a life of their own, so the prospects of putting a more appropriate management in place in time to save the company were limited at best. In any event, it was felt that the government would find it hard to justify letting WorldCom emerge from Chapter 11 with its debts written off and prepared once again to become predator rather than prey: this aspect of the Chapter 11 process, it was felt, was all very well in the light of historically poor decision making in an adverse environment, which could potentially be remedied without the need to liquidate a company, but was not appropriate in the context of fraud.[38]

At the end of the day, therefore, it was at best debatable whether WorldCom was worth saving, and if it was not, and a break-up appeared to be the most sensible outcome, there were allegedly plenty of parties interested in picking up the pieces, although some claimed that the international operations were not particularly desirable since they were unprofitable and faced too much competition insofar that they comprised a backbone but not any local access lines. For the moment, however, WorldCom hung on grimly although the catalogue of dubious decisions continued to mount up. The board attempted to respond to severe criticism of Bernie Ebbers' severance package (see note 22) which came, inter alia, in a report by from Richard Breeden (see note 31) which was particularly critical of the role played by Stiles Kellett (who subsequently resigned from the board). The board also sought a replacement for John Sidgmore as CEO, although this was carefully not mentioned in connection with his increasingly possible involvement in the earlier stage of the fraud. In mid-September, WorldCom moved to restate its accounts for the third time, although in this case it was a matter of $2 billion of 'aggressive' accounting – pushing the rules to the limit but not beyond. Evidently, WorldCom now took the view that the best policy was to declare all possible accounting issues rather than have them uncovered by outsiders.[39]

At the end of September, David Myers entered a guilty plea, stating that he was acting under orders from Scott Sullivan. Subsequently, Buford Yates pleaded guilty to two felony charges, blaming his superiors and claiming that he had objected to his orders (even though he had nevertheless carried them out), and Betty Vinson and Troy Normand followed suit in mid-October. Although Bernie Ebbers still remained unindicted – partly because he never sent e-mails and rarely touched a computer, and hence it was difficult to find hard evidence of a 'smoking gun'[40] – it was alleged that, in addition to $408 million loaned by WorldCom which was backed by property, Mr Ebbers also received a $679 million loan from a Citigroup subsidiary, backed by WorldCom shares, and that this both gave Citigroup an incentive to promote the stock and also allegedly brought in profitable work on behalf of WorldCom.[41]

In early October, WorldCom announced that it had accumulated a $1 billion cash pile and would now need no more than $1.5 billion of debtor-in-possession financing – it had not yet used any of that initially made available. Nevertheless, its prospects of emerging from Chapter 11 were dampened somewhat in early November when the SEC published an amended, expanded, complaint which stated that WorldCom had misled investors from at least as early as 1999 until the first quarter of 2002, during which period it had overstated reported income by approximately $9 billion.

On a more positive note, Michael Capellas, formerly president of Hewlett-Packard, agreed to take on the role of chairman and CEO at WorldCom,[42] but the task he faced was made no easier by the tactics of a group of bondholders, led by a distressed-debt investor, David Matlin, which was attempting to buy up sufficient outstanding debt to enable it to control the outcome of the bankruptcy or, at least, to represent a blocking one-third minority with the power to veto arrangements. In general, bondholders appeared to favour a debt-for-equity swap that would allow WorldCom to emerge from Chapter 11 as quickly as possible. Their cause was assisted by a settlement between the SEC and WorldCom at the end of November – a separate matter from the criminal and civil cases being pursued against named individuals – whereby WorldCom pledged not to engage in any fraudulent activity; consented to ongoing scrutiny by an independent monitor of its corporate governance, policies, plans and internal controls; and consented to a review of its internal accounting by an outside consultant approved by regulators. WorldCom neither admitted nor denied wrong-doing, but would be subject to a substantial fine.[43]

In January 2003, Lucy Woods, who headed the international division, resigned, but this was not thought to presage the bankruptcy of the division even though it was still consuming large quantities of cash. Not surprisingly, CEO Capellas was unwilling at this stage to set out too many hard details of the restructuring plan that was scheduled to be filed by mid-April, nor the implications for staffing levels, but he did announce the creation of a corporate ethics office. By early February, it had become clear that a further 5,000 employees – 8 per cent of the residual workforce – would lose their jobs, that line costs and sales and general administration expenses would be cut by 13 per cent and that WorldCom would retain a presence in eight US locations as well as Hong Kong and Britain. However, the main bombshell landed in mid-March when WorldCom declared that it would be taking almost $80 billion in charges to write off the entire $45 billion value of goodwill and reduce the value on its books of property, equipment and other intangible assets from $44.8 billion to $10 billion. Only AOL Time Warner had ever written off a larger sum in the course of one financial year.[44] Nevertheless, with $2.5 billion in cash on hand at the end of December, and net losses running at under $100 a month on average, the write-off was cosmetic rather than operationally significant.

At the end of March, the *Wall Street Journal* claimed that accounting irregu-larities could be as high as $11 billion, although the numbers would not be officially released until the summer. It alleged that in 2001 WorldCom had moved significant lumps of its expenses – perhaps in excess of $3 billion – over to MCI and that MCI executives had raised objections but had been rebuffed. On a more positive note it was suggested that WorldCom would emerge from Chapter 11 with as little as $2–4 billion of net debt and over $1 billion in cash on its balance sheet, but although that would provide a safety margin, early estimates of the amount of business lost to rivals AT&T and Sprint indicated roughly $2 billion over a nine-month period.[45] Although executives were anxious to emerge from Chapter 11 as quickly as possible, they were obliged to wait until the financial results for the previous three years were restated and approved.

The reorganization plan

On 14 April, WorldCom filed its reorganization plan which, inter alia, would give WorldCom bondholders 36 cents on the dollar for the $26 billion outstanding with payment in the form of new equity. MCI bondholders would get 80 cents on the dollar for the $2.6 billion outstanding and Intermedia bondholders would get 94 cents on the dollar for the $1 billion outstanding. MCI and WorldCom trade creditors, owed $2.8 billion, would get 36 cents on the dollar and Intermedia trade creditors 83 cents on the dollar; but MCI and WorldCom junior bondholders would lose their entire $750 million investment, while Intermedia junior bondholders would recover 46 cents on the dollar. Payment would vary with different classes of creditors getting debt, a mixture of cash and equity or a mixture of debt and equity. These arrangements did not prove satisfactory to many MCI bondholders and trade creditors who argued that MCI had operated much as it had before being taken over and that it still owned substantially the same assets. Hence, its bondholders and creditors should be entitled to the majority of the new equity[46] which would in practice be going to the likes of MatlinPatterson Global Opportunities Partners (17 per cent) and Financial Ventures (12.64 per cent).

In May 2003, still technically registered as WorldCom Inc. even though it proposed to re-emerge post-Chapter 11 as MCI Inc. and was trading as MCI, the company agreed to pay a fine of $500 million to settle the fraud case brought by the SEC.[47] Under a new provision of federal law, the money will at least partly be restored to shareholders. Although the SEC considered the fine to be very large, rivals predictably tended to see it as puny relative to the scale of the fraud while some analysts wondered about the point of fining a company that had been declared bankrupt. Nevertheless, District Judge Rakoff ruled in early July that a further $250 million in post-bankruptcy stock would have to be set aside in fines – the largest ever levied by the SEC but modest in relation to shareholder losses. Ratification by the Federal Bankruptcy Court is awaited.

In early June, two reports on the fraud at WorldCom, one prepared by bankruptcy court examiner Richard Thornburgh and the other, appointed by the WorldCom Audit Committee, by lawyer William McLucas, were published simultaneously.[48] These reports are too substantial to analyse in detail in this study, and in essence provided only a limited number of new insights into what had been going on at WorldCom. However, they did suggest that rather more people had been involved than previously thought, and resignations followed including that of Susan Mayer, the senior vice president and treasurer. Even so, evidence against Bernie Ebbers remained elusive.

It seemed probable that BellSouth would be acquiring MCI's broadband Internet assets – subject to court approval – for the bargain price of $65 million, but Nextel Communications upped the ante to $144 million when the assets were auctioned at the end of June: a poor return, nevertheless, on assets that cost WorldCom over $1 billion. Of more significance, perhaps, was evidence that MCI would struggle post-Chapter 11 despite its cleaned-up balance sheet. In early July 2003, it was forced to readjust its financial forecasts for 2003 and 2004 to take account of a much reduced growth rate in revenues. It blamed this not only on falling prices, customer defections and increased churn but also on a new 'do not call' law which prohibits telemarketers from cold calling anyone registered on a 'do not call' database. However, MCI's cash reserves had risen to $4.2 billion.

A small part of this was needed to acquire the outstanding 39 per cent of Digex that MCI did not already own together with some Digex preferred stock, and rather more to pay off a $436 million claim registered by Verizon Communications for money owed pre-Chapter 11. As most of this had subsequently been collected and withheld by Verizon, only a net $60 million needed to be paid over. Similar settlements with other trade creditors should now follow. Nevertheless, despite its written-off debts, MCI is by no means home free. Its competitors are relentlessly attacking it with some success, not merely acquiring its customers but persuading the government temporarily to exclude MCI from bidding for its contracts and inducing the FBI to investigate allegations that MCI disguised the origins of long-distance calls in an attempt to avoid paying termination charges to local operators.[49] The logic of this escaped Lex,[50] who pointed out that the line between 'least cost routing' and illegal activities was ill-defined and had not previously elicited complaints, and that, in practice, punishing the company meant punishing creditors and employees.

In September 2003, Bernie Ebbers was finally caught up in a criminal indictment filed by the Oklahoma attorney-general which also cited five other executives and the company itself. The fact that his shares were now truly next to worthless, as shown in Figure 7.2, may have been a greater cause of concern.

Conclusions

WorldCom was the classic example of a company that lived or died according to the mantra of growth – in the 23 quarters between 1994Q1 and 1999Q3 there were 16 occasions on which year-on-year revenue growth exceeded 50 per cent. While it lasted, the strategy of serial acquisitions was a fail-safe

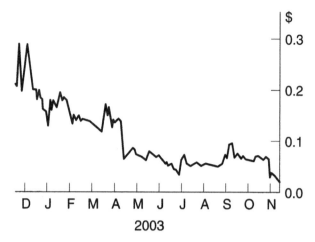

Figure 7.2 WorldCom Inc. WorldCom Group share price, December 2002–November
2003 (dollars).
Source: Daily share prices in the *Financial Times*.

method for achieving such growth and, given the use of stock rather than
cash as the takeover currency, one that avoided the sorts of problems spelt
out in the Vivendi Universal case study. Unfortunately, the old adage that
what goes up eventually comes down was sure to intrude at some point, and
when it did WorldCom predictably suffered more than its peers. Its solution –
the move into the US consumer long-distance market via the purchase of
MCI – certainly added to the revenue stream, but this was a business under
stress and, whilst it was possible to maintain revenues, this could only be
done via an erosion of margins. As elsewhere, switching to ebitda served to
divert attention from profitability and cash flow, but that was standard
practice in the dot-com era. WorldCom's contribution to the weird and
wonderful world of telecommunications accounting started off with a strong
affection for pro forma accounting and a fondness for lending huge sums at
cheap rates to its CEO, but it was never going to be brought to the brink of
extinction by such technicalities. Nor indeed, was the alleged fraud itself
overly dramatic – after all, a company valued at over $100 billion should be
able to survive $4 billion of misallocated costs if its trading performance is
up to par.

Unlike at Enron, where evidence of fraud brought down the company,
WorldCom was already more or less a penny stock by the time the accounting
irregularities were revealed. The restated accounts for 2000 indicated that
the company was already in serious trouble. As noted above, one major
difficulty lay with the complexity of the organization – too many companies
had been acquired over too short a period to ever have any real prospect of
melding them together into a cohesive whole, even assuming there was a

serious desire to do so. Given that so many operated outside the USA, the problem of control was necessarily exacerbated. Once Chapter 11 was declared the various bits of the WorldCom empire were always likely to adopt an 'every man for himself' mentality: bankruptcy tends to be treated as a far more serious outcome outside the USA compared to within it. But even in the USA employees tended to remain loyal to their original employer – most notably after WorldCom's entry into Chapter 11. MCI employees, in particular, considered themselves to be much better organized than their WorldCom counterparts. The failure to assign clearly defined responsibilities to each part of the organization – a problem by no means confined to WorldCom – had long made it difficult for customers to know which division to deal with.

For many analysts, the personality of Bernie Ebbers was a contributory factor in WorldCom's fall from grace, in part because he was insufficiently interested in melding together the various acquisitions. Although it has yet to be proven that he was complicit in the fraud – it does have to be said in his favour that he hung on to his WorldCom shares to the bitter end, in the process ruining himself – his tendency to suppress all criticism of the company was difficult for critics to handle so long as WorldCom continued to pump out optimistic data about its operations, yet by the time the company realized that he had become a liability rather than an asset it was already too late. Replacing Bernie Ebbers with John Sidgmore as CEO was also problematic. So long as he was able to disassociate himself from the original accounting irregularities, it was possible for him to promote his message that WorldCom was under new management and that the problems were being resolved. However, once the second set of irregularities was revealed he struggled to maintain his clean hands image and several directors plotted successfully to have him removed.

The WorldCom fraud has raised numerous questions about corporate governance. The fraud, unlike at Enron, was really quite straightforward, involving as it did reserves used to reduce costs and costs reclassified as capital expenditure. Furthermore, it was carried out by a relatively small group of senior executives. Clearly, however, this was known to a good number of employees, but evidently these were largely prevented from whistleblowing by threats from above. Understandable enough, perhaps, when jobs were on the line, but why was the board of directors so supine? Seemingly, it was prepared to remain happily ignorant of what was going on: for example, the deal with EDS, involving $1.65 billion, was approved in 20 minutes without a written record and announced before it was officially confirmed by the board. Equally, the purchase of Intermedia was effectively passed on the nod based on a single sheet of paper.

The Chapter 11 bankruptcy process appears superficially to give WorldCom a second chance to use its sheer size to control its markets, and its competitors have complained long and loud that it should not be allowed to emerge in one piece with its debts largely forgiven. However, their pleas have tended to fall on deaf ears since it is evident that WorldCom's unwieldy structure – itself a major contributor to its fall from grace – can hardly be set right within a matter of a few months. Equally, there are those who believe that there are more accounting scandals hidden away that need to be sorted out. The board of directors is having to be rebuilt,[51] as are financial reporting systems.[52] Even the name is to go, being replaced by that of MCI although it is tarnished in its own way by its history of being known for cut-price long-distance services. How many customers will desert is a moot point as many contracts have yet to reach their renewal date, but big users of data tend not to contract with only one supplier anyway so desertions will probably be limited to parts of renewed contracts so long as the company appears to be maintaining its network. Furthermore, WorldCom began raising its consumer prices once it entered Chapter 11, and tried to stabilise corporate prices, and its competitors were only too happy to follow suit rather than try to undercut it across the board. By its very nature, the situation at the end of 2003 is hard to call. For a start, WorldCom faces nearly $80 billion of class-action suits led by the New York State Common Retirement Fund and representing most of those who bought shares, bonds or notes of WorldCom between 29 April 1999 and 25 June 2002. It has to emerge from Chapter 11,[53] consolidate the various businesses left in operation, eliminate unprofitable contracts and set prices that generate profits in the face of severe competition. It is a tall order and it is a matter of wait and see.

Part III

Illustrative application of strategic modelling III

All three companies described in the following chapters are media companies. They are, however, all drawn from different countries. Vivendi Universal (Chapter 8) is French, though its expansionary strategy did result in it having a considerable presence in the United States. The reverse is true for AOL Time Warner (Chapter 9), which is largely an American company with some European investments. The KirchGruppe (Chapter 10) is German to the core even though it owned a smattering of investments overseas.

Across all three companies a series of common themes are identifiable. As befits the media industry, 'larger than life' characters populate each of the three companies. The re-invention of Compagnie Générales des Eaux as Vivendi Universal is inextricably linked with Jean-Paul Messier, whereas many of the media industry's leading barons such as Rupert Murdoch and Silvio Berlusconi feature in the decline of the KirchGruppe, as does, of course, its eponymous founder Leo Kirch. As is demonstrated in Chapter 10, Kirch thought that he could use his connections with German bankers and politicians to prevent the collapse of the KirchGruppe – not that leaning on politicians for favours is exclusively a Germanic preserve.

AOL Time Warner is somewhat different in this respect. The main protagonists in the takeover of Time Warner by AOL, Gerald Levin and Steve Case respectively, are not really 'larger than life' characters although they have both featured prominently in the media over the past several years. The best-known and arguably most extroverted of the senior executives associated with the takeover was Ted Turner (although his role is now much diminished), who made who made much the most memorably colourful comment when the merger was announced. Nonetheless, both Case and Levin drove the merger forward to completion, overcoming regulatory concerns and increasingly sceptical commentators on the way. Not surprisingly, both played the ultimate price when the new entity failed to live up to expectations – they lost their jobs and were widely vilified.

A second common theme is that all three companies operated in a broad range of markets. The range of markets in which AOL Time Warner was (and in essence still is) active ranged from music to film production, cable-TV networks, publishing and, of course, Internet access. Vivendi Universal was also in many of the same markets, as well as in telecommunications and waste management (reflecting its broader industrial roots). The most limited operationally of the three companies was the KirchGruppe, which operated in just the publishing and TV markets but these are in practice the most directly influential in respect of, for example, public opinion.

In each case, the span of businesses contributed, to a lesser or greater extent, to the tribulations that they faced. In the case of AOL Time Warner, the anticipated synergies between the new media-focused AOL and the old media-focused Time Warner failed to materialise. Instead, and somewhat surprisingly, the takeover by AOL resulted in the disparate divisions of Time Warner co-operating with one another better than ever before. This failure of synergies to emerge between the two parts of the merged company has led many to question whether convergence as popularly envisaged will ever be realized.

As Vivendi Universal expanded further into the media sector, questions were increasingly asked why the company continued to maintain a presence in the waste management market. One explanation could be that Messier was too distracted by the task of leading Vivendi Universal's expansion into new business areas to find a solution to the lack of synergies, or, alternatively, the business may have been retained due to its profitability. Although several factors contributed to the collapse of the KirchGruppe, one important issue was the company's expansion into the German pay-TV market which resulted in huge losses that profits elsewhere could not offset.

Financial issues have contributed significantly to the shaping of strategies in all three cases. Despite frantic efforts on the part of Leo Kirch, the KirchGruppe collapsed because it was unable to fund its operations through borrowing. Not only had the group pledged all of its available assets as collateral on loans, but its profitability was also insufficient to support the loss-making parts of the group. As is shown in Chapter 8, the large debts that Vivendi Universal amassed as it expanded into new markets contributed to both the fall of Messier and the unravelling of the company's American presence. Although AOL Time Warner was by no means deficient when it came to indebtedness – in 2002 it had some $27 billion of long-term debt – the main financial challenge it faced was reconciling the massive amounts of goodwill (see glossary) associated with the merger with the less optimistic environment in which the company was operating. AOL Time Warner eventually opted to write off nearly a $100 billion of goodwill, exposing in the process the fragility of the takeover and differences between the various divisions.

One way that Vivendi Universal, AOL Time Warner and the KirchGruppe sought to overcome the problems that they faced was through deal making. Leo Kirch continued to manoeuvre and propose deals right up until the company collapsed, whereas Vivendi Universal cut its debt burden through divesting assets and engineered its exit from the USA through unravelling its relationship with Barry Diller and selling the freed-up assets to NBC for cash and stock. Although AOL Time Warner is the product of a very large deal, the company has not really demonstrated a tendency to make deals – perhaps as well since its record is somewhat flawed. Its relationship with Bertelsmann had to be unwound in order for regulatory approval for the takeover to be granted, and AOL Time Warner has tried twice to address adverse conditions in the music market through selling Warner Music.

If we turn to look at AOL Time Warner more closely, the models depicted in Chapter 2 serve to illuminate different aspects of the strategy adopted. If we use the strategic states model suggested by Pehrsson, then attention is focused on the number of markets and the extent to which products are tailored to customer requirements. As readers may recall, the strategic states model provides a framework for understanding the interplay between, on the one hand, the number of markets in which a company is present, and, on the other, the degree to which products have been tailored to meet the needs of customers. A company may be present either in a handful of markets or in many markets, while the products that it sells in these markets may be tailored to the needs of its customers to a lesser or greater extent.

Depending on the interplay between these, a company will choose from one of the following four strategies: price, distribution, relations and responsiveness. These are pure strategies that are combined depending on the interplay between the number of markets where a company is present and the degree to which it has tailored its products to meet the needs of its customers. For example, if the company is present in only a handful of markets and has not extensively tailored its products to the needs of its customers, then strategies primarily based upon prices will be adopted although the company will also have recourse to strategies based upon relationships.

Underpinning the bringing together of AOL and Time Warner is the notion of convergence. That is, the boundaries between previously separate markets blur so that, in essence, they become a single market. Closely related to this notion is the idea that services will be integrated and customized to meet the needs of consumers. Technological advances such as digitization and fibre optics have served to encourage convergence. Prior to the takeover, AOL effectively operated in just a handful of markets and entered into limited tailoring of its products to meet the needs of customers. Furthermore, AOL did not own its own telecommunication networks and had only a limited presence in the content market. Consequently, in both of these areas AOL was reliant on others.

Thus, from the perspective of AOL, acquiring Time Warner was a very attractive prospect as it would rectify its shortcomings in both of these areas: AOL would thereby gain access to the extensive cable-TV and content businesses of Time Warner. When it came to justifying the takeover, especially once stock prices began to fall and the regulatory approval process dragged on, the repeated mantra was that of convergence. In terms of the strategic states model, the intention was that the takeover would enable AOL to move from the bottom-left quadrant to the top-right quadrant of Figure III,

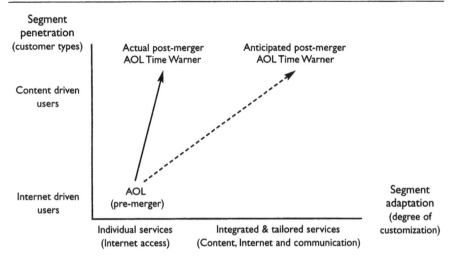

Figure III Business strategy development.

adapted from Figure 2.10. Such a move would change the basis on which AOL competed from price and building relationships with distributors to the services and products that it offered.

However, as the figure demonstrates, this did not happen in practice. Why was this the case? Firstly, the merged company was not able to deliver the synergies that it promised. The Time Warner half of the company resented its status as the junior partner even though its revenue stream was larger, while the AOL half (as the acquirer) considered itself to be in charge: its market value was, after all, much greater than that of Time Warner when it took it over. This antagonism ensured that the two halves did not work well together, thereby inhibiting the development of integrated services.

This lack of co-operation compounded the problems emanating from the AOL part of the company. Quite simply, the walled garden (restricted content) of AOL could not compete with the wealth of content freely available elsewhere on the Internet. The lack of co-operation with the former Time Warner divisions meant that customers were not being satisfactorily locked in by virtue of the portal's (largely unique) content. Perhaps more worryingly was the price-based competition that AOL faced in its core dial-up Internet access market. In a nutshell, AOL was considerably more expensive than some of its competitors. Not only did this limit the growth potential for AOL, but it also placed pressure on the company to reduce its prices as well.

Thus, the use of the strategic states model helps to explain why AOL was so eager to acquire Time Warner. The model also points to why the takeover was unable to live up to initial expectations. At the same time, the model also hints at those areas where the performance of what is now Time Warner (with AOL as a division) must be improved.

Vivendi Universal

Français, oui, Yankee, non

Background

The French company Compagnie Générale des Eaux was originally formed as a water utility in 1853. In 1998, it adopted a new name, Vivendi, designed to reflect the fact that it by now held a diversified portfolio of assets with interests in water, energy, waste management, transport, telecoms, media, construction and property. In March 1998, a merger was agreed between Vivendi and Havas, France's then largest publisher of books and business information titles. This was completed in May, whereupon Havas became part of Vivendi's media and communications division, comprising holdings in telecommunications, publishing and multimedia, audio-visual and Internet.

Vivendi was the largest shareholder in Canal Plus at the beginning of 1999, with a stake in excess of 34 per cent. It announced in June 1999 that it was buying the rest of Pathé, in which it already held a 26.6 per cent stake. The offer constituted three Vivendi shares in exchange for two Pathé shares. Vivendi intended to retain the pay-TV business and to sell the other assets to Fornier. Via this transaction, Vivendi acquired a 16.7 per cent stake in UK satellite operator BSkyB and became its second-largest investor after majority owner News Corporation – subsequently raising its stake to almost 25 per cent by acquiring the holdings of Granada and Pearson in July. Given BSkyB's strong position in the UK, and the strength of Canal Plus elsewhere in Europe, they looked to fit well as potential partners, so the announcement of talks leading to a possible merger came as little surprise. However, the regulatory hurdles were immense, as was rapidly made clear by the European Commission, and Canal Plus was determined to achieve clear management control, so it came as no real surprise when the merger talks were abandoned. In July, News Corp. reiterated that it had no intention of relinquishing control of BSkyB. Vivendi subsequently increased its stake in Canal Plus to 49 per cent by acquiring the shares held by Richemont for €1.4 billion.

Vivendi thus had an incentive to renew the merger discussions with BSkyB, although the latter remained unlikely to enter negotiations that would end up with it playing a subservient role to Vivendi. A link between the companies via News Corp.'s new digital business, initially called Platco, became a possibility. It was rumoured in May 2000, that Vivendi would be offered a 10–12 per cent stake plus board representation, with Vivendi folding its BSkyB holding into Platco. Platco was renamed Sky Global Networks in June, with a view to a flotation. However, News Corp. appeared by July to have gone off the idea of a link with Vivendi, and was allegedly looking to financial investors for backing.

In the meantime, VivendiNet (a 50:50 joint venture between Vivendi and Canal Plus) and Vodafone announced that their new 50:50 Internet joint venture, initially called MAP, would begin offering an e-mail service in May 2000 linking mobile phones and PCs. In June, MAP was launched under the renamed Vizzavi banner to provide e-mail, search facilities, information, entertainment and e-commerce. It was to be the default home page for the companies involved and utilize mobile phone, PC, TV and personal digital assistant platforms. Content would primarily be provided by VivendiNet (via Canal Plus, Havas and Havas Interactive). It would operate initially in France, Germany, Italy and the UK, with the existing Vodafone and Vivendi operating companies being rolled up into Vizzavi and offered a 20 per cent stake in the national subsidiaries. In order to pacify the European Commission, Vivendi agreed to dispose of its 55 per cent stake in AOL France to allow competitors unrestricted access to its platform and subscribers to change their default page away from Vizzavi. On this basis, the Commission cleared the venture in July 2000. It took until March 2001 for agreement to be reached on transferring the AOL France stake to AOL.

The creation of Vivendi Universal

In a further development, Vivendi, Canal Plus and Seagram of Canada agreed to merge in June 2000, with the resultant entity, to be called Vivendi Universal, owned 59 per cent by Vivendi shareholders, 29 per cent by Seagram shareholders and 12 per cent by Canal Plus shareholders. Vivendi offered 0.7 shares for each Seagram share, equivalent to a nominal value of $77.35, with an adjustment factor set at +/−12.5 per cent to allow for deviations in the two companies' share prices between the offer and completion dates. The premium to Seagram's pre-offer price was almost 50 per cent and the total cost was $34 billion plus $4 billion of inherited debt, but the immediate effect in the financial markets was to reduce the Vivendi share price by one-quarter from €115 to €89 and the Seagram share price to $60. The assets acquired from Seagram included Universal Studios, the world's largest music company, Universal Music (incorporating PolyGram acquired in 1999) and 43 per cent of USA Networks.

Each shareholder in Canal Plus was offered two Vivendi shares plus one share in a new Canal Plus company, equivalent to roughly €250, for each share held. The reason for this arrangement was that under French law Vivendi could not increase its existing 49 per cent stake in another domestic broadcaster, but could buy the entire film production business and all overseas activities of Canal Plus – hence the need to hive off the domestic broadcasting into a separate company in which shares could be issued to existing Canal Plus shareholders. The other parts would be acquired via an all-paper offer. Altogether, it cost €12.5 billion to take full control of Canal Plus.

In a further part of the overall transaction, Vivendi announced that it planned to float an initial 30–40 per cent of its water and waste management business, Vivendi Environnement, with the rest following later. A 27.7 per cent stake was duly listed on the Paris Bourse in July 2000 at a price of €34. The Seagram's drinks business, worth $6–7 billion, would also need to be sold, with the advantage of thereby clearing the debts inherited with Seagram.

The deals, seen by some as a wireless version of AOL Time Warner because of Vivendi's ownership interest in the likes of French mobile operator SFR and its Vizzavi venture, were subjected to careful scrutiny in both the USA and EU. At the end of July, the French broadcasting regulator (CSA) cleared the proposed takeover after Vivendi agreed to adjust the new structure by awarding ownership of the subscriber base of Canal Plus to Canal Plus Programmes. This new entity, which would incorporate all of the regulated businesses of Canal Plus, would be only 49 per cent owned by Vivendi Universal in order to conform with existing law preventing a single company from owning a controlling stake in a TV company. The residual part of Canal Plus would become a wholly-owned subsidiary of Vivendi Universal.

In August 2000, the Seagram purchase failed to be challenged by the Federal Communications Commission in the USA and hence passed by default. In November, the deal was approved by the European Commission after Vivendi agreed to sell its stake in BSkyB within two years – subject to the Commission approving the buyer – since BSkyB had links to the Fox film studio in the USA, and to offer competitors access to the new group's film production and co-production rights. Vivendi also agreed to let rival Internet portals have access to Universal's online music for five years to avoid the danger that Vizzavi would become dominant in the online music market and as a portal.[1] Once all of the various companies' shareholders had approved the deal, Vivendi Universal – hereafter simply Vivendi – was able to begin trading in mid-December 2000. By this time, however, a certain lack of faith among shareholders combined with difficult market conditions meant that Vivendi shares were trading roughly 40 per cent below the level at the time the offer was made in June (see Figure 8.1).

Early struggles

In February 2001, Jean-Paul Messier, who had been chairman and CEO of Vivendi since its formation, delivered a speech containing the following excerpt which sounded remarkably similar to the sentiments expressed at the launch of AOL Time Warner:[2]

> Our strategy is quite simple: begin with the consumer! Our goal is not to collect businesses. Our goal is to anticipate the needs for entertainment

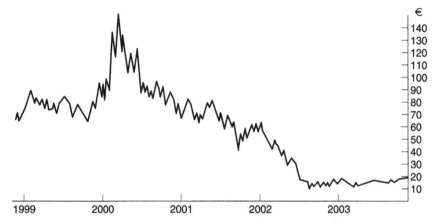

Figure 8.1 Vivendi Universal share price, 1999–2003 (euros).
Source: Daily share prices in the *Financial Times*.

and education, and to respond to these needs more efficiently than our competitors. . . . Our portfolio is totally focused on five key contents for tomorrow's Internet: education, games, music, sports, movies. Our access businesses are focused on the multi-distribution channels that will undergo the strongest growth for the Internet. . . . Our unique combination of key contents and distribution and packaging skills gives us a tremendous competitive advantage. It allows us to leverage our brands through aggressive cross marketing.

At the time, the company was organized into two parts: Media and Communications and Environmental Services. The former, in turn, was divided into five segments: Music, Publishing (VUP), TV and Film, Telecoms and Internet. Although it had no interests of consequence in radio or broadcast TV, it was probably true to say that Vivendi had the broadest range of operations of any media conglomerate at the time, roughly on a par with AOL Time Warner.[3] However, aside from any other matters, conglomerates are extremely difficult both to finance and manage, so the as yet unanswered question was whether Mr Messier was up to the job.

On the whole, the financial markets were initially very positive and, as shown in Figure 8.1, Vivendi's share price twice stemmed the downwards trend that was the common pattern of all TMT companies during mid/late 2000, rising from roughly €80 to €90 on both occasions. The news, in respect of both the restructuring and the company's finances, was mostly positive. In February, for example, Vivendi placed 32.3 million bonds exchangeable into Vivendi Environnement shares after five years on a one for one basis, equivalent to a 9.3 per cent stake, raising €1.8 billion.

It was also of interest that Vivendi retained links to AOL. In March 2001, as noted above, Vivendi agreed to sell its 55 per cent stake in AOL France to

AOL for $725 million, payment to be in the form of AOL Europe junior preference shares yielding a 6 per cent dividend. During April 2003, these shares would be redeemed in return for either cash, publicly traded AOL Europe common stock or AOLTW stock. However, a looming issue was that although several parts of the jigsaw had been assembled – for example, Vizzavi, Canal Plus and the AOLTW deal – Vivendi needed to complete additional deals either in the form of joint ventures or acquisitions. By selling off part of its stake in hived-off Vivendi Environnement (which would take with it a chunk of Vivendi's aggregate debt) or in BSkyB, Vivendi would at least be able to raise cash for the latter purpose, but whatever these arrangements its priority was to strengthen its US distribution networks via a link with either a telco, a mobile network, an Internet portal or a broadband cable operator. It was widely believed that Vivendi would prefer to increase its 43 per cent stake in USA Networks. Vivendi also needed to build a presence in the US educational sector similar to that it enjoyed in France. In Japan, moves were afoot to build on the relationship with Sony, initially in relation to Duet,[4] a joint venture online music service, but would possibly spread to a link with Sony's film studio, Columbia.

In May, the family of Edgar M. Bronfman, Jr. – now Executive Vice Chairman of Vivendi – which had acquired very large quantities of Vivendi shares in exchange for their holding in Seagram, decided to dispose of 16.9 million of these shares in order to diversify their portfolio now that the lock-up period had passed. The shares were acquired by Vivendi at an average price of €75.1. The Bronfman family and related charities still retained 6.1 per cent of the outstanding equity, but the financial markets saw this as a bad omen and the share price subsequently fell to a low of €40. This also reflected the take-over bid for Boston-based educational publisher, Houghton Mifflin, agreed in June 2001 at a price of $60 a share or $1.7 billion in cash overall plus the assumption of the publisher's net debt. The purchase was to be financed largely by the anticipated divestiture of VUP's Professional Information Division and free sheets. Once consummated, on 6 July, the merger left Vivendi as the second-largest educational publisher in the world.

The TV and Film division underwent further restructuring. Vivendi and News Corp. agreed to merge their pay-TV and digital distribution activities in Italy, respectively Telepiù and Stream. In the Nordic countries, Canal Plus sold its stake in the regional satellite platform Canal Digital, while securing a long-term exclusive distribution agreement for its Nordic premium channels. Canal Plus also re-organized its French premium channel. Further, in movie and TV production and distribution, Universal Pictures and StudioCanal were combined and StudioCanal acquired a controlling interest in Expand, France's leading, and Europe's third-ranked, producer of TV programming. It was anticipated that the outstanding publicly-owned shares in StudioCanal would be bought in.

On the telecoms front, SFR was awarded a third-generation mobile licence, albeit at the rather excessive price of $4.5 billion. Since only two applications were made for the four licences on offer, the price was subsequently reduced significantly to tempt other participants. Vivendi also acquired a stake in Maroc Télécom for $2.1 billion, obtaining control via board representation. In late May, Vivendi also acquired US-based MP3.com, the leading distributor of music on the Internet, for $372 million. Its shareholders were invited to accept $5 per share either in cash, part-cash plus Vivendi shares or exclusively the latter subject to an overall cap of $186 million in cash. Any shares issued would be treasury shares rather than new stock. The objective was to tie in MP3.com with Duet, which was shortly to be launched and had signed a distribution agreement with Yahoo!

In July 2001, Vivendi defied the slow-down in the advertising market (unlike AOLTW) by announcing what in the circumstances looked to be sparkling results for the half year.[5] However, less sanguine analysts were quick to point out that AOLTW was making progress in integrating its media empire around an Internet backbone, in which respect Vivendi was definitely a laggard. So far, there was little to show for Vivendi's efforts in this area. For example, although Vizzavi had access to some 80 million potential customers, only 530,000 had signed up in the UK and Netherlands by end-March 2001 and there had yet to be a launch elsewhere. One major difficulty was the poor performance of WAP handsets. Vizzavi continued to talk confidently of breaking even in 2003, but although six million customers eventually signed up by December 2001, reflecting, in part, the acquisition of Vizzavi Spain, projected revenues for 2002 remained hopelessly below target at $45 million.

It was possible to argue that AOLTW was US-centric and that Vivendi, Houghton Mifflin notwithstanding, remained transatlantic. This meant that there still remained an opportunity for the creation of a truly global media empire. As it happens, this just happened to be what Rupert Murdoch, chairman of News Corp., had in mind. The chosen vehicle would be Sky Global Networks, the holding company for Murdoch's international satellite TV businesses including BSkyB in which Vivendi still held a stake worth roughly $3 billion. Vivendi had been obliged to agree to dispose of this stake within two years to get permission from the European Commission to buy Seagram, but preferred not to dispose of it in the open market because of its size and, hence, the downwards pressure it would exert on the BSkyB share price. Instead, Vivendi preferred to seek an asset swap, preferably for BSkyB's minority stake in USA Networks. However, accepting that this was not to be forthcoming in the near future, Vivendi authorized the placement of $1.5 billion of BSkyB shares in December 2001 – equivalent to 35 per cent of Vivendi Universal's holding – in the form of equity certificates that would be convertible in October 2002.[6] At much the same time, the US Federal Trade Commission approved a consent decree clearing the way for the sale of the Seagram Spirits and Wine business to Diageo and Pernod Ricard for $8.1 billion.

In mid-December, there was an extraordinary burst of activity involving Vivendi. One element was an agreement with News Corp. to withdraw the planned merger between their Italian pay-TV interests, given the expectation that it would anyway be rejected by the regulators. As in the case of the Seagram purchase, regulators did not seemed to be enthused by any connection between Mr Murdoch and Mr Messier. Not content with his somewhat complex relationship with Mr Murdoch, Mr Messier also flagged the possibility of a link between the European programming and distribution assets of Canal Plus and John Malone's Liberty Media Corp. which controlled, inter alia, Dutch cable operator UPC.[7]

However, Mr Messier simultaneously announced a deal involving another media magnate, Barry Diller of USA Networks. In this case, what was proposed was that Vivendi would, in effect, swap its 43 per cent stake in USA Networks together with almost $4 billion in cash, bonds and shares, for control of two high-quality but mature cable networks, USA Network and Sci-Fi, serving a population of 160 million households. The total cost worked out as approximately $10.3 billion, with over half covered by the USA Networks stake plus $1.6 billion in cash and a further $1.6 billion in Vivendi shares issued to Liberty Media, equivalent to a 3.49 per cent stake.[8] A further $750 million was in the form of a commercial note issued to USA Networks. As part of the deal, Mr Diller would become Chairman and CEO of the enlarged TV and Film division – to be known as Vivendi Universal Entertainment (VUE) – with a 1.4 per cent stake but no contract at Vivendi. The fact that the division was being run by the co-founder of Canal Plus in 1984, Pierre Lescure, who was widely extolled in French cultural circles on account of Canal Plus bankrolling roughly 80 per cent of the highly active French film industry, indicated the potential for internal disarray about the role of Yankee philistines to add to that engendered by Mr Messier's decision in the aftermath of the Seagram takeover to move his domicile to New York, not to mention his assertion that 'the French cultural exception is dead'.[9] For Mr Diller it was, however, something of a homecoming given that, in 1997, it was Seagram that had sold him the USA Network, Sci-Fi and what became Studios USA.

The final element was the announcement that Vivendi would be buying just over 10 per cent of EchoStar Communications Corp. for $1.5 billion in cash. EchoStar would issue new shares with downside protection at $26.04 reserved for Vivendi independently of the outcome of the ongoing attempt by EchoStar to buy General Motors' subsidiary Hughes Electronics, the parent of satellite operator DirecTV.[10] The purchase would be partly financed by the $1.2 billion raised from the sale of 9.3 per cent of Vivendi Environnement. As a result of the investment, EchoStar agreed to broadcast at least five new channels created by VUE to its six million DISH Network satellite subscribers, who would also have access to Universal pay-per-view movies in relation to which EchoStar would pay VUE a fee per subscriber. In return, EchoStar obtained access to the 'MediaHighway' technology devised by Canal Plus for its G2 set-top box in Europe where it had pioneered interactive TV.[11]

Mr Messier, not surprisingly, was rather pleased with his month's work: previously, he asserted, US investors 'were not taking us seriously as a credible player. We were seen as an exotic French company.' From that point on, Vivendi would be 'recognised as a tier one media player'. The USA would account for 40 per cent of Vivendi's media turnover in 2002 as well as 60 per cent of its non-telecoms ebitda, but was this major re-orientation of activities going to pay dividends?

Causes for concern

The obvious place to begin an assessment of Vivendi's prospects at the beginning of 2002 is with the share price. Did the financial markets approve of Mr Messier's dealings? As can be seen from Figure 8.1, they were certainly excited by the prospects given the surge in the share price from roughly €40 to €60 during the second half of 2001, and in the immediate aftermath of the full sequence of announcements the price rose briefly above €60. However, it did not take long before the markets became distinctly underwhelmed by the reality, with the share price turning tail and continuing to fall steadily until it reached a mere €10.

There were many reasons for this, aside from the issuance of 55 million treasury shares worth €3.3 billion in early January which triggered a 5 per cent drop – despite ameliorating the debt position – because Mr Messier had previously promised to cancel them, thereby improving earnings per share. For example, the question could be asked why, if Mr Messier believed that content was king, he was willing to pay EchoStar a premium to distribute it. The answer appeared to be that until VUE was ready to roll as part of Vivendi, Mr Messier did not yet have any attractive US TV content to distribute. This was in principle only true in the short term, but the problem was that analysts took the view that, even with the VUE content and distribution, all was not well. For one thing, the USA Networks channels would be obliged to renew their own carriage deals with pay-TV operators. For another, should EchoStar fail to secure DirecTV – as most analysts predicted given the regulatory issues – Vivendi Universal would be linked to an operation which reached only 7 per cent of US households and would have no independent broadcast network of its own.

Other critics wondered why, earlier in 2001, Mr Messier had chosen to buy Houghton Mifflin rather than dealing with his lack of a US distribution network. At the time he appeared to set little store by this deficiency while emphasizing the virtues of multi-channel communication, yet towards the end of the year it had become a dominating theme. What did this say about the clarity of Mr Messier's vision?

But the most obvious source of concern were the financial implications of so many acquisitions in so short a time.[12] In particular, there was the matter of debt which, as shown by the accounts for 2001 in Table 8.1, had risen to €27 billion by the year end, in the process creating massive interest charges.

Table 8.1 Vivendi Universal financial summary, year ending 31 December (€ million)[a]

Summary	2002	2001	2000
Total revenue	58,150	57,360	41,580
of which:			
Vivendi Environnement	*30,038*	*29,094*	*–*
Vivendi Universal[b]	*28,112*	*25,404*[b]	*15,286*
of which:			
Cégétel	*7,067*	*6,384*	*–*
Universal Music Group	*6,276*	*6,560*	*–*
Universal Entertainment	*6,270*	*4,938*	*–*
Canal Plus	*4,833*	*4,563*	*–*
Maroc Telecom	*1,487*	*1,013*	*–*
Other[c]	*1,385*	*1,269*	*–*
Universal Games[d]	*794*	*657*	*–*
Operating income	3,788	3,795	1,823
Net interest expense	(1,333)	(1,455)	–
Income (loss) before exceptionals, etc.[e]	(954)	1,867	1,061
Net exceptionals	1,049[f]	2,365	3,812
Income tax	(2,556)	(1,579)	(1,009)
Goodwill amortization	(1,277)	(1,688)	(634)
Goodwill impairment	(18,442)[g]	(13,515)[j]	–
Net goodwill	20,500	37,600	47,133
Net income (loss)	(23,301)[h]	(13,597)[h]	2,299
Earnings/(loss) per basic share €	(21.43)	(13.53)	3.63
Total assets	69,300	139,000	150,738
Net debt	12,337[i]	37,100	25,514[k]
of which:			
Vivendi Universal	*12,337*	*21,352*	*–*

Source: www.vivendi.fr and http://finance.vivendiuniversal.com/finance/financials

Notes:
[a] The accounting data are extremely complex – the 2002 accounts when downloaded fill 647 pages! The figures recorded are 'actuals' in accordance with French GAAP. At 31 December 2002, Vivendi Universal applied the option proposed in paragraph 23100 of the French rules 99–02 and presented the results of businesses sold during 2002 on one line to the consolidated statement of income as 'equity in earnings of disposed businesses'. Disposed businesses include all of Vivendi Universal Publishing's operations excluding Vivendi Games, publishing activities in Brazil, the consumer press division (the disposal of which was completed in February 2003) and Comareg (the disposal of which was awaiting completion). [b] The total of 57,360 is achieved by adding in 2,862 of VUP assets sold during 2002. [c] Principally comprised of Vivendi Telecom International, Internet, Vivendi Valorisation and VUP assets not sold during 2002. [d] Formerly part of Vivendi Universal Publishing. [e] Exceptional items, income taxes, goodwill amortization, equity interest and minority interest. [f] Restricted in 2001 to unusual items of a non-recurrent nature. In 2002, these represented mainly capital gains on disposal or dilution of interests in BSkyB (€1.6 billion), Environnement (€1.4 billion), European publishing operations (€330 million), Canal Digital (€172 million) and Vizzavi Europe (€90 million) less capital losses on disposal of Houghton Mifflin (€822 million), EchoStar (€674 million), VUP B2B/Health (€298 million) and Telepiù (€360 million). [g] Including €5.4 billion at Canal Plus, €5.3 billion at Universal Music and €6.5 billion at VUE. [h] The largest up to that point in French corporate history. [i] The net debt of Environnement was deconsolidated as a result of significant stake reductions during the year. [j] Including €6 billion at Canal Plus, €3.1 billion at Universal Music, €1.3 billion at Universal Pictures and €600 million at Vivendi Environnement. [k] Compared to €22,833 million in 1999 but only €6,502 million in 1998.

True, Vivendi had been careful not to pay cash for everything, but even the widespread use of equity to buy other companies' shares at a premium to their ruling price creates acres of goodwill which need to be amortized, and, unless the stock market is subsequently buoyant – which was certainly not the case in 2001 – recognition of impairment on a potentially heroic scale. On the plus side, Vivendi had occasionally used existing treasury stock (authorized for issue but held in reserve) rather than new shares to finance acquisitions, had yet to issue a profits warning, and the sale of the Seagram drinks business was expected to bring in $8 billion during 2002, but could the losses be reined in?

Even the nature of the organization that had been created gave cause for concern. Because it gave every indication of becoming a conglomerate, Vivendi ran the risk of being valued at much less than the sum of its parts. Its growth also appeared to be dependent upon maintaining the stream of acquisitions. To offset these factors, Mr Messier needed to prove that the new acquisitions would create synergies. He himself had extensive experience as a banker involved in M&A activity, but would the strong personalities he had acquired along the way bend to his will? Few thought this likely as these included, for example, Barry Diller, known as much for his temper as for his business acumen. Furthermore, he had been granted a stake in VUE with a guaranteed value of $275 million, and it was arguable whether he would respond by putting most of his efforts into the running of his other interests. He also had a patchy relationship with the Bronfman family – Edgar Bronfman Jr. had resigned his executive position at Vivendi in the run up to the USA Networks deal.

Finally, there was the issue of the strategy in Europe which had faded into the background somewhat during the forays into the USA. On the face of it, Vivendi had little business trying to compete in telecommunications. Cégétel and SFR might be major players in France, but were not active elsewhere in Europe. For its part, Canal Plus continued to lose money outside France and Vizzavi was going nowhere fast despite investment of €1.6 billion and the backing of Vodafone.

Or, perhaps, the final issue was why Vivendi Universal still owned the majority of Vivendi Environnement.

The plot unravels

In mid-February 2002, Vivendi officially announced that it had agreed to buy Stream.[13] However, on 1 March, the Italian anti-trust authority halted the deal for 45 days while it investigated its implications. While the outcome was awaited rumours began to fly about a far more interesting development, namely the possible ousting of Mr Messier. This seemed to be inconceivable to some – had he not inherited a grey utilities business seeped in the traditions of the French civil service and transformed it into this very modern conglomerate with fingers in all sorts of 'new economy' pies? Well, 'yes', came the reply, but his ego and boundless ambition came at a price, and if it was the price of a Vivendi share it was rather low and getting progressively lower. Significantly, however, it was not just disgruntled shareholders who had lost patience but top executives, and, in mid-April, Denis Olivennes, a trusted aide and possible successor who felt that the goalposts were constantly being moved at Canal Plus, tendered his resignation. This was rapidly followed by the firing of the Canal Plus CEO, the popular Pierre Lescure, and his replacement by Xavier Couture from broadcaster TF1.[14]

Unfortunately for Mr Messier, this coincided with the run-up to the French presidential elections and all of the candidates were quick to express their disgust at his behaviour, as were myriad film stars and Vivendi employees. Having just written off half of what he had paid for Canal Plus, and having now made what he perceived as his once-and-for-all move to stamp his authority on its operations, it was Mr Messier who emerged with his reputation – and possibly his job – on the line.[15] Suggestions that the Vivendi Universal share price would rise were he to be dismissed appeared to be supported by news that value investor Vincent Bolloré had acquired a half per cent stake at €37 per share. The simultaneous announcement that Vivendi had sold 75 per cent of its healthcare and business publishing assets for €1.2 billion plus a conditional deferred payment to a Cinven/Carlyle/Apax Partners consortium was either good (since it would reduce the net debt) or bad (since it was much less than had originally been expected) depending upon one's point of view.

The Vivendi AGM was scheduled for 24 April 2002. It was expected to be a torrid affair, but Mr Messier was provided some protection by his willingness to waive his share of a massive new stock option scheme valued at up to €2 billion if the Vivendi share price had failed to recover to its value on 1 January 2002 by the end of September. However, it was clear that shareholders wanted him to concentrate upon debt reduction while the French establishment would not tolerate any further disposal of shares in Vivendi Environnement which meant that, in effect, there was little latitude for either disposals or acquisitions and that the share price would continue to suffer from the conglomerate discount.

A particular issue therefore arose in relation to the telecommunications interests since Mr Messier wanted to take control of Cégétel and SFR and rebalance Vivendi towards this sector when the existing shareholder pact expired in September. In contrast, many analysts thought that Vivendi should quit the sector altogether as it lacked economies of scale. In the event, the first-quarter results for 2003 revealed that the Telecoms Division was the only one to be showing any growth. Furthermore, Vizzavi was proving to be a serious disappointment despite attempting a new business model that provided improved benefits to content providers, and it was generally accepted within Vivendi that the best option was now to sell out to Vodafone.

Although Mr Diller expressed public support for Mr Messier, he was known to harbour ambitions to run a US television network. He was alleged to be angling for a merger between a hived-off VUE and NBC, the TV network owned by General Electric, but such a move would signify the break-up of Vivendi and the reversal of Mr Messier's strategy. At a public meeting, held at the end of April, a heckler was applauded when he responded 'your resignation' when Mr Messier rhetorically asked what the answer was to the company's problems. Mr Messier's own suggested answer was 'transparency', but this did not go down with investors who noted that whereas the share price stood at €35, the company was committed to buying back 19.7 million shares at between €60 and €80 during 2002 and a further 3.1 million at €50.5 in January 2003.[16] It also suffered an embarrassing credit downgrade by Moody's from Baa2 to Baa3, its lowest investment grade, to which Mr Messier responded by reiterating the company's commitment to debt reduction and specifically to lowering debt to less than three times ebitda by the end of 2002. However, Moody's noted that payment of cash upon completion of the agreed acquisition of USA Networks would bump up the debt substantially in the short term.

In early May, with the European Commission having finally approved the sale of the 27 per cent stake in TV channel operator Multithématiques, which formed part of the package whereby Liberty Media would exchange various assets for a stake in Vivendi, the question was whether Mr Malone would raise objections to the fact that the Vivendi shares were now worth so much less than they were at the time the deal was originally agreed. However, Mr Malone accepted that he had negotiated a deal which took no account of subsequent share price movements. This did not mean, however, that he was exactly happy with the way Mr Messier was running the company.[17] Not long after, News Corp. notified Vivendi that it would if necessary go to court to force completion of the agreed merger between Telepiù and Stream which Vivendi was seeking to terminate on the grounds that the regulators had set ten onerous pre-conditions for the deal to be authorized. To add fuel to the fire, Canal Plus Technologies had filed a lawsuit against Mr Murdoch's digital encryption company, NDS, alleging that it had cracked its technology and disseminated it over the Internet so that it could be pirated. With Mr Murdoch also up in arms – although he was somewhat mollified by the fact that Vivendi had severed its final ties with BSkyB by placing its remaining 13 per cent stake on the market, raising a much-needed $2.4 billion – it could be said that Mr Messier certainly knew how to annoy his main rivals.[18]

He could also be said to be his own worst enemy. Having announced at the recent AGM that he had no intention of reducing the stake in Vivendi Environnement, he now began to suggest that reducing it below 50 per cent would be a good idea as it would allow Vivendi to deconsolidate its €14 billion net debt. Needless to say this idea was hugely unpopular among the political elite, who were appalled at the possibility of foreign control and whose response was a veiled warning that French municipalities might be able as a consequence to cancel their all-important contracts. Mr Messier pointed out that any disposal could be restricted to, say, other French banks and utilities, and that he would be willing to stand down as Chairman of Environnement. With a major board meeting about to take place, Mr Messier's survival appeared to be in the balance.

In the event, the eight-hour meeting did not result in his departure. On the other hand, it did not produce a clear strategic blueprint either and the share price promptly fell sharply. On a more positive note for the company, Standard & Poor's withdrew the threat of a credit downgrade to 'junk' given the cash inflow from the BSkyB stake, and Mr Messier was personally able to celebrate the award of a bonus worth 250 per cent of his salary for 2001 which he offered to invest in Vivendi stock.[19]

Progress was forthcoming in relation to Vivendi Environnement with a Vivendi board decision – announced shortly after the close of the presidential election to reduce controversy – gradually to reduce its holding to 40 per cent via the disposal of a 15 per cent stake followed by a rights issue. The Environnement share price settled at €32.50, exactly the level at which it had begun life two years earlier.

However, this was insufficient to save Mr Messier. His strategy falling apart at the seams, Mr Messier decided to fall on his sword before he was pushed – at least two banks, allegedly pressurized by the political establishment, intended to withhold further loans unless he was removed – and on 2 July announced that he would be standing aside in favour of Jean-René Fourtou, vice-chairman of drug group Aventis. Mr Fourtou, who would be appointed initially for a six-month period, would immediately undertake a strategic review. The share price rose by 10 per cent, but it seemed extremely unlikely that the financial market's preferred solution – the sale of Cégétel and Vivendi Environnement – would transpire due to political considerations. The prospect of Canal Plus falling into foreign ownership was also clearly off limits, which certainly constrained what could realistically be done to pay down the debt. As €1.8 billion of this was about to fall due, and there was only €2.4 billion available in cash and unused credit lines, securing new sources of liquidity was clearly a matter of some urgency,[20] although the prompt placement of a 15 per cent stake in Environnement which, combined with a fully underwritten rights issue, would reduce the Vivendi Universal stake to 42 per cent, was a move in the right direction, permitting the deconsolidation of roughly €18 billion of debt.

Let the fire sale begin

In practice, the disposal of the Environnement stake for €1.5 billion notwithstanding, matters were even more urgent than they seemed, and the term 'crisis' began to be bandied about. The immediate trigger was Moody's decision to downgrade Vivendi's €19 billion of debt to a 'junk' rating of Ba1 – Standard & Poor's was content to reduce its own rating to the lowest investment grade of BBB – for the time being – thereby forcing some institutions to sell off their Vivendi shares. The credit agencies estimated that

Vivendi needed to refinance €6 billion of debt falling due by the end of 2002 and a further €2.8 billion falling due during the first half of 2003. Given the predicted cash shortfall, it was widely held that there would need to be a fire sale of assets, possibly including one of the five divisions in its entirety. The share price promptly fell a further 25 per cent.[21]

Predictably, the company's new board – which included the newly installed Claude Bébéar, the honorary chairman of Axa and a close friend of Mr Fourtou, who was given the specific responsibility for financing a rescue plan, and Henri Lachmann, chairman of Schneider Electric, to lead the strategy workforce – chose to put some of the non-core assets on the block to begin with, including the recently acquired stake in EchoStar and some shares in DuPont and overseas telcos (see Table 8.2). These were to be added to the

Table 8.2 Vivendi Universal on the block, August 2002–February 2003

On offer	Details	Value (€ million)
Definite		
Canal Plus	51 per cent	c. 2,000
Canal Plus International	Non-French pay-TV including Telepiù	c. 2,000[a]
Canal Plus technologies	89 per cent of decoder manufacturer	190 achieved
Express-Expansion	Newspapers and magazines	200 achieved
Houghton Mifflin	US publisher	1,567 achieved
Paris St Germain	Football club	?
Vizzavi	50 per cent of Internet portal	143 achieved
Odds and ends[b]	Property, industrial etc.	?
Possible		
DuPont	16.4 million shares	c. 700
EchoStar	10 per cent	1,037 achieved
Maroc Télécom	35 per cent	c. 1,500[c]
Recreation	Theme parks	at least 1,500
Universal Music	Global music group	at least 7,000
Universal Pictures	Hollywood studio	at least 4,000
USA Networks	Cable operator	at least 5,000
To be kept		
Canal Plus	49 per cent	c. 2,000
Cégétel/SFR	Controlling stake in mobile operator	at least 6,000[d]
Vivendi Environnement	40.6 per cent	1,856 achieved[e]
Vivendi Universal Publishing	European/Latin American publishing	1,138 achieved

Notes:
[a] Telepiù was provisionally sold for €871 in October 2002. The payment of the cash element of €457 million was made in April 2003. [b] Including Mr Messier's New York apartment, a Venetian palazzo, a French château, a Chinese orange juice maker and an aircraft leasing company. Achieved sales in 2002 were 25 per cent of B2B/Health for €150 million, 0.8 per cent of Lagardère for €44 million and 6.7 per cent of Vinci for €143 million in July 2002; 34 per cent of Sithe Energies Inc. for €319 million in December 2002; and unspecified others for a total of €186 million. In April 2003, Viventures Partners was sold for €9 million and in May, Comareg was sold for €135 million and Vivendi Telecom Hungary for €325 million. [c] In early May 2003, Vivendi Universal decided instead to buy a further 16 per cent for €690 million under the terms of a put option when it received no satisfactory offers for its existing stake. [d] Vivendi Universal bought BT's stake in early December for an additional €4 billion. [e] For one half, with options to purchase the other half for roughly €2 billion.

disposals already accomplished during the first half of 2002 in the form of B2B Publishing for €900 million, real estate for €100 million and Canal Plus Nordic TV for €270 million. Meanwhile, a value of €12 billion was placed on the Universal Music Group – although it was accepted that regulators were rarely willing to countenance mergers between large music groups so the list of potential buyers was short – and of €20 billion on VUE in which Barry Diller and Edgar Bronfman, Jr were expected to take an interest. Although the French assets were clearly more controversial, a value of €9 billion was placed on Canal Plus assuming it was to be bought by TF1, Lagardère or investor Vincent Bolloré. As for VUP, that was potentially worth roughly €6 billion. In total, this represented more than twice Vivendi's market value, which was hardly a vote of confidence. Nor indeed, was Philips decision to write down the value of its 3.5 per cent stake in Vivendi by €1.5 billion.

As if its problems were not sufficient to be going on with, Vivendi now found itself accused in *Le Monde* of accounting irregularities, although it transpired that the company's accounts had in fact accorded with French accounting rules and that the financial markets had known why there was a question mark over the accounts all along.[22] While more of a storm in a teacup than a scandal of Enron proportions, the newspaper report still managed to send the share price down a further 40 per cent, ending below €20 for the first time. The general nervousness surrounding Vivendi did, however, provide News Corp. with an opportunity to slash its offer price for Telepiù – to €1 billion for the core business and €500 million for future Italian football rights and two terrestrial TV licences in Italy – on the grounds that it could not attract other investors at the original price.

The first strategic decision announced by Mr Fourtou was the breaking up of Canal Plus and the sale of its international operations. Excluding Telepiù, some €2 billion was expected to be forthcoming. In mid-August, the board approved a plan to dispose of at least €10 billion of assets, of which half would go by mid-2003. Houghton Mifflin would be top of the list. It also approved the cancellation of 20.9 million treasury shares linked to stock option plans and announced that it was negotiating a €3 billion credit facility with the company's banks. However, in the short term it was obliged to reveal the results for the first half of 2002 which included a net loss of €12.3 billion and a write-off of €11 billion of goodwill, largely relating to the Seagram purchase – excluding the write-off and exceptionals, the loss was accordingly trivial. Nevertheless, this was met with a credit downgrade to junk by Standard & Poor's and a drop further into junk territory by Moody's. The share price unsurprisingly hit what was to prove to be its all-time low.

Mr Fourtou responded by pledging to tell the truth in future about Vivendi's situation, but Lex was unimpressed since Mr Fourtou seemed to think that the truth encompassed the latitude to delay asset sales.[23] Still, he decided to cease any further investment in Vizzavi and entered negotiations to sell Express-Expansion, the stable of flagship magazines including *L'Express*

– which was not, however, on the official list for disposal because of the potential political fallout.[24] The sale was completed on 31 August to Socpresse, owner of centre-right newspaper *Le Figaro*, for over €300 million shortly after the disposal of the 50 per cent stake in Vizzavi to Vodafone for €143 million. At the same time, Blackstone and Thomas H. Lee, two US private equity groups, submitted a joint offer for Houghton Mifflin.

In mid-September, Vivendi was able to confirm that it had agreed the €3 billion short/medium-term bank loan facility – of which €1 billion was needed to repay the emergency loan granted in July – albeit at a high rate of interest. This gave the company some breathing space, but it clearly needed to press on with its disposal programme, commencing with the sale of Canal Plus Technologies to Thomson Multimedia for €190 million. Although it had not intended to prioritize the sale of its European publishing assets, preferring to concentrate on Houghton Mifflin, these attracted the attention of French private equity groups PAI and Eurazeo, as well as media and aerospace group Lagardère – all of which, to the joy of politicians, were French. Meanwhile the situation at VUE became much cloudier when it was revealed that covenants in the deal with USA Networks effectively prevented any change in VUE's structure without the approval of Mr Diller who owned a 5.44 per cent stake via his USA Interactive company in addition to his personal stake, and that VUE had promised not to sell any USA Networks assets for 15 years.[25]

In October, the sale of Telepiù to News Corp. for €871 million – comprising €457 million in cash and €414 million in inherited debt – was finally agreed subject to regulatory clearances. This was much less than had originally been expected and Vivendi felt it necessary to announce that it would not conduct a fire sale of its other assets. This meant that it felt obliged to reject all of the offers for Houghton Mifflin as inadequate and proceed with the sale of the European and Latin American publishing interests to Lagardère at an agreed price of €1.14 billion. Because of the distinct possibility that the deal would be rejected by the antitrust authorities, and in order to ensure it got the cash, Vivendi actually sold the assets to Natexis Banques Populaires to sell on at its leisure.

The need for cash suddenly became much more acute when Vodafone offered to buy out the other minority shareholders in Cégétel/SFR or, alternatively, to buy out Vivendi's stake as well. Vivendi relied upon these companies for the majority of its operating profits, so it was extremely reluctant to let them come under the control of Vodafone. This could be avoided by exercising its pre-emption right to buy only the 26 per cent stake in Cégétel held by BT at the price tabled by Vodafone – €4 billion – while leaving Vodafone to mop up the stake held by SBC. On the other hand, accepting the Vodafone offer would remove its immediate debt problems at a stroke. Analysts regarded this as a 'no-brainer' and unanimously advised Mr Fourtou to take the €6.8 billion on offer. Needless to say, the assets being French, Mr Fourtou got the courts to extend the deadline for acceptance to mid-December and set about raising the money to buy out BT, in part by agreeing a bid for Houghton Mifflin from a private equity consortium including Thomas H. Lee and Bain Capital at the previously unacceptable price of €1.57 billion (comprising €1.20 billion in cash plus €370 million of debt taken on). Moody's promptly downgraded Vivendi's credit rating to Baa3. In early November, Vivendi announced that it would also renege on its commitment to retain its stake in Environnement, initially by placing 20.3 per cent with a small group of companies to be found by investment banks. These companies would take over the commitment not to dispose of the Environnement shares before the end of 2003, and would have the option to double their stakes before the end of 2004. Pending the ability to name the companies, Vivendi launched a three-year €885 million convertible bond – at €12.7 – with a massive yield of 8.25 per cent. The companies were subsequently named as a consortium led by Electricité de France, almost all French, which paid €1.86 billion in total or €22.5 per share compared to a market price of €25. They were given the option to buy an equal number of shares at €26.5.

Shortly after, Vivendi announced that it had received an informal offer from Marvin Davis, a Texan oil billionaire, to buy the whole of VUE for $15 billion plus $5 billion of debt taken on. This was rebuffed as inadequate since analysts' calculations indicated a price lying between €20 billion and €25 billion plus debt, excluding the computer games business which was not being sold along with the publishing assets and was valued at €1.4 billion.[26] While Mr Davis retired to reconsider his position, Vivendi moved to buy the BT stake in Cégétel at the beginning of December for €2.7 billion in cash plus €1.3 billion of inherited debt. It also announced its intention to demerge VUE in 2003 either by listing it separately or selling it outright. Meanwhile, the collapse of EchoStar's takeover bid for Hughes meant that a change of plan was needed, and the decision was taken to convert the existing convertible preference stock into ordinary shares to be followed by a possible disposal. However, the latter would depend on EchoStar's share price since Vivendi was guaranteed the $26 per share it paid provided it held on to the shares for two and a half years after conversion. In the event, it decided not to wait and sold the stake for $1.04 billion, registering a loss of $430 million in the process. That meant that roughly €4.3 billion had been raised from Environnement, Houghton Mifflin and EchoStar during the Christmas period, leaving Vivendi with €13 billion of debt.

Back to basics in 2003

In early January 2003, the deal-making picked up once again with an agreed offer worth $450 million for Vivendi Telecom Hungary from American International Group and GMT Communications Partners. Vivendi also signed a letter of intent to sell its 49 per cent stake in Polish telco Elektrim Telekomunicacja (ET) – itself holding a 51 per cent stake in mobile operator

PTC – to Polsat for €600 million. This would leave Vivendi with a direct 10 per cent stake in ET parent Elektrim. Nevertheless, the credit rating agencies refused to return Vivendi Universal to investment grade status unless there were further disposals. It was also noted that Vivendi's debt pile was denominated in euros while any US disposals would produce dollars. With the euro now beginning to strengthen against the dollar, any offer made in dollars would be expected to fall in value prior to completion of the deal.

At the end of January some progress was made in relation to pay-TV in Spain when Sogécable, jointly owned by Canal Plus and Spanish publishing group Prisa, agreed to merge with Telefónica's Via Digital. Canal Plus would be left with a 16.4 per cent stake in an enlarged Sogécable, but the best that could be hoped for initially would be a reduction in the losses previously recorded. In contrast, Mr Fourtou effectively set out to alienate Mr Bronfman Jr. by putting the Seagram collection of art up for sale. For his part, Mr Diller resigned as chairman of VUE in order to avoid any possibility of conflicts of interest should he become involved in bidding for VUE assets.

The results for 2002, announced in early March (see Table 8.1), made fairly grim reading and appeared to reflect those of a year earlier with the massive loss of €23.3 billion – once again, a French record after France Télécom had temporarily snatched that unwanted title. This was very largely accounted for by goodwill impairment charges at Canal Plus (€5.4 billion) – sufficiently severe to forestall any thought of an initial public offer or trade sale[27] – Universal Music (€5.3 billion) and VUE (€6.5 billion). Total revenues were up slightly but the operating position was basically unchanged. Only on the net debt front was there a clear improvement because Environnement's €15.7 billion net debt was now deconsolidated and sales worth many billions of euros had been effected.

To these could be added €257 million of warrants in USA Interactive sold in February, at which time the fairly modest amounts due for Express-Expansion and Canal Plus Technologies were also received. However, despite these inflows and €4 billion of cash in hand, the financial situation was more precarious than it seemed due to the need to redeem €3.4 billion of bonds. Hence, at the end of March 2003, with its total debt in the €15–17 billion region, Vivendi took steps to protect its dwindling cash reserves by restructuring its debt and raising an additional €3.5 billion ($3.72 billion) of liquidity. It announced the issue of €1 billion of seven-year, high-yield bonds through a privately placed offer and signed a €2.5 billion three-year loan with eight banks. It reiterated its target of €7 billion of asset disposals during 2003 and a debt target of €11 billion by the year end. It also predicted that its credit rating would move from 'junk' to investment grade no later than the first half of 2004. But who would be buying the assets on offer?

At the end of March, initial offers were tabled for Universal Games, valued at between €1 billion and €1.5 billion with Microsoft and Sony Corp. leading the bidders. At the end of April, it also became known that African operator, MSI Cellular, had made a bid for the majority stake in Kenyan mobile operator, KenCell, being divested by Vivendi. However, these positive signs in relation to the debt position were rapidly cancelled out by rumours that Vivendi would face a potential $2.7 billion tax liability inherited with the purchase of Seagram in respect of its return of DuPont shares in 1995,[28] and what with potential billion dollar penalties if it sold VUE (payable to the Bronfman family) or the cable TV channels (payable to Mr Diller – see below), it seemed as though progress would be patchy and quite possibly litigious. The situation was not helped by the revelation that Mr Messier had earned €5.6 million in 2002 – 10 per cent more than in 2001 – even though he had lost his job and the company had made a record-breaking loss.

Early April saw the sale of private equity fund Viventures Partners for €9 million to EGlobal Asset Capital, and at the end of the month the cash element of the Telepiù sale, amounting to €457 million, was finally forthcoming. These sums paled beside the rumoured $6 billion being offered by Apple for Universal Music. However, the accounts for the first quarter of 2003 indicated that the Division's revenue had fallen by 19 per cent compared to a year earlier, so the rumour was greeted with general scepticism. The €135 million paid by the France Antilles Group for Comareg in late May was scant consolation, and the €325 million finally forthcoming for Vivendi Telecom Hungary somewhat less than expected. In contrast, not merely did Vivendi decide not to proceed with the sale of its stake in Maroc Télécom in view of the unacceptable offers received, but was obliged under the terms of a put option to acquire a further 16 per cent for €690 million.

In early May, Vivendi's lawyers came up with a proposal for a sale and buy-back of the US entertainment assets in order to avoid the potential break-up liabilities of up to $2 billion. These liabilities were in the form of payments to USA Interactive and its chairman, Barry Diller, which together controlled 6.9 per cent of VUE. Mr Diller, the former chairman of VUE, had secured the payment guarantees to minimize potential tax liabilities arising from the €12.4 billion ($14 billion) sale of his US entertainment assets to Vivendi in 2002. Although Vivendi disputed the size of the liabilities, it hoped that if bidders for assets such as Universal Television – comprising TV production, distribution and the USA and Sci-Fi channels – agreed to acquire the whole of VUE and subsequently resold the non-TV businesses back to Vivendi, no compensation at all would become necessary. This was, however, disputed by almost everyone outside Vivendi. Aside from the consortium led by Mr Davis, which had already tabled an offer of roughly $20 billion for the whole of VUE plus Universal Music, the US TV network owned by General Electric, NBC, appeared to be the most likely participant in such a deal and, indeed, had opened negotiations (although it was not interested in Universal or the theme parks), with Liberty Media, Viacom and MGM the only others judged to have both the financial muscle and interest to participate. For his part, Mr Bronfman Jr. was known to be trying to put together a consortium but was not expected to succeed. Meanwhile, US private equity group, Blackstone, was negotiating in relation to the theme parks. There was a suggestion that any bidder for the whole of VUE would in practice only bid for a majority stake, thereby reducing the financing needed and avoiding tax penalties for Vivendi. A deadline of 23 June was laid down for offers to be tabled, which it transpired had to be in respect of the whole of VUE, with a view to choosing a list of three preferred bidders in July. Viacom immediately declined to bid, but it was observed that whoever acquired VUE would probably sell off certain parts afterwards so there would potentially be a good deal of behind-the-scenes negotiating before the issue was finally unravelled and, indeed, Viacom subsequently returned to express an interest in the cable networks.

The first-quarter results of 2003, announced in June, revealed operating profits of €844 million, a net loss of €319 million and net debt of €15.3 billion. The company reiterated its full year earnings targets. However, the operating loss at Universal Music, where sales fell by 20 per cent during the quarter, was a source of concern.

In mid-June, Mr Diller gave notice to Vivendi Universal that USA InterActive had exercised its right of first refusal and would purchase the remaining 28.28 million warrants to acquire USAi shares that Vivendi held for a total consideration of $407.4 million. Vivendi was left with a holding of 56.6 million shares in USAi. Shortly thereafter, the headquarters of Universal Studios and other property in California was declared to be under offer for $260 million. At the end of June, Vivendi sold its 26.3 per cent stake in Spanish 3G licensee, Xfera, to its other shareholders for a symbolic one euro. Investors were no better pleased by the news that a New York tribunal had awarded Mr Messier a severance package of $23.6 billion (€20.6 billion), even though this had been arranged with only one non-executive just before his departure and not agreed by the full board. The award predictably became bogged down in litigation.[29]

A board meeting in early July decided that Universal Music would not now be sold, partly because it was unlikely to achieve a satisfactory price and would crystallize tax liabilities – and accordingly rejected the bid from Mr Davis that included it. All other bidders were asked to resubmit offers for the whole of VUE by the end of August. Vivendi appeared to be leaning towards NBC which had proposed an equity-sharing partnership, combining its network and cable channels with VUE and offering Vivendi the option of an IPO or trade sale at a later date.[30] However, NBC was not entirely acceptable because of the absence of a cash element in the proposed deal and it was replaced by Comcast in Vivendi's affections – but not for long, as Vivendi responded to what it perceived as under-valuations by threatening not to sell to anyone and Comcast withdrew.[31] With Liberty Media also dropping out, the front-runner then appeared to be a consortium led by Edgar Bronfman, Jr. since it was willing to provide $8 billion in up-front cash. However, it was unwilling to match Vivendi's $14 billion asking price so in the end it was NBC that entered exclusive negotiations based upon an offer of $3.8 billion in cash up front (of which $3.3 billion would go to Vivendi), $1.7 billion in debt reduction and a 20 per cent stake in the merged company to be called

NBC Universal; which it would have the option to sell in three tranches commencing in 2006 with a possible disposal of $3 billion plus a further $4 billion in each of the following two years. Vivendi took it upon itself to unravel the relationship with Mr Diller without needing to draw upon the cash, mainly by selling its holding in USAi. Vivendi Universal expected to retain control over the Studio Canal cable network and the computer games unit, but raised the possibility of a disposal of its stake if its value rose sufficiently.

Meanwhile, Vivendi would create a telecoms group based around SFR and an entertainment group based around Universal Music and Canal Plus even though the latter offered no obvious synergies. On the one hand, the telecoms group was about to shrink in size as Vivendi accepted the offer of €700 million in cash from Deutsche Telekom for its stake in Polska Telefonia Cyfrowa (PTC) of Poland, with payment due at the beginning of 2004, while on the other Vivendi expressed the intent to increase its stake in Maroc Télécom from 35 to 51 per cent by exercising an option to purchase provided by the government.

The first-half figures announced in September 2003 revealed healthy operating profits at three of the four main units – telecoms, pay-TV and VUE – but Universal Music slid into loss as did Universal Games as less profitable game console sales rose relative to personal computer titles. Comparisons across the board with a year earlier were problematic because the size and structure of the company had changed significantly. The sale of VUE was expected to lead to a reduction in net debt below €5 billion by the end of 2004. The amount of cash involved in the sale was not reduced and the deal was finally signed on 8 October although it was expected to take six months for full regulatory clearances to be achieved. Additional cash would hopefully be forthcoming from the sale of the Newsworld International cable network – omitted from the VUE deal – to a group of investors led by Al Gore for €70 million ($82 million). On a less positive note, Vivendi's hopes of selling its stake in Poland's PTC were dashed, at least temporarily, when partner Elektrim refused to accept the price being offered.[32]

In an interesting development in late September, given the previous antipathy between the companies, Mr Fourtou announced as part of the presentation of first-half results which in other respects were satisfactory, with Canal Plus moving into profitability for the first time since 1996, that 'Our strategy is clear. We are part of the Vodafone family.' By this he appeared to mean that Vivendi would be tapping into the purchasing and marketing clout of partner Vodafone, and introducing an equivalent to the popular Vodafone live! portal. This sparked rumours that this was the initial step along the path leading to a takeover of SFR by Vodafone. In mid-October, substance was added to the rumours when Vivendi and Vodafone announced that they had agreed in principle to merge Cégétel's various units including SFR, Cofira and Transtel into the Cégétel Group and rename it SFR. As a result, Vodafone would hold 43.9 per cent of SFR and Vivendi would hold

55.8 per cent, with the remainder held by some minority shareholders of Cofira. In addition, Cégétel and French railway operator SNCF would merge the two units of their fixed-wire businesses, with Cégétel taking a 65 per cent stake in the merged entity. These arrangements were expected to release tax credits leading to a €400 million improvement in cash flow.[33]

Conclusions

The financial affairs of Vivendi Universal are complicated – its annual report for 2002 is extraordinarily lengthy. Much of the conglomerate put together by Mr Messier was assembled quickly and must have involved the company's accountants working overtime to meet publication deadlines. Unfortunately, a good deal more overtime will be needed to prepare the accounts for 2003 which will have to grapple with the dismantling of Mr Messier's empire. Mr Messier was nicknamed J6M, standing for 'Jean-Marie Messier, Moi-Même, Maître du Monde'. He took pleasure in this and used it for the title of his autobiography. However, at the time of his resignation he did accept that he had done 'a bit too much, a bit too quickly', and even that his media profile had been 'excessive'.

Mr Messier was by background deeply imbued with the traditional French approach to business and its links to the state. However, he chose to 'go Hollywood' and blow a breath of Yankee fresh air into the dull affairs of the French utility he headed without really appreciating how risky such a venture would be. This was not merely because the French establishment was far from ready to welcome such a disruptive force into its midst, but also because it threw him up against some of the shrewdest operators in the media. At one time or another – and eventually all at the same time – he took on Mr Murdoch, the French political and cultural establishment, US investors and the Vivendi board – from which it might reasonably be concluded that he was rather bad at relationships. This was not helped by his unpredictability: for example, he was adamant that he would not sell Environnement then did precisely that.

On the other hand, it can be argued that business is not a popularity contest and that those portrayed as the 'bad guys' often win out in the end. Mr Murdoch, for example, tends to fight battles he can win in the end, but Mr Messier just appeared to like to fight regardless of the outcome. Had he been right in his crucial assumption about the prospects for TMT companies compared to utilities – which he shared with many others – all would probably have been forgiven, but as it was he took a big bet on the Internet that didn't pay off. In retrospect, it can be argued that he was good at putting together deals but that these were chosen with insufficient care with the result that there was a lack of a workable grand strategy. Hence, as soon as the business environment began to deteriorate it was easy for analysts to pick holes and drive down the share price. The crucial problem, given that Mr Messier was trying to assemble a media conglomerate, was the lack of synergies: the strong set of US entertainment assets sat uncomfortably with Canal Plus and there was no obvious logic to the stake in Cégétel/SFR especially given the poor performance of Vizzavi. Furthermore, Houghton Mifflin's educational content did not gel with the film and music businesses. As for Vivendi Environnement, this was a legacy without any synergies.

The new board of Vivendi represents the return of the old guard of French capitalism. Mr Fourtou is on the boards of Axa and Schneider; Messrs Fourtou, Henri Lachmann and Bernard Arnault – a recently outgoing director – are all members of Mr Bébéar's private club. What this means is that bankruptcy will be avoided at all costs. In mid-May 2002 the incoming French government made no secret of the fact that it would protect Vivendi from foreign predators. The Minister for Culture went on record as follows: 'The purchase of this group by a foreign company would have incalculable consequences. It would threaten the cultural diversity to which we are so attached . . . we would seek to block or control such a sale within the limits permitted by the law'. However, the reality is that although the fire sale is eventually going to remove any fears about the company going out of business, it is still going to leave that which cannot be sold off at an acceptable price, which is hardly the recipe for a profitable operation. The accumulation of too much debt made it impossible to move forward. Unfortunately, it may be that the removal of much of that debt will also achieve the same result. What hampered Vivendi Universal above all else was the inability to achieve a sufficient cash flow from its valuable assets. The position remains that it has full ownership only of its music assets, and while, for example, moving to majority ownership of Cégétel/SFR is a step forward in cash flow terms, the position remains unsatisfactory. Furthermore, unless a new structure can be devised that satisfies the financial markets, they will continue to treat the company as a messy conglomerate, thereby depressing its share price and leaving its debt rated as 'junk'.

Chapter 9

AOL Time Warner

AOL + Time Warner = AOL Time Warner = Time Warner + AOL

Introduction

America Online (AOL) was founded in 1985 to provide content and services to residential customers via dial-up modems – it changed its name from Quantum Computer Services in 1989 and was first publicly traded on the New York stock exchange in 1992. Typically for the time, AOL restricted its subscribers to its own e-mail service and content, but the subsequent growth of the Internet led AOL to add access to the World Wide Web. Because its Internet interface was user-friendly, and its extensive marketing proved highly successful, AOL was able to grow rapidly during the 1990s, achieving roughly a 40 per cent market share by the end of the decade. By comparison, its main rivals, Earthlink and Microsoft's MSN, had market shares well below 10 per cent. AOL did not produce its own content, but rather sought to provide access for its subscribers to the widest possible array of content produced by others. Its market power was such that it was increasingly able to charge prospective content providers a fee to become a 'preferred provider', and on the face of it, AOL's business model appeared to be working very well.

The late-1990s were characterised by an upsurge in merger and acquisition (M&A) activity.[1] A notable feature of takeover activity during 1999 was that it was largely confined to linkages between companies in related fields – for example, equipment manufacturers buying specialist technology, or fixed-wire/cellular/cable network operators expanding their networks in a variety of ways. Internet companies were also active, but the big deals, of which there were few, were amongst themselves: For example, Yahoo! offered $4.7 billion for Geocities in January, and $5.7 billion for Broadcast.com in April, while CMGI offered $2.3 billion for Alta Vista in July.

AOL ended 1999 worth $169 billion, its share price having soared during the year as shown in Figure 9.1. The only problem was that much of the market value of Internet companies like AOL was what Walt Disney executives preferred to term 'Mickey Mouse' money, with no foundation in physical assets. An alternative way of looking at this issue was to express 'new economy' or Internet dollars in terms of the (much lower) number of real world dollars for which they could be exchanged. However, AOL was not a significant offender in this respect as it was financially sound.

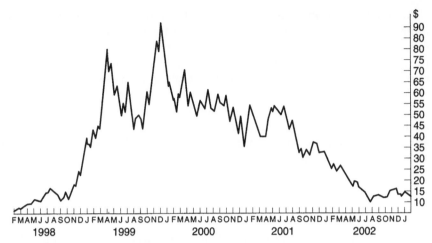

Figure 9.1 AOL Time Warner[a] share price, January 1998–January 2003[b] (dollars).

Source: Daily share prices in the *Financial Times.*

Notes:
[a] The company is now known as Time Warner Inc. [b] During 2003 the share price traded in the narrow $10–16 range.

All looked to be going smoothly for AOL, but at the very beginning of 2000 sentiment suddenly turned against the Internet sector and analysts began to talk openly about the possibility that the Mickey Mouse money would disappear as quickly as it had previously appeared. Precisely at this point, on 10 January, AOL made an audacious attempt to convert its Mickey Mouse money into real money by launching the sector's largest ever takeover bid for Time Warner. This chapter seeks to analyse the strategic thinking behind the takeover and the reasons for its extraordinary outcome – the writing off of nearly $100 billion of assets by the merged company in 2002 alone.

Multimedia and convergence

The bid for Time Warner could be seen as a major step on the road to the delivery of multimedia. Technically, multimedia, as the name suggests, refers to the provision of a service through two or more media (channels of communication). However, the term has come to be used more commonly in the context of sending multiple services along a single medium such as copper wire or fibre-optic cable. Multimedia has accordingly been defined as 'the integration of a variety of audio-visual presentation methods into a single framework, using a personal computer as the "platform" or basis'.[2] An alternative is to think of multimedia in terms of content, software, hardware and network or, as Oftel, the UK regulator, expressed it, content creation, service provision, consumer equipment and distribution network (the 'pipe').[3]

Although the term 'multimedia' is widely bandied about, often giving the impression that multimedia applications are freely available, that is still far from the truth. Some of the confusion surrounding the issue can be ascribed to the largely independent growth of different elements in the multimedia mix, and in particular to the development of regulatory bodies set up to deal exclusively with specific elements.

'Convergence' is another concept that is difficult to pin down. It tends to mean different things to different people in the context of multimedia, as was made evident by the lengthy analysis in the European Commission's 1997 Green Paper on the convergence of the telecommunications, media and information technology sectors[4] (see Adstead and McGarvey[5] and Katz[6]). According to the Green Paper (p. 1), 'the term convergence eludes precise definition, but is most commonly expressed as:

- the ability of different network elements to carry essentially similar kinds of services, or
- the coming together of consumer devices such as the telephone, television and personal computer.'

It may be noted that this definition is not fundamentally different to those proposed by the *Financial Times* and Oftel cited above, so there is an implication that 'convergence' is simply another version of 'multimedia'.

There are two quite distinct elements in a multimedia system, namely hardware and software. For sound historic and economic reasons, companies traditionally specialised in one or the other. Hence, on the one hand, there are electronics, telephone, cable TV and satellite companies, and, on the other hand, news and entertainment companies and film studios. To move across from one to the other by building up a new business from scratch is wholly impractical – hence the continuous pressure to merge the two together, a process that can be described as 'vertical value-chain convergence'.[7] In recent years, this pressure has been exacerbated for both traditional hardware and software companies by the rise of the Internet, given its ability to act as a conduit for multimedia services. However, the Internet is different in at least one major respect, namely the fact that it is largely user-driven with the users generating a substantial part of the content.

Background

Even without the benefit of hindsight, the underlying justifications for early attempts to achieve convergence could be seen to be based upon hypothesis at least as much as upon fact. It was assumed, for example – though it was by no means self-evident – that the first players into the market would be the winners. It was also assumed that investing in networks would be economically viable even though the number of competing networks, utilizing a variety of different technologies, was growing rapidly. In practice, not all were persuaded. The then chairman of Viacom memorably claimed that 'software is king, was king and always will be king' before proceeding to take over Paramount Communications, Blockbuster Video and MTV. As for the networks, they could be leased. Unfortunately, if he was correct then the Disney purchase in August 1995 of Capital Cities/ABC was clearly a strategic error, especially since Disney's commanding reputation for entertainment software hardly necessitated a captive distribution network. In the event, the weakness at ABC badly held back Disney during 1999. Problems arising from conflicting cultures and egos, together with the need to move the enlarged business to a single location, proved to be more severe than expected. However, these problems could be said to have been more to do with implementation than a lack of strategic foresight.[8]

A further acquisition of significance was the offer in August 1995 by Time Warner – a company which had yet to make a profit – for the 82 per cent of Turner Broadcasting that it did not yet own. Subsequently, Time Warner came to be worth more than Disney, but where was it going? A clue was offered in January 1997 when Time Warner announced its Full Service Network, a fusion of the television, computer and telephone to provide a high-speed interactive network delivered via cable. Time Warner thought that the winning formula was to combine convenience with choice – represented by full video-on-demand, sport-on-demand, home shopping and banking, Internet access, and cheap telephony. However, the trial in Orlando served only to prove how expensive such a system would be to set up[9] and the experiment was discontinued. Subsequently, Time Warner preferred to develop its own Internet hub, Pathfinder, rather than buy a ready-made success story such as Lycos or Excite, but Pathfinder also proved to be unsuccessful.

Even Viacom seemed to have become confused about its ultimate objectives since, in September 1999, it launched a takeover bid worth $36 billion for fellow media company CBS that was strangely reminiscent of Disney's earlier criticized, foray. During the interim period, the world's largest media companies had seemingly become engaged in an attempt to develop into jacks of all trades. Certainly, there was a natural logic in producing something – TV and film production – and subsequently distributing it through the maximum number of channels – terrestrial TV, cable TV, satellite TV, cinema, radio, publishing, the Internet, theme parks, shops and music – especially since each indirectly advertised the existence of the others. Time Warner was involved in everything bar satellite TV and radio, whereas Disney only missed out on satellite TV. Viacom/CBS would still miss out on satellite TV, theme parks and music, but although the move might seem logical to the companies, it was bound to appear to the antitrust authorities more like a crude attempt to secure market power.

At the end of 1999, Time Warner, chaired by Gerald Levin, was valued at $81 billion and Disney at $66 billion – on the face of it far too costly to acquire and, in any event, there was no reason to suspect a move to link up the physical and online worlds. Early in 1999 Lycos had proposed a link-up with USA Networks and was rewarded with a 30 per cent fall in its share price – hardly a good omen. However, two factors could not altogether be overlooked: first, Internet companies such as AOL and Yahoo! were awash with Mickey Mouse money and needed to turn it into real money; second, it was increasingly appreciated that the Internet was either a threat or a step on the road to fame and fortune.

In the event, what transpired was the then largest takeover bid in history. Allegedly a 'strategic merger of equals', the deal involved the creation of a new company called AOL Time Warner (AOLTW), with its proposed holdings as set out in Table 9.1, worth $327 billion on 10 January 2000, the day it was announced. In practical terms, AOL shareholders were to receive 1.5 shares in the new company for each existing AOL share, whereas Time Warner shareholders were to receive one new share for each existing Time Warner share. This meant that AOL shareholders would end up with 55 per cent of the new company and hence effective control – an interesting variant on the term 'equal', although AOL did enter the deal worth twice as much on paper as Time Warner. The financial markets' response was to raise Time Warner's share price from $65 to $90 and to lower AOL's share price from $73 to $71, thereby valuing each Time Warner share at a notional $106.

In certain quarters the excitement could scarcely be contained. Ted Turner, founder of CNN and now vice-chairman of Time Warner with a 9 per cent stake, famously went on record with the assertion that he approached the deal 'with as much or more excitement than on that night when I first made love, some 42 years ago'.[10] Steve Case, AOL's chairman and chairman-elect of AOLTW, took a more cautious line, noting that 'there were a lot of cooks' involved in the deal.

As is usual in deals involving Internet money, real money valuations were hard to pin down. It appeared that AOL was offering a notional premium of nearly 70 per cent to acquire Time Warner, but, as the Lex Column was quick to point out,[11] the reality was that AOL was exchanging its Internet money for real money at a very attractive rate of exchange, and hence was getting a discounted bargain, rather than over-paying, given that Time Warner was expected to contribute 85 per cent of AOLTW's revenues and 80 per cent of AOLTW's cash flow. According to Lex, the projected ebitda[12] was 35 for 2001 – twice the rate for old media companies but well short of the 150 previously

Table 9.1 AOLTW holdings

Type	Main holdings
Cable networks	Time Warner Cable
Films	New Line Cinema, Warner Brothers
Magazines	*People, Sports Illustrated, Time*
Music	Atlantic, Spinner, Winamp, Warner Brothers Records
Online services	America Online, CompuServe, Netscape
Television	CNN, Home Box Office, The WB Network

projected by AOL for 2000. This, it observed, indicated that sky-high Internet company valuations were heading back to earth.

The strategic benefits for AOL were easy to identify. It hoped to acquire lots of new content, improve relationships with major advertisers and access to broadband cable. Time Warner stood to exact a much higher share valuation for its shareholders, to become much the largest media company in the world, to retain equal board and managerial representation, and to become the media company with the best-developed Internet strategy. Cross-promotion would drive down the cost of acquiring new subscribers to a range of services.

The deal was bound to attract detailed scrutiny from regulators both in the USA and Europe. Time Warner was already rolling out a fast Internet access via cable service branded as Road Runner, in which it held a 38 per cent stake, and it was immediately obvious that AOLTW would be rejected by the regulators if it tried to shut off access to Time Warner's cables by other Internet service providers (ISPs). This struck some as ironic given AOL's lengthy campaign to force AT&T to open up its cables to the likes of AOL. By keeping Road Runner independent as a rival to Excite@Home[13] and by guaranteeing access to all-comers, AOLTW hoped to have headed off its major potential difficulty. Overlaps in other areas were unlikely to cause much concern, although cable franchises would need regulators' approval to be transferred.

In Europe, the object of most attention was AOL Europe, AOL's existing roughly 50:50 joint venture with Bertelsmann of Germany which had taken a 5 per cent stake in AOL in 1995. This operated in nine countries and four languages and had almost three million subscribers at the end of 1999, effectively making AOL the only US Internet service provider with anything approaching global reach. AOLTW would inevitably compete with this venture as well as with the 50:50 joint venture AOL Australia, particularly in relation to Bertelsmann's music interests and publisher Random House. There was also a question mark over other links such as those with Cégétel and Canal Plus of France. However, AOL needed non-English content in Europe, and there was nothing new about a business model that had companies co-operating in certain markets while competing in others. The likely outcome was expected to be the flotation of part of AOL Europe thereby allowing Bertelsmann to reduce its stake in the venture, but in the event AOL gave Bertelsmann a put option (right to sell its stake at a pre-determined price) and Bertelsmann also reduced its stake in AOL to 0.7 per cent.

Musical chairs

Not content with its involvement in the world's largest takeover bid, Time Warner was simultaneously involved in the creation of the world's largest music group. On 23 January 2000, its subsidiary, Warner Music, announced a 50:50 joint venture with EMI of the UK, to be called Warner EMI Music, pooling their recorded music and music publishing businesses. Depending upon which measure was to be adopted, the proposed Warner EMI could be said to exceed a 25 per cent share of both the music publishing and recorded music markets, and hence attracted the attention of regulators in both Europe and the USA.[14]

Two years previously, EMI had engaged in merger discussions with Seagram of Canada, owner of Universal Music, that had come to nothing, and had been viewed as a takeover candidate ever since. However, this was not strictly a takeover bid. A new company, Warner EMI, was to be created with control vested in Warner. In return for ceding control, EMI shareholders would retain their shares and receive a cash payment of £1 (worth roughly $1.50 at the time), equivalent to a 15 per cent mark-up on the ruling share price. EMI would retain its separate listing, holding its stake in Warner EMI, its 43 per cent stake in HMV Media Group and other minority investments. If the EMI share price were to rise above £9 ($13.5) for a period of 15 days at any time during the ensuing three and a half years, Time Warner would be entitled to take an 8 per cent stake in EMI. In one sense EMI shareholders would be worse off than with a full takeover bid since that would almost certainly have needed payment of a 30 per cent premium to the ruling share price. However, they would be getting some cash and retaining an interest in a pure music business rather than being paid in full in Time Warner shares that were difficult to value because of its own takeover.

The logic behind the joint venture was that online sales of CDs by retailers were set to boom, followed in a few years by increasing use of direct downloading of tracks from the Internet. Companies accordingly needed to prepare themselves for the digital age, which in effect meant cutting the costs of distribution and preserving relations with artists. As with AOLTW, Internet issues were of paramount concern and music businesses could find themselves being referred to in future as content providers.

Regulatory skirmishes

The AOLTW deal appeared to reaffirm the claim that 'content is king'. Despite being left behind in the wake of the deal, Disney, CBS and their ilk could at least take heart from this supposition. However, it was by no means all good news. Towards the end of 1999, NBC launched NBCi and Disney launched Go.com. NBCi was formed by bringing together NBC's online activities, Snap.com and Xoom.com. Go was formed by bringing together Disney's online activities and Infoseek, a second-tier portal. Neither was perceived as having a clear strategy and both struggled to trade at above the issue price – a very poor performance for any dot.com company in 1999.

Whether this meant that they should themselves look for a suitor was a moot point given that there were very few candidates. Yahoo! was 'available', but its high valuation suggested that it would be predator rather than prey. Meanwhile, there was reason for old media companies to avoid pressing the panic button. At the end of the day, most existing deals between themselves and AOL to supply content were long-term, and AOL could hardly afford to try to break its contracts. Furthermore, those companies reaching customers via AOL had a vested interest in continuing to do so. Just how long these arrangements could continue was nevertheless a difficult issue. The established model of aggregating content via exclusive and non-exclusive alliances, and using programming skills to hold users within a specific portal or 'walled garden' rather than their going walkabout on the wider Internet, was unlikely to be discarded without careful thought. However, Time Warner could provide the type of content that AOL was already acquiring from elsewhere – for example, it had an alliance with Viacom's popular Nickelodeon and MTV businesses[15] – and which it inevitably had an interest in promoting wherever possible.

Immediately after the deal was announced AOL's share price fell roughly 10 per cent, to $65, equivalent to $97 per Time Warner share, and by early March the AOL share price stood at $59 (see Figure 9.1). The attractions of the deal for Time Warner shareholders were therefore beginning to pall, but at $84 – buoyed up by excellent financial results for 1999[16] – the Time Warner share price still stood comfortably above the pre-bid level and its managers presumably realized that they would never get a better opportunity to short-circuit the process of adapting the business to the world of the Internet. As for AOL shareholders, they could take the view that a further bout of Internet frenzy in 2000 similar to that in 1999 would leave the AOL share price at a level that would facilitate the purchase of Time Warner for far fewer AOL shares than had been offered this time around. Presumably, shareholders nevertheless noted that Steve Case and other AOL executives were clearly not of that opinion, and that they could even be suffering the odd bout of uncertainty about the company's prospects in a world of free Internet access and inadequate access to cable. On the whole, therefore, neither set of shareholders had much incentive to duck out of the transaction, and both accepted on 23 June.

In any event, the financial markets had become so volatile that it had become extremely difficult to assign values to companies in the 'new economy'. Even had market sentiment remained positive, the challenges were substantial. For example, there would be the need to restructure the companies; to digitize much of Time Warner's content; to find innovative ways to market it over the Internet; to ensure that the cable networks could carry it without loss of speed; and to integrate Time Warner's offerings without damaging relations with existing content providers. On the one hand, there was the need to seek synergies to save money, yet on the other, there was the need to maintain a competitive environment in order to keep both existing allies and the antitrust authorities happy.

This was always going to be difficult. In June, AOL's dominance of the instant messaging[17] market was troubling the FCC, which kept demanding additional information concerning the AOL link with Time Warner. Further, although Time Warner announced a non-binding 'memorandum of understanding' that it would open up its cables to multiple ISPs, this provoked a somewhat sceptical response from the FCC. Although a letter of intent was signed in June with Juno Online, the third-largest ISP in the USA, to give it access to the cables, this would not become effective until the issues surrounding Road Runner's existing contracts were resolved. The FCC appeared to be fairly satisfied about the matter, but it was anticipated that a 'consent decree' would nevertheless need to be signed to ensure that Time Warner did not renege on its offer in order to satisfy the Federal Trade Commission, which somewhat surprisingly stepped into the fray to bring this about.

Meanwhile, in Europe, the Warner Music link with EMI was set back when, also in June, the European Commission announced a full four-month inquiry into the merger, expressing its concerns that AOL could become the 'gatekeeper' for online music distribution; that the relationship with Bertelsmann clouded the picture and needed to be examined carefully; and that AOL would have preferential access to the leading source of music publishing rights and repertoire in most EU states. In particular, the combined entity would control roughly 50 per cent of all music publishing in Sweden and more than 70 per cent in Finland.

In September, the European Commission published a preliminary objection to AOLTW and Warner EMI Music. The Commission had to resort to the little-used concept of 'collective dominance' to support its claim that Warner EMI Music would create an oligopoly in the music market that would allow the remaining companies to collude on prices and act as 'gatekeepers' in restricting the ability of potential competitors to download music online because, in the case of AOLTW, it was already attracting the majority of prospective customers. It was, however, debatable whether conventional measures of market dominance, such as market shares, should be used in the context of 'new economy' takeovers. While the antitrust authorities in the USA needed to grapple with whether vertical integration of content and network was directly comparable to other forms of vertical integration, the European Commission's somewhat hostile attitude to AOLTW appeared to be placing itself into a situation that its US counterparts found difficult to understand because the cable networks were exclusively located in the USA.

The Commission, having received undertakings from Time Warner and EMI, but underwhelmed by the argument that independent record labels provided competition, then drafted a decision to block the merger, claiming that the undertakings were 'behavioural in nature' and 'could not address the anti-competitive concerns . . . which arise from the simple knock-on effect on the music publishing markets of the creation of a dominant player'. Based upon collecting societies' data, it estimated that Warner EMI Music would have a market share for mechanical rights of between 29 and 76 per cent and for performance rights at between 25 and 68 per cent.

In early October, Warner Music and EMI announced that they were willing to sell both the Virgin record label and Chappell Music Publishing, constituting a large part of the Warner Chappell music publishing business, a concession that the independent music companies had previously said would satisfy their concerns. However, the Commission seemed certain to block the deal anyway so Warner Music and EMI withdrew their proposal in order to prevent a formal veto being recorded. This cleared the way for the Commission to approve AOLTW given that the central issue concerning cable access was not relevant in relation to Europe. The key concession by AOL was its agreement to sever all links with Bertelsmann – notably its 50:50 joint venture AOL Europe and AOL Compuserve France involving Bertelsmann, Cégétel and Canal Plus.

The overall situation had become somewhat clearer because Time Warner argued that the existing arrangement, whereby Road Runner had exclusive rights to its cables until the end of 2001, could probably be renegotiated in the light of the decision by the Department of Justice that AT&T should sell its stake in Road Runner as a condition of approval for its takeover of MediaOne which held the stake. For its part, Time Warner made it clear that it would rather give up on the AOL deal than be forced to sell its cable interests to achieve it. In mid-October, the European Commission duly approved the merger subject to setting up an independent monitor to verify that all links with Bertelsmann had been severed.

In mid-December, the FTC unanimously approved AOLTW for an initial five-year period, subject to conditions. In the first place, AOLTW was obliged to open its cable network to competing ISPs, including one ISP prior to AOL's launch of its own cable service and at least two others within the subsequent 90-day period subject to capacity and technical constraints. Under an agreement signed with the second-largest US ISP, EarthLink, in November, a provisional date of mid/late 2001 had already been pencilled in for EarthLink to launch a service, so that date would in effect also determine the launch date for AOL. Second, AOLTW was prevented from interfering with subscribers' use of interactive TV services provided by other suppliers. Third, in order to prevent AOLTW from abandoning Digital Subscriber Line (DSL) provision[18] in places where it preferred to concentrate on cable access, AOLTW was obliged to provide a uniform DSL service in areas both where it provided cable access and where it did not.

The parallel, but as yet incomplete, FCC investigation was not expected to cause any further problems of note, and the share price of both companies bounced slightly. In anticipation of a ruling that AOL (with 21.5 million users at the time) would be forced to interconnect its instant messaging system with those of Yahoo! (10.6 million) and Microsoft's MSN (10.3 million), the latter announced that they had created the IMUnified consortium to speed up the process of introducing a single protocol covering inter-operability.

Nevertheless, in the run-up to Christmas, AOL was trading down at $37 and Time Warner at $55 – in both cases a low for the year and a far cry from the prices at the time the deal was first announced. This reflected a profit warning by Time Warner in relation to its film, music and advertising revenues – much in line, it had to be said, with conditions across the industry in general. In contrast, AOL was trading successfully. Given the high proportion of earnings expected from the former Time Warner businesses, this indicated that AOLTW would merit a downward rerating even after this share price fall.

At the same time the distribution of cable interests between Time Warner and AT&T was finally unravelled. Time Warner announced that it would be taking full control of Road Runner, relieving AT&T of the problems of overlap with Excite@Home. At the time Road Runner had 1.1 million customers – a figure dwarfed by the 26 million customers for AOL's narrowband service. The first step – buying back the Road Runner stakes held by Microsoft and Compaq, plus associated restructuring charges – was costed at $570 million. Subsequently, Time Warner and AT&T would divide up Road Runner's customers and network between themselves, with roughly 720,000 existing subscribers using Time Warner's cables staying with that provider and the rest going to AT&T. Road Runner would probably be maintained as a separate broadband access provider, running alongside the equivalent AOL service in a manner reminiscent of AOL's parallel (and cheaper) narrowband CompuServe brand acquired in 1998.[19]

Somewhat surprisingly, the FCC investigation dragged on into mid-January 2001 as it became clear that a majority could not easily be found for any particular plan of action. In the event, although the FCC demanded that AOL open up its instant messaging system to rivals as 'advanced' services – essentially non-text services such as video-conferencing images – were launched, it did not make this a requirement in relation to existing text messaging. The condition would apply either for five years or until an interoperability standard was agreed. Further, AOLTW would not be permitted to pressurize consumers to subscribe to its own Internet service and would be obliged to let unaffiliated ISPs choose their own home page and bill their customers direct. Finally, AOLTW would be obliged to negotiate in good faith with ISPs of all sizes in all locations. AOL traded up at $47 and Time Warner up at $71. AOLTW was duly listed on the NYSE on 11 January 2001.

Post-merger tribulations

At the end of January, AOLTW announced its results on the basis that it had been trading as a single company during the previous financial year. These showed that AOL's subscription, advertising and e-commerce businesses were growing at over 10 per cent a year whereas Time Warner's music division was losing sales market share and its film and network TV divisions were weak. This was somewhat ironic given that AOL had been seen as the problem during 2000 given the widespread crash in Internet-related stocks, whereas Time Warner's share price had borne up surprisingly well. Overall, AOLTW lost $3.9 billion ($2.4 billion in 1999) on sales of $36.2 billion ($32.5 billion in 1999). AOLTW accordingly announced that it would be cutting 2,000 jobs in addition to the 400 already announced at CNN News – roughly 3 per cent of the overall workforce. However, analysts took a generally very cautious stance on the company's prospects in 2001 although, in the event, these turned out to be perfectly satisfactory so far as the first quarter was concerned, with AOLTW weathering the meltdown in advertising expenditure in good shape and predicting that it would meet its targets for the full year.

In April 2001, AOLTW entered discussions with NTL, the largest cable operator in the UK with 8.5 million subscribers in the UK, France, Germany, Sweden and Switzerland, with a view to finding a means of entry into the European market. In May, AOLTW announced that it had struck a deal with High Speed Access similar to those already agreed with EarthLink and Juno Online and meeting the condition that two ISPs in addition to EarthLink had to be granted the right to use AOLTW's cables.[20]

By late June, AOLTW subsidiary, AOL's ISP service, had reached 30 million users, of which six million were located in 16 countries outside the USA, and the monthly fee was increased by $2 to $23.90. A new version, AOL 7.0, was announced with a launch date of September. However, the longer-term prospects were uncertain. On the one hand, they were deteriorating because it was evident that Microsoft was busy evolving from friend to foe. As part of a deal signed in 1996, AOL had agreed to build its service around Microsoft's Internet Explorer web browser in return for a prominent position within Windows. This was no longer the case in respect of the new platform, Windows XP, due to be launched in October. This did not prevent PC manufacturers from choosing to load AOL's software in their machines, so the immediate impact would not necessarily be severe, but it did mean, for example, that Microsoft would attempt to transfer users of AOL's instant messaging service over to its own, bundled up in Windows XP. Furthermore, Microsoft chose to undercut AOL's ISP charges even though this was likely to lead to accusations that Microsoft was once again abusing its monopoly position, and, unfortunately, users would inevitably suffer because what they wanted were compatible, not competing, standards.[21]

AOL was able to announce a marketing deal with AT&T Wireless to include the development of a new service which would be delivered via the latter's new GSM/GPRS network. It also invested $100 million in a strategic alliance with Amazon.com and spent roughly $1.5 billion buying IPC Media, the UK's leading consumer magazine publisher. However, 2001Q2 results reported in July indicated that AOLTW was beginning to suffer from economic slowdown in the USA and the accompanying slump in advertising revenue, and although pre-tax losses fell sharply and ebitda rose, the share price fell by almost 10 per cent. In effect, the markets were saying that they were not fully persuaded about the rationale for creating AOLTW, and were waiting for significantly improved performance to become convinced.[22]

At the end of July, AOLTW announced that it had contracted Qwest to be a primary provider of dial-up and broadband access and that, in return, Qwest would purchase advertising from AOLTW. KPNQwest would separately provide the same services in Europe. In August, AOLTW created a new division, AOL Interactive Services, to develop interactive TV and video-on-demand subsequent upon initiating a trial service in South Carolina. Although trials during the 1990s had been a failure, it was argued that the arrival of broadband access via cable plus a reduction in the cost of technology now made such services potentially economic. It also announced a third round of job cuts, this time at its AOL Internet unit. At the end of September, in the aftermath of the attack on the World Trade Center, AOLTW announced that it had made a $734 million net loss on turnover of $9.2 billion for the quarter to end-June 2001 and issued a profit warning. With only 35 per cent of revenue derived from advertising, AOLTW was less affected than other media groups, but expected conditions to deteriorate during the final quarter. This proved to be correct, with the net loss coming in at roughly $1 billion. This stemmed in part from more aggressive provision of free-usage promotions designed to fend off competition from MSN, and the termination or renegotiation of three- to five-year advertising contracts signed when online prices were at their peak. AOLTW's share price promptly fell back below $30.

In November, the AOL unit announced that it had reached the 32 million subscriber mark, partly driven by the launch of the new upgraded AOL 7.0. Analysts, however, took a generally dim view of the growth of net subscriber additions and of the prospects for revenue per subscriber. The launch of the first Harry Potter film, also in November, appeared to put some much-needed gloss on AOLTW's tarnished image since it was the first real test of whether all the parts of the company were pulling in the same direction and of the potential for cost savings by keeping as much activity as possible, especially promotional, in-house. However, here again there was a tendency to concentrate on the negative aspects such as the resistance at Time Inc. and CNN to any suggestion that their journalistic integrity should be subservient to the needs of the corporate body.[23]

On the whole, the situation was finely balanced at the beginning of 2002, but it was not to last. The main blow came in the form of the inevitable need to write down the value of AOLTW since the takeover, a reduction estimated at no less than $40 billion. At the end of 2000, the two constituent companies were together worth $178 billion (of which AOL represented $100 billion), but this figure was now much too high. Naturally, this had no direct bearing on AOLTW's cash flows, but it was hardly good for confidence. Neither, for that matter, was the announcement that AOL would be paying $6.75 billion to Bertelsmann in return for its 49.5 per cent stake in AOL Europe. This sum had been written into a put option entered into at the time – March 2000 – that Bertelsmann bought the stake and Bertelsmann understandably wanted out before the option expired in mid-January. The only trouble was that the stake was now worth less than $2 billion – AOL Europe had made a loss of $600 million on revenues of $800 million in 2001 – and the settlement would require payment in cash. Richard Parsons, the co-chief operating officer who had been chosen to replace CEO Gerald Levin in May, took the opportunity to announce that AOLTW would in future 'deliver' rather than 'over-promise'- but how?[24]

It was widely accepted that the main strategic challenge to be addressed would be how to replicate AOL's dominance in dial-up Internet access in a broadband world.[25] So far, the AOL online service seemed to be acting as little more than a giant marketing machine for Time Warner Entertainment. However, Mr Parsons remained undaunted, claiming that he subscribed '100 per cent to the theory, the strategy and the vision that drove the merger . . . convergence is not only coming, it's here.'[26] Rather more tellingly, Bob Pittman, the chief operating officer, noted that much of the short-term benefit of the merger was emanating from closer co-operation between former Time Warner divisions, rather than from a combination of old and new media. The financial markets, for their part, remained profoundly unimpressed, and as shown in Figure 9.1, the AOLTW share price declined almost continuously from January to August 2002, bottoming out at roughly $10 – little more than 10 per cent of its peak value, although it had to be said that in that respect AOLTW was by no means exceptional.

Not only was AOLTW struggling to make ground in broadband, but its dial-up service was also suffering because the proportion of non-paying subscribers had risen from seven to 15 per cent, primarily as a result of 'bundling' deals with computer manufacturers whereby they provided free access for up to one year with new machines. It also needed to turn around the loss-making AOL Europe as part of its plan to raise the proportion of revenue raised overseas from the 17 per cent recorded in 2001 to nearer one half. Although this implied a need for acquisitions, all that had been managed so far was the purchase of UK consumer magazine publisher IPC for $1.6 billion – AOLTW had lacked the firepower to compete with Comcast for AT&T Broadband in 2001 and its net debt of well over $20 billion did not give it much room to manoeuvre now.[27]

What was progressively emerging during the early months of 2002 was resentment among the old Time Warner divisions at the drag AOL was exerting upon the merged company – a neat reversal of the arguments put forward to justify the takeover. It was even suggested that the best thing for AOLTW would be to spin off AOL. Given that Steve Case, AOL's founder, remained in the chairman's seat, these suggestions were couched in a semi-humorous manner – at least for the time being. However, John Malone of Liberty Media, with a 4 per cent stake in AOLTW, asked regulators to remove restrictions on the voting rights attached to his shares, and Ted Turner's love affair with AOLTW was clearly on the wane.

The restructuring of Time Warner Entertainment

AOLTW was obliged to embark upon some restructuring during 2002, and Time Warner Entertainment was the logical place to begin. The position was that AOLTW owned 74.49 per cent of the Series A Capital and Residual Capital and 100 per cent of the (junior) Series B Capital while the rest of the first two categories was held by AT&T. However, AT&T's interest was to pass to Comcast in November 2002 as a result of the agreed takeover by Comcast of AT&T Broadband. The initial step was for 2.13 per cent of the Series A and Residual Capital to be acquired by AT&T at the end of May as the result of an existing call (right to buy) option. In August, AOLTW agreed to acquire the whole of TWE's content assets, including Warner Bros. and Home Box Office as well as its interests in The WB Network, Comedy Central and Court TV. In addition, almost all of AOLTW's interests in TWE and all of its interests in cable TV systems held through wholly-owned subsidiaries would be contributed to an existing subsidiary of Comcast that would become a subsidiary of AOLTW and be renamed 'Time Warner Cable Inc.' Comcast would then receive $2.1 billion in cash plus AOLTW common stock worth $1.5 billion at the time of the asset transfers and would retain both a 17.9 per cent economic interest in Time Warner Cable and a 4.7 per cent economic interest in TWE. Overall, Comcast would end up with a 21 per cent economic interest in Time Warner Cable which would have $8.1 billion of net debt and be prepared for an initial public offering. Regulatory approvals were expected in early 2003.[28]

There was also a complicated restructuring, completed in December 2002, of the TWE-Advance/Newhouse Partnership.[29] The effect of this was to transfer the Advance/Newhouse interest in broadband ISP Road Runner to TWE, thereby raising its stake from 65 per cent to 82 per cent, while transferring 2.1 cable subscribers to Advance/Newhouse – a significant chunk of AOLTW's 12.9 million subscribers.[30]

Personnel and other matters

In April 2002, Robert Pittman (ace marketer) took over the reins of the AOL division from Barry Schuler (ace technologist) – the job he had held before the takeover – in addition to his duties at AOLTW. This did little to cheer the financial markets which valued AOLTW at the time at a 27 per cent discount to its break-up value – mainly because the AOL division was valued at only $7 a share. Clearly, Mr Pittman needed to drum up some advertising revenue and sell the virtues of the AOL division to the rest of AOLTW. Unfortunately, this proved to be a less than enjoyable process and he resigned in mid-July, to be replaced by two Time Warner veterans, Don Logan – appointed chairman of a newly formed Media and Communications Group – and Jeff Bewkes – appointed chairman of the new Entertainment and Networks Group (see Table 9.2). Two things were clearly being signalled: first, that convergence was 'out' and decentralization was 'in'; second, that AOLTW would henceforth be run by old media rather than new media personnel.

Meanwhile, there was the little matter of the record $54 billion accounting charge relating to the loss of market value since the merger (see Table 9.3)

Table 9.2 New company structure

Media and Communications Group	Entertainment and Networks Group
America Online	Home Box Office
AOL Time Warner Book Group	New Line Cinema
AOL Time Warner Interactive Video	Turner Broadcasting System
Time Inc.	Warner Bros.
Time Warner Cable	Warner Music Group

Table 9.3 AOLTW balance sheet 2001 and 2002, year ending 31 December ($ million)

	2002 Historical	2001 Pro forma[a]	2001 Historical
Subscriptions	18,959	16,809	15,657
plus Advertising and commerce	7,680	8,461	8,260
plus Content and other	14,426	13,232	13,307
equals Total revenues	41,065	38,502	37,224
Less			
Total costs	(35,402)	(32,681)	(37,106)
Impairment of goodwill	(45,538)	–	–
Equals			
Operating income (loss)	(39,875)	5,821	118
plus Cumulative effect of accounting change	(54,235)	–	–
plus Other expenses			
Equals			
Net income (loss)	(98,696)	472	(4,934)
Basic income (loss) $ per share	(22.15)	0.11	(1.11)
Current assets	115,450[b]		208,504
of which:			
Goodwill	36,986		127,420
Long-term debt	27,354		22,792

Source: www.aoltimewarner.com

Notes
[a] In order to enhance comparability, pro forma financial statements for 2001 are presented supple-
mentally as if IPC and the remaining interest in AOL Europe had been acquired, Road Runner had been
consolidated and FAS 142 had been applied at the beginning of 2001. AOLTW adopted FAS 142 in
January 2002, the effect of which was to require it to stop amortizing goodwill and certain intangible
assets with an indefinite useful life, and instead to account for impairment on an annual basis. The
accounting charge of $54 billion above arose in its entirety from a reduction in goodwill associated with
the takeover. The $45.5 billion arose from the annual impairment review for 2002 and consisted of AOL
($33.5 billion), cable ($10.5 billion), music ($650 million) and carrying value of music brands ($850
million). [b] This is comprised of cable ($37.7 billion), networks ($31.9 billion), films ($16.4 billion),
publishing ($14 billion), AOL ($7.8 billion), music ($6.1 billion) and corporate ($1.6 billion).

and, in August, news that the Securities and Exchange Commission and Department of Justice, which had launched separate investigations into AOL's accounting for online advertising deals, might also investigate other divisions – including, as it transpired, one into the circumstances surrounding hugely profitable executive share sales during 2001. The share price promptly dropped to $10 amid near-record trading volumes (see Figure 9.1).[31]

On a more positive note – although some saw it as negative – AOL signed an agreement with Comcast in August to secure distribution via the latter's broadband cable network. According to best guesses, AOL was paying $38 a month per subscriber, yet with Comcast charging $39.95 to its own customers it was hard to see how AOL could compete after adding on its own costs. AOL subsequently signed up with Covad Communications to access its DSL network, also acquiring call options on 3.5 million Covad shares.

By mid-September the calls for the resignation of chairman Steve Case – the last senior executive from the former AOL left on board and by now a somewhat shadowy figure behind the scenes – were growing ever louder, but under the terms of the merger he needed only three supporters on the 14-person board to remain secure. His departure might have helped morale but was unlikely to make any discernible difference to strategy where Mr Parsons sought to protect AOLTW's credit rating – threatened by its continuing high level of debt – by promising an initial public offer of Time Warner Cable as soon as market conditions permitted. Should that fail to transpire in the medium term, non-core businesses such as Comedy Central – a 50:50 joint venture with Viacom – and Court TV – jointly controlled by Liberty Media – would be sold off. The Atlanta Braves, Hawks and Thrashers might also have to go on the block and/or DC Comics. However, talk of a spin-off of AOL, either along the lines of the division of the original AT&T into AT&T, Lucent and NCR or as a dividend payment to shareholders, was promptly squashed.[32]

AOL 8.0 was launched in October with a promise that irritating pop-up advertisements would be suppressed. AOL also set out to develop a service specifically aimed at small businesses, an area in which its previous forays such as NetCenter had failed to take off. Indeed, AOL had even had to withdraw its e-mail facility for Time Warner because it could not cope with the massive files being transferred.[33] An important objective was to build on the popularity of its free instant messaging service, AIM, which had 180 million registered users, with a view to the introduction of paid services providing companies with more control and security. Another objective – the move to broadband – was initiated in radio with the Broadband Radio @AOL service in November. However, margins on broadband, at 18 per cent, were much less than on dial-up, at 55 per cent, and AOL continued to be plagued with personnel problems, with James De Castro resigning after only seven months spent trying to revive AOL, allegedly because Jon Miller had been preferred to him as CEO.

Above all else, there was a recognition that it was time to be pragmatic, to cast aside hopes of forced co-operation between the various fiefdoms in AOLTW and to introduce, gradually, content from AOL's sister divisions such as CNN, *Time* magazine and HBO into AOL's offerings – a strategy based on collaboration rather than synergy. Given that most executives now had share options instead of cash bonuses built into their remuneration packages, they certainly had an incentive to collaborate,[34] but thorny issues such as whether content providers should charge AOL for their services refused to go away. Interestingly, no one any longer talked about the threat potentially posed by AOLTW's ability to keep popular content in-house – the company no longer had any choice but to flog anything to anyone, however close the rivalry.[35]

In an attempt to attract potential customers who were unwilling to pay a monthly fee of over $20, AOL introduced a pre-pay card providing 500 minutes of dial-up access for $15 over a maximum period of 18 months. It also began to develop plans to obtain a bigger share of the e-commerce revenues derived from its customers and purged the advertising team whose questionable deals were continuing to be investigated.

What was joined shall be parted

In early December 2002, AOLTW attempted to put the previous two years behind it and look forward to a new era. Unfortunately, the first thing that had to be admitted was that the prognosis for the overall advertising spend was at best poor and that AOL's revenues would probably halve during 2003 as it weaned itself off old contracts and set up new initiatives. As Jon Miller put it, in a 'multiband' world AOL customers would no longer come to it exclusively via dial-up Internet connections but increasingly via broadband (often the cable networks of rivals to AOLTW) and mobile devices. There was a manifest risk in directing much of Time Warner's content to AOL on an exclusive basis – for example, online subscriptions to publications – but if AOL was forced to rely on cable systems its parent did not own then it had to provide customers with a justification for signing up to AOL rather simply using the cable operators' own free portals. It proposed to offer a 'Bring Your Own Access' package for $14.95 a month for customers signing up on another company's cable or DSL network.

AOLTW would not undertake any complex or 'transforming' deals for some time, but still intended to proceed with an IPO of Time Warner Cable, while retaining a minimum 70 per cent stake for itself. Talks were also on-going to merge CNN with Disney Corp.'s ABC. Despite the difficulties encountered during the previous attempt to acquire EMI, AOLTW still remained interested in principle in such a deal although the regulatory environment remained hostile. In any event, net debt remained excessively high and shareholders remained disgruntled – the share price looked to have settled in the $10–15 trading range. As for employees, they remained 'sullen but not mutinous'.[36]

In early January 2003, AOLTW's CFO, Wayne Pace, flagged the probability of a substantial asset write-down while assuring shareholders that this would not threaten compliance with debt covenants – independently calculated to require shareholder equity of $50 billion – or liquidity. Standard & Poor's warned of a possible credit rating downgrade from BBB+ as did Moody's from Baa1, but it was generally assumed that AOLTW would not take a major hit unless it knew that its ratings would not be affected. To general surprise, Steve Case then announced that he would stand down at the AGM in May – seen as a victory for a disillusioned, and now much poorer, Ted Turner, although the financial markets took little notice. The chairman's role was passed to CEO Dick Parsons, but given that Mr Case would remain a board member there remained a distinct possibility of continued in-fighting between ex-AOL and ex-Time Warner executives. Further confusion was added by the resignation of the head of CNN which immediately followed, albeit for unrelated reasons.

At the end of January, AOLTW's fourth-quarter earnings statement revealed that the write-down – primarily relating to the reduced value of AOL – would be a record-breaking $45.5 billion and the total loss for 2002 an astonishing $98.7 billion (see Table 9.2). AOLTW pointed out, however, that in general it had met or bettered analysts' expectations and that it expected to reduce net debt during 2003 to $20 billion. Asset disposals would include the stake in Time Warner Cable, the book division and the recently completed sale of $800 million of shares in Hughes Electronics.[37] Ted Turner simultaneously announced that he would be standing down as vice-chairman in May, although he would retain his 3.4 per cent stake in AOLTW and possibly a seat on the board.

One major issue to be addressed was the fact that AOL's subscriber base had fallen for the first time ever during the previous quarter – a problem common to all major dial-up service providers. AOL's response was to introduce new paid-for services such as an online music subscription services, MusicNet, and a facility to check e-mail via voice mail. It also began to tinker with discounted access such as a $10 monthly service with Wal-Mart Stores with limited access to content.[38]

In mid-February, AOLTW abandoned its attempt to merge its Cable News Network division with ABC News, arguing that it could not cope with the complexities of integrating the two organizations at a time when the priority was to pay off debt and boost morale. The sale of the book division, expected to achieve $400 million on the back of a record year in 2002, also looked to be in trouble, with the likes of Harper Collins and Simon & Schuster refusing to bid and Random House thinking in terms of a much smaller sum. Eventually, only Perseus Books Group was left in the frame with a mooted offer of around $300 million.

At the end of March, the SEC raised further issues about AOL's accounting practices in respect of two advertising deals with Bertelsmann involving $400 million of revenues between the first quarter of 2001 and the last quarter of 2002. The SEC alleged that the money should have been accounted for as a reduction in the purchase price of AOL Europe rather than as revenues, a claim refuted by AOLTW. More bad news came, first, in the form of an admission that AOL's US subscribers had fallen to 26.5 million at the end of 2002, higher than a year earlier but down from the September figure with every expectation that dial-up subscriptions were on a declining trend; and, second, by way of a lawsuit filed by two institutional investors alleging that leading investors who participated in the creation of AOLTW had used 'tricks, contrivances and bogus transactions' to inflate the share price. Among those cited were Steve Case, Gerald Levin, Ted Turner, Bob Pittman and, inevitably, Ernst & Young, the auditors.

Shortly thereafter, AOLTW achieved the sale of its half share in the Comedy Central cable TV network to partner Viacom for $1.23 billion, and immediately entered into exclusive talks with a single bidder, David McDavid, a car dealership millionaire from Texas, for its loss-making Atlanta sports teams with a mooted price of $350–400 million. Taken in addition to the free cash flow of $1 billion achieved in the first quarter, it appeared that CEO Dick Parsons had made such a solid start to repairing the AOLTW balance sheet that issues such as the sale of the book division could be postponed.

At the end of May, AOLTW and Microsoft agreed to settle their outstanding – not to mention long-standing – litigation over Netscape. Microsoft agreed to pay $750 million to AOL which, in turn, agreed to use Microsoft's Windows browser – Internet Explorer. Microsoft also agreed to distribute AOL's Internet access software when distributing its own software to manufacturers of small PCs while continuing to compete in the Internet access market via its own MSN service. The payment would make a small dent in the net debt of $26.3 billion.

AOLTW and Bertelsmann also appeared to be settling their differences which had been exacerbated by Bertelsmann's refusal to proceed with the purchase of AOLTW's consumer books division. In response, AOLTW had cancelled discussions about the possible acquisition of Warner Music but these were re-opened in mid-June, subsequent to which Bertelsmann subsidiary Random House renewed its interest in the consumer books division. At that time also, progress was being made with the disposal of the seven factories manufacturing CDs and DVDs via an agreed sale to Cinram International of Canada for just over $1 billion. In addition, the Atlanta Hawks were duly sold in mid-September for $250 million, but to a group of investors rather than to Mr McDavid.

In late July, AOLTW reported mixed news for the second quarter. On the one hand, Warner Bros. was very profitable, free cash flow was buoyant at $2.5 billion, net debt was down to $24.2 billion (with another $1 billion to come) and an IPO of Time Warner Cable was no longer a priority. On the other hand, it remained locked into its accounting dispute with the SEC and

AOL had lost 846,000 subscribers, of whom 380,000 were scrapped as they were paying nothing for one reason or another.[39] While AOL was charging $23.90 a month, basic services could be bought from the likes of NetZero and Juno for $9.95 a month.[40] However, broadband subscriptions were up by 170,000 and the launch of AOL 9.0 on 31 July at a cost of $250 million was seen as the vital step to build on this relative success.[41] In the light of this, the head of AOL asked Mr Parsons to consider dropping AOL from the company's name in order to emphasize its divisional status and this was agreed by the board on 17 September. From mid-October 2003, the company was known once again as Time Warner and traded as TWX rather than AOL.[42] Time Warner's publishing division was renamed as Historic TW Inc.

In late September, AOLTW and Bertelsmann made one final attempt to hammer out the terms of an all-paper 50:50 merger between Warner Music and BMG which warned, however, that it was neither willing to forgo control nor inject any cash to make up any shortfall in its valuation compared to that of Warner Music. At this point EMI returned to the fray with an unspecified new offer but which was rumoured to provide much more cash than that of BMG. At the time of writing a further offer, from a consortium led by Edgar Bronfman Jr., is favoured to win the day.

Conclusions

As noted, AOLTW was worth $327 billion at the time of the takeover bid but not much more than half that figure when the deal was finally consummated roughly a year later. One year further on and the company's value fluctuates around the $60–70 billion level. AOLTW is not the only company to have fallen in value on an epic scale, as the Vodafone case study demonstrates, nor does such a fall necessarily mean that there is nothing left to salvage. Ted Turner's love affair may be over, but there are still real assets left in the hands of family members. The as-yet unanswered question is what will become of them.

The short but extremely active history of AOLTW has had profound effects upon the accepted doctrine surrounding the concepts of multimedia/convergence/value chain management. As demonstrated above, these are somewhat elusive and overlapping concepts, and there is accordingly a need to determine their meaning within a real world context. AOLTW superficially looked much more like a real multimedia/convergent company than anything that had preceded it, and was accordingly expected to provide a blueprint for the early years of the new millennium. In the event, the AOLTW experience has proved to be unique and, many would argue, uniquely awful.

Nevertheless, it may be argued that the vision was not of itself all that faulty, but rather its execution and its abysmal timing. Not everyone was enthused by the new structure introduced in mid-2002, arguing that the world inhabited by the old Time Warner was characterized by independent fiefdoms, everlasting inter-departmental negotiations, much backstabbing and long lunches which incoming AOL executives would be unable to control. Others argued the opposite – that AOL's brash business methods had no lasting value and that they would destroy the well-established and successful business culture at Time Warner. In reality, both camps were right, and this was exemplified by the role played by Steve Case. The issue here, however, was not so much a clash of management style between old media and new media, but rather the unsuitability of introducing a strongly entre-preneurial style into a mature company. Once the takeover was consummated Mr Case simply did not have the appropriate skills to oversee the melding together of such different cultures.

Ironically, perhaps, what this failure to meld the two companies has meant is that neither culture has been destroyed, and both arguably have a reasonably bright future. Certainly, the results for 2002 were more than satisfactory given the environment at the time, but it is necessary to bear in mind that the omens for 2003 are probably less auspicious than for 2002: for example, no obvious blockbuster films to match Harry Potter and Lord of the Rings sequels, and ongoing problems in the music division.

One peculiarity of the current position is that AOL may be almost worthless if judged by the value put on it by the financial markets, but it still has 35 million subscribers and 37 per cent of the dial-up market – vastly more than its competitors. Naturally, it can be argued that the dial-up market is saturated, that AOL has only 5 per cent of the broadband market and that the market for advertising remains depressed – all those bankrupt dot.coms were heavy advertisers. It seems a touch ironic that Time Warner's greatest attraction for AOL remains the content that it will be able to send down those broadband pipes, whereas AOL's greatest attraction for Time Warner – the potential to revitalize its old media properties in a new media world – is now seen as almost an irrelevance. In fairness, AOL is tackling this issue, having created a team of 100 people working on broadband for which it had 2.7 million subscribers in early April 2003. The new 'AOL for Broadband' is emulating the likes of Yahoo! and MSN in offering services to broadband users rather than simply providing the high-speed connection, but whether subscribers will pay an additional $14.95 a month to another ISP simply to access AOL content, even the enhanced version provided by AOL 9.0, remains to be seen – MSN charges only $9.95 extra. The prospects are better in persuading dial-up customers who pay $23.90 a month to add AOL for Broadband for an additional $1.05 a month.[43]

The ever-revolving door through which the architects of AOLTW have been fairly summarily ejected may or may not prove to be a good thing. Messrs Case, Levin, Pittman and Turner have been sacrificed, but will their qualities be missed in the longer term?

Despite the currently devastated share price, a large number of people have done very well out of the takeover – especially those who sold out long ago. It is clear in retrospect that there was only a brief window of opportunity for the conversion of Mickey Mouse money into real assets, that AOL successfully climbed through it, and that it will not reappear for the foreseeable future. Whether this will prove to have been the saving of AOL, or merely the means by which either AOL or Time Warner or both are brought to their knees, only time will tell.

Chapter 10

The KirchGruppe

The House comes tumbling down

Introduction

Over a 46-year period Leo Kirch created a media empire, the KirchGruppe, built around films, television, football and Formula 1. With a reputation for opaque accounting, but able to lean on influential German businesspeople and politicians to assist it through hard times, the KirchGruppe appeared to be impervious to economic downturns and, as of early 2002, the companies involved employed a total of 10,000 people and had a combined turnover of more than €6 billion. However, within a remarkably short period of time thereafter, all of the holding companies of the KirchGruppe were declared to be insolvent. Although this case study demonstrates that the behaviour of the KirchGruppe was closely tied in with the long-standing and excessively protective 'German' way of doing business,[1] which undoubtedly had the consequence that the KirchGruppe's deep-rooted problems were kept away from the public gaze and left unremedied until it was too late to save the company, the fact remains that strategic errors were made and risks undertaken – and not only by the KirchGruppe itself – on a scale that would have brought down any equivalent organization trying to trade through a prolonged recession.[2]

Background

The KirchGruppe structure evolved to become extremely complex. Hence, it is helpful as a starting point for the purposes of the analysis that follows to divide the KirchGruppe into a small number of separate businesses.

Films

At the beginning of the 1950s, Leo Kirch came to understand that as television developed it would demand large supplies of films, series and other programme material. In 1955, he founded Sirius-Film and set about buying the rights to films in many European countries. In 1956, he secured the rights to a number of successful Italian films and was able to market these in Germany. In 1959, he bought the rights to 400 US films from

United Artists/Warner Brothers and, as a result, was able to meet the growing demand for such products by the then German television companies ARD and ZDF. Leo Kirch invested early in the production and co-production of films and TV series. During the period 1959–63, the central involvement of the group in the film industry was led by Beta Film and Taurus Film. By 1996, the KirchGruppe controlled, through a variety of deals with US studios, the rights to 15,000 films and 50,000 hours of TV series, children's programmes, documentaries, operas, concerts and shows including, for a ten-year period, the pay-TV rights for Disney films. As a result of these deals, the KirchGruppe built up a strong relationship with the US studios.

Television

The KirchGruppe developed extensive interests in commercial satellite and cable television companies. This began in 1984 with an early involvement in pay-TV with the Swiss company Teleclub and the spread into free-to-air TV via involvement in Sat 1 in 1988. In 1990–91, together with Bertlesmann and Canal Plus, the KirchGruppe established the first German pay-TV company. In 1992, it took a controlling interest in both NDF, the most successful German production company for TV series and films, and in DEFA, a leading producer of documentaries, while in 1993, together with Telecinco of Spain, it established DSF, the first German TV sports channel financed by advertising. In October 1999, the group launched the digital pay-TV channel, Premiere World – with Rupert Murdoch's News Corporation taking a 22.03 per cent stake in KirchPay-TV via its BSkyB subsidiary (see Figure 10.1) – which began transmission in March 2000 and subsequently took a controlling interest in Sat 1 and ProSieben. In June 2000, with the assistance of Axel Springer who took an 11.48 per cent stake protected by a put option,[3] these were merged to become a listed subsidiary of KirchMedia – ProSiebenSat.1 Media – subsequently to become Germany's largest free-to-air TV company.

Leo Kirch's attention increasingly shifted towards the pay-TV market and he began to accumulate the rights to a number of films and performance rights suitable for this purpose, including those to soccer World Cup transmissions. The KirchGruppe was successful in purchasing the exclusive rights to live transmissions of German First and Second Division football matches and this was extended for another four years in May 2000. These matches are shown on Premiere World. In February 2001, the KirchGruppe acquired a 58.3 per cent stake in SLEC Holdings, which controls the rights to the transmission of Formula 1, for roughly €2 billion.

Publishing

The KirchGruppe also developed an interest in the printing and publishing industry. As noted by Tryhorn,[4] most of the involvement centred on the

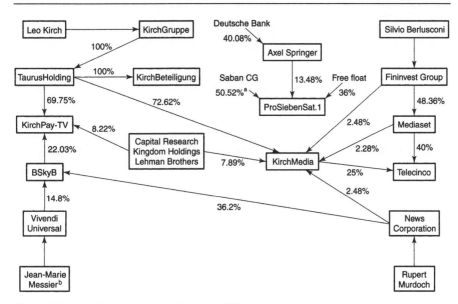

Figure 10.1 KirchGruppe linkages, October 2003.

Notes:

[a] 88.52% of the voting rights. [b] Replaced on 2 July 2002 by Jean-René Fourtou.

group's links with Axel Springer. Somewhat ironically, Leo Kirch's attempt to encroach upon the preserve of the long-established incumbent publishers was met by the kind of bitter opposition from Germany's media establishment that he subsequently reserved for those trying to encroach on his own interests. However, after fighting a protracted battle with shareholders to wrest control from Axel Springer's widow, he eventually acquired a 40 per cent stake in the company which gave him access to influential titles such as *Bild Zeitung*, Germany's top tabloid, and the prestigious broadsheet *Die Welt*.

The KirchGruppe structure in 2002

As shown in Figure 10.2, the KirchGruppe consisted at the beginning of 2002 of a wholly-owned holding company, TaurusHolding, and three strategic business units called KirchMedia, KirchPay-TV and KirchBeteiligung. However, this disguises somewhat the true complexity of the group which consisted of 150 public companies and somewhere between 200 and 400 corporate entities and separate business vehicles, many of which were not audited.

KirchMedia

KirchMedia was historically a profitable operation. It held the transmission rights for the Bundesliga and the World Cup Tournaments for 2002 and

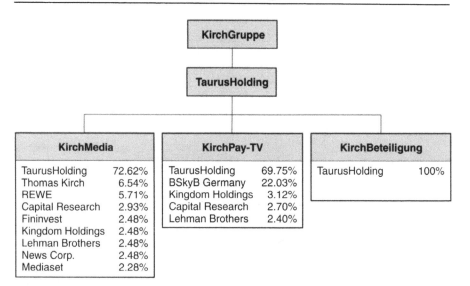

Figure 10.2 The KirchGruppe organization chart.

2006 and was also the home of the film rights held by the group. The ownership of KirchMedia included Silvio Berlusconi, with holdings via his private Fininvest Group and its subsidiary Mediaset, and Rupert Murdoch (via his minority, controlling stake in News Corp. which owned 2.48 per cent). Roughly one-third of its revenue came from selling pay-TV rights to KirchPay-TV.

KirchPay-TV

The financial problems of the KirchGruppe largely originated with KirchPay-TV, the home of Premiere World. It had struggled to acquire subscribers because roughly 90 per cent of German households could receive 30 free-to-air channels, often via cable. TaurusHolding owned 69.75 per cent of KirchPay-TV. Significantly, Rupert Murdoch acquired a put option allowing him under specified circumstances to demand that TaurusHolding repurchase the 22.03 per cent stake in return for €1.7 billion in cash.

KirchBeteiligung

The third business unit, KirchBeteiligung, was a wholly-owned subsidiary of TaurusHoldings. This unit contained the 40.33 per cent stake in Axel Springer Publishing, as well as a 77 per cent stake in the television transmission rights for Formula 1 racing.

The crisis unfolds

Although by no means its first, the difference between the crisis of 2002 and its predecessors was that whereas previously Leo Kirch somehow managed to engineer a rescue for his group, not least because he was well connected in financial and political circles, the sheer scale of the problem this time around – involving, according to the end-2001 balance sheet, €5.6 billion of bank debts and €2.3 billion of other liabilities but in reality at least €13 billion allowing for, inter alia, the series of put options – served to defeat him. The heavy reliance upon bank debt by the KirchGruppe was unusual for a modern corporation because raising funds via the issue either of shares or bonds is much cheaper; but the crucial aspect was that when Leo Kirch did seek to bring in new capital by tapping private investors, he allowed them to protect their investments with put options which, needless to say, he never expected them to exercise.

The beginning of the current crisis can strictly be traced back to early in December 2001, when the first rumours began to spread that Rupert Murdoch's News Corporation had ambitions to refinance, and take control of, the ailing KirchMedia. It was alleged that it would threaten the exercise of its put option to serve as a mechanism for the collapse of the KirchGruppe with a view to obtaining some of its assets, in particular ProSiebenSat.1, at a knockdown price, and that it might also make a move on Premiere World which was expected to need a further €2 billion of investment if it was to reach break-even. News Corp. was quick to deny the rumours, but few analysts were convinced since Murdoch's interest in the German TV market was well known and circumstances had never been more conducive to such a move. Warned of these intentions, Leo Kirch sought to raise capital to defend his company. Unfortunately, the previously compliant banks not only refused to extend additional credit but Dresdner Bank went so far as to demand repayment of a €500 million loan by the end of the month. With many of its other assets already pledged as collateral, the KirchGruppe offered to sell its stake in the Spanish TV company Telecinco, worth roughly €500 million, whereupon Dresdner Bank demanded that the stake be used as collateral in return for extending the repayment deadline to April 2002. Deprived in principle of this source of funds, Leo Kirch sought to persuade Axel Springer Publishing to agree to defer the exercise of a put option which would otherwise require the KirchGruppe to repay €750 million in January 2002 in return for the Springer stake in ProSiebenSat.1. At the end of January 2002, Axel Springer Publishing rejected his request for help and announced that it would exercise its option. This lack of co-operation was not surprising in view of the unhappy relationship that had existed for some time between the two companies, stemming from the time when Leo Kirch had, against the owner's wishes, successfully bought a large shareholding in Springer. However, it also has to be borne in mind that ProSiebenSat.1 had issued three profit warnings during 2001 and outraged minority shareholders with a proposal to merge the company with heavily indebted KirchMedia.

The situation was to worsen markedly in February when the director of Deutsche Bank, Rolf Breuer, questioned the creditworthiness of the Kirch-Gruppe in an interview with Bloomberg TV. This resulted in a refusal by Dresdner Bank to extend the credit that was due to be repaid in April, and a threat that it might even seek its early repayment.

Continued suspicions about the intentions of Rupert Murdoch also caused the relationship with BSkyB to worsen and the KirchGruppe representative on the BSkyB Board resigned. Mr Murdoch obstructed a plan to assist the KirchGruppe, and indicated that he would be seeking to reclaim his investment in Premiere World and would under no circumstances consider investing more funds in the venture. This continued pressure from foreign sources resulted in Chancellor Schröder, the Director of the Deutsche Bank and the managing directors of Bertelsmann arguing on the pages of *Der Spiegel* for a German solution to the crisis. The HypoVereinsbank responded with an offer to help the KirchGruppe by purchasing its 40 per cent holding in Axel Springer Publishing for roughly €1.2 billion. This could be viewed as a Bavarian as well as a German solution – and the offer was subsequently supported by, inter alia, Bayerische Landesbank and Commerzbank.

Leo Kirch rejected the need for any further assistance since he was already well advanced with discussions concerning the sale of Telecinco and was convinced that this would raise all of the funding required by the Kirch-Gruppe. Nevertheless, the offers kept coming in, with Bernie Ecclestone offering €800 million for the Formula 1 rights – much less than Kirch had paid to acquire them – while Hunziger was intent on buying the news agency DDP.

However, the crisis refused to subside and, on 14 February 2002, Leo Kirch met with his bankers in Munich to discuss the financial situation. A KirchGruppe spokesman denied that the DZ-Bank based in Frankfurt had demanded the repayment of a €400 million credit. At the same time, Deutsche Bank was meeting with other KirchGruppe creditors in Frankfurt and let it be known that it was sceptical about the possibility of a rescue bid for the company. The following day, the HypoVereinsbank and four other banks assisted the KirchGruppe by announcing that they were willing to continue their financial support, linked to a combined offer for the Springer stake. As a result of this move, Deutsche Bank also softened its attitude and participants spoke about an orderly retreat from the crisis. As part of this process, the KirchGruppe transferred to the DFL (the parent company of the Bundesliga) the sum of €100 million that had fallen due at this time in respect of the transmission rights for the Bundesliga. The KirchGruppe duly announced on 22 February that the planned merger between ProSiebenSat.1 and KirchMedia would no longer go ahead in June as planned but would be delayed until such time as the financial situation at KirchMedia had been improved. This delay created additional problems for the KirchGruppe because nearly all of the minority shareholders would be able to exercise their put options to return their stakes in KirchMedia if it failed to be floated on the stock exchange in June, and this would cost the KirchGruppe in excess of €833 million plus interest charges.

The pressure on the KirchGruppe increased further in March due to a number of factors. In the first place, although Axel Springer Publishing suggested that it was ready to assist in the search for a comprehensive solution to the crisis, it went on to note that it had prepared a legal complaint in relation to the KirchGruppe's apparent reluctance to repurchase the Springer stake in ProSiebenSat.1. For their part, the banks asked the KirchGruppe either to sell or close Premiere World in order to avoid bankruptcy. In response, the KirchGruppe announced that, as a last resort, it would be prepared to sell Premiere World and the Formula 1 transmission rights and to consider the sale of the television rights for the 2006 World Cup in Germany. It also announced some other measures including confirmation that the merger of KirchMedia and ProSiebenSat.1, slated for June, would not take place and that Premiere World would be restructured and would be earning profits by January 2004. As a result of these measures, the banks announced that they would in principle be prepared to provide a cash injection of €800 million provided that Leo Kirch was prepared to give up majority control of KirchMedia. In addition, the HypoVereinsbank granted a credit of €255 million to ProSiebenSat.1.

On 26 March, media industry experts suggested that KirchMedia was about to be taken over by a consortium involving Rupert Murdoch and Silvio Berlusconi. Leo Kirch had already indicated that he was prepared to cede control of the group and, as a result, the banks appeared to be willing to see Murdoch and Berlusconi take stakes of up to 20 per cent in return for their contribution to the €800 million recapitalization. The following day it became clear that KirchMedia also required a bridging loan of €150 million to avoid immediate insolvency. However, in the event, the banks could not agree among themselves on the terms for a loan. Furthermore, the complications were not merely financial. Although, technically, Germany has no restrictions on foreign ownership of media assets, politicians in Berlin were becoming very nervous about the possible major involvement of Silvio Berlusconi in the German media market. Chancellor Schröder stated that it was 'not unproblematic' when the head of government of a friendly partner state of Germany gained influence via his private business interests over the German media sector.

As the various pieces of the KirchGruppe slipped towards insolvency, the interested parties continued to search for a solution. On 2 April, Rupert Murdoch made one last effort to reach a solution by inviting the bankers to discussions in Los Angeles, but only one top manager from the four major creditor banks was able to be present at the discussions and these duly ended without achieving anything worthwhile. The Hollywood studios also intervened at this point by announcing that they were willing to lower the price they were asking for their films in exchange for a share in the KirchGruppe. At the Kirch HQ, contingency plans were put in place for KirchMedia to be declared insolvent. A spokesperson argued that they wanted to be sure that they could put forward a rescue plan since, according to their understanding of the position, they would have eight weeks (following insolvency) to convince the court that they had a sustainable solution.

The impact of the KirchMedia insolvency

The KirchGruppe announced the insolvency of its core business, KirchMedia, on 8 April 2002, and it was confirmed that Leo Kirch was prepared to stand down as chairman. The position of KirchPay-TV initially remained unclear. The insolvency had consequences for all of the main stakeholder groups.

The banks

The insolvency would have a variable effect upon the main creditor banks – much depended on how well loans were secured and to what extent they had already been written down in balance sheets. Deutsche Bank and Dresdner Bank seemed likely to escape most lightly. Deutsche Bank might have recourse to the 40 per cent stake that the KirchGruppe held in Springer Publishing and this would more than cover the credit of €700 million that it had extended to the KirchGruppe, while Dresdner Bank might or might not have access to the KirchGruppe's much sought-after stake in the Spanish TV company Telecinco – it had made the loan to TaurusHolding whereas the assets were held by KirchMedia. As for the stake in SLEC, this appeared to have been pledged to Bayerische Landesbank, JP Morgan and Lehman Brothers.

Many of the banks had cause to worry because their loans were partly secured against the film rights held by the KirchGruppe. It was questionable how much such rights were worth, given that new films had not been added to the library for some time because of the financial situation at the Kirch-Gruppe. Furthermore, KirchMedia owned distribution rights rather than film rights in many cases and the pay-TV rights could only be sold to Premiere. These banks initially seemed to lack the resolve to do much about the potential losses at the KirchGruppe, in part because the latter was continuing to make interest payments. In any event, the Bayerische Landesbank – the biggest creditor by far and 50 per cent owned by the state of Bavaria – could rely on the Bavarian Government to step in if it faced major problems.

The minority shareholders

Leo Kirch was not the only loser from the crisis. Rupert Murdoch and News Corp. had also lost out, at least for the moment. In December 2001, Murdoch planned to use his option to return his shares in Premiere World as the way to force a takeover of large slabs of the KirchGruppe. This would have enabled Murdoch to make his long-desired entrance into the German media industry. However, an insolvency of the group would have the effect of rendering worthless his option to resell his shareholding in Premiere World to the KirchGruppe, and the fact that it did not work out the way it was planned was in many ways Murdoch's own fault. He could have made his demands as early as January 2002 because the number of subscribers to Premiere World was below the target originally agreed, and at that time he could either have disposed of his stake in the company or taken control of Premiere World. However, Murdoch decided to postpone his put option in return for a 2.48 per cent stake in KirchMedia, and on 8 April these shares had become worthless.

Murdoch nevertheless remained the most likely person to replace Leo Kirch because the short-list of global media moguls was indeed short. Certainly, there were no real German contenders given that the Bertelsmann Group was disqualified by competition policy rules. If foreign investors needed to be let in, then Rupert Murdoch/News Corp. was definitely regarded by the German establishment as the lesser of two evils compared to Silvio Berlusconi/Fininvest. The German political establishment was simply not prepared to allow the head of another state to participate in the German media industry.

Axel Springer Publishing also did rather badly out of the insolvency. The KirchMedia administrator – Wolfgang van Betteray – was very sceptical about the status of the company. Springer tried to exchange its stake in ProSiebenSat.1, once worth €767 million, for a share in the restructured KirchMedia, but van Betteray argued that these shares were now worthless so Springer would be obliged to invest new money if it wished to participate. It might have been willing to do that if it could have obtained a blocking minority stake of 24.1 per cent, perhaps in conjunction with contributions from other shareholders such as Rupert Murdoch, but at the time Springer did not have the money to invest. Deutsche Bank was left to decide, together with Friede Springer, what was to become of the Kirch shareholding in Axel Springer Publishing, since it could not be ruled out that KirchBeteiligung would also become insolvent. Springer continued to argue with the administrator concerning the value of its shares, and it was expected to be able to retain its 11.5 per cent stake in ProSiebenSat.1.

The politicians

The political dimension of the crisis was important. In particular, the Bavarian minister, Edmund Stoiber, viewed the demise of the group as a challenge to his model of Bavarian capitalism. Since a large number of jobs were at stake, this was also a concern for the then Federal Chancellor, Gerhard Schröder, who wanted to be seen as economically competent. Herr Stoiber defended the loans given to the KirchGruppe by the Bayerische Landesbank since he believed that the KirchGruppe investments in Bavaria were crucial for the development of Munich, initially as the centre of the

German media industry with 100,000 jobs and eventually as the centre of the European media industry. For this reason, he was pleased to support the Bayerische Landesbank's credits to KirchMedia.

Towards resolution

In mid-May, the European Broadcasting Union stepped in with an offer to buy the European broadcasting rights for the 2006 World Cup for €525 million – €10 million more than the price originally paid by the KirchGruppe. Although the rights had been transferred to a Swiss-based KirchGruppe subsidiary just prior to the bankruptcy of KirchMedia, the latter's administrator was legally empowered to reclaim them. What was not clear, however, was whether Fifa was in a position to then reclaim them for itself and reassign them to the EBU.

At the end of May, Rupert Murdoch formally requested that TaurusHolding redeem the BSkyB stake in KirchPay-TV. Technically its put option did not fall due until October, but the failure to hit operational targets plus the breaching of banking covenants triggered clauses permitting earlier redemption. Clearly, Murdoch was unlikely to get his hands on any immediate cash, but BSkyB was thereby raised towards the top of the list of creditors should anything eventually be salvaged from the ruins of KirchPay-TV. The three other major investors were also expected to trigger their put options.

A deadline of 10 June was set by the KirchMedia management for minority shareholders and creditors to agree on a recapitalization, to include a debt-for-equity swap. This would then enable the stake in ProSiebenSat.1 and the film library to be transferred to a new company free of liabilities. Some 82 bodies registered an interest in some or all of the constituent parts of KirchMedia, the assets of which would be opened up to bids in July or early August. The US film studio Columbia TriStar opened discussions with Commerzbank and publisher WAZ Gruppe with a view to making a joint bid for the great bulk of KirchMedia and they were favoured to win the auction although the consortium membership was still under negotiation and did not have exclusive bidding rights. It was also riven by internal dissent over who was to take management control and the need for an exit strategy via a partial flotation of the revived KirchMedia at a later date.

Commerzbank – expected to take a 40 per cent stake in the bidding consortium – calculated that an offer would have to be in the region of €3 billion for a company carrying €3 billion of debt. Although KirchMedia as it stood was only worth a maximum of €2.5 billion, the bidders would be obliged under German law to buy out the minority shareholders in ProSiebenSat.1 for roughly €900 million. As of mid-June, the consortium's main rival appeared to be the Axel Springer and Heinrich Bauer consortia, but the make-up of the Commerzbank consortium then suffered a severe blow when the WAZ Gruppe withdrew.

Meanwhile Clemens Vedder, a well-known German corporate raider, expressed an interest in the Alex Springer stake, even though Springer declared its first-ever loss for the 2001 financial year. His approach followed that of, inter alia, BC Partners which offered €1 billion – but all were rebuffed. For his part, Leo Kirch attempted – probably with little hope of success, although a court awarded him control over the shares until August – to prevent Deutsche Bank from gaining control over the shares, while Friede Springer, who controlled a majority of the shares in conjunction with other heirs of Axel Springer, attempted to impose conditions on transfers of voting rights – which allegedly required the authorization of the Springer board, even though KirchBeteiligung was a major stakeholder.[5] Furthermore, several other banks with outstanding loans were unwilling to see the stake transferred to Deutsche Bank – although Commerzbank itself abruptly withdrew its proposed involvement in the purchase of the Springer stake in May – fearing that it would subsequently auction it off for a sum sufficient only to recover its own loan, so the matter was still some way from resolution.

Any hopes that the remaining parts of the KirchGruppe could soldier on were dashed in mid-June when both TaurusHolding and KirchBeteiligung filed for insolvency, and the task now remained to identify the parts of the KirchGruppe that could be saved. Many of the film rights would have to be sold at a loss, which would almost certainly be bad news for the payments due to the content providers like the Bundesliga clubs. Other viable parts of the business, such as ProSiebenSat.1, could be restructured, perhaps under the control of News Corp. which had made a success of BSkyB, while loss-making ventures, such as KirchPay-TV, would have to be closed unless a buyer could be found. Not surprisingly, such a solution was unlikely to find favour in Germany where a more traditional approach was favoured involving some kind of deal with the banks which would minimize evaluation and disclosure of the viability of parts of Kirch, together with guarantees and soft loans from public bodies.

In September, Springer scored a victory in a Munich court when it ruled that Leo Kirch could not sell his stake without Springer's consent. He was also barred from stripping the shares of their voting rights and moving them to a trust with a view to selling them to the WUZ Gruppe, Springer's profitable rival which had allegedly offered between $800 million and $900 million for the shares. Meanwhile, Springer was negotiating a strategic partnership with Ringier of Switzerland which, given a price in excess of the WUZ offer to Kirch, would be tantamount to a merger. When the WUZ Gruppe dropped its offer shortly thereafter, and Ringier raised its demands, this seemed even more to be the intent. For its part, Deutsche Bank reserved its position, although it had conducted preparatory work on placing the shares, recognizing that it would make more money if a friendly deal was struck between Springer and Ringier which would be free of regulatory issues and generate substantial synergies.[6] It was suggested that Ringier could sell on part of its acquired stake to Friede Springer who was anxious to raise her stake beyond 45 per cent in order to terminate conflicts with other family members.[7] What subsequently emerged was a complex plan whereby Springer would first buy Ringier, and Ringier shareholders would then use the proceeds to acquire 90 per cent of Leo Kirch's stake in Springer, with the other 10 per cent being handed over to Friede Springer. Unfortunately, this indicated that the Kirch stake in Springer was worth only $600 million whereas Deutsche Bank was looking for a much larger sum, and although Ringier was smaller than Springer, its management wanted to exercise more control than Friede Springer was willing to concede on the grounds that, unlike Springer, it was profitable. With CEO Michael Ringier raising the ante by insisting that Ringier was worth more than previously suggested, and that he would not let the company fall under the control of Friede Springer, it was hardly surprising that negotiations had stalled by the month end.[8]

Elsewhere in the Kirch empire, with the due date for bids approaching rapidly, and with a view to easing the situation, all interested parties in KirchMedia were authorized to submit bids for its main sporting rights – the 51 per cent stake in ISPR (part-owned by Springer) and KirchSport – which were attracting interest in their own right. On that basis, bids were expected to fall below the $2.7 billion price tag now placed on the whole of KirchMedia. The surviving interested parties appeared to be, respectively, TF1, the French TV group, in association with US Media entrepreneur Haim Saban; Columbia Tristar, part of Sony together with Commerzbank; and a group of existing shareholders led by Lehman Brothers – but neither the list nor the amounts on offer could be pinned down with any certainty.[9] It was also unclear whether bidders would be obliged to buy out the minority shareholders in ProSiebenSat.1 – somewhat surprisingly, publication of the auction documents revealed that Springer had a pre-emption right over 16.5 per cent of KirchMedia's 52.5 per cent stake in ProSiebenSat.1 in the event of its sale. Furthermore, Springer executives were militating to exercise a major role in ProSiebenSat.1, allegedly to prevent overcharging by other parts of the Kirch Empire. As if to prove the general fluidity of the situation, a new bidder for KirchMedia suddenly appeared in the form of publisher Heinz Bauer, backed by the HypoVereinsbank.

Meanwhile, the sports rights came under separate offer by its management, backed by entrepreneur Robert Louis-Dreyfus, and a consortium led by Leo Kirch, while, for its part, bids for the pay-TV unit Premiere appeared to be forthcoming from the same people interested in Deutsche Telekom's cable businesses: Goldman Sachs, Primera, Apax Partners, Warburg Pincus; and Liberty Media with Apollo and Blackstone.[10]

Needless to say, even these complex scenarios were not to prove the dividing line between the end of the negotiations and the beginning of the auctions. For example, BAFin, the German financial markets regulator, notified the bidders for KirchMedia assets that, under the terms of the new takeover code introduced in January, the consortium members would be treated as a 'concert party'. Hence, since they would be bidding for over 30 per cent of its equity, they would have to bid for the whole of the assets of ProSiebenSat.1, including the 36 per cent free float worth $740 million – to which would have to be added the outstanding $1.3 billion of debt. Nevertheless, the sports rights were sold off by way of a management buy-out by Kirch Sports Group for an undisclosed sum in October.

For its part, Deutsche Bank grew weary of the negotiations with Ringier and announced its intention to auction the Springer stake in early October – the end of September constituting the last date authorized by the courts for Leo Kirch to come up with an alternative solution. Since due diligence could not be completed that quickly, Deutsche Bank was in practice going to have to wait some weeks for a realistic bid, potentially allowing the Ringier impasse to be resolved. In any event, the Vinkuliering still hung heavily over the heads of the parties concerned.[11] On 8 October, Deutsche Bank put paid to speculation and probably avoided any further problems with the other creditors by itself buying the stake for $670 million as the sole bidder, announcing that it intended subsequently to either sell on the shares or arrange a flotation.

As for KirchMedia, here the waters were muddied by the re-appearance of Mediaset as a bidder in conjunction with TF1 and Mr Saban, given that it was controlled by Silvio Berlusconi, the then Italian prime minister.[12] KirchMedia creditors expressed a clear preference for the bid by the Bauer consortium, which allegedly was offering roughly $500 million in cash for the 36 per cent stake in ProSiebenSat.1 while proposing to roll the film library's debts into a new vehicle without any additional financing. However, Mr Saban promptly submitted an overbid worth $800 million plus between $200 million and $400 million to settle the film library's debts; although the administrator refused to put this offer before the creditors, hoping to sign the deal with Bauer by Christmas and conclude it by the end of March.[13] This partiality by the administrator proved discouraging to Springer, which announced in mid-December that it intended to exit the television business in favour of the print media. Somewhat oddly, Springer had just strengthened its own hand by getting a court to agree that the $750 million it was calling in by exercising its put option could be exchanged for a large chunk of KirchMedia's stake in ProSiebenSat.1, but it now seemed intent of selling of its own 11.48 per cent stake in the latter.[14]

There was a real sign of progress when Premiere was finally sold off to the private equity house Permira in mid-December, with the deal pencilled in for completion in early 2003. Permira itself would take a 70 per cent stake, paying in cash, with creditor banks converting outstanding loans into a further 20 per cent. Georg Kofler, the new CEO, and two other managers would acquire the residual 10 per cent stake. It was forecast that Premiere would reach break-even in early 2004 and would now have sufficient cash to last until that point was reached.[15] Almost immediately afterwards the Bauer consortium purchase of the ProSiebenSat.1 stake for $720 in cash was agreed, and there was talk of the additional purchase of the Springer stake as well as an open offer for the free float. However, the Bauer consortium pointed out that the deal was conditional upon its acquisition of the majority of the film rights, which was less than straightforward because the various creditor banks had opposing views as to how best to get (part of) their money back.[16] Whereas the creditor banks were being asked to roll-over old Kirch debts, most of them wanted to exit at the earliest opportunity. What also needed to be taken into account, in the event, was the return of Haim Saban's consortium to the bargaining table with a much enhanced offer of $2.1 billion. Its offer was supported by the US government, which may or may not have been sensible but appeared to have put pressure on the administrator not to ignore the consortium a second time, although he remained adamant that the Bauer offer was the best available. However, regulators began to drop hints that the Bauer consortium bid could break the rules governing media ownership in Germany.[17]

On 11 March, the Bauer consortium suddenly withdrew, stating that it refused to be drawn into an auction. It was claimed privately that Heinz Bauer wanted nothing to do with Haim Saban's 'American methods', particularly 'the relentless media leaks'. For its part, KirchMedia pointed out that it preferred the Saban offer anyway. However, there were still some issues arising from TF1's role since it was thought to need a rights issue to raise the $420 million it was allegedly contributing. On 16 March, it was confirmed that the Saban offer had been accepted, the first time a major media asset in continental Europe had been taken over by a non-resident. The first tranche of the fee would be roughly $525 million – negotiations over the film library were ongoing and would raise the total cost to around $2 billion – but TF1 would not be party to it unless it came up with shareholder backing to provide the requisite funds before the deal was closed. Haim Saban also indicated that he had not yet decided whether to make an open offer for all outstanding ProSiebenSat.1 shares even though he would hold over 30 per cent. Nor was it clear whether stock market regulators would enforce an open offer, leading minority shareholders to complain to the regulator in May.

Shortly afterwards, the situation finally became clearer. The Saban Capital Group (Saban CG) would acquire a 36 per cent stake in ProSiebenSat.1 carrying 72 per cent of the voting rights. Springer would then trade its pre-emption right on a further 16.52 per cent in return for a 2 per cent stake. This would ultimately leave Springer with 13.48 per cent, Saban CG with 50.52 per cent and a free float of 36 per cent.[18] As for the film library and film rights, these would also be sold to Saban CG for an unspecified sum subject to the agreement of the creditors and regulators. They would then be transferred to a new vehicle without any additional financing and, given the existing debts to banks and other creditors of $1.4 billion, there would be a gradual repayment of debt depending upon the KirchMedia cash flows. At the end of April, the cartel office unconditionally cleared the offer for

ProSiebenSat.1,[19] with TF1 offering to commit up to $170 million to the various purchases. Meanwhile, Haim Saban continued to negotiate over the film rights and also with the likes of private equity groups Blackstone and Thomas H Lee about their taking stakes worth between $500 million and $800 million in a holding company set up to acquire the Saban stakes. However, the banks expressed their unhappiness at arrangements whereby Saban CG would pay only $78 million initially and nothing further until 2006, and prospective partners, aside from TF1, were scarce on the ground as they felt that Haim Saban was trying to impose unreasonable terms as well as being deterred by the weak dollar (raising the price in euros) and the threat of recession in Germany.[20]

The creditors accordingly drew up an alternative plan whereby they would take control of ProSiebenSat.1 and contribute to a recapitalization of up to €300 million, which would also be funded by proceeds from the recent sale of KirchMedia assets. They would then hold on to the assets for roughly two years before attempting to sell ProSiebenSat.1 without the film library. This was just as well since, on 3 June, Haim Saban withdrew his offer. This was partly triggered by a ruling by the German takeover regulator that Mr Saban would have to tender for the whole of ProSiebenSat.1 unless he could make out a case that the target company was a 'Sanierungsfall' – a restructuring case deemed to be in need of the funds that would normally go towards a full bid. As Lex pointed out,[21] it was hard to understand why there was such reluctance to buy the superficially valuable assets represented by ProSieben.Sat.1. Although in the short term it faced a vicious circle whereby falling advertising revenue meant programming costs needed to be cut; which resulted in a loss in audience size, which resulted in a loss of revenues, etc., this could be overcome by additional investment and better scheduling. On a positive note, the Kirch Media administrator and ProSiebenSat.1 CEO proposed a deal whereby the latter would have cheap access to the film library for a period of ten years, payment coming from the advertising revenue generated from the programmes. However, while this would benefit ProSiebenSat.1 in the short term, it could rebound on it if the advertising market turned up appreciably.

The recapitalization of ProSiebenSat.1, split evenly between KirchMedia and creditor banks, was approved by its shareholders in mid-June, and led to a sharp upturn in its share price from roughly €4 to €6. However, in a surprising move, Mr Saban returned with a revived offer in mid-July. He was backed by a consortium of private equity groups, but his offer was only initially in the €6 to €7 range compared to his original offer of €7.50 and he did not want to be forced to make an offer to all ProSiebenSat.1 shareholders. So would the KirchMedia creditors take the money and run or continue with their plan to recapitalize ProSiebenSat.1? Predictably, they accepted the offer when it was raised to €7.50 a share (excluding the film library) at a total cost of €1.3 billion ($1.48 billion), to include €525 million for the 36 per cent KirchMedia stake, €280 million of new financing, plus a public offer for the ProSiebenSat.1 preference shares trading at roughly €5.60 which would not otherwise be converted to ordinary shares.[22]

Conclusions

The peculiarly German dimension notwithstanding, the demise of the Kirch-Gruppe is at heart a not uncommon tale of what the *Financial Times* refers to as 'old-fashioned imperial over-reach involving new-fangled technologies and financial instruments'.[23] The trouble with collections of media assets is that they are rarely all profitable, let alone at the same time. Thus, for example, KirchMedia depended entirely upon free-to-air TV broadcasting (ProSiebenSat.1 and Telecinco) for its pre-tax profits during 2001. The other assets lost money and devoured cash. While profits from trading film rights continued to underpin the KirchGruppe, they had to be offset against the heavy interest payments resultant from its reliance upon bank debt.

In essence, Leo Kirch was taking a number of calculated risks. In the first place, he took the risk that interest payments would always comfortably be covered by earnings. Second, he took the risk that the banks would always be compliant, and that political pressure would be placed upon them, especially in Bavaria, at times when they became less amenable. Third, he took the risk that he could attract large amounts of private capital via the issuance of put options which he would never be called upon to honour.

Certainly, he was not the only person to be totally wrong-footed by the sharp decline in advertising revenue during 2001, with its consequence that ProSiebenSat.1's market value was heavily depressed. Nevertheless, Leo Kirch built up his empire in a traditionally continental manner by acquiring a number of minority stakes or majority stakes lacking the crucial element of control. When conditions were auspicious, and the profits were rolling in, this made little difference overall. However, in adverse conditions it meant that the KirchGruppe was no longer in full control of its destiny. Leo Kirch's strategic approach was also flawed in other respects. For example, given the success of BSkyB in the UK, a smaller market than Germany, it is perhaps surprising that Premiere acquired so few subscribers. However, the UK market is not dominated by cable and there are only a handful of free-to-air channels. Add in poor customer service and poor construction of tariffs and the recipe for failure at Premiere was well and truly mixed.

Furthermore, and not uncommonly for a media company, the Kirch-Gruppe's accounts lacked transparency, although they were probably the most opaque of all. Under such circumstances, the banks were at best careless about checking the status of their collateral. It was suspected in many quarters – and subsequently proven in certain cases – that Leo Kirch was using the same assets as collateral for more than one loan. For example, the stake in Springer was extended as collateral to five banks. After debacles along the lines of Long Term Capital Management, one might have expected major banks to seek out the overall picture before committing themselves to a significant share of the total exposure.

The demise of the KirchGruppe has achieved several things. In particular, it has managed the not inconsiderable achievement of pitting against one another not merely political parties (Social Democrats versus Christian Democrats/CSU) but financial institutions (in general, those based in Frankfurt (Deutsche Bank) versus those based in Munich (HypoVereinsbank and Bayerische Landesbank)) and business interests (those favouring the opening up of corporate Germany versus those favouring solutions hatched up in the traditional 'smoky rooms'). But is it a pointer to what is about to happen elsewhere? In part the answer must be that it already has happened elsewhere on a more limited scale – witness the demise of ITV Digital in the UK, the bankruptcy of NTL and the problems at Telewest and UPC. However, the really interesting question as the KirchGruppe saga unfolded was the fate of Vivendi Universal (which is addressed in detail in a separate case). As Figure 10.1 above shows, media empires tend to be inter-linked, so serious damage at one inevitably has negative implications for the others. Because the German dimension has been absent elsewhere, it is unlikely that there will be another collapse along the lines of the KirchGruppe, but even a cursory examination of the problems at other media groups indicates that the KirchGruppe should not be treated as unique.

It is not appropriate to dwell too much on the German dimension because it is not specific to the telecommunications sector. Nevertheless, anyone intent upon forecasting the future shape of the media industry in Europe cannot ignore the tendency to support 'national champions' against outsiders on the continent (though not in the UK). After the debacle of Deutsche Telekom's abortive bid to acquire Telecom Italia, it is hardly surprising that a company such as Mediaset, with its direct connection to the Italian prime minister, should raise hackles, but the KirchMedia administrator certainly seemed intent upon handing the company on a plate to the exceedingly Germanic Bauer consortium come what may.

Given the simultaneous collapse of so many organizations, a radical restructuring of the European media industry must surely be imminent, and xenophobia is hardly going to assist in the process. However, a widespread refusal in continental Europe to let the matter be decided according to Anglo-Saxon business practices is by no means the only contentious issue: There is also the need to overcome concerns over accounting fudges if not outright fraud and a straightforward lack of resources among 'suitable' buyers whose share prices have fallen heavily and whose cash piles have been depleted to prop up the many unprofitable parts of their own empires. At least in the short term, therefore, the banks are likely, albeit unwillingly in many cases, to end up holding significant chunks of the European media industry. In the longer term, the all-important issue is whether the likes of Rupert Murdoch and Liberty Media's John Malone (who has fingers in a great many pies including a significant stake in News Corp.) will be permitted to muscle their way into the continental media industry and turn it into yet another outpost of the dreaded 'popcorn culture'. So far, the omens are not good with Liberty Media's failed attempts to acquire cable assets from Deutsche Telekom a case in point.

In conclusion, we have apparently not yet seen the end of the Kirch-Gruppe saga although the major decisions have now been made. Once the KirchGruppe is no more there will need to be a period of careful management to bring its independent pieces onto a stable footing. Only time will tell whether this will prove to be an opportune time to embark upon this particular voyage of discovery.

Part IV

Illustrative application of strategic modelling IV

In this final set of chapters we look at two quite different companies united by the fact that their understanding of the future did not materialize. Cable & Wireless (Chapter 11) thought that IP-based services would rapidly replace the more traditional telecommunication services while Marconi (Chapter 12) aggressively entered the IP equipment market just before the bottom was to fall out of the Internet and telecommunications markets. In other words, both companies made large bets on how the future would develop that did not come to fruition – at least not before their finances imploded under the strain.

An integral component of the changing fortunes of Cable & Wireless (hereafter C&W) and Marconi is leadership, or, perhaps more accurately, the changes in management that new senior executives brought about. In the case of Marconi, the conservative management style of Lord Weinstock was replaced by that of Lord Simpson. As Simpson set about transforming Marconi, he cast side the conservatism of the Weinstock era and dramatically sold the core defence interests to BAe. This sale provided Simpson with the cash that subsequently funded the expansion of Marconi into new markets.

As events turned against Marconi, the management of the company increasingly found themselves at odds with one another. If nothing else, the resulting blame game highlighted the divisions within the management. However, if there were divisions, how was Simpson able to enact his chosen strategy? On the one hand, Simpson was Weinstock's chosen successor and this gave him a certain degree of creditability. One the other hand, the board did not appear to restrain the senior management in their actions. Having said this, many analysts welcomed Simpson's strategy and this would have limited the ability of the board to restrain, let alone criticize, the cash-based acquisition strategy on which he embarked.

The situation was somewhat different in the case of C&W. For many years, the management of C&W had been criticized for their inaction. This abruptly changed with the appointment of Dick Brown, who began to transform the company through buying and selling 21 businesses for around $20 billion in a handful of years. This policy was continued and deepened by Graham Wallace who, in essence, moved C&W out of residential and voice telephony markets into business and IP-based service markets. A rising share price and supportive comments by analysts suggested that the strategy adopted was the right one.

However, most good things tend to come to an end. While a combination of factors did conspire to derail the new strategy of C&W, the problems faced were compounded by some of the management decisions taken. For example, the decision by Wallace to acquire Web-hosting businesses was questioned by many, not least because this was a very competitive market and the businesses acquired were loss-making. Second, the shares accepted in part payment for Hong Kong Telecom from PCCW were retained only to see their value plummet. Again, the logic for retaining the stake was widely questioned by analysts. The shares were ultimately sold for a small fraction of the value initially placed on them. As Wallace was closely associated with all of these decisions, he understandably sought to defend his actions and solve the increasingly pressing set of problems that C&W was facing. Having failed to do so, Wallace was replaced by Francesco Caio in 2003.

It is interesting to note that although both Marconi and C&W funded their acquisitions from the capital raised from selling their existing businesses, there was one fundamental difference between the two companies: Marconi used all its available capital to fund its expansion into new markets whereas C&W did not. This meant that when the chosen strategies of the two companies went against them, C&W had more breathing space in which to react. Not only did this enable the company to think through a new strategy more fully and comprehensively than it would have been able to do if on the verge of bankruptcy, but it could also use its remaining resources to avoid bankruptcy. In contrast, without the luxury of financial reserves, Marconi was forced into bankruptcy.

The strategy of C&W can be understood through reference to the growth share matrix. As we stated in Chapter 2, the growth share matrix provides a framework for management to manage the portfolio of businesses within the company. The framework is composed of two axes. On the vertical axis is the growth rate of the market in which the business operates, while on the horizontal axis is a measure of the relative competitiveness of the business unit in this market. Both axes are divided into 'high' and 'low' to form the four cells of the matrix: stars, cash cows, question marks and dogs.

In essence, the strategy of C&W was quite simple. The company would address the frequent criticism that it was nothing more than a loose collection of investments around the world through selling many of these and re-investing the proceeds in new markets such as those that are IP-based. One motive for the sales was that C&W was a minority shareholder in these investments, and as a consequence lacked control. Another motive was that these investments were located in the slower-growing, and lower-valued parts of the telecommunications industry.

Using the terms of the growth share matrix, how can this strategy be understood? Those businesses to be sold were the cash cows, whereas those that would receive the additional investments due to their promise were stars. As shown in Chapter 11, C&W was able to raise substantial sums from the sale of numerous businesses around the world. C&W partially benefited from the widespread appreciation of value across the TMT sector. The resulting cash mountain was then used by C&W to fund its expansion into new markets; that is, into stars. However, this description is static in nature and does not take into account how events transpired.

The description is inaccurate because the new businesses did not produce the anticipated level of revenues or, for that matter, profits. The competitive nature of many of the markets that C&W entered ensured that expectations were not met either initially or over time. This can be illustrated in respect of the expensively acquired American web-hosting businesses. As a consequence, a gap appeared between what C&W was saying it would deliver and what it actually did deliver. The businesses were re-organized in an attempt to stem their losses and move them into profitability. That several re-organizations were entered into suggests that the confidence that C&W management had in these businesses was misplaced, and that a more appropriate description of them would, in fact, be question marks and not stars.

Stemming the losses, both in the USA as well as in IP-based markets elsewhere, was central to these businesses becoming star businesses, with all that this entailed. The problem became ever more pressing as the cash mountain raised through the sale of the assets dwindled away, and was compounded by the introduction of competition into the Caribbean market where C&W was often a monopoly provider and hence it represented a cash cow. As the cash mountain was used up to fund the move of C&W into new markets, the Caribbean became the most important source of capital for the company, but the removal of its monopolies meant that the region could no longer be relied on to provide sufficient capital for use elsewhere in C&W. In other words, the cash cow is increasingly unable to fund the IP-based strategy that management believes will transform the company, but the opposite side of the coin is that C&W has finally got to grips with the need to dispose of its dogs such as its American network, so all is not yet lost.

Through the use of the growth share matrix, attention is drawn to how a company may be transformed through using cash cow businesses to expand into new markets. In the case of C&W this strategy was very attractive, especially as it would ensure that long-standing criticisms of the company would be tackled head on, and new, valuable markets entered in the process. However, as events demonstrated, this is easier said than done. The new markets that C&W entered proved not to be stars but rather, at least initially, dogs, whose problems could not be resolved through continued investments.

Chapter 11

Cable & Wireless

Cavalier & wasteful

Introduction

Cable & Wireless (hereafter C&W) is one of the world's longest-lived telecommunications brands, having been in existence for roughly 130 years. By the end of 1997, it was the one hundred and eighty-seventh most valuable company in the world. One year later, it was ranked 153 and worth $22.7 billion, and a year after that it was ranked 143 and worth $41.1 billion. This sharp increase is clearly shown in Figure 11.1, where the share price soars at the end of 1999. Its value had fallen back slightly to $39.9 billion by the end of 2000, although its rank had risen to 133. Its value peaked in March 2000 at over $60 billion, yet by the end of 2001 it was worth a mere $7.7 billion and not even ranked among the 500 most valuable companies in the world. Nevertheless, even that dismal performance could not compare with the collapse of the share price to 40p in December 2002 – a level last seen 20 years previously – with C&W's debt reduced to junk status.

To lose $60 billion in value might appear to be careless at best – although Vodafone and others have lost a great deal more. However, the interesting question is not 'how much?' but 'why?', and it is this question that is addressed below. It is a salutary experience to open the Annual Report and Accounts for 2002 where the then CEO, Graham Wallace explains (p. 5) that 'the underlying competitive strengths of our businesses, combined with our cash position, provide a sound basis for improvements in future profitability and cash flow', and compare it with p. 8 where the somewhat astounding fact is reported that 'including all exceptional items and goodwill amortisation, losses per share were 187.4p'. So how was so much value destroyed and this venerable company brought so low?

Background

The global perspective

Until fairly recently it was possible to argue that C&W was best regarded as a global alliance of sorts, in that it had a stake in companies supplying terrestrial and mobile telephony throughout the world. In the mid-1990s, its

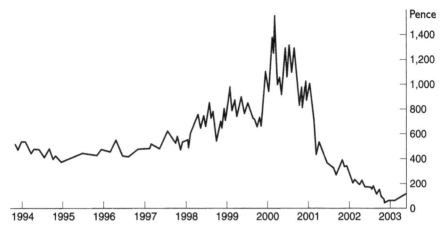

Figure 11.1 Cable & Wireless share price, 1993–2003 (pence).
Source: Daily share prices in the *Financial Times*.

major holding was a 54.2 per cent stake in Hong Kong Telecom (HKT). In the UK it operated as Mercury Communications, and in the USA it operated as CWI. Other interests encompassed, inter alia, Optus Communications (Australia's second-largest carrier); Tele2 (Sweden's second-largest carrier); Barbados External Telecom and Barbados Telephone Co.; Batelco (Bahrain); Grenada Telecom; TOJ (Jamaica); CTM (Macao); Dhivehi Raajjeyge (Maldives); St Kitts and Nevis Telecom; YITC (Yemen); Telecom of Dominica; FITL (Fiji); Eastern Telecom (Philippines); Solomon Telekom; Telecom Vanuatu; Petersburg Long Distance (Russia); and TSTT (Trinidad and Tobago).[1] In fact, allowing for its links with NTT, Toyota and Itochu in Japan, the Ministry of Posts and Telecommunications and the Shanghai and Guangdong operators in China, and Bell South in Australia, C&W had particular strengths in parts of the world where other ostensibly global alliances such as Concert and Global One were relatively weak. On the other hand, it had no substantive connections with any of the world's major carriers, and hence was weak in Europe and the USA where the other alliances were relatively strong.

In 1995, Veba of Germany took a 10.5 per cent stake in C&W (costing $1.35 billion) to seal a strategic alliance, named Vebacom, with a view to offering strong competition in the German market.[2] C&W, in turn, took a stake in Vebacom. In May 1996, C&W announced that it was in the process of developing a tripartite joint venture between Veba, itself and Stet, the then Italian incumbent, which would subsequently take a stake in C&W of up to 15 per cent. However, in October, events took an unexpected turn when RWE defected to the Vebacom camp,[3] thereby making the latter a major force to be reckoned with in the biggest European market[4] and providing C&W with a decent foothold in Europe outside the UK.

The most pressing problem was the need for C&W to come up with a strategy for its highly profitable holding in HKT prior to the hand over of the colony to China in June 1997. The Chinese Ministry of Posts and Telecoms requested that it be given a stake in HKT with C&W retaining control, and a 5.4 per cent stake was duly sold to China Telecom for $1.2 billion in July 1997, with the possibility of further transfers in return for improved access to the Chinese market via share swaps. Despite this, C&W was explicitly excluded from participation in the flotation of 25 per cent of China Mobile (Hong Kong) in October 1997 into which China had transferred several mainland mobile phone companies.

The UK connection

The British fixed-wire incumbent, British Telecommunications (BT), was split off from the Post Office towards the end of 1981. At the time of its initial privatization in late 1984, and for a considerable time thereafter, BT was protected by the fact that only one significant competitor, Mercury, 80 per cent owned by C&W and 20 per cent by Bell Canada International, had been licensed (in 1982) on the grounds that open competition would result in the destruction of new entrants rather than of the entrenched former monopoly.[5] Mercury, understandably, chose to cherry-pick the most valuable parts of the network, comprising businesses in major cities, and especially the City of London, and the relatively profitable long-distance and international markets. The regulatory review conducted by the Office of Telecommunication (Oftel) in 1991 led to the abolition of this cosy duopoly, and effectively opened the market to any network, existing or to be laid down, with the proviso that no new international network would be licensed.[6]

Mercury was originally perceived primarily as a major network operator that, by under-cutting BT, would attract large numbers of residential customers and effectively become a second incumbent. However, in December 1994, Mercury announced that it intended to withdraw from most residential services unless delivered in partnership with cable companies, sell off its payphones, contract out its directory enquiries and shut down its multimedia activities and customer premises equipment. It also abandoned plans to provide wireless in the local loop and chose instead to concentrate upon the business market. The root of the problem lay partly in the fact that the price gap between BT and Mercury had become quite modest from 1992 onwards, especially for businesses that could obtain volume discounts from BT, and partly in the aggravation involved for customers wishing to switch suppliers given the absence of number portability at that time. It was somewhat ironic that Mercury became the victim of a two-way squeeze between, on the one hand, an incumbent forced by the regulator's price cap to cut its costs and, on the other hand, new entrants such as cable companies let loose by the decision to terminate the duopoly agreement.

Despite the advances made during the initial decade post-privatization, BT's global reach was by no means complete, and it remained relatively weak outside the European Union. Hence, a strategic link with an operator in the Far East such as C&W had obvious attractions. As noted previously, C&W was itself an assorted collection of telecoms alliances, depending heavily upon its stake in HKT, the 'jewel in its crown', for its profits. In 1995, an internal split over strategy led to the resignation of senior executives and effectively put C&W into play. It was approached by BT in November 1995 with a view to a merger. The biggest difficulty was that under Hong Kong stock exchange rules, a bid for C&W would also have obliged BT to buy out the 42.5 per cent of shareholdings in HKT not owned by C&W, thereby raising the overall cost of a merger to an unacceptable $26 billion. It was therefore proposed that C&W would instead acquire BT by issuing new shares. This would also have had the benefit that, by retaining the name C&W, there would in theory have been no need to renegotiate all of C&W's arrangements with individual governments in the 50 or so countries in which it operated. A second obvious problem was that the merged group would have needed to dispose of both its 80 per cent stake in Mercury and its 50 per cent stake in UK mobile operator Mercury One-2-One in order to avoid regulatory problems in the UK.

A further difficulty was that BT already had an alliance with Viag while at that time, as noted above, C&W had an alliance with Veba, called Vebacom, in which C&W had a 45 per cent stake. Hence, one of these alliances would have had to be dismantled. There was also a question mark concerning the UK government's 'golden share' in C&W,[7] not to mention some uncertainty concerning Beijing's attitude towards Hong Kong Telecom after its takeover of Hong Kong in 1997 and the uncertain reaction by the US authorities to C&W acquiring BT's stake in long-distance operator MCI. In the face of these difficulties, and given C&W's determination to be fully valued, the proposals initially came to nothing. Negotiations were revived, but they were finally terminated in May.

No longer cabled

C&W's decision to reinvent itself as a niche player in business markets was unlikely to resolve its difficulties because such markets were constantly being entered by new competitors. Its response, which enabled it to carry calls via its own long-distance network without the need to pay interconnection fees to BT, was to enter the cable market via the complex merger that created Cable & Wireless Communications (CWC). In October 1996, C&W (in the guise of Mercury) joined up with Nynex CableComms, Bell Cablemedia and Videotron to form a holding company (CWC), the UK's then biggest cable company. Bell Cablemedia bought a 60 per cent stake in Videotron Holdings, while its parent, Bell Canada, joined with C&W in making an offer for Bell Cablemedia. Nynex CableComms was folded into CWC at a notional value of $2.5 billion, and C&W paid $250 million to buy the 5 per cent of Mercury it still did not own from Bell Canada. The total value of CWC was estimated at approximately $8 billion but, in order to secure ownership (52.6 per cent) and management control, C&W had only to put up $580 million in cash. Having received clearance from the European Commission on 11 December 1996, CWC was floated at the end of April 1997. It traded under the name of Cable & Wireless.[8]

In the short term, CWC was heavily dependent upon telephony for its revenue, but it eventually decided to forgo the use of telephone lines and signed up with Network Computer (NCI) to provide a 200-channel service using its cables, with a national service intended to come on stream early in 1999, thereby permitting Internet access at between 20 and 100 times the speed of existing modems. The biggest loser would initially be Telewest, but the next largest operators included International CableTel, which paid $360 million in March 1996 to acquire NTL – under which name it subsequently traded – the former transmission arm of the Independent Broadcasting Authority, thereby becoming a national operator at a stroke. By June 1996, there were only three remaining companies of any size – CWC, Telewest and NTL.

Early in 1999, Telewest opened exploratory talks with C&W with a view to buying parts of CWC. However, in July 1999, C&W confirmed that it had also entered negotiations with NTL and France Télécom with a view to selling to them the residential cable interests of CWC (CWC Consumer Co), representing three-quarters of its value, for roughly $12.5 billion, while retaining the old Mercury long-distance network (CWC Data Co). NTL's decision to pursue a joint approach with the French carrier reflected the fact that it was loaded down with debt and C&W wanted to be paid partly in cash.

At this point in time, CWC, NTL and Telewest were roughly equal in size, so the issue was whether there would be further mergers. The eventual deal, announced on 26 July 1999, had three components. The first consisted of an offer by C&W for the 47.4 per cent of CWC not already in its ownership at a cost of just under $10 billion. The second consisted of an offer by NTL for CWC Consumer Co in the form of 54.4 million new NTL shares (equivalent to a 12 per cent stake), $4.5 billion in cash and $3 billion in assumed debt. For reasons of tax efficiency, Bell Atlantic was permitted to take its payment exclusively in NTL stock, while C&W was able to take mostly cash. The third consisted of a cash injection of $5.5 billion into NTL by France Télécom in return for a 25 per cent stake in the enlarged company. The takeover was finally given a clean bill of health in March 2000.

Strategic issues

For most of the period since its flotation,[9] Cable & Wireless had seen its share price lag the FTSE All-Share index, and even during 1998 it barely bettered the index during a period when BT's share price rose nearly twice as fast. This could partly be attributed to the fact that it no longer provided demonstrably cheaper services than other carriers. Furthermore, it had jettisoned the Mercury brand name and those of its cable TV partners, and was looking relatively pedestrian compared to the nimble WorldCom. The lowest point in its fortunes was probably in 1995, when the then chairman and chief executive were dismissed after a damaging boardroom dispute – note the static share price in Figure 11.1. The company's response was to appoint Dick Brown as chief executive. He duly set about restructuring in no uncertain manner. On the one hand, he acquired new interests, 21 in total worth $20 billion,[10] including a 49 per cent stake in C&W Panama, costing $650 million, on the grounds that it offered more certainty of return than an investment in mainland USA. On the other hand, he proposed a multi-billion dollar disposal of minority holdings by the end of 1998 where C&W lacked control or direct influence, including its stakes in Bouygues Télécom and the South African carrier MTN.

C&W was very active outside the EU after the beginning of 1998. In March 1998, for example, it sold its 22.3 per cent stake in Occel of Colombia; in April it disposed of most of its East European interests including PLD Telecom, PeterStar and Belcel to News Corp;[11] and in August it sold its 18.5 per cent interest in MTN for $400 million.[12] In November, it moved to raise its stake in the now renamed C&W Optus to 52.8 per cent.[13]

The most interesting development during the first half of 1998 was the proposed link with Telecom Italia, announced in May, which included the transfer of the stake in Bouygues Télécom and part of the stake in C&W West Indies and C&W North America.[14] However, Telecom Italia withdrew from the latter transactions in July, and was unable to buy the stake in Bouygues Télécom because its majority shareholder, Bouygues, exercised its pre-emptive right to the stake[15] which was offered to it by CWC on identical terms to those negotiated with Telecom Italia. The link was formally severed in November, partly as a result of the resignation of Gian Rossignolo, the Telecom Italia president, who was the driving force at the Italian end.[16]

In statements made in mid-1998, C&W gave the impression that it did not intend to compete directly with incumbents in the EU, but rather to target business customers and niche markets in the main cities. It would use its international connections to become a global transport company.[17] This would represent a move away from C&W's historic image as a holding company for a jumbled collection of overseas assets. C&W remained fairly dependent upon its revenues from Hong Kong Telecom – at the time roughly 30 per cent of the total – but this dependence was shrinking and the missing link in its global aspirations related to the acquisition of a service provision facility in the USA. Although that route was felt to be prohibitively expensive, C&W surprised the markets in May 1998 by putting in a successful bid to acquire the Internet backbone business of MCI for $625 million.[18] When the European Commission subsequently insisted on the sale of MCI's entire Internet operation as a condition for authorizing the WorldCom merger with MCI, C&W secured the retail businesses as well, paying $1.75 billion in all.[19]

Dick Brown commented at the time that 'we have bought the future'. Certainly, C&W had now gained, at a stroke, an established position in the USA; its brand image had received an enormous boost on a global scale; and it had opportunities to expand in the fast-growing data transmission business. It immediately seized one by winning a three-year network management contract with the UK subsidiary of America Online.[20]

In November 1998, C&W announced that it would be investing $1 billion over five years to build a fibre-optic network linking over 40 cities in 13 countries – a much grander design than that revealed in mid-year. To this end, it had formed a partnership with Hermes Europe Railtel and was also buying $100 million of 'dark fibre'[21] from Global Crossing, an independent company developing a global network. However, it would lease existing capacity to make the final connections.[22]

The abrupt departure of Dick Brown in January 1999 left the company in better shape but still without a clear strategy given the failure of its Italian linkage and the lack of progress in China. It had an interest in 54 businesses in 33 countries and, on a pro-rata basis, three million customers. However, it still had an image problem compared to the likes of AirTouch and Vodafone. With the share price for ADRs in New York fluctuating around $11 at the end of 1998, but a break-up value of perhaps $14, C&W was expected to attract the attention of predators in the existing atmosphere of 'anything goes' mega takeovers. Shrugging such concerns aside, C&W's new boss, Graham Wallace, announced in April 1999 that C&W would be getting out of businesses where it had neither influence nor control, and hence that it would be selling its Global Marine business to Global Crossing for $900 million, mostly in cash.[23] He claimed that the ultimate objective was to turn C&W into a specialist business-to-business service provider with a truly global reach. To this end, C&W would be increasing its annual investment to over $5 billion a year.

In an attempt to bolster its Far Eastern influence, C&W launched a hostile takeover bid in March 1999 worth $560 million in cash for IDC of Japan where its 17.7 per cent stake was under threat from another, friendly, bid by NTT.[24] It also launched a hostile $964 million takeover bid for AAPT, Australia's third-largest carrier, having previously acquired a 10.6 per cent stake from Singapore Telecommunications.[25] C&W was ultimately successful in acquiring IDC once it had raised its own offer slightly,[26] whereas the Australian bid was unsuccessful because the C&W offer price was comfortably over-bid by Telecom New Zealand.[27] It nevertheless remained the case that many of C&W's remaining overseas assets did not fit in with its new strategy, even including C&W HKT which was an integrated service provider yet provided the bulk of C&W's profits. The company was accordingly sold off to PCCW at the beginning of 2000.[28]

Also in March 1999, One-2-One was put up for sale by joint owners C&W and MediaOne. A value of $17 billion was bandied around but no trade buyer was willing to countenance this price and all had dropped out by July.

However, it came as no great surprise when Deutsche Telekom, fresh from the rebuff in its attempt to take over Telecom Italia, made a successful offer in early August. The offer comprised roughly $11 billion in cash plus $2.4 billion in assumed debt and the repayment of $390 million of shareholder loans, and was completed at the end of September. The gross profit on C&W's stake worked out at $5.6 billion, equivalent to $2.50 a share, despite which the C&W share price fell back to under 700p compared to nearly 1000p at its peak earlier in the year.

As previously noted, in July 1999 C&W acquired the 47 per cent of CWC that it did not already own and simultaneously sold CWC's residential cable assets to NTL rather than Telewest. This left C&W with Data Co, effectively the old Mercury, and it was expected that this would be merged with C&W Europe in due course. This would simplify C&W's operations since it had previously struggled to meld the business services of the two companies given their partially separate structures. While this move appeared to unravel the master plan devised by Dick Brown, it served to focus C&W upon its business services and the two deals generated a gross profit of at least $2.5 billion. The downside was that the slimmed down C&W looked to be a more attractive target for a predator than it had been previously. However, it was not destined to remain a cheap target for long

The good times roll

A quick glance at Figure 11.1 demonstrates only too clearly how the financial markets responded to the prospects for C&W at the beginning of 2000 – although it has to be borne in mind that they felt the same way about almost everything connected with the TMT sector at this time. Within the space of a few months in early 2000, the C&W share price doubled as C&W was perceived to be getting its strategy on course. Divested of CWC, it agreed with Compaq Computer to invest $500 million over five years in a global joint venture designed to provide an end-to-end e-commerce service for small and medium-sized businesses. This would be the first to offer a full range of services – Internet access, website hosting and renting application software, electronic procurement, unified messaging, remotely managed network computing services for PCs and servers and Internet telephony. C&W thereby hoped to become a leading application(s) service provider (ASP). Normally, subscribers to an ASP pay a monthly fee for a software package running on machines 'hosted' in a remote data centre. However, the twenty such centres to be built by C&W would provide a more extensive portfolio of services.[29]

C&W's plans to become Europe's leading provider of business Internet services, at a total cost of $1 billion, initially progressed nicely. It acquired ISPs Xpoint in Austria, ISDnet in France, Unidata and DSNet in Italy, Intercom in Spain, and agri.ch and Petrel Communications in Switzerland to add to its existing INS in the UK, ECRC in Germany and pi.se in Sweden. Not only would the ISPs bring a great deal of business traffic onto its networks but they would enable C&W to develop services such as Web-hosting. Its core IP network was extended at a cost of $500 million to encompass 18 cities by April 2000, with an eventual target of 200 cities in 2002. In the USA, WorldCom's attempt to take over long-distance carrier MCI initially failed to satisfy the Federal Communications Commission, and a new deal was struck that also obliged MCI to dispose of its retail customers, on which basis the Commission authorized the takeover in July. This meant that a new negotiation for the expanded Internet interests had to take place, which resulted in C&W paying a total of $1.75 billion, as noted previously. The newly merged MCI WorldCom now controlled roughly 20 per cent of the US Internet backbone compared to 31 per cent for C&W. For the time being, C&W could claim to own one-twelfth of the world's fibre-optic capacity and status as the third-largest carrier of international traffic.

A new decade dawns[30]

At the dawning of the new decade/century all appeared to be well in the world of C&W. The share price was rising like a rocket as the company settled into its new existence as a business-oriented Internet and data services operator with a strong balance sheet (as shown in Table 11.1). With lots of cash in the bank as a result of the disposals noted above, and more to come from CWC and C&W HKT, and gearing (percentage of debt to equity) at a lowly 11 in March 2000 (down from 87 a year earlier), the future seemed rosy. Most of the revenue came from the UK (£2.78 billion), Hong Kong (£2.25 billion) and Australia (£1.65 billion), and the decision was made to re-organise the company as of 1 June 2000 into C&W Global, C&W Optus and C&W Regional (mainly the Caribbean holdings). The numbers for 2000 nevertheless failed to excite since, after stripping out acquisitions and disposals, growth appeared to be no better than average for the sector, and the share price fell back sharply. However, as Lex noted[31], growth could be expected to speed up and hence C&W 'looks good value for investors and would-be predators'.

In June 2000, C&W strengthened its position in the ASP market by forming an alliance with Microsoft to launch software applications for small businesses accessible remotely over the Internet.[32] A month later, it teamed up with Nokia Networks to launch hosted applications to mobile operators, ISPs, dot.coms and companies wishing to exploit wireless data technologies[33] and bought five additional small Internet companies for £67 million (bringing the total for the year to 22).[34] However, the first clear signs of rumbling discontent in the Caribbean became public in August[35] and led to a second collapse in the C&W share price which had recovered well during the early summer. In Barbados, Trinidad and Tobago and the Windward and Leeward Islands, C&W was under increasing pressure to give up its lucrative fixed-wire, mobile and international monopolies – in Jamaica, the government was refusing to pay compensation for premature termination of the

Table 11.1 Seven-year financial record, year ending 31 March (£ million)

	1997	1998	1999	2000	2001	2002	2003
Group turnover[a]	6,050	7,001	7,944	9,201	8,099	5,911	4,391
as revised[b]					7,851	5,748	
Group operating profit/loss before exceptionals[a]	1,538	1,651	1,602	1,020	178	(824)	(452)
Exceptionals	0	(250)	46	(1,370)	(444)	(4,359)	(5,548)
Group operating profit/loss[a]	1,538	1,401	1,648	(350)	(266)	(5,183)	(6,075)
Other exceptionals	0	837	198	4,452	3,670	142	(475)
Profit/loss pre-tax	1,418	2,184	1,822	4,024	3,632	(4,718)	(6,373)
Profit/loss post-tax	1,131	1,940	1,463	3,574	3,112	(5,029)	(6,409)
Minority interests	454	652	555	(150)	258	94	124
Profit/(loss)	677	1,288	908	3,724	2,854	(5,123)	(6,533)
Assets	9,669	12,915	17,487	21,528	24,267	16,308	–[c]
Liabilities	4,358	7,402	9,490	10,403	7,884	6,885	–
Equity shareholders' funds	3,749	2,964	4,571	8,096	15,252	9,024	2,149
Diluted earnings/(loss) per share	29.5p	55.6p	37.5p	150.9p	103.5p	(187.4p)	(280.4p)
Dividends per share	11.1p	12.3p	13.5p	15.0p	16.5p	16.5p	1.6p
Net cash					–	2,629	1,619

Source: Cable & Wireless Annual Report and Accounts 2001, p. 81 and 2002, p. 77; Annual Report 2003, pp. 41, 43, 85.

Note:
[a] Excluding share of joint ventures and associates. [b] It is not possible to reconcile the accounts for 2003 directly with those for 2001 and 2002 published in 2002 due to revisions for the two previous years (only) in the 2003 Annual Report (see pp. 43–4). Some idea of the scale of the revisions can be seen here and others are available by reference to the (somewhat different) five-year summary published in the 2003 Annual Report, p. 41. [c] The net total for 2002 is given as £9,357 million and the net total for 2003 as £2,520 in the 2003 Annual Report (p. 85).

fixed-wire and mobile monopolies in November 1999 – and was engaged in various actions relating to access in the British Virgin Islands, St Lucia and Dominica.

In October, C&W selected Nortel Networks for a £1 billion network and outsourcing project which would include the implementation of a global voice over IP (VoIP) platform. Voice traffic would be migrated onto the network over a three-year period. By the end of November IP nodes had been established in Amsterdam, Frankfurt, London, Paris, Sydney and Tokyo, and during 2002 a total of 200 points of presence would be established. Meanwhile, IDC was building a 10,000 kilometre fibre-optic backbone in Japan to connect up 80 cities and, in the USA, C&W Global, Compaq and Microsoft launched C&W a-Services in September.

Publication of the half-year results to September 2000 revealed a net increase in cash of £8,212 million, of which half represented net asset disposals – mainly CWC and C&W HKT. The net cash position was accordingly turned around dramatically to show £4,188 million (£7.1 billion in the bank less debts of £2.9 billion) and the share price steadied to end the year close to 1,000p.[36] On the face of it, C&W's cash-positive position was a rarity in the telecommunications sector at that time, and although heavy investment of roughly £3 billion on the international IP network was pencilled in for 2001, the talk among fund managers was largely about whether C&W should return its surplus cash to shareholders. As Lex put it,[37] C&W 'is no longer a laughing stock. Nor is it a mediocre investment trust. . . . C&W provides a vehicle for investors excited about corporate data and Internet services.' However, somewhat prophetically, Lex added that 'there is plenty of execution risk'.

Annus horribilis I

As shown in Figure 11.1, C&W's share price suffered its third severe collapse at the beginning of 2001. A number of factors accounted for this. In particular, the situation in the Caribbean continued to cause problems. In February, C&W announced its intention to depart the St Lucia telecommunications market on 31 March, complaining that the government had enacted new legislation and licensed a new operator before C&W's licence was due to expire. A similar situation (liberalization plus licence termination) was already in force in St Kitts and Nevis, Grenada and Dominica and was pending in St Vincent and the Grenadines. The response of the Organization of Eastern Caribbean States (OECS) was to threaten to evict C&W from four other islands, and C&W rapidly backed down. During March, C&W and the OECS negotiated a phased dismantling of C&W's monopolies and the start of the liberalization process, signing an agreement in early April, which was generally seen as leading to a big reduction in C&W's profits in the area, which were a quarter of the total at the time.[38]

Meanwhile, in February, C&W put a sale sign on its remaining stake in PCCW, which had fallen heavily in value due to a collapse in the latter's value, and on its stake in C&W Optus which, unlike the PCCW shares, immediately provoked keen interest,[39] and the prospects of these disposals at depressed prices put further downward pressure on C&W's share price. However, the worst damage was done by the announcement in March that revenues in the USA were falling due to a sharp (annualized at 50 per cent) decline in the price of Internet traffic, while in Japan the price of international calls had fallen by 40 per cent in under a year. As a result, C&W intended to cut its workforce by 4,000[40] – equivalent to roughly 22 per cent of the C&W Global workforce – resulting in a charge of £350 million during the second half of 2001 on top of a write-down of £450 million in respect of obsolete equipment. The share price promptly fell from 678p to 545p,[41] followed by a further 58p the next day: so much for the execution risk. C&W promptly postponed its network roll-out in Japan and pulled out of the broadband Internet market in the UK. However, it managed to avoid a debt downgrade.

There were the odd bits of good news. For example, in February, the Global.net broadband Internet access service for businesses, previously available only in Japan and the USA, was extended to Western Europe, while in March C&W was selected by Vodafone to carry its global voice traffic. However, there was an increasing clamour for the cash pile to be returned to shareholders rather than invested in poorly performing businesses. This could be seen as a classic case of City short-termism since its denizens had been applauding C&W's strategy only a year previously. However, the numbers did look a little strange. C&W had cash deposits of £4.2 billion plus stakes in NTL (£0.64 billion), PCCW (£1.07 billion) and C&W Optus (£2.76 billion). Since the market value of the company at the end of March amounted to £12.4 billion, all of C&W's operations were effectively valued at a mere £3.73 billion – less than its cash in hand.[42] This was potentially increased at the end of March when it was offered £3.1 billion for its C&W Optus stake by Singapore Telecom, mostly in cash, which it accepted.

The first signs of a boardroom clear-out now appeared with the media claiming that the 70-year-old chairman, Sir Ralph Robins, should depart. For now, the CEO, Graham Wallace, seemed to be secure, although major stakeholders were alarmed that the two main strategic options – pouring more money into C&W Global, even though it appeared to be years away from profitability, and simply sitting back for now while minimizing short-term losses – both looked likely to burn through the cash mountain. The sale of the US and Japanese operations was much favoured by analysts, but since it effectively represented an acknowledgement by senior management that their strategy had been a miscalculation, they were unlikely to comply. Indeed, they determined to spend a good deal of the cash on acquisitions, initially, and unsuccessfully, attempting to execute a friendly takeover of US web-hosting company, Exodus Communications.[43] After a part-disposal of its NTL stake for £100 million, C&W had over £7 billion gross available for acquisitions, and the first purchase for $340 in cash and debt was Californian Web-hosting and content delivery specialist Digital Island,[44] which had been valued at $11 billion 18 months earlier. Although C&W already had 22 data centres around the world, these mostly dealt in simple collocation, whereas the acquisition of (loss-making) Digital Island would enable C&W to move into more complex, and hence higher value, Web-hosting. However, the markets were not enthused by acquisitions and C&W's share price fell further, as it did in mid-May when C&W reported that gross margins in the USA had fallen from 48 to 18 per cent.

Graham Wallace successfully sought shareholders' permission to buy back 15 per cent of C&W's shares should there be no further suitable acquisitions, and admitted that the company had mistakenly been chasing revenues instead of margins. Nevertheless, publication of the results for the year ending 31 March 2001 were well received, despite the operating loss, if only because the cash pile still existed and things could have been a lot worse – as, indeed, they were for most other carriers. Graham Wallace's strategy appeared to be to take the cash pile post the sale of C&W Optus of around £6 billion plus £2.5 billion in marketable securities, and invest £2–3 billion in C&W Global plus £700 million in Digital Island. The first claim on the residual would be acquiring local access in the USA and some would be returned to share-holders. In contrast, analysts preferred all of the cash to be returned followed by a takeover by a Baby Bell such as 5.4 per cent shareholder Verizon Communications.

One of the ironies of C&W's situation was that in holding back from further acquisitions on the grounds that valuations had further to fall, Graham Wallace was effectively announcing his expectation that the same would be true of C&W. When C&W Global predicted that its revenue would be 5 per cent lower in the second half of 2001 compared to 2000 this did not accordingly come as much of a surprise, but the share price still fell to a nine-year low of 275p, equivalent to a market value of £7.8 billion. According to analysts' calculations, this meant that, after allowing for net cash and investments, C&W Regional was worth roughly £1.9 billion, while C&W Global was worth only £1 billion – and that did not take account of the probable fall-out from the terrorist attacks in early September.[45]

Bowing to external pressure, C&W finally agreed in mid-November to hand back £1.7 billion to shareholders via a special dividend of 11.5p per share[46] plus a buy-back of up to 15 per cent of the outstanding shares, which would still leave £3 billion in the bank. The results for the first half ending 30 September contained no surprises[47] – although it was somewhat alarming to see revenue falling at C&W Global which was being touted as a growth business – but plans to invest a further £2 billion over the next two years meant that the cash pile would shrink to £1 billion. Graham Wallace remained sanguine, claiming that there was still more than enough cash to bring C&W Global to cash flow positive and pursue takeovers. He added that 'either by superb foresight or good luck we have come out of a variety of sectors at very good values'[48] and the share price actually looked to be ending the year in better shape than might have been expected. Neverthe-less, it could not withstand the purchase of Exodus Communications – a loss-making business in Chapter 11 bankruptcy in the USA – for $850 million in cash in late November which was seen by analysts as risky and long term.[49] Even though C&W was taking on only the best 30 of Exodus's data centres and doubling traffic on C&W's under-utilized Internet backbone, most accordingly advised investors to head for the exit door.

Annus horribilis II

The situation at the beginning of 2002 was that C&W appeared to be suffer-ing from a dose of schizophrenia. The C&W Regional networks, despite the difficulties outlined previously, used old-fashioned technology in unsophistic-ated markets to generate very large amounts of cash. C&W Global, on the other hand, used sophisticated technology in sophisticated markets to move ever further away from reaching free cash flow break-even. The consequent renewal of the decline in the share price was not helped by the revelation that C&W was caught up in the 'hollow swaps' scandal, whereby spare capacity was exchanged with other carriers and the 'sales' side of the ledger recorded as generating revenue even though no cash actually changed hands. The C&W finance director, Robert Lerwill, responded that this was not illegal, that US accounting standards were being met in full and that relatively little revenue was involved, but the markets understandably were not amused and he was subsequently replaced by David Prince while remaining head of C&W Regional.

By mid-May, the share price had fallen to 200p and the market value of the company to £7 billion. It was widely argued that senior heads needed to roll, and the first of these predictably turned out to be that of chairman Sir Ralph Robins – he was duly replaced by David Nash – who had gone on record the previous year with the claim that 'we are immeasurably better off for having committed ourselves to the IP sector'. That this was at best questionable was revealed in the half-year financial figures published in May which, while meeting reduced expectations, recorded a substantial pre-tax loss and stated the need to write-off £4 billion of assets and goodwill.[50]

In September, Graham Wallace announced three measures to boost cash flow and profit at C&W Global: the disposal of the US retail voice business to Primus Telecommunications for $32 million; further reductions in investment; and concentration on high-growth, high-margin customers. However, he also announced further falls in revenue which analysts interpreted as effectively a fourth consecutive profit warning. Nor were they impressed by his continued assertion that C&W Global would become cash flow positive in the fourth quarter of 2003–2004. After redoing their sums, they concluded that C&W Global now had a negative value on the balance sheet and demanded that the strategy should be abandoned in the USA together with the resignation of Graham Wallace. Despite the recent purchases there, dealing with the USA market was the clear priority with three possible options:

- *Close the entire operation:* Cost of £800 million; savings of £290 million a year.
- *Sell the entire operation:* Cost of £400 million; savings of £180 million a year plus sale proceeds.
- *Restructure the entire operation:* Cost of £280 million; save £325 million a year.

All of these estimates were precisely that, with many believing the costs of closing down to be much higher than those quoted. Not surprisingly, the latter option was the one ultimately chosen, with the strategy adjusted to encompass withdrawal from low-margin Web-hosting and data services for small and medium-sized companies and concentration on large contracts with multinationals. Applied throughout C&W Global, albeit concentrated on the USA and UK, the restructuring would run up an unexpectedly large bill of £800 million, mostly to cover the ending of leasing deals with other network operators and write-downs on surplus property.

The restructuring, duly announced in November, involved cutting a further 3,500 jobs in the USA and Europe and the number of global data centres from 42 to 23; but savings of £400 million a year in operating costs plus £200 million a year in investment were promised. Calls for the resignation of Graham Wallace were rejected by the board which was rewarded with a share price collapse to 83p, implying that C&W was worth less than its cash in the bank of £2.2 billion. Both Wallace and Nash claimed to be astonished that finally biting the bullet and acceding to the wishes of the financial markets had resulted in a massive dumping of C&W shares, but analysts argued that it was not a clean solution and that either further losses could be racked up in the USA or huge additional closure costs could be incurred.[51] This was borne out when the internal strategic review discovered that far from owning £897 million of leases, the true figure was actually £2.2 billion, of which £1.8 billion were held by C&W Global.[52] The remaining £2.2 billion net cash could thus disappear within a short space of time. For its part, Verizon Communications decided to bail out even though its stake was now worth less than £200 million.

Clearly, further boardroom changes were needed, but in practice it was not Graham Wallace but chairman-designate David Nash who resigned at the end of November (to be replaced in January 2003 by Richard Lapthorne). Unfortunately, this attempt at a sacrificial lamb was rapidly overtaken by the one kind of bad news the company could least afford: namely further revelations of non-disclosure. In this case it was triggered by a credit ratings downgrade by Moody's which awarded C&W's debt the status of 'junk', meaning that it could no longer be held by certain types of investment bodies which would have to dispose of it at depressed prices.[53] What had not previously been disclosed – on the grounds, claimed C&W, that its auditors considered such a downgrade to be a 'remote possibility' at the time, given that its debt was rated A3, three grades above the cut off for 'junk' – was that, at the time when One-2-One was sold to Deutsche Telekom, C&W had agreed that should such a downgrade occur it would provide £1.5 billion of collateral against potential tax liabilities arising from the sale.[54] The downgrade accordingly meant that C&W would either have to obtain a bank guarantee for £1.5 billion or ring-fence that sum in cash. Since this amounted to nearly three-quarters of its cash pile, the C&W share price understandably plummeted by 43 per cent[55], valuing the company at a mere £1 billion[56], even though C&W insisted that the cash would not be needed. As a result, C&W's capitalization fell below that required to retain its status as a FTSE 100 constituent.

As if this was not bad enough, a leaked confidential company report revealed that C&W Regional was struggling to compete with new entrants such as Digicel, which had already overtaken it in Jamaica, because it had a poor image with subscribers and was suffering from personnel defections and low morale. Although its mobile operations were generating considerable revenue growth and prospects remained reasonably good, the competitive threats were soon to pile up with liberalization already due in Jamaica in March 2003, in Barbados within the year and in Trinidad and Tobago. Meanwhile, in St Lucia, St Vincent and Grenada, C&W was finally forced to accept having Digicel – and later AT&T – deliver calls to fixed-wire destinations for the first time in February 2003.[57]

Out of the woods in 2003?

The prognosis in mid-January was that, at least temporarily, C&W had been given breathing space by Richard Lapthorne's appointment as non-executive chairman which was widely applauded by the financial markets and resulted in a 10p rise in the share price. Graham Wallace was expected to depart shortly, to be replaced, it was alleged, by the former CEO of Mercury, Duncan Lewis. He duly resigned as part of a general management reshuffle and the C&W share price rose to 64p, valuing the company at £1.5 billion.[58] However, Mr Lewis refused to consider the job, preferring to consider the possibility of participating in a break-up bid by a private equity company, but for the moment none were interested as they were deterred by the high risks involved, including change of ownership clauses linked to Caribbean licences which might have obliged C&W to renew its applications.

C&W subsequently sold half of its 30 per cent stake in Singaporean mobile operator MobileOne for roughly $70 million. This news paled besides the revelation in early February 2003 that C&W had been unofficially approached by PCCW, backed by Texas Pacific, with a view to a takeover bid worth £1 a share in cash – nearly double the market price at the time. PCCW would take on C&W Regional while Texas Pacific would take on C&W Global. However, given a combination of PCCW's insistence on examining C&W's books prior to a formal 'friendly' bid – a 'hostile' approach would have precluded access to the books and hence would have been somewhat unwise – and less than pleasant memories of the purchase of C&W HKT which had left C&W holding a large quantity of heavily-indebted PCCW's now largely worthless shares, it was hardly surprising that PCCW was told to go away in no uncertain terms. The financial markets barely marked up the C&W share price, indicating that they did not think the approach was serious, and PCCW duly announced that it would make no further contact with C&W.[59]

It was noted that major shareholders were bailing out, discouraged by the valuations – generally in the order of 45–50 pence – put on C&W until such time as it could recover the disputed funds. Prudential, Barclays, Fidelity[60] and in particular Franklin Resources, which had raised its holding to 10 per cent in June 2002, had become steady sellers towards the end of 2002. However, they had cause to regret this as the share price shot up 22 per cent on 24 March 2003 when the new chairman revealed that C&W had agreed to pay £380 million to the tax authorities to settle outstanding company tax liabilities for the ten years to the end of March 2001. In return, the ring-fenced cash would once again become available. The share price also rose sharply on 1 April (see Figure 11.2) when C&W announced the appointments of Francesco Caio as its CEO and Kevin Loosemore as its COO. It also stated that it would withdraw from domestic-only operations and focus upon providing a service to multinational companies across Europe. It had accordingly entered into an agreement with European data service provider IP-e-Ye and Swiss carrier Smart Telecom to sell its domestic-only businesses in Belgium, the Netherlands, Russia, Sweden and Switzerland, although the sums involved were trivial.

On 27 May, Graham Howe, former deputy CEO of Orange, and Kasper Rorsted of Hewlett-Packard, were appointed as non-executive directors – subsequently to be joined by Lord Robertson in the capacity of executive deputy chairman to replace Winfried Bischoff who announced that he would resign in July.[61] On 29 May, the share price rose back through £1 – a level last seen in November 2002 and nearly three times the 37p low seen on 9 December. However, the results for the year to 31 March 2003 proved to be far from uplifting, involving as they did a record £6.5 billion loss, suspension of the dividend and the announcement of withdrawal from the USA as well as 1,500 redundancies in the UK. On the other hand, cash reserves stood at £1.6 billion, and, despite a refusal by Mr Caio to spell out his intentions in detail, the share price remained resilient since the withdrawal from the USA

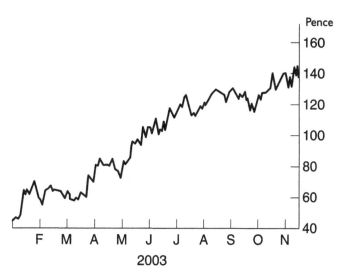

Figure 11.2 Cable & Wireless share price, 2003 (pence).
Source: Daily share prices in the *Financial Times*.

where a loss of £255 million had been sustained, and consequent refocusing upon the UK and C&W Regional appeared to inject a dose of realism in comparison to the Wallace years. The markets were also pleasantly surprised by Mr Caio's observation that C&W was making most of its money from voice telephony, even though he acknowledged that it was a declining market. Nevertheless, although C&W Regional remained extremely profitable, unravelling the previously opaque accounts had revealed that the UK operation, far from being profitable as was widely assumed, had sustained an annual loss of £303 million on declining sales – hence the need for job losses there. Mr Caio's remedy broadly appeared to encompass supporting companies such as Tesco that were launching own-brand telephony services and becoming more service oriented. He also made business units accountable for targets based on pre-tax profit rather than ebitda.

In the 2003 Annual Review and Summary Financial Statement, Richard Lapthorne summarized the revised strategy as incorporating: (1) a new, simpler organization that does away with the C&W Global and C&W Regional distinctions; (2) a devolution of responsibility to country-based chief executives; (3) a clarification of the lines of accountability; (4) a restructuring of the UK business; (5) a complete withdrawal from the USA by the least-cost route; and (6) a shift of focus from building infrastructure to serving customers. In operational terms what this meant was broadly as follows: C&W would sell off, support management buy-outs (MBOs) of, or outsource substantial parts of its business. The first two options would apply in the likes of France, Germany, Italy (agreed in May 2003) and Spain, in addition to the countries noted above.[62] The agreement with IP-e-Ye would typify the latter option, whereby IP-e-Ye would resell C&W's international network services while C&W would resell IP-e-Ye's network integration services. The obvious danger with this approach was that large companies had previously been persuaded that the only way for an operator to guarantee quality of service was by controlling the entire network, yet here was C&W stating that it would be able to maintain quality while reducing radically the number of controlled points of presence (already down from 30 to 11 in Europe).

In June, C&W also withdrew from its long association with the fixed-wire market in Hong Kong by selling its remaining 14 per cent stake in PCCW for £233 million. It subsequently issued a convertible bond worth £275 million, equivalent to roughly 7.5 per cent of its share capital, sold its German domestic business to Arques for an undisclosed sum and its French domestic business in France to Tiscali for €5.6 million and agreed severance pay with Graham Wallace amounting to the better part of £1 million. Net cash holdings at the end of June amounted to £1.6 billion. In July, Moody's downgraded C&W bonds to Ba3 from Ba1, but the share price had enjoyed such a dramatic upsurge in recent times that news of this kind appeared to do little to dent confidence.

In late July, C&W Jamaica announced that its Caribbean operations had suffered because of devaluations in the US and Jamaican dollar and ongoing liberalization. However, it was fighting back by launching a GPRS service in Jamaica over a network also enabled to provide enhanced data (rates) for GSM evolution (EDGE). Altogether, the roll-out would eventually encompass twelve countries in the Caribbean which would all initially be switched from TDMA to GSM. However, all that C&W would reveal about its proposed exit from the USA was that it was 'making progress'. This, it subsequently turned out, was in relation to a proposed management buy-out with backing from Blackstone.

Conclusions

Like Marconi, C&W spent the three years 1999–2002 unerringly transforming itself from a diversified and rather dull conglomerate into a company focused on a part of the telecommunications sector that is particularly prone to overcapacity and over-optimistic forecasts with, however, one difference: Marconi spent everything it had and ended up virtually bankrupt whereas C&W never got around to spending its entire pile of cash – and hopefully never will. On the other hand, what C&W did buy was questionable. Altogether, by the end of 2001, C&W had acquired £16 billion in cash plus various shareholdings in SingTel, NTL and PCCW. In turn, £9 billion had been spent on investment and acquisitions and a further £2.4 billion had been swallowed up in tax, interest payments and dividends. This left cash in the bank but the core business, C&W Global was shrinking instead of growing, partly because half of the revenue came from other telecoms companies which were either shrinking in size or going bankrupt. Unless that was remedied, C&W appeared to have no prospects other than to burn its way through its cash pile and end up as another Marconi.

Between the end of 2000 and the end of 2002, the cost per megabyte of IP traffic fell from £400 to £170. There was nothing C&W, acting alone, could have done about that, but the indictment of its management is that they saw it coming yet refused to take avoiding action. Having committed themselves to a major change in strategy, the board, and especially the executive directors, were unwilling to tarnish their reputations by acknowledging that they had got their timing wrong, dumping most of the loss-making IP businesses and falling back on the profitable C&W Regional operations. Indeed, top management appeared to be fixated by the fact that the cash cushion would see them through, come what may. The Annual Report for the year ending 31 March 2002 is full of revealing quotes to that effect, but one need proceed no further than page 2, where Sir Ralph Robins opens with the claim that 'our strong balance sheet and strong position in our chosen markets continue to distinguish C&W from almost every other telecoms company'. But for how much longer?

Undoubtedly, the Achilles' Heel in recent times has been C&W's somewhat cavalier approach to corporate governance. Not only did it engage, albeit in a modest way compared to the likes of Global Crossing, in the technically legal but highly dubious practice of 'hollow swaps', but it took what can only be described as a very conservative approach to rules on non-disclosure: that is, it disclosed nothing it could get away without disclosing.[63] Fortunately, under Mr Caio's regime, this should now be remedied.

As noted, the old-style C&W was treated by the investment community as something of a joke, approximating to an investment trust. Certainly, few among them questioned the sense in selling off many of the company's subsidiaries at peak prices, but many questioned whether C&W HKT should have been included and almost everyone questioned how the proceeds were being used. At the end of the day, what this case study suggests is that it is ultimately better to run a not-much-admired company as well as possible than to be carried away with grandiose ideas that destroy the reputations of all concerned – not to mention quite staggering amounts of wealth which, at the end of the day, largely formed part of ordinary people's pension funds. Having acknowledged that it was making most of its money from voice telephony, and that since only a few large multinationals needed a global telecoms provider it would be better off pulling in its horns to serve mainly UK businesses and those supplied by the former C&W Regional, C&W seems to be recovering gradually and avoiding the fate of Marconi. It is at least certain that it will never go bankrupt in the style of WorldCom, although the costs associated with shutting down the US operation will eat heavily into the cash pile. Overall, C&W is not fully out of the woods yet – the losses in the UK must also be addressed as a priority and may never show a profit – and undisclosed liabilities may yet come back to haunt it.

Chapter 12

Marconi

Come back Weinstock

Introduction

On 2 December 2000, *The Economist* ran a story[1] entitled 'Reinventing Marconi' which opened as follows: 'In three years, George Simpson has turned Britain's stodgiest industrial company into a high-tech communications business'. On 6 July 2001, the *Financial Times* devoted a full-page spread to Marconi which contained a story entitled 'Heroic duo's reputation hit below waterline'.[2] Evidently, the fall had been rather swifter than the rise, but a more accurate picture can be obtained by reference to Figure 12.1, which plots the share price over the past ten years or so. What this reveals is that Marconi's share price was extremely stable from the beginning of 1993 until the end of 1997, around the 250p mark. During 1998 and 1999 it roughly doubled, before taking off like a rocket at the end of 1999 to peak at 1,100p in January 2000. A sharp fall to 700p in April was followed by a further surge to roughly 1,250p in September. At the time of *The Economist* article the share price was well below its peak – albeit moving sharply upwards – and it may seem on the face of it, therefore, a rather odd time to be lauding the company's progress; but as most of the other case studies show, TMT stock prices in general were heading downwards at the time. Nor was there anything exceptional about the ongoing decline, but the drop in early July 2001 was both very sharp, accompanied by an extraordinary trading volume of over 500 million shares and, as subsequent history has shown, indicative of a company in near-terminal condition.

On the face of it, the story represented by Figures 12.1 and 12.2 has clear parallels with that recounted in the case studies on Cable & Wireless and Vivendi Universal, but with the difference that the former was a carrier while the latter was a media company, whereas the story of Marconi's rise and fall primarily concerns the equipment manufacturing sector. In every case the story concerns men with 'heroic' vision and an inability to understand why the markets lost faith in their ability to deliver it, and who were ultimately cast out – albeit well-rewarded – for their strategic shortcomings. However, it is easy to lay blame with hindsight, and the markets certainly supported Marconi's strategy during the late 1990s, so our purpose in what follows is to unravel the story and assign responsibility in as even-handed a way as possible.

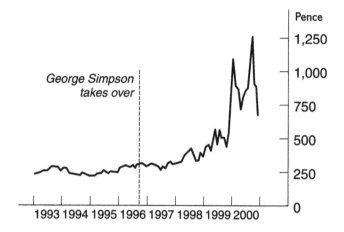

Figure 12.1 The Simpson effect.

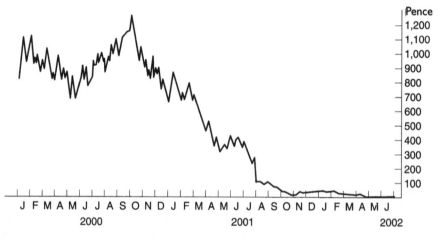

Figure 12.2 Marconi plc share price, 2000–2002 (pence).
Source: Daily share prices in the *Financial Times*.

Background

Once upon a time there was the General Electric Company, set up in 1886 and from 1963 run by Arnold Weinstock, who created a manufacturing giant during the 1960s through a series of takeovers, commencing with that of his father-in-law's electrical goods company. Interestingly, given his reputation in retrospect, the later-to-become Lord Weinstock was seen at the time as a dashing young industrialist who took control of a series of engineering companies going nowhere fast such as Associated Electrical Industries and

English Electric. As a result, the renamed GEC acquired a product list that included semiconductors and telephone exchanges, as well as a wide range of defence equipment. By virtue of factory closures and redundancies, GEC was able to produce a series of solid results and acquired a reputation for solid management in consolidating those initial gains. Rather than continue to expend cash on takeovers, Lord Weinstock preferred to set up joint ventures with the likes of Alsthom and Siemens. However, by the late 1980s many of GEC's markets were under attack from low-cost factories based overseas, and it became ever-more dependent for its profits on its protected domestic customers, particularly the Ministry of Defence and the then Post Office. While duly noting the growth potential in related sectors such as computers, consumer electronics and the provision of support services rather than hardware, Lord Weinstock preferred to take a conservative line – sticking to his knitting – to the extent that he failed to make a move to buy the then British Aerospace in the aftermath of its disastrous rights issue, although this could be excused by his reasonable expectation that such a takeover would anyway be rejected by the antitrust authorities.

Lord Weinstock was subsequently succeeded by his personal choice, George Simpson, a Scottish accountant who had worked for the then British Leyland – renamed Rover Cars – and British Aerospace – renamed BAe – after it acquired Rover in 1988. Although this was superficially at a knock-down price, Rover continued to struggle and George Simpson made his reputation by persuading BMW to pay £800 million for Rover in 1994 (only to regret its impetuosity for years thereafter). He also managed to sell Lucas, of which he was subsequently CEO, to Varity of the USA just before it suffered severe market turbulence. After he moved to GEC there was a falling out among the top executives at BAe where, in the light of substantial consolidation in the US Defence industry, the CEO advocated a merger with DASA, a subsidiary of Daimler-Benz, while the chairman, Sir Richard Evans, favoured an all-British merger between BAe and the defence electronics interests of GEC and its Marconi subsidiary. Towards the end of 1998, at a time when negotiations to sell these interests to Thomson-CSF of France were well advanced, George Simpson and Sir Richard suddenly announced that they would in fact be demerged and sold to BAe instead for over $10 billion in the form of BAe shares which would be awarded pro rata to shareholders. That done, George Simpson made the historic decision to concentrate upon restructuring GEC as a telecommunications business. To this end, GEC bought US-based Reltec and Fore Systems, the former for $2.1 billion in cash in March 1999 and the latter for $4.2 billion in cash in April 1999 – cash being required in both cases because Marconi was not listed in the USA. These companies specialized in manufacturing switches and optical fibres, and to support them GEC also bought a number of smaller software companies and consultancies such as MSI (for $680 million, half in cash, in April 2000) and US-based RDC. GEC also bought out the stake held by Siemens in its circuit-switched telecoms business trading as GPT.[3] Ultimately, in gross terms, Marconi spent a sum not far short of what it earned from the sale to BAe.

Towards the end of 1999, GEC changed its name to Marconi after the eponymous inventor of radio and moved the headquarters of its communications business to the USA. Noting that its major rivals, Cisco Systems, Nortel Networks and Lucent Technologies – all based in North America – preferred to outsource much of their manufacturing while concentrating upon high-valued-added activities, Marconi determined to follow suit. Nevertheless, along with its peers, Marconi's market value began to soar as the financial markets wholeheartedly took on board the claim that the 'Internet will transform the future of work'. At the end of 1998, Marconi was the one hundred and eighty-sixth largest company in the world by market capitalization. One year later it was one hundred and twentieth but valued at $45 billion, roughly twice as much. Most of this was accounted for by its telecoms businesses, although Marconi retained some of its legacy from its GEC days such as medical electronics systems and petrol pumps. Interestingly, the markets pressurised Marconi to dispose of these on the grounds that they offered only limited opportunities for growth, pricing Marconi's shares at a discount to pure telecoms rivals such as Alcatel and Nortel Networks, but George Simpson argued that he had to have relationships with end-customers and that these could be created via the sale of vending machines and petrol pumps to the likes of Coca-Cola and Exxon. Hopefully, these customers would then become interested in using fibre-optic links to individual machines to determine when, for example, a vending machine had broken down or needed restocking.

Matters of high finance

George Simpson, like Bernie Ebbers at WorldCom, relied heavily on his chief financial officer, John Mayo, who was first in line to succeed him as CEO of Marconi when he retired in 2001. John Mayo had made his name when organizing the spin-off of Zeneca from ICI, and had enhanced it while masterminding the acquisitions and disposals that underpinned the creation of Marconi as it stood in 2000. The collapse in the share price after Marconi was floated on the Nasdaq stock exchange in October 2000 was unhelpful, but, as indicated, simply appeared to reflect the experience of TMT stocks in general, and the share price remained well above the 250p of Lord Weinstock's reign. Nevertheless, the fact that Marconi's three larger rivals, all well-established in the world's largest market, were also suffering was not necessarily much of a consolation as orders began to evaporate. Equally, there was a noticeable trend towards wireless networks which were supplied by other manufacturers such as Ericsson, and even though wireless needed to connect up with fixed-wire networks at some point, the excess supply of fibre in fixed networks was growing larger by the day. Still, Marconi was able to respond that its customers were mainly the bluest of blue chips and that, unlike its rivals, it had never become heavily involved in the game of providing cheap vendor finance in order to secure sales.

Although Marconi remained sanguine, at least in official statements,[4] analysts increasingly began to talk in terms of a possible takeover, particularly by a company such as Cisco Systems which had the resources but lacked the optical switches made by Marconi.[5] John Mayo's skills could prove useful in such a context, it was felt. Meanwhile, he oversaw the purchase of integrated access device manufacturer Mariposa Technology for $268 million in September 2000, and set in hand plans for the partial flotation of Fibreway, Marconi's fibre optic network, during the first quarter of 2001. The financial figures for the first half ending in September 2000, released at the end of November, indicated significant revenue growth on a like-for-like basis, with operating profit following suit, but when heavy charges for goodwill amortization and exceptionals were set against these, the result was a pre-tax loss of $100 million.

But was this a symptom of an increasingly deep-rooted malaise or merely a reflection of market trends? Was John Mayo correct in arguing that Marconi had good longer-term prospects because it was focused on businesses 'that have the golden thread of communications running through them?' At the end of 2000 Marconi tended to be given the benefit of the doubt, with, for example, Martin Dickson in the *Financial Times* concluding that short-term difficulties should not be seen as detracting from the achievement of Lord Simpson (as he was by then) and John Mayo 'in executing one of the boldest and most successful metamorphoses of a British company in the past decade'.[6] Interestingly – echoes of Cable & Wireless here – he applauded Marconi's 'no-brainer' strategy of spending the company's notorious £3 billion cash mountain. Lord Weinstock's cries of horror were, unsurprisingly given the times, relegated to the back pages.

Seeking to gain a foothold in the mobile sector as it progressed towards 3G, Marconi agreed in February 2001 to take a $60 million stake in US-based ArrayComm, developer of smart antenna technology designed to boost network capacity. It also received a boost when BT announced in mid-March that Marconi would be the sole supplier of technology to its core optical network in a contract initially worth well over $1 billion, although it remained unclear whether it had been forced to cut its prices to the bone to beat off a challenge from Nortel Networks. However, analysts were rapidly beating a retreat from positions held only months earlier and began to berate Marconi for failing to respond to the market downturn which had led its rivals to announce profit warnings of varying severity. Although Marconi was less exposed to the fast-deteriorating US market, it seemingly could hardly emerge unscathed given that nearly half of its revenues were generated there, and analysts rushed to cut their earnings forecasts. Just as Marconi's success in the USA was initially seen as a mark of its successful strategy, so now it was leading analysts to question whether Marconi had overpaid for acquisitions to gain entrance to a party that had just broken up.

Certainly, having spent its windfall from the sale to BAe, it was no longer in a position to buy itself out of trouble even assuming profitable but cheap targets were available.[7]

Needless to say, Marconi did indeed need to make cut-backs, announcing in April that it would be cutting some 3,000 jobs, equivalent to 6 per cent of its global workforce, of which 1,200 would be in the UK. Nevertheless, it blamed the job losses on plans to re-organize the company into three divisions – networks, wireless and enterprise – rather than on a slowing in demand for its products, and claimed that its results for the year to end-March 2001 would be on target, with operating profits, before exceptionals, of roughly $800 million. Perhaps recognizing that, although it was strongly positioned in the SDH market, it could scarcely be seen as a technological market leader in multiple markets, the three new 'customer facing divisions' were put forward as being distinguished by differences in 'solutions' as against product ranges. Sceptical analysts responded that it was more likely a strategy to prevent like-for-like comparisons in the future and that John Mayo's definition of Marconi's position as 'the world leader in optical networking outside the USA' was less than helpful. Nevertheless, the absence of bad news was sufficient to drive up the share price from 300p to 400p by the end of April – the very last such increase, though few would have believed it at the time.

In mid-May, Marconi promised to make disposals to generate working capital, commencing with its medical systems business and possibly including ipsaris, its fibre-optic network. A target in excess of $2 billion was pencilled in. The accounts for the year ending 31 March (see Table 12.1) made gloomy reading. As well as a sharp upsurge in the use of working capital to £1.07 billion from a meagre £164 million the year before, operating cash flow showed an outflow of £106 million compared to an inflow of £610 million. These figures reflected a sharp upturn in inventory levels, as Marconi had increased capacity to meet rising demand the previous autumn only for it to evaporate by the spring. Overall, turnover had risen from £5.7 billion to £6.9 billion, but there was nevertheless a pre-tax loss of £61 million compared to a profit of £523 million after goodwill, amortization and exceptional items of £723 million. The 'notorious' cash mountain was by now a (somewhat less) notorious debt mountain.[8]

In late July, Marconi effected a reverse takeover of Easynet Group, a loss-making and cash-deficient ISP, by folding ipsaris into it as an alternative to the now-abandoned plan of a flotation. Marconi exchanged its 91.8 per cent in ipsaris for 77.5 million Easynet shares (equivalent to a 10 per cent stake) valued at £235 million (see Table 12.2) – somewhat less than the £400 million that Marconi had so far invested in it.

Abandoning ship

By that time the sale of the medical systems business to Philips for £780 million had also been agreed,[9] but Lord Simpson was a far from happy man.

Table 12.1 Five year summary of consolidated results,[a] year ending 31 March (£ million)

	2003	2002	2001	2000	1999
Total Group turnover	2,002	4,567	6,942	5,724	4,090
in respect of:					
continuing operations	1,914	3,479	5,181	5,724	4,090
discontinued	88	1,088	1,761	–	–
Total Group operating					
(loss)/profit	(858)	(6,293)	57	(115)	448
in respect of:					
continuing operations[b]	–	(463)	754	750	508
Goodwill amortization	(114)	(440)	(673)	(765)	n/a
Exceptional items	(374)	(5,223)	(32)	(107)	n/a
(Loss)/profit before tax	(1,328)	(5,664)	(70)	523	976
in respect of:					
continuing operations[c]	–	(668)	653	654	576
(Loss)/earnings per					
ordinary share[b]	(17.2p)	(23.2p)	15.1p	16.9p	13.1p
Dividend per ordinary					
share	–	–	5.35p	5.20p	n/a
Retained (loss)/profit	(1,144)	(5,875)	(435)	380	259
Goodwill	597	877	5,395	4,397	1,220
Tangible assets	243	522	1,142	758	470
Investments	63	250	591	1,626	1,223
Stocks/contracts	234	720	1,721	946	616
Debtors	613	1,297	2,683	2,250	1,432
Net monetary (debt)/					
funds	(3,617)	(2,865)	(3,167)	(2,145)	624
of which:					
bonds	–	(1,765)	–	–	–
bank credit	–	(2,470)	–	–	–
cash and liquid resources	1,158[d]	1,370	–	–	–

Source: Marconi Group Annual Report and Accounts for the year ending 31 March 2002, pp. 40, 76; Marconi Corporation, Group Preliminary Financials, 31 March 2003 at www.marconi.com

Notes:

[a] Figures for 2001 quoted in the text refer to those declared at the time which have subsequently been adjusted. Figures for 2002 which appear in the 2003 accounts differ in a number of respects from those reported in 2002 which have been left as originally cited. [b] As used above, continuing operations – defined to exclude goodwill amortization and exceptional items – reflects the historical track record of those businesses, both Group and share of joint ventures (but excluding associates), which form part of the Marconi Group as at 31 March. All prior year comparatives assume that the FRS17 standard for pension accounting had been adopted. The income received by the Group from its stake in Alsthom (formerly GEC Alsthom), which was equity accounted until 30 September 1998, and those businesses previously disposed, have been excluded from the figure for 2002. [c] Excluding goodwill amortization and exceptional items. [d] £783 million when adjusted for payments associated with the restructuring.

Table 12.2 Directors' merry-go-round

Name	Comment
Atkinson, K.	Non-executive – appointed 16/12/02
Benning, P.	CFO – appointed 24/07/03
Bonham, D.	Chairman (interim) – appointed 20/04/01. Resigned 16/12/02[a]
Castell, Sir W.	Non-executive – term ended October 2002
Clubb, I.	Non-executive – appointed 13/03/03
Devaney, J.	Chairman – appointed 16/12/02
Donovan, M.	COO.
Dunn, Baroness	Non-executive – resigned 11/04/02
Flaherty, K.	Non-executive – appointed 13/03/03
Hare, S.	Former CFO – appointed 10/04/01. Resigned 13/11/02
Holden, C.	CFO (interim) – apointed 13/11/02
Hurn, Sir R.	Former Chairman – resigned 04/09/01
Koepf, W.	Non-executive – appointed 16/12/02
Mayo, J.	Former Deputy CEO – resigned 06/07/01
McWilliams, D.	Non-executive – appointed 19/08/03
Meakin, R.	Resigned 01/03/02
Parton, M.	CEO.
Rudge, Sir A.	Non-executive – resigned 16/12/02
Seitz, Hon R.	Non-executive – resigned 16/12/02
Simpson, Lord	Former CEO – resigned 04/09/01
Stapleton, N.	Non-executive – term ended October 2002.
Thomas, A.	Appointed 11/04/02 – resigned 13/03/03

Note:
[a] Derek Bonham was appointed interim Chairman in September 2001. After resigning in December 2002 he remained on the board of Marconi plc until it was re-listed.

His protégé, and subsequently his deputy, John Mayo, was proving elusive, and when he contacted the head of each division personally, their reports indicated that the financial situation had deteriorated badly since the beginning of the year. This meant, in turn, that GEC's optimistic presentations to analysts would prove to be undeliverable, quite possibly inducing accusations of creating a false market in GEC's shares. Lord Simpson contacted his chairman, Sir Roger Hurn, who summoned an emergency board meeting for 4pm the following Wednesday. Meanwhile, Philips wanted to release the news about its purchase in order to avoid creating its own false market, but to publicize the sale on Tuesday followed by a profits warning on Wednesday would unquestionably be seen as creating a false market, so the most sensible option was seemingly to ask for a temporary suspension of trading in GEC shares. At the board meeting there were angry exchanges between John Mayo – whose people skills were no match for his financial sleight-of-hand – and other board members, and the following morning he was obliged to issue a profits warning and plans for 4,000 further redundancies, including 1,000 managers, via a conference call to analysts.[10]

As shown in Figure 12.1, the share price promptly collapsed from a pre-suspension 245p to 100p with 225 million shares changing hands, roughly 10 per cent of those in issue. On the face of it, the problems of a medium-sized TMT company which, as John Mayo continued to argue, was performing roughly in line with its rivals, hardly seemed to warrant the extraordinary media response,[11] but the former GEC was close to the heart of British investors and Lord Weinstock, one of their favourite industrialists, who had retained the title of Chairman Emeritus of Marconi, was deeply unhappy and let the media know it. Clearly, heads needed to roll, and although John Mayo, as deputy CEO, hoped to pressurize Lord Simpson to lead the way to the exit by buying £220,000 of Marconi shares,[12] he was the one forced to resign as he had lost the confidence of the board. Marconi's website was altered to convey the message that the company was 'transforming the economics of doing business'. While this had the ring of truth about it, it was clearly not in the manner intended.

Needless to say, the rest of July was somewhat unpleasant for all concerned. First, the credit agencies put Marconi on credit watch, with some analysts fearing a potential downgrade to 'junk' status. Second, two US legal firms filed class-action lawsuits against the company and its senior board members. Third, although Lord Weinstock was willing to support Lord Simpson's staying at the helm in the short term, he, along with major investors, demanded that a new CEO be found within three months. Furthermore, although both Lord Simpson and other board members promptly bought large numbers of shares to prove their faith in the company's prospects, this merely meant in practice that they would lose all their investment in due course. Given that Marconi's main rivals had all issued multiple profits warnings, few commentators seriously believed that Marconi's first would also be its last, but on 18 July the board successfully faced down a shareholder revolt at its AGM, promising that a two-month strategic review would come up with an adequate response to the criticisms vented by shareholders.

August proved to be only a little better, as a further drop in the share price to a 20-year low of 70p in mid-month meant that Marconi was in line to be dropped from the FTSE 100 index, and many analysts expected the price to drop further – although none predicted just how bad things were about to become. Net debt worsened to £4.4 billion as the company continued to haemorrhage cash but, somewhat surprisingly, its bankers proved happy to roll over its credit facilities without introducing any covenants.[13]

Clearly, costs needed to be trimmed, and in that respect at least Lord Simpson could be trusted, although few believed that he knew enough about technology – he had relied on John Mayo in that respect – to create a vision for the future. A target for net debt was fixed at £2.5 billion in March 2002, and £1 billion was pencilled in from the disposal of General Domestic Appliances (GDA), Marconi's joint venture with GE making white goods (£300 million or so), Gilbarco, the petrol pumps business, and Video Jet, a bar-code printing business (worth perhaps £400 million). The problem was that non-core businesses had generated £110 million of operating profit during the 2000/2001 financial year and would be unlikely to achieve their true value if regarded as fire sales. Many analysts favoured the closure of some of the telecoms equipment businesses, essentially those where Marconi had little prospect of achieving critical mass, but few expected anything so radical to emerge from the ongoing strategic review.

The new CEO revised the target for net debt to £2.7–3.2 billion – still equivalent to a gearing ratio (debt to equity) of well over 100 per cent – but rejected the idea of a rescue rights issue on the grounds that credit facilities were more than adequate to see the company through its crisis. He also set out to reduce the operating cost base to an annual run rate of £1 billion, down from £1.4 billion one year previously. According to the finance director, Steve Hare, this was not a 'severe crisis [but rather] a challenging set of circumstances'.[14] They were certainly too challenging for Alcatel, which promptly ruled out any possibility of a merger even though, at 38p a share, Marconi was now worth a mere £1 billion. However, several market professionals bought holdings on the grounds that the share price would either revive significantly or the company would go bust,[15] and the banks declined to withdraw agreed lending borrowing facilities by invoking the standard 'material adverse change' clause in their contracts, even though many had handed Marconi bonds over to their 'junk bond' desks – technically, the credit agencies had yet to downgrade them although this inevitably took place shortly thereafter.

On 30 August, Marconi reassured its union representatives that it would be making no further redundancies, yet on 4 September it announced a second profits warning, stating that sales had fallen by 12 per cent to £1.13 billion during the quarter to 30 June 2001 and that, far from breaking-even during the half-year to end-September as promised at the time of the first profits warning, it now had no prospect of recovering from an operating loss of £227 million in the first quarter.[16] It added that it would be writing off up to £3.5 billion of goodwill arising from recent acquisitions, and would be carrying provisions of £500 million against its inventory plus a further £150 million for doubtful debts. There would therefore need to be an additional 2,000 redundancies, bringing the total to 10,000 during the financial year. The unions were understandably not amused. Nor were investors who saw the share price fall below 55p, implying that an astonishing £33 billion (roughly $50 billion) had been cut from the company's market value in under one year. Lord Simpson was possibly not amused at being forced to resign, but he had no cause to complain about his pay-off of £1 million plus a further £1 million in pension rights. He was replaced by Mike Parton,[17] head of Marconi's networks divisions. The Chairman, Sir Roger Hurn, followed him out the door to be replaced, on a temporary basis, by Derek Bonham, former CEO of the Hanson Group. The company was ejected from the FTSE 100 shortly afterwards.[18]

The new strategy unfolds

At the end of September 2001, Marconi announced that it had agreed to sell its 1.5 per cent stake in Lagardère for $64 million (£43 million) – few even knew of its existence, dating back to GEC days – but the share price continued its inexorable fall, particularly subsequent to a very cautious SEC filing associated with its American Depositary Receipts, and the first analyst went on record with the opinion that Marconi's shares were worthless. It was predicted that the ensuing sales would, in addition to those cited above, include property worth £100 million and its 70.1 per cent stake in Easynet, now worth perhaps £125 million, but since Marconi did not own a majority of the voting rights this was expected to prove hard to sell.

In the run up to its mid-October trading update on the second quarter and first half of 2001, the share price rose sharply to 25p, driven in part by the purchase of several million shares by a friend of Lord Weinstock, industrialist Sir Alan Sugar. In the event, the figures served to reassure, even though they benefited from profits earned by the about-to-be-sold medical systems subsidiary – the European Commission approved the sale on 17 October. Operating profit was positive at £5 million. However, net debt fell by only £100 million from £4.4 billion to £4.3 billion and although the new CEO claimed that the company's finances had been 'stabilized', he was somewhat downbeat about prospects for the year ahead.[19]

In late October, Barclays Bank and HSBC, Marconi's largest lenders, took charge of an operation to restructure Marconi's borrowings, with the particular objective of an extension beyond 2003. With the sale of the medical systems business finally completed, and the share price back up at 35p, Marconi's situation no longer looked to be desperate, and the situation was eased further by news that private equity firm Duke Street Capital was weighing up bids of roughly £150 million for Gilbarco and £800–900 million for GDA, and, in mid-November, by the sale of the first batch of 12 properties for £66.8 million. However, on 13 November, Marconi wrote off its entire investment in Fore Systems, rendering it one of the most disastrous overseas purchases ever by a UK company. It also wrote off part of its investment in Reltec such that total write-offs for the first half amounted to £3.5 billion, resulting in an overall pre-tax loss of £5.1 billion. Equally ominously, Group turnover fell 19 per cent to £2.6 billion, but it said something about expectations that the share price rose on the day, partly because cash flow was positive.[20]

In mid-December, with the Marconi share price now touching 50p equivalent to more than three times its level in early October, Bookham Technology – a company with more profits warnings to its name than Marconi – agreed to buy Marconi's optical components business in a share exchange worth roughly £19.7 million, with Marconi promising to buy large quantities of Bookham components in return. Analysts were baffled by Marconi's willingness to be paid in shares, and several recommended

Table 12.3 Main asset purchases and disposals,[a] December 2000–April 2003

	Date	Comment
Telit Networks/Telit Mobile	21/12/00	Acquired for £11.1 million/£29 million
TI-Projekte	25/01/01	Acquired for undisclosed sum
Harman Info. Technology	April 2001	Acquisition
Inviscid Networks (19.9%)	April 2001	Acquisition
Enargeia Global Networks	May 2001	Acquisition
Northwood Technologies	24/05/01	Acquired for £19 million
Netscient Ltd	May 2001	Acquisition
Alsthom (5.67%)	19/06/01	Sold
ipsaris	26/07/01	Exchanged for 70.1%[b] of Easynet Group valued at £235 million
Lagardère (1.5%)	Sept. 2001	Sold for £43 million
Marconi Medical Systems	19/10/01	Raised £729 million, representing a profit on disposal of £155 million
Siemens Telecommunications	27/11/01	Sale of 21.5% stake raised £20 million
Lottomatica (3.7%)	05/12/01	Sold for £25 million
Marconi Optical Components	01/02/02	Exchanged for 9.9% of Bookham Technology valued at £19.7 million
Marconi Commerce Systems	01/02/02	Raised £225 million, representing a profit on disposal of £29 million
Marconi Data Systems	05/02/02	Raised £283 million, representing a profit on disposal of £181 million
General Domestic Appliances	08/03/02	Sold to Merloni Elettrodomestici for £120 million in cash
Surplus properties	Various	Sold for £116 million
Applied Technologies	12/07/02	Sold to 3i for £57 million
Marconi Mobile	03/08/02	Sold to Finmeccanica for £387 million
Private Mobile Networks	05/03/03	Sold to Finmeccanica for £2 million plus £13 million of debt taken on
Marconi Online	05/03/03	Sold to Coca-Cola Amatil for £1 million

Source: Marconi Group. Annual Report and Accounts for the year ending 31 March 2002, pp. 26, 66–7; media reports.

Note:
[a] In addition, 25 per cent of Marconi Communications South Africa was exchanged for a 30 per cent holding in African Renaissance Holdings. For details of acquisitions and disposals during 2000 see Annual Report and Accounts 2001, p. 36. In some of the cases cited the purchaser took on debt as well as paying the stated amount to Marconi. [b] However, although this figure is quoted on p. 66 of the 2001/02 Annual Report and Accounts, the figure on p. 7 and p. 26 is 71.9 per cent (49.9 per cent of voting rights).

shareholders to sell immediately as Marconi's best outcome was no better than mere survival. Nevertheless, Marconi seemed to be making real progress with its debt reduction strategy when it subsequently agreed to sell Marconi Commerce Systems (formerly Gilbarco) to Danaher for £225 million, announced the sale of its half share of Hotpoint, part of its GDA joint venture, to Merloni for £130 million and bought back 7 per cent of its outstanding bonds with a face value of £152 million for £80 million. As a result, Marconi could now concentrate upon the third element in its debt reduction strategy, namely cost reduction.[21]

A further £10 million of property was sold to Ashtenne Holdings in early January 2002 followed immediately by its Data Systems (formerly Video Jet) ink-jet printing business to Danaher for £277 million. This meant that Marconi now had roughly £1.5 billion of cash in the bank, but analysts were concerned that with the disposal of a number of cash-generative businesses, Marconi would struggle to generate cash from those that remained – which consisted largely of the core communications division. On 15 January their fears were confirmed when CFO Steve Hare declared that 'we don't expect to see any improvement in the market for the whole of 2002'. As a consequence, Marconi now sought to break-even on turnover of £675 million, well down on its original target of £800 million, and announced a further 4,000 job losses which implied that entire product lines would need to be closed down. The deadline for completion of the restructuring exercise was set at March 2003. Analysts argued that it was impossible to tell whether Marconi would survive until its turnover was stabilised, and the share price fell back to 24p.

At this point, released from his legal obligation to keep silent, the disgraced John Mayo decided to exact some revenge by accusing the new CEO (correctly, as it happens) of responsibility for creating the massive inventories which had helped bring Marconi to its knees. This formed part of a three-page attempt to rewrite Marconi's history while under the control of Lord Simpson,[22] in the course of which, inter alia, he claimed that the company had, against his advice, rejected potential takeover bids worth as much as £25 billion. However, his claim that Lord Weinstock had run GEC with weak financial controls which he had inherited from Weinstock in 1997, that GEC was not compliant with the US Foreign Corrupt Practices Act thereby delaying the Nasdaq quotation while the matter was rectified which forced Marconi to make acquisitions with cash, that the GEC cash mountain was a myth – it had only amounted to £1 billion, of which one-half constituted payments in advance – and that Lord Weinstock had failed to create shareholder value, evinced a hollow laugh from those who believed that Messrs Simpson and Mayo were amongst the UK's greatest-ever exponents of value destruction. As it happens, John Mayo was willing to admit that he had contributed to some mistakes, namely: that he should have pressed for Marconi to sell its defence business and keep the cash rather than demerging it and letting shareholders have the benefit; that he should have sought agreement to enforce much tighter working capital control in the communications division in the year to July 2001; that he should have advocated the sale of all non-core businesses at the time of the sale of the medical systems business; and that he should have advocated that Marconi should wait until the bottom of the cycle to make major takeover bids. He was careful to point out that as the finance director at GEC, and later as the deputy CEO at Marconi, he could insist on nothing: the board as a whole was ultimately responsible on every occasion.

Marconi's board chose not to respond publicly, but it was made known that there had never been a takeover proposal actually on the table in 2000 and analysts generally took the view that someone responsible for a company's finances should not try to avoid all responsibility for bad financial controls.[23] Marconi promptly bought back a further £200 million of bonds for £110 million, although its debt was downgraded to an even lower grade of 'junk'.

From a high of over 40p in early January, the Marconi share price sagged continuously in the absence of any positive news, reaching 18p on 20 March. On 22 March, it collapsed to 7p amid the greatest volume of trading in its history after revealing that it had backed out of a proposed new financing facility with its creditors due to the continuing deterioration in its main markets.[24] Analysts interpreted Marconi's behaviour as testimony to uncertainty as to whether the business would generate sufficient profits to meet the higher interest costs associated with any debt restructuring. While it was already clear that the repayment of roughly £900 million by March 2003 would defeat the company without something being done in the interim, neither a deeply discounted rights issue nor a further debt placement could provide a solution, so the matter was ultimately in the hands of the banks and a debt-for-equity swap seemed on the cards. This would, in turn, lead to a fight between the banks and bondholders as to who would have first call on Marconi's assets – for the time being the banks had the upper hand, since Marconi had agreed to give up £2.4 billion of untapped borrowing facilities and put the £2.2 billion it owed the banks 'on demand' to gain some breathing space – so it was viewed as a positive step when Marconi invited bondholders to participate for the first time in restructuring talks at the end of March.

At the end of April another loss was declared for the fourth quarter ending in March and plans were outlined to take a further exceptional charge of between £700 million and £800 million during the second half, mainly relating to Reltec. Turnover was at half the level of a year previously, but, more positively, net debt was down to £2.9 billion. Marconi also announced that it had agreed to restrictions on £850 million of cash held by banks outside its main lending syndicate and an increase to 2.25 per cent over Libor in respect of the interest charge on its syndicated loans. Rumours that the top management were all about to be dismissed were firmly denied – it wasn't likely that quality replacements could anyway be found – but it was confirmed that Derek Bonham would step down from his position as interim chairman once a suitable replacement was contracted. A 102-page five-year business plan prepared by consultancy LEK was presented to creditors for consideration. The share price fell to 3.5p.

At the end of June, the long-expected debt-for-equity swap was confirmed in principle, effectively wiping out the holdings of existing shareholders,[25] as well as a proposed de-listing from the Nasdaq. On a more positive note, a further £57 million was raised in July with the sale of Marconi Applied Technologies to 3i, but this did little to offset the increase in net debt by £152 million to £3 billion during the first quarter of 2002/2003. The sale in early August of most of the defence communications business, Marconi

Mobile, to Finmeccanica for £387 million, almost all in cash, was rather more helpful, although it effectively signified the end of the process of non-core disposals since the only remaining asset of any value was the outdoor power and plant business (essentially Reltec). Understandably, further lay-offs became inevitable, with a further 1,000 in the UK announced shortly afterwards.

At the end of August, the refinancing package was announced. Creditors would exchange £4 billion of debts for 99.5 per cent of the equity plus £260 million in cash (subsequently raised to £340 million) and loan notes due in 2008 worth £900 million (as well as a share of the proceeds of future asset sales); while existing shareholders would get 0.5 per cent of the equity plus four-year warrants that would allow them to purchase a further 5 per cent subject to Marconi's market value rising to £1.5 billion. The ongoing Marconi – its shares now trading at 1.8p – would be left with net debt of £300 million (subsequently lowered to £186 million at somewhat higher interest rates) and cash of £635 million (subsequently lowered to £602 million) restricted in its use to funding working capital requirements and security against continuing liabilities. The restructuring would be completed by January 2003 at which point Marconi plc would be liquidated and the shares would be re-listed in London and New York as the Marconi Corporation.[26] What would remain would essentially be a regionally-based (in Europe and North America) second-tier equipment supplier focused on its core product lines – particularly SDH – and established customers, such as BT, which accounted for 20 per cent of turnover.

Second-quarter turnover reported at the end of October revealed a further fall to £482 million, but job cuts had raised the gross margin back above 20 per cent of turnover, with more to come. At 2.2p a share, Marconi was now worth £100 million. In early November, it symbolically vacated its grand Mayfair HQ and moved downmarket, albeit temporarily, to the Euston Road. Subsequently, CFO Steve Hare was invited to depart, possibly unfairly as he had supervised the disposal of non-core assets but was being treated as the fall-guy for the failure to close the original refinancing deal in April 2002, even though it was rejected by the entire board. In mid-December, Derek Bonham finally stood down as interim chairman to be replaced by John Devaney and several other adjustments were made to the composition of the board (see Table 12.2). Further positive news came in the form of £45 million in cash by way of settlement of a long-standing dispute with RT Group, the rump of the collapsed Railtrack network. However, first-half figures to the end of September remained fairly dismal, with turnover down to £992 million, core orders down 40 per cent on a year previously and losses before interest, tax, depreciation and amortization at £156 million. With exceptional restructuring costs of £186 million and interest payments of £133 million, it was fortunate that disposals had amounted to £387 million. Marconi stated that it aimed to break-even at the operating level with turnover of less than £1.9 billion, and that its headcount in March would now be lower than expected, at 14,000.[27]

With the completion date for the restructuring being pushed back first to April 2003 and then to May, some additional modest sums were raised in early March through the sale of the Private Mobile Networks unit and Marconi Online (see Table 12.2). The 780-page restructuring document was finally published in mid-March, together with acknowledgement that Marconi had run up £75 million in fees, largely to law firms, and was subject to the approval of the High Court and creditors. In addition to the figures quoted previously the new business plan committed Marconi to achieving turnover of £1.7 billion in 2003/2004 with quarterly break-even starting at £520 million and declining to £450 million a year hence. Profitability would have to wait until 2004/2005.[28]

Arise Marconi Corporation

The High Court approved Marconi's debt restructuring plans in mid-May and a re-listing of its equity as Marconi Corporation was pencilled in for the 19 May. The Corporation's core activities were defined as the provision of optical networks, broadband routing and switching and broadband access technologies and associated installation, maintenance and other value-added services. Holders of the old Marconi plc shares received one new share in Marconi Corporation for every 559 old shares plus one share warrant – exercisable if the shares reached £1.50 – for every 56 old shares. Altogether, one billion new shares were issued, of which over ten per cent were traded on the first day of issue as many previous holders of debt in Marconi Plc took the opportunity to bail out. Having risen to 61.5p, the share price fell back slightly to leave the Corporation valued at just under £600 million. The history of the share price subsequently is shown in Figure 12.3, where it is now quoted against a somewhat different re-listing price. However, the crucial point is that it has roughly doubled since re-listing, leaving the Corporation valued at £1.2 billion.

At the end of May, it was just like the old days as Marconi announced that turnover would drop to below £400 million during the first quarter of 2003/2004 compared to £426 million in the previous quarter – blamed primarily on instability in the Middle East and the Sars outbreak – and that a further 500 jobs would need to be cut by March 2004. The full year financial review to 31 March 2003 (see Table 12.1) was difficult to compare to that one year previously, but the obvious features were a more than halving of turnover, a huge reduction in exceptionals and a consequent fall in pre-tax losses to £1.3 billion, much as expected. Margins were on the mend and costs were under control, largely due to a headcount reduction from 34,300 at 31 March 2001 to 15,300 two years later. Core break-even turnover was accordingly reduced from £1.7 billion to £1.5 billion for the coming year. Cash flow was positive, and the gross debt position after the restructuring of £808 million was further reduced via the sale of 36 million shares in Easynet, a broadband provider, for roughly £40 million in early July. As Marconi

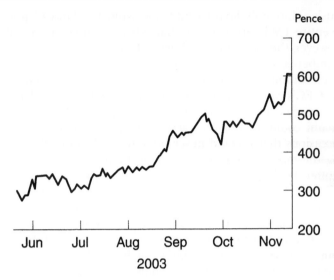

Figure 12.3 Marconi Corporation share price, 2003 (pence).
Source: Daily share prices in the *Financial Times*.

Corporation had emerged with £783 million in cash, it effectively had no net debt and had net assets of roughly £400 million.[29]

This fairly happy story did not last long. First-quarter results for 2003 revealed a deteriorating situation, with net cash down to £5 million and a £24 million bill looming for share options during 2003 alone. The company could do little bar make optimistic noises about the medium-term outlook. On a slightly more positive note, it was revealed that Marconi had sold its last wholly-owned non-core asset, Marconi Mobile Access SpA to Finmeccanica. In August, it also sold Gamma Telecom Holdings for £5.6 million following up in September with the sale of the residual 40 per cent stake in Easynet for £56 million. On the whole, this news scarcely justified the sharp upturn in the share price, but TMT stocks were coming back into favour and there was a general willingness to buy into anything with a cleaned up balance sheet and a management without grandiose ideas.

Conclusions

The cry of 'cash is king' once more reverberates around the financial markets, and how dearly some investors must wish that GEC had kept faith with Lord Weinstock's strategic vision. On the other hand, he personally chose George Simpson to be his successor so that vision was arguably flawed in certain key respects. Nevertheless, he was never the follower of fashion typified by George Simpson and his peers, especially those in the TMT sector, and it is most unlikely that he would ever have followed fashion from a position of weakness even if the markets had forced him to 'modernize'.

Obviously, Marconi's board could not avoid the kind of pressures that beset the entire TMT sector, and to that extent was no more culpable than its peers. However, the likes of Cisco, Lucent Technologies and Nortel Networks were incumbents with significant market shares in particular technologies, whereas telecommunications had only recently been but one fairly minor feather in GEC's cap. Naturally, this does not of itself imply that incumbents cannot be caught up, or even overtaken, by upstarts, but there was no way that Marconi could achieve this across the board: indeed, it admitted on several occasions that it could never hope to catch up its three main rivals. Becoming the market leader in any one technology such as SDH was never going to offer much protection against a severe market downturn, at least not via organic growth. Even the fabled cash mountain was worth only $5 billion or so which was but pocket money in relation to the sums changing hands at the end of the 1990s – even assuming that John Mayo was less than truthful in claiming that in fact the mountain was more like a molehill. Furthermore, by moving to make acquisitions before it had achieved a Nasdaq listing, Marconi was obliged to pay cash for acquisitions at a time when rivals could get away with offering vast numbers of their own shares – although it is possible that it would have had to pay even more than the already over-inflated prices using its own stock.

Defenders of Lord Simpson – and especially, as noted, the somewhat self-serving John Mayo – continued to roll out the 'there was no other choice' argument until it was only too clear that if the outcome was near bankruptcy, then almost any other choice would have been better, especially sitting on the cash pile, but in fairness that is to ignore the tremendous pressure exerted upon the likes of GEC and C&W by the financial markets to take up some of the allegedly wonderful opportunities open to them. It is noteworthy that the sale of GEC's core defence business fetched a very good price. It is equally noteworthy that the banks lent roughly £5 billion, largely as a five-year loan in March 1998,[30] on favourable terms and without imposing the usual covenants in the event of poor performance. Lord Weinstock would probably have resisted the siren calls to borrow and spend to the bitter end, although his board might have become extremely fretful – he had hoped to be succeeded by his son but he died young – but markets are more forgiving when their favourite sons are recalcitrant and it does have to be said that other 'old-fashioned' companies have also taken a severe battering: in March 2003, for example, ICI's share price halved overnight.

Those of a less forgiving bent remain convinced that even if the strategy of switching towards telecommunications was justifiable – on the grounds that, at best, it was somewhat arbitrary but the choices were limited – the timing was completely wrong. Their view is that piling into a market that is already looking 'peaky' is invariably a mistake, and that if European companies are willing to buy American companies for inflated prices this merely indicates that other potential American bidders have a much better idea of what things are worth. Lord Simpson would doubtless disagree – as John Mayo did in practice – given that, for example, he acquired Fore Systems on a multiple of three times sales which was well below the average paid by the likes of Nortel Networks while spending much larger sums.

Overall, there can be no doubt that Marconi's strategy was insufficiently well thought through, involving too much expensive deal making and too little care taken in managing the results. The board did not appear to be up to the job, failing – perhaps forgivably – to foresee the sharp downturn in business and, less forgivably, utterly unable to respond in time when it was only too obvious. It also failed to maintain good communications with the financial markets, which understandably felt aggrieved.

In conclusion, therefore, the picture is not exclusively one-sided and one must resist the urge to rewrite history. This is not because there is no blame to be laid, but rather because it should not be laid at too few doors. The history of the TMT sector since the late 1990s indicates only too well that there are large numbers of 'villains' – including analysts over-keen to hype, corporate financiers over-keen to do deals, bankers over-keen to lend, institutional shareholders over-keen on short-term shareholder value, the financial press over-keen on creating 'heroes', boards of directors less than keen on good corporate governance and managers less than keen on managing[31] – and remarkably few 'heroes'. Lord Simpson was neither totally incompetent – the first half of the strategy, disentangling the old GEC, was carried out fairly effectively – nor did he engage in illegal activities, although the delay in announcing the appalling figures for the first quarter of 2001 was certainly less than wholly honest dealing.[32] On the other hand, he would have been better advised to stick to the industries where he had gained his experience. Like so many others who thought the TMT sector was ripe for the picking by anyone with any kind of decent past record as an industrialist, nothing could have been further from the truth. However, some do now see Marconi as a recovery story. For example, Fidelity Investments, the largest US mutual fund, has wound down its large holding in C&W and replaced it with a 7.4 per cent stake in Marconi. In practice, both have been enjoying an excellent run of late.

Glossary

American depository receipt The standard unit in dollars for quoting overseas company shares in the USA.

Bear raid Deliberate selling of a company's shares intended to trigger a sharp fall in the share price with a view to profitable repurchase at a later date.

Broadband Defined by speed of data transfer. Often taken to imply a minimum of 384 thousand bits per second (kbps), but may fall short of this in practice.

Bundling The practice of marketing more than one service in a single package.

cdma2000 A version of third-generation mobile telephony (3G) popular outside Europe.

Chapter 11 The US bankruptcy code.

Chinese boxes Whereby control is exercised via the first in a string of companies, each owning a small proportion of the next in line.

Convergence The ability of different network elements to carry essentially similar kinds of services.

Convertible bond A bond which can be converted into shares at specified future dates.

DSL A technology whereby the capacity of existing copper wires is greatly increased to permit the transfer of data as well as voice.

EDGE A development of GSM providing greater data transfer speeds than GPRS but less than W-CDMA – hence sometimes referred to as 2.75G.

European Commission The administrative arm of the European Union.

Gearing The ratio of debt to equity.

Golden share A single share conferring special rights on its holder, the government.

Goodwill The difference between the value of an asset at the time it was acquired and its current market value.

GPRS The uprated version of GSM designed to carry data, often known as 2.5G.

Growth stock A share valued for its ability to provide capital growth rather than dividend income.

GSM   The standard digital technology for voice used throughout Europe. By far the most popular 2G technology worldwide.

Hard core   A group of supposedly loyal institutional shareholders holding between them a significant proportion of a company's share capital.

Hollow swap   Whereby capacity that is exchanged between operators is credited as a sale generating revenue.

Hotspot   A specific location providing very high rates of data transfer, usually via a lap-top PC. If connected together, also known as a W-LAN or Wi-Fi.

Incumbent   A company that has been established in the marketplace over a significant period of time; often defined by the existence of a licence.

Initial public offer   The first occasion on which a company's shares are put on sale to financial intermediaries and/or the general public.

Instant messaging   This enables Internet users to view a 'buddy list' installed via software on their PCs, and to send messages to any of them who are connected at the time with the message appearing instantly on the recipient's screen.

Junk   Term used to describe interest bearing securities below investment grade yielding high rates of interest which cannot be held as assets by certain financial intermediaries.

Local loop   The connection from the local exchange to a set of domestic/business premises.

Lock-up period   Period during which shares acquired as part of a takeover bid cannot be sold.

MVNO   A mobile operator providing an 'own-label' service largely over another operator's network.

New economy   Incorporating modern digital technology; relating to the Internet.

Organic growth   Growth that takes place internally without recourse to external acquisitions.

PCN   The version of GSM operating in the 1800 MHz band.

Portal   A site initially accessed by Internet users that offers a range of services including news, Internet search, e-mail and financial and other information.

Pre-emption right   The right to acquire a stake in a company before it is offered to other parties.

Put option   The right to sell a share at a predetermined price on or before a specified date.

Proportionate subscriber numbers   Gross subscriber numbers multiplied by the percentage ownership in each network.

Rights issue   Where a batch of new shares is issued at a discount to the price that the existing shares are trading at in the market.

Synchronous digital hierarchy   A data transmission technology using fibre-optics.

TDMA   A mobile technology prevalent in the USA (but absent in Europe) which is often being switched to GSM as a prelude to the introduction of 3G.

Tracking stock   This is hived off from the parent company and pays dividends linked only to its own performance. Its shareholders do not have ownership rights and cannot prevent managers from putting the interests of the parent company before those of holders of the stock.

Treasury shares   Shares authorized for issue but held prior to issue in a company's Treasury Department.

UMTS   The European version of W-CDMA.

W-CDMA   The version of third-generation mobile telephony (3G) favoured in Europe, where it is known as UMTS, and parts of the USA and Asia.

White Knight   A third party that steps in to assist a company subject to an unwelcome takeover bid.

Wi-Fi   Wireless Fidelity is the technology used in W-LANS or hotspots.

W-LAN   A wireless local area network capable of high rates of data transfer within a restricted area; a group of connected hotspots.

Notes

I Structural overview

1 The tables necessarily collect the data at one particular point in time, but interested readers can easily update the data for themselves by checking the daily share prices in the *Financial Times*. The pros and cons of using capital values rather than revenues or profits are set out in the *Financial Times* FT500 supplement of 11 May 2001, p. 2.

2 Originally formed by France Télécom, Deutsche Telekom and Sprint (pre-demerger), it is now the sole preserve of the first-named with both European telcos about to sell off their stakes in Sprint FON.

3 As in respect of Olivetti's successful takeover of Telecom Italia.

4 Hence, for example, Deutsche Telekom's failed bid for Telecom Italia, Telefónica's failed attempt to take over KPN and Telnor's failed merger with Telia.

5 The additional shares issued by the purchaser are exchanged for those of the target, and hence incorporate the existing market value of that target. However, a bidder normally has to pay a considerable premium over and above the pre-bid share price, and this can be expected to have a depressing effect upon the bidder's own share price.

6 Prior to the end of 2000, the classic exponents of this strategy were WorldCom among telcos and Cisco Systems among equipment manufacturers. To these could, over a much shorter period, be added Vodafone among wireless companies.

7 Needless to say it works in reverse. When Vodafone's share price falls, index trackers need to hold fewer Vodafone shares and more of any other FTSE-100 constituent rising in value. It should also be borne in mind that when a company is taken over using the bidder's equity, the target's shareholders may not want the bidder's shares because, for example, it is listed abroad. As they dispose of their unwanted shares the price is depressed until such time as the overhang is cleared. During the late 1990s recipients of, say, shares in WorldCom or Cisco tended to hold on to them, helping to maintain the bidder's share price, but over the past year or two shares in companies even with the reputation of Vodafone have tended to be dumped in large quantities. A similar pattern is expected with VoiceStream shareholders receiving shares in Deutsche Telekom.

3 British Telecommunications (BT)

1 For a detailed history of the company, see Curwen, P. (1997) *Restructuring Telecommunications: A Study of Europe in a Global Context*, London: Macmillan Press. Details of BT licences, applicable European Union Directives and the role of

regulators can be found in BT Annual Report and Form 20–F 2003, pp. 18–23. To ease comparisons with other case studies some of the financial data are expressed in dollars. For most of the period under consideration the pound was worth between $1.40 and $1.60, and hence a conversion at £1 to $1.50 will yield fairly accurate valuations in both currencies throughout the text.

2 See BT 1999 Annual Report and Form 20–F, p. 31.

3 Stonham, P. (1998) 'Takeover frenzy in telecoms: the case of MCI WorldCom. part one: competitive strategies', *European Management Journal*, **16**(3), pp. 318–26; 'Takeover frenzy in telecoms: the case of MCI WorldCom. part two: financial bids', *European Management Journal*, **16**(5), pp. 562–72.

4 See Curwen, P. (2002) *The Future of Mobile Communications: Awaiting the Third Generation*, London: Palgrave, pp. 178–9.

5 See chapter on AOL Time Warner.

6 See the various Annual Reports and Forms 20–F, notes to the financial statements.

7 However, the first option was at that time a preferred option where the government remained the major shareholder.

8 It may be noted that by early 2000 BT had risen steadily up the ranks to become the twenty-second largest company in the world with a market value of roughly $160 billion.

9 A brief discussion of all acquisitions and disposals can be found in the BT and BT Group Annual Reports and Forms 20–F, for example: 2000, pp. 73–4; 2001, pp. 99–100; 2002, pp. 10–11, 101–3, 148–51.

10 For a review of regulation in the UK and EU see BT Group Annual Report and Form 20–F 2002, pp. 18–23 and 'Happy birthday, BT', *The Economist*, 6 July 2002, p. 38.

11 Because of the division of BT into BT Group and mmO₂, as well as the rights issue of 19 November 2001, it is difficult to make valid comparisons between share prices over the longer term. The table below, extracted from the BT Annual Report and Form 20–F 2000, p. 144 and BT Group Annual Report and Form 20–F 2001, p. 141 attempts to provide a useful summary expressed in pence per ordinary share, where the second pair have been adjusted to take account of the rights issue.

Year ended 31 March:	High price	Low price	High price	Low price
1997	461	326	n/a	n/a
1998	685	380	481	266
1999	1,119	630	784	442
2000	1,513	889	1,081	623
2001	1,172	469	822	329
2002	n/a	n/a	421	216

12 British Telecommunications plc is now a wholly-owned subsidiary of BT Group and holds virtually all of its businesses and assets. In the financial year to 31 March 2002 almost 90 per cent of BT Group revenues were derived from operations within the UK.

13 It may be noted, however, that BT Group and mmO₂ entered into a number of agreements to define the continuing relationship between the groups. These included that BT Group: agreed until November 2004, to promote on an exclusive basis the mobile products and services of O₂ UK to the UK business market; agreed until 31 March 2003, not to offer mobile products and services to the UK consumer market solely under the BT brand, but would be able to offer bundled fixed and mobile products; and that parts of mmO₂ would be able to use certain BT trademarks and brands until 31 March 2003.

14 See BT Group Annual Report and Form 20–F 2002, pp. 8–9 for a more detailed exposition of the seven strategic priorities.

15 See Reddall, B. (2002) 'BT plans cut-price broadband, may work with AOL', www.totaltelecom of 24 April.

16 Earnings before interest, tax, depreciation and amortization.

17 The requisite licences were shortly to be issued by the Radiocommunications Agency – see Budden, R. (2002) 'BT steals a march with wireless Lan', *Financial Times*, 10 April, p. 28. The first hotspots, trading as BT Openzone, were opened in June 2002, with the full commercial launch pencilled in for 1 August – see Nuttall, C. (2002) 'BT launches public wireless network', http://ft.news.com of 24 June and "BT ramps up WiFi offering," www.cit-online.com of 31 January 2003. BT Group also re-entered the consumer mobile market on 1 October 2002 under the 'Mobile Sense' brand, a decision seen as somewhat at odds with the previous demerger of mmO_2 and less than promising given the existence of five well-established competitors. In February 2003, BT Group was also authorized to act as a reseller for T-Mobile in the UK.

18 See Budden, R. (2002) 'BT pleases City as it bucks telecoms trend', http://news.ft.com of 17 May.

19 'BT Group', the Lex column, *Financial Times*, 17 May 2002.

20 See Arnold, M. and R. Budden (2002) 'BT targets £100 million from new directory services', http://news.ft.com of 6 August.

21 See Budden, R. (2002) 'BT Group shares hit by weak first quarter', http://news.ft.com of 25 July.

22 See Loades-Carter, J. (2002) 'BT faces cuts to wholesale broadband prices', http://news.ft.com of 10 September. The proposal included backdating to August 2001. As of August 2002, BT Group had a 31 per cent share of Internet access to the business market with Freeserve on 14 per cent, but only 18 per cent of the consumer market with Freeserve on 20 per cent and AOL on 18 per cent. The regulator specified a 50 per cent price cut for PPCs but only 20 per cent for line rentals in December 2002.

23 See articles by M. Pesola at http://news.ft.com of 7 November 2002.

24 The open offer was necessitated by the acquisition of a stake in excess of 30 per cent, and although pitched at a discount to the market price, BT Group was happy to sell its stake even at one-third of what it had paid for it in April 1999. The total value raised would be £132 million, payable in January 2003. As of 31 March 2003, BT was left holding stakes in four satellite entities, 16.6 per cent of LG Telecom, 11.9 per cent of an enlarged StarHub and 23 per cent of Albacom.

25 See Tassell, T. and R. Budden (2003) 'BT may face £1.5bn pension deficit', http://news.ft.com of 13 February and Budden, R. (2003) 'BT plans £1.5bn injection to cover pension gap', http://news.ft.com of 23 February – see note 27 below.

26 In addition to this reduction for the IPStream Home 500, the monthly charge for the IPStream Office 500 was cut from £40 to £18 per month and the IPStream Office 2000 from £80 to £38 per month. Subscriber numbers at the time were given as 800,000, with 67 per cent of homes able to obtain the service. In July 2003, the regulator also ordered BT to cut its wholesale unmetered Internet access charges by 17 per cent, backdated to June 2002. Interestingly, the justification was that BT could provide the service more efficiently due to its network upgrades.

27 Accounting for pensions is complicated. There is the Funding Valuation (£2.1 billion according to BT) which is used to set the annual contribution rate, SSAP24 which smooths out assets and liabilities over the long term and FRS17 which calculates the total deficit at a point in time assuming future returns based upon bond yields (£9.0 billion pre-tax or £6.3 billion post-tax according to BT).

However, the Funding Valuation is very sensitive to assumptions about predicted rates of return on fund assets which are assumed to consist largely of shares – see Cohen, M. (2003) 'BT pension fund valuations fall short of making sense', http://news.ft.com of 23 May and BT Annual Report and Form 20–F 2003, pp. 112–16.

28 The millionth broadband subscriber was signed up in June 2003 with a target set for 80 per cent population coverage by the year-end. BT also announced a new broadband product called BT Yahoo! Broadband which would become available in September and incorporate BT Openworld for non-business users. On the mobile front, BT announced the forthcoming launch, subject to signing up a carrier, of its 'BluePhone' – a mobile handset that would revert to a fixed-wire device in the environs of the home, thereby greatly reducing the cost per minute for outgoing calls. An innovation of BT Mobile is free calls to the family home provided they last less than two minutes.

29 See Budden, R. (2003) 'With growth prospects poor and core revenues under attack, BT faces up to a future as a utility', http://news.ft.com of 22 May.

30 See Lindsay, R. (2002) 'mmO$_2$ shares and bonds mauled on bleak market outlook', www.totaltele.com of 26 April.

31 See Budden, R. (2002) 'Share price slide surprises mmO$_2$ boss', http://news.ft.com of 29 May.

32 See Reddall, B. (2002) 'mmO$_2$ tops H1 forecasts, starts earning', www.totaltele.com of 19 November. In the event, the Competition Commission recommended in January 2003 that mmO$_2$ cut its termination charges for calls originating on both by 15 per cent on or before 25 July 2003 and by price inflation minus 15 per cent from 2003 to 2006.

33 For a pithy hatchet job on BT's strategy since privatization, see Kay, J. (2003) 'Investors, rejoice: BT is back where it started', http://news.ft.com of 29 May.

34 See BT Annual Report and Form 20–F 2003, p. 11. A discussion of 'new wave' business is to be found on pages 11–12.

4 AT&T

1   See 'Lex: AT&T' at http://news.ft.com of 23 January 2003.

2   See Commission of the European Communities (1998) 'Initiation of proceedings (Case No IV/JV.15 – BT/AT&T)', *Official Journal of the European Communities*, C390/21.

3   See www.bt.com/World/news, NR9861. See also Office of Telecommunications (1999) *BT/AT&T Proposed Joint Venture*. A Consultative Document, Oftel, London, June.

4   Tracking stocks pay a dividend based upon a specific subsidiary but give the shareholders no ownership rights and managers are not obliged to give shareholders priority over the interests of shareholders in the parent company. Research indicates that tracking stocks do less well over time than subsidiaries that are spun off (see *The Economist*, 5 August 2000, p. 92).

5   That is, he had been paid entirely with AT&T shares.

6   See the AOL Time Warner case study.

7   See AT&T Financial Report 2001, p. 76.

8   *Idem.*, pp. 1–2.

9   This constituted something of an act of revenge. In March 1999, Comcast had bid $53 billion plus $7 billion of debt taken on for MediaOne, only to be beaten at the post by a bid from AT&T – although Comcast did receive $1.5 billion in compensation for withdrawing its own bid. Bearing in mind that AT&T had also paid $37.5 billion plus $11 billion debt taken on for TCI in October 1998, not to

mention its other outlays for smaller cable networks – perhaps $100 billion in all – Comcast's offer was a blatant attempt to acquire the entire package of cable assets for what it was previously prepared to pay for MediaOne alone. As noted in the text, there had until recently been a limit on the market share that a cable company could acquire, but the decision by the courts to strike this down effectively opened the way for the Comcast bid. A particular issue was that Brian Roberts held 87 per cent of the Comcast voting shares even though he held an overall economic interest of only 2.4 per cent, worth roughly $1 billion. By leaving AT&T shareholders with 51 per cent of the merged company there would be no change in ownership and control, and AT&T shareholders would therefore avoid tax liabilities. However, Mr Roberts would still control 45 per cent of the voting shares.

10 Earnings before interest, tax depreciation and amortization
11 Even though AOL and Time Warner had previously agreed to open their own networks in order to gain approval for their proposed merger from the FCC.
12 See AT&T Financial Report 2001, p. 54.
13 *Idem.*, p. 53.
14 *Idem.*
15 *Idem.*, pp. 52, 64.
16 Naturally, what the other case studies actually tend to show in practice (cf, AOLTW, C&W, Vivendi, BT, etc.) is that a refusal to change course eventually costs the jobs of a good many senior executives.
17 See 'AT&T: Size matters', *The Economist*, 23 February 2002, p. 89.
18 See AT&T quarterly report for the period ending 30 September 2002, p. 11.
19 A possibility that would be triggered if the share price traded below $1 for a specified period. See *Idem.*, p. 7 and http://news.ft.com of 31 May 2002 where it was pointed out that with AT&T shares trading at under $12, and the assets to be transferred to AT&T Comcast valued at just under $10, the residue of AT&T was being priced at $2 a share or roughly $7 billion in total. A further factor is that the Dow Jones Index is weighted by absolute stock prices rather than market capitalization, and hence AT&T stood to be ejected.
20 See AT&T quarterly report for the period ending 30 September 2002, p. 12. The creation of AT&T Comcast required a reshuffling of the debt held by the various parties, including the repayment of intercompany debt by AT&T Broadband to AT&T – see *Idem.*, p. 50.
21 *Idem.*, p. 31.
22 *Idem.*, pp. 13, 51.
23 See www.totaltele.com of 16 March 2003, http://news.ft.com of 31 May and AT&T quarterly report for the period ending 30 September 2002, p. 51.
24 See www.totaltele.com of 15 October 2002 and 20 January 2003.
25 See AT&T quarterly report for the period ending 30 September 2002, p. 51.
26 See *Idem.*, p. 50, www.totaltele.com of 2 April 2002, 16 September 2002 and 15 November 2002, and http://ft.news.com of 21 October 2002.
27 See www.totaltele.com of 7 January 2003. AT&T Latin America was subsequently forced into Chapter 11 bankruptcy by creditors, with AT&T continuing with its sale to Southern Cross subject to a penalty payment of $750,000 for not meeting the April deadline.
28 See www.att.com/news for the news release of 23 January.
29 See also the Vodafone case study for a similar criticism.
30 AT&T and BellSouth spent much of 2003 in discussions about a potential merger and were in a position to proceed quickly by October. However, plans were then put on hold, possibly because of adverse market reactions – see Larsen, P. and Politi, J. (2003) 'BellSouth ends AT&T deal talks', http://news.ft.com of 29 October.

5 Telecom Italia

1 See Dixon, H. (1999) 'Chinese Boxes may hold the key', *Financial Times*, 4 March, p. 32.
2 Since Tecnost was responsible for operations distinct from its role as a holding company, the former were hived off into Tecnost Sistemi, which became an Olivetti subsidiary in February 2000. It was later transferred to Olivetti Lexikon, which was itself rebranded as Olivetti Tecnost in January 2001 – see www.olivetti. com.
3 See *Financial Times* (2001) 'Pirelli/Telecom Italia', 27 September and 17 October (Lex Column).
4 The regional administrative court reversed the ruling by the stock market regulator, Consob, in February 2002 on the grounds of procedural flaws as against a lack of merit – see www.totaltele.com of 10 April 2002.
5 See www.totaltele.com of 13 November 2001.
6 Although undesirably large, this nevertheless represented a gearing ratio (debt divided by equity) of under 50 per cent at a time when those of Deutsche Telekom and France Télécom were twice as high. In part, this could be attributed to Telecom Italia's reluctance to bid for 3G licences in the UK and Germany.
7 Although Olivetti was obliged to consolidate Telecom Italia's accounts, Pirelli was not obliged at the time to consolidate those of Olivetti (see note 2 above).
8 The write-off included €2.1 billion in respect of international operations, including €700 million in respect of 9Télécom in France, and €900 million in respect of Seat PG – see www.totaltele.com of 15 February 2002 and 26 March 2002 and www.cit-online of 15 February 2002.
9 See www.totaltele.com of 8 October 2002.
10 See www.totaltele.com of 5 June 2002.
11 See www.ft.com of 5 November 2002.
12 See http://news.ft.com of 11 June 2002.
13 See http://news.ft.com of 28 August 2002 and www.totaltele.com of 12 September 2002.
14 See www.totaltele.com of 5 September 2002.
15 See www.cit-online of 7 November 2002.
16 See www.totaltele.com of 12 September 2002 and of 21 January 2003. The proposed purchase was scrapped in July, necessitating the payment of a €55 million penalty – see www.totaltele.com of 1 August 2003.
17 See www.Olivetti.com. This web site contains, inter alia, annual summaries of developments in the Olivetti Group for 2000, 2001 and 2002. The Tiglio transactions are to be found in the latter.
18 Mr Gnutti had been a board member of Telecom Italia in the days when it was headed by Mr Colaninno.
19 See www.news.ft.com of 19 December 2002.
20 See www.totaltele.com of 20 December 2002.
21 See www.totaltele.com of 9 December 2002.
22 See www.totaltele.com of 30 December 2002. A full list of transactions executed in 2002 can be found in 'Evolution of the Olivetti Group in 2002' at www.olivetti.com.
23 See Kapner, F. (2003) 'Shareholders critical of Telecom Italia plan', 'Lex: Telecom Italia', http://news.ft.com of 10 and 12 March and www.totaltele.com of 12 March.
24 'Lex: Seat Pagine Gialle', http://news.ft.com of 11 June 2003.
25 There has been only one other instance when Telia took over Telenor in December 2002, but the latter was a comparative minnow by the standards of European incumbents.
26 A practice often referred to as taking place in the *salotto buono* or drawing room.

6 Vodafone

1 The euro (€) fell fairly steadily against the dollar throughout much of the period under discussion, falling as low as $0.83. Conversion into dollars has been undertaken as appropriate at the rate ruling at the time specified.

2 See Annual Report and Accounts for the year ended 31 March 2002, p.9.

3 *Ibid.*, p. 9.

4 *Ibid.*, pp. 8, 16.

5 *Ibid.*, p. 14.

6 *Ibid.*, p. 8.

7 *Ibid.*, pp. 8–9 and 13–14.

8 *Ibid.*, pp. 7–9.

9 See http://news.ft.com of 5 February 2002.

10 Annual Report and Accounts for the Year ended 31 March 2002, p. 8.

11 See *Financial Times*, 8 January 2002, p. 21.

12 See Warner, B. (2002) 'Mobile giant has bought Vivendi's stake in their portal JV', www.totaltele.com of 30 August 2002.

13 Annual Report and Accounts for the year ended 31 March 2002, p. 9.

14 The General Packet Radio Service is best viewed as a half-way house between 2G and 3G, providing higher data speeds than 2G via an 'always-on' connection on a packet-based network.

15 In mid-1999, there were roughly 15 billion shares in issue. This then shot up to 30 billion and, early in 2000, to 60 billion. By mid-2001, there were almost 70 billion in issue – hence, at £1.50 or so apiece, yielding a total value of roughly £100 billion ($145 billion) for the entire company.

16 See Budden, R. (2002) 'Losing a reputation for walking on water', *Financial Times*, 13 April, p.14.

17 Selling the shares 'short' with a view to driving down the price and repurchasing them more cheaply at a later date.

18 See Lex (2002) 'Crossed lines', *Financial Times*, 4 May.

19 See Reddall, B. (2002) 'Vodafone shares bounce despite huge loss', www.totaltele. com of 26 May. See also http://news.ft.com of 28 and 29 May and www.cellular-news.com of 28 May for comments on the results

20 20 May 2002, p. 24.

21 See http://ft.news.com of 26 June 2002.

22 The position in March 2003 can be seen in Table 6.1. See also, for example, www.cellular-news.com of 29 November 2002.

23 The convoluted negotiations are covered in media/web articles on an almost daily basis during October, November and December 2002 – see, for example, www.cellular-news.com of 4 December.

24 See Lex in the *Financial Times* of 11 November 2002.

25 See Budden, R. (2002) 'Good reception for Vodafone but mixed signals for future', *Financial Times*, 13 November 2002, p. 25

26 See www.cit-online.com of 18 December 2002.

27 The various acquisitions are set out in the Annual Report and Accounts for the year ending 31 March 2003, pp. 4–6.

28 See Plender, J. (2003) 'Big feet, shrinking values, surreal numbers', http://news. ft.com of 2 June 2003.

29 The Vodafone live! portal was launched in most countries with the Sharp GX10 as well as the Nokia 7650 and Panasonic GD87 handsets. It was also compatible with the Sharp GX10i, SonyEricsson T610 and Nokia 3650. The latest handset is the Sharp GX20, introduced in Sweden in October 2003.

30 Loades-Carter, J. (2003) 'Vivendi and Vodafone simplify Cegetel holdings', http://news.ft.com of 14 October.

7 WorldCom

1 See www.worldcom.com/global/investor_relations/financials.
2 Behind AT&T, Sprint and MCI. The background to the WorldCom story can be found in Catan, T. *et al.* (2002) 'Bernie Ebbers: before the fall', http:// financialtimes of 18 December and 'Bernie's undoing: how the deals ran out', http://financialtimes of 19 December.
3 The 1996 Telecommunications Act in the USA set in motion a restructuring process of which WorldCom's activities were but one part. An overview of this process can be found in Curwen, P. (1997) *Restructuring Telecommunications: A study of Europe in a global context*, Basingstoke: Macmillan Press, Chapter 13.
4 To support this, Bernie Ebbers espoused a rough-and-ready image that included blue jeans, cowboy boots and pick-up trucks.
5 Naturally, objections were raised periodically in certain quarters, and the Securities and Exchange Commission objected, for example, to the planned write-off of $7 billion after the purchase of MCI. Nevertheless, the SEC eventually accepted a $3.1 billion write-off. The key aspect of pro forma accounting was that it involved stripping all post-merger charges and other one-off expenses out of a company's results to show what was claimed to be a clearer picture of underlying performance. However, the more sceptical view was that by taking excessive charges against profits, bigger reserves were created than were strictly needed which could be fed back into the profit and loss account when reported earnings were otherwise going to turn down – a practice known as 'cookie jar' accounting.
6 This was sufficient to outbid BellSouth, although the latter's unofficial offer was not made public at the time.
7 See, for example, *Common Market Law Reports*, *Antitrust Reports*, April 2000, pp. 655–6 and August 2000, pp. 198–200; 'WorldCom and Sprint admit defeat', *Financial Times*, 14 July 2000, p. 1.
8 Because regulatory approval when WorldCom acquired MCI was contingent upon WorldCom spinning off some Internet holdings to C&W, in which respect it was so remiss that C&W was able to obtain compensatory damages in the courts.
9 See, for example, 'Disconnected', *The Economist*, 1 July 2000, pp. 91–2.
10 Known in WorldCom as 'generation D'.
11 Digex was separately being pursued by both Exodus Communications and Global Crossing – see www.totaltele.com of 4 September 2000.
12 The same strategy was being adopted by AT&T.
13 Whereby, although a customer does not have a dedicated private network but is rather using a leased part of the public network, its data are treated as though they are passing along a dedicated network.
14 See www.totaltele.com of 1 November 2000.
15 See Waters, R. (2000) 'Pyrrhic court victory for WorldCom', *Financial Times*, 15 December, p. 34.
16 See Molony, D. at www.totaltele.com of 19 January 2001 and 5 February 2001.
17 See www.totaltele.com of 16 February 2001.
18 See Bögler, D. and R. Waters (2001) 'Ebbers has good reason to dig deep for Intermedia', *Financial Times*, 23 March, p. 33.
19 See www.totaltele.com and http://news.ft.com of 7 February 2002.
20 See http://news.ft.com of 15 April 2002.
21 See Waters, R. (2002) 'Grubman pulls support for WorldCom', *Financial Times*, 23 April, p. 26.
22 Bernie Ebbers was kept on in the new role of chairman emeritus and retained the interest rate subsidy on his consolidated loans of $408.2 million – WorldCom was borrowing at 7.3 per cent but charging him only 2.2 per cent – for a further five years, as well as a $1.5 million annual pension right and other benefits.

23 See Budden, R. and R. Waters (2002) 'WorldCom bankers eye global assets', *Financial Times*, 3 May and 'All eyes on WorldCom International', http://news.ft.com of 8 July.

24 Scott Sullivan was followed out the door by David Myers, senior vice president and controller, who resigned. Myers reported to Sullivan and assisted in the preparation of the financial statements.

25 Generally Accepted Accounting Principles – see www.totaltele.com of 26 June 2002 and the general discussion in the *Financial Times* of 28 June 2002, p. 22.

26 WorldCom issued a statement on 1 July explaining the background to the uncovering of the alleged fraud – see http://news.ft.com of 1 July 2002. Significantly, the reclassification of costs took place after the end of the financial quarter when executives knew the exact difference between actual performance and promises made to Wall Street.

27 This is one of the issues addressed in a major analysis of the situation at WorldCom on pp. 21–4 of the *Financial Times* of 27 June 2002. There were several reasons why WorldCom stood to gain from its behaviour: the amounts concerned could be depreciated over time rather than being accounted for as an immediate cost item, thereby inflating net income; declared ebitda (earnings before interest, taxes, depreciation and amortization) was considerably larger than it would otherwise have been; ebitda margins were overstated; capital expenditure was overstated – historically a helpful sign although in this case, with the markets looking to see signs of economies, the benefit was that the cut in investment would otherwise have appeared to be too large to maintain the future of the business; line costs were understated.

28 Except insofar that raising reported profitability created an additional tax burden which eroded net cash flow.

29 It is an irony of the Chapter 11 bankruptcy process in the USA that whereas it is very difficult to obtain additional financing outside bankruptcy because new lenders tend to be left to fight over any leftovers with existing bondholders, once in Chapter 11 a new lender can supply 'debtor-in-possession' financing which has to be repaid before all other claims.

30 As it had been in respect of Enron as it hurtled towards self-destruction.

31 At this point the other directors comprised John Sidgmore (CEO), Bert Roberts (chairman), Max Bobbitt, Stiles Kellett, Carl Aycock, James Allen, Judith Areen and Gordon Macklin. After its Chapter 11 filing WorldCom added Nicholas Katzenbach and Dennis Beresford. The restructuring team comprised Dick Thornburgh, a former attorney-general, and Richard Breeden, former head of the SEC, neither of whom had experience of the telecommunications industry. Stiles Kellett resigned in October 2002, and John Sidgmore, Bert Roberts, Francesco Galesi, Max Bobbitt, Carl Aycock and Judith Areen resigned in December 2002.

32 See http://news.ft.com of 8 July 2002.

33 Mostly difficult to identify because they held 'bearer bonds', but America's largest pension fund, the California Public Employees Retirement Scheme, admitted to $330 million of unrealized losses on WorldCom bonds and a further $230 million on WorldCom shares. It should also be noted that some bondholders held MCI and Intermedia bonds rather than those of WorldCom, and sought to protect their interests against any actions that could harm the value of these businesses.

34 See Larsen, P. and A. Hill (2002) 'WorldCom unearths new $3.3 billion fraud', http://news.ft.com of 8 August 2002.

35 Needless to say, redundancies subsequently surfaced, starting with 2,000 international jobs – 25 per cent of the staff – in mid-September.

36 See Backover, A. and M. Kessler (2002) 'Internal rifts threaten WorldCom',

www.ecommercetimes.com of 27 August. It may be noted that mere entry into Chapter 11 is insufficient grounds for the cancellation of contracts.

37 UUNet executives claimed that Internet traffic would double every 90–100 days. They exaggerated! See Tessier, J. (2002) 'WorldCom's Internet backbone has important role', www.newsfactor.com of 3 September.

38 See Fonow, R. (2002) 'Why WorldCom won't survive', www.totaltele.com of 5 September.

39 See http://news.ft.com of 19 September 2002.

40 See Hall, J. (2002) 'Ebbers' technophobia makes WorldCom probe harder', www.totaltele.com of 15 October.

41 See Rayner, A. (2002) 'Citigroup loan to Ebbers cited in lawsuit', *The Times*, 15 October, p. 29 and Larsen, P. (2002) "Court report sheds light on WorldCom's ways", http://news.ft.com of 5 November.

42 His appointment was ratified only after a lengthy spat concerning the (extremely generous) level of his compensation package.

43 See Kennedy, S. (2002) 'Court oks partial settlement in WorldCom case', www.totaltele.com of 27 November.

44 See Moules, J. *et al.* (2003) 'WorldCom will take an $80 billion write-down', http://news.ft.com of 13 March.

45 See Hall, J. (2003) 'WorldCom seen emerging with slim debt load', www.totaltele.com of 11 April.

46 See www.totaltele.com of 24 April 2003.

47 Securities and Exchange Commission v. WorldCom, Inc, No. 02–CV-4963 (JSR) of 26 June 2003.

48 For the Audit Committee Report see http://eol.finsys.com/edgar (209 pages). This contains, for example, a potted history on pages 44–55 and a summary of improper adjustments to line costs on page 55. In 1999 and 2000 these took the form of releases of previously set aside 'accruals' (reserves). This is explained on pages 61–6. For commentary, see media reports on 10 June 2003.

49 See Larsen, P. (2003) 'FBI to widen MCI probe', http://news.ft.com of 13 August. A full list of all outstanding investigations into MCI can be found at www.boycottworldcom.com/scandal

50 See Lex at http://news.ft.com of 3 August 2003.

51 Five new board members were appointed at the end of August including David Maitlin, bringing the total to nine. Once a non-executive Chairman is elected, Michael Capellas will revert to the sole title of CEO.

52 At the end of August, Richard Breeden published 76 directives designed to make MCI's corporate governance 'squeaky-clean'.

53 Judicial approval for the Plan of Reorganization was received on 1 November 2003. Creditor claims and other settlements are still outstanding, but the company is expected to emerge with $2.3 billion in cash and $5.8 billion of debt. The new 12-person board and the use of MCI as the trading name would commence on 1 January 2004.

8 Vivendi Universal

1 *The Economist*, 21 July 2001, p. 74.

2 www.vivendi.fr/vu2/en/news/00000677.

3 A comparison of seven conglomerates at a somewhat later date can be found in 'Tangled webs', *The Economist*, 25 May 2002, pp. 81–3.

4 *Common Market Antitrust Law Reports*, December 2000, pp. 1007–8.

5 www.vivendiuniversal.com/vu2/en/news/00000776. Needless to say, the company preferred to concentrate upon the sharply upwards trend in ebitda (earnings before interest, taxation, depreciation and amortization) rather than the more

tricky-to-achieve profitability. According to CEO Messier, the results confirmed 'the robustness of our businesses, with limited exposure to advertising; the benefits of a truly global position; and the fast progress of the reorganization and implementation of our recent merger'.

6 See Harding, J. (2001) 'Vivendi Universal sells $1.5bn of BSkyB shares', *Financial Times*, 14 December, p. 22.

7 Canal Plus and UPC already had a joint venture in Poland where they had merged their satellite platforms earlier in 2001. They were also linked via separate stakes in USA Networks.

8 As of 31 March 2003, Liberty Media's stake was the third largest, exceeded only by that of the Bronfman family with 4.23 per cent and Philips with 3.57 per cent. No other shareholder held over 2 per cent – see http://finance.vivendiuniversal.com/finance/market/shareownership.

9 The term 'cultural exception' refers to the welter of quotas and subsidies through which France in particular protects its creative industries from Hollywood competition. The comment was accordingly badly received in France – President Jacques Chirac called it a 'mental aberration' – and he was forced to retract somewhat, claiming that 'I will not be an apostle of US cultural domination, but I want to be able to compete on a level playing field'. One of the curious features of the situation at Canal Plus was that whereas it was obligated by its charter to give 9 per cent of its revenues to support French film production, those revenues were dependent upon the successful flogging of football matches, political satire, Hollywood films and a bit of porn to its paying customers – see Parmentier, G. (2002) 'Canal Plus: slaughtering a sacred cow', http://news.ft.com of 1 May.

10 It was not without interest that Hughes had just previously rejected an approach to purchase EchoStar from Mr Murdoch.

11 For information on the various dealings see, for example, Johnson, J. (2001) 'Vivendi to buy USA Networks subsidiary', *Financial Times*, 17 December, p. 23; 'Veni vidi Vivendi', *The Economist*, 22 December, p. 87; Grimes, C. and J. Harding (2001) 'Vivendi agrees $1.5 bn investment in EchoStar', *Financial Times*, 16 December, p. 18; Lex in the *Financial Times* of 14 and 16 December; Johnson, J. and C. Grimes (2001) 'Messier thrives on Vivendi's frantic pace', *Financial Times*, 21 December, p. 23.

12 In fact, there was also widespread concern about the accounts themselves since a plethora of acquisitions always makes it difficult to make valid year-on-year comparisons. In addition, Table 8.1 is prepared according to French GAAP which is somewhat different from the more widely accepted US GAAP – for example, an additional €1.8 billion of goodwill amortization for 2001 which was declared at the end of April 2002 was attributed to the 'mechanical effect' of a switch to US GAAP. The only issue on which Mr Messier was prepared to comment was whether there were unpleasant liabilities hidden off-balance-sheet. He said that this was not the case.

13 At $600 per subscriber, many at Canal Plus considered the price to be excessive by a factor of ten, thereby at a stroke putting paid to any realistic hopes of bringing Canal Plus back into profit within two years – the target set for Mr Lescure and Mr Olivennes.

14 Mr Lescure is alleged to have claimed that he had never 'met as big an ego as Messier' – see Harding, J. and J. Johnson (2002) 'Vivendi's ego left facing fall-out from dual sacking', *Financial Times*, 17 April, p. 28. However, outside Canal Plus itself, his reputation as a manager was poor – see 'Canal Plus: Rebels with a cause', *The Economist*, 27 April 2002, p. 73.

15 It was argued that if he was dismissed the Vivendi Universal share price would rise sharply – see Johnson, J. and J. Harding (2002) 'Messier fate lies with Vivendi board', *Financial Times*, 18 April, p. 28.

16 Johnson, J. (2002) 'Goodwill write-off pushes Vivendi to €17bn loss', http://news. ft.com of 30 April.

17 Harding, J. (2002) 'Malone set for $1bn hit on Vivendi deal', *Financial Times*, 6 May, p. 19.

18 Kapner, F. (2002) 'Pay-TV ruling gives Vivendi escape route', http:/mews.ft.com of 14 May.

19 It was possible to argue that the sum involved was fairly trivial compared to the $18 million 'golden parachute' to which Edgar Bronfman, Jr. was entitled when he resigned his executive duties in March.

20 Johnson, J. and J. Harding (2002) 'Vivendi battles to avoid default on €1.8 billion debt', *Financial Times*, 5 July, p. 1.

21 Johnson, J. and A. van Duyn (2002) 'Messier era ends with junk downgrade', *Financial Times*, 3 July, p. 26.

22 See Johnson, J. (2002) 'Regulator seizes Messier messages', http://news.ft.com of 10 September and the subsequent accusations about misleading accounting statements in Ratner, J. (2002) 'Vivendi faces two more probes in the US', http:// news.ft.com of 3 November.

23 See the Lex commentary on Vivendi Universal in the *Financial Times* of 21 August, 2002 and 'Vivendi Universal: Plus ça change', *The Economist*, 28 September 2002, p. 83.

24 Johnson, J. (2002) 'Vivendi secretly looking to sell off magazine stable', *Financial Times*, 21 August, p. 5. The attitude to the sale of French publishing assets such as Larousse and Le Robert was similar. Curiously, French politicians had been only too keen to applaud Vivendi when it acquired the American Heritage dictionary as part of Houghton Mifflin, but when it came to the possibility of a role reversal, became positively xenophobic – 'cultural expropriation' was how it was seen by former culture minister, Jack Lang.

25 Burt, T. (2002) 'Vivendi's Diller considers break-up', http://news.ft.com of 22 September.

26 Larsen, P. and J. Johnson (2002) 'Vivendi and suitor put price on illusion', http://news.ft.com of 24 November.

27 Burt, T. (2003) 'Loss-making Canal Plus plans restructuring', http://news.ft.com of 9 March.

28 Henni, J. and G. Poussielgue. (2003) 'Vivendi faces IRS penalty', http://news.ft. com of 1 April.

29 See Johnson, J. (2003) 'Vivendi in uncharted legal waters', *Financial Times*, 12 July, p. M5, 'Vivendi in legal move to halt €20m for Messier', http://news.ft.com of 12 August and 'SEC moves to block $23 million payoff to Messier,' http://news. ft.com of 17 September.

30 Larsen, P. (2003) 'Vivendi talks as bidders get frustrated', http://ft.news.com of 17 July.

31 Larsen, P. (2003) 'Comcast rules out bid for Vivendi US assets', http://ft.news.com of 14 August.

32 Major, T. (2003) 'Deutsche Telekom pulls out of mobile talks', http://news.ft.com of 28 September.

33 Loades-Carter, J. (2003) 'Vivendi and Vodafone simplify Cegetel holdings', http://news.ft.com of 14 October.

9 AOL Time Warner

1 See Chapter 1.

2 *Financial Times*, 17 October 1994, p. x.

3 Office of Telecommunications (1995) *Beyond the Telephone, the Television and the PC*, Oftel, London, pp. 10–11.

4 Commission of the European Communities (1997) *Green Paper on the Convergence of the Telecommunications, Media and Information Technology Sectors, and the Implications for Regulation*, COM (97) 623 final, CEC, Brussels.

5 Adstead, S. and P. McGarvey (1997) *Convergence in Europe: the New Media Value Chain*, London: Pearson Professional.

6 Katz, M. (1996) 'Remarks on the economic implications of convergence', *Industry and Corporate Change*, 5(4), pp. 1079–96. See also Katz, M. and G. Woroch (1998) 'Introduction: convergence, regulation and competition', *Industry and Corporate Change*, 6(4), pp. 701–18.

7 Williams, N. and E. English (1997) *Current Trends in World Telecoms*, London: FT Telecoms and Media Publishing, p. 25.

8 'Two sharks in a fishbowl', *The Economist*, 11 September 1999, pp. 83–4.

9 Waters, R. (1997) 'Time for some results', *Financial Times*, 14 May, p. 17.

10 Quoted in Hill, A. and R. Waters (2000) 'Media titans in $327bn merger', *Financial Times*, 11 January, p. 1.

11 'WhatsUpDoc.com', *Financial Times*, 11 January 2000, p. 24. Major articles on the merger have also appeared as follows: 11 January, p. 29; 12 January, p. 34; 17 January, p. 24.

12 Earnings before interest, tax, depreciation and amortization. For a further analysis of the financial flows associated with the takeover see Loomis, C. (2000) 'AOL +TWX = ???', *Fortune*, 7 February, pp. 35–7. She calculated that AOLTW would initially have a P/E ratio of 300 although that, like many other conventional measures when set in a 'new economy' context, might not matter much. She also observed, however, that if AOLTW was to deliver the expected 15 per cent rate of return over a 15-year period, then the capitalization of AOLTW would need to have reached $2.4 trillion by the end of the period. She concluded that this was not economically feasible.

13 Thereby necessitating a restructuring exercise no later than the end of 2001 when AT&T would be obliged to divest its own interest as a condition for its takeover of MediaOne.

14 There is a detailed discussion of the deal in *Financial Times*, 24 January 2000, p. 24 and 29 January 2000, p. 18. The deal attracted the attention of potential counter-bidders, and a consortium of three companies including Telefónica indicated that it would be making a cash bid worth $9 billion. However, it was unable to raise the necessary finance before the EMI shareholders meeting on 26 June which accepted the Warner offer.

15 AOL's main content providers include Canal Plus, CBS Sportsline, Dow Jones, Dun & Bradstreet, Economist Intelligence Unit, MTV, Nickelodeon, Reuters, Standard & Poor's and Ziff Davis.

16 See *Financial Times*, 3 February 2000, p. 30.

17 A piece of software is loaded into a personal computer that allows a list of 'online buddies' to be installed. Instant messages, faster than e-mail, can then be exchanged with any of them who are logged on. AOL introduced the service in 1989 and added the 'buddy list' feature in 1996. The short message service is the equivalent for mobile devices. The Federal Communications Commission (FCC), on 12 June, sought additional information on AOL's instant messaging software, its ownership interest in Hughes Electronics Corp. and Time Warner's deployment of high-speed Internet, telephone and digital cable services. On 23 June it sought additional information, especially concerning AOL's proposed interactive TV service, AOL-TV. This issue is analysed in Faulhaber, G. (2002) 'Network effects and merger analysis: Instant messaging and the AOL-Time Warner case', *Telecommunications Policy*, 26(5–6), pp. 311–33.

18 DSL is a technology whereby the capacity of existing copper wires is greatly increased to permit the downloading of data rather than the transmission of voice.

19 See www.aoltimewarner.com/corporate_information/timeline for a potted history of AOLTW.

20 High Speed Access pulled out in September, and AOLTW subsequently sought to replace it with Junction Services, New York Connect.net and South Texas Internet Connections.

21 See 'From Friends to Foes', *The Economist*, 23 June 2001, pp. 86–7.

22 See *Financial Times*, 30 October 2001, p. 32.

23 See Grimes, C. (2001) 'Harry Potter and the sales team', *Financial Times*, 16 November, p. 12.

24 See Kapadia, R. (2002) 'AOL Time Warner expects charge of up to US$60 bn', www.totaltele.com of 8 January; Lex Column (2002) 'Down to earth', *Financial Times*, 7 January.

25 The reasons for this are discussed in Waters, R. (2002) 'Surfing alone', *Financial Times*, 27 April, p. 19.

26 See Grimes, C. and R. Waters (2002) 'Deflated expectations', *Financial Times*, 9 January, p. 19.

27 See Kapadia, R. (2002) 'Global media – Europe seen as AOL Time Warner road to growth', www.totaltele.com of 21 March.

28 Extensive financial data are to be found on the www.aoltimewarner.com web site. Information on restructuring is to be found in the 'notes to supplemental consolidated financial statements'.

29 In March 2002, the partnership served seven million cable customers, had $9 billion of total assets and generated annual revenues of $3.5 billion. TWE owned roughly two-thirds and A/N one-third.

30 These and other more minor restructurings had implications for AOLTW's consolidated accounts. These are discussed in Waters, R. and C. Grimes (2002) 'A media giant finds the future less rosy', *Financial Times*, 28 March, p. 25 and Kapadia, R. (2002) 'AOL Time Warner loses some control in Newhouse revamp'," www.totaltele.com of 25 June.

31 See, for example, Waters, R. and T. Burt (2002) 'Controversy haunts AOL six years on', *Financial Times*, 15 July, p. 8 and Grimes, C. (2002) 'AOL inflated ad revenues by nearly $200 million', http://news.ft.com of 23 October.

32 See Shook, D. (2002) 'How to undo AOL Time Warner', www.commercetimes.com of 4 November.

33 Followed a week later by Microsoft's own upgrade, MSN 8, costing $21.95 a month for dial-up compared to $23.90 for AOL 8 and with a link-up to Walt Disney – see Kapadia, R. (2002) 'MSN launches new service, sets sights on AOL', www.totaltele.com of 25 October.

34 Richard Parsons has so far resisted pressure to re-price options to put them back 'in the money'.

35 See 'AOL Time Warner: you've got trouble', *The Economist*, 30 November 2002, pp. 52–3.

36 See Kapadia, R. (2002) 'AOL Time Warner cable spin-off in, complex deals out', www.totaltele.com of 11 December.

37 For a sceptical response, see Lex (2003) 'AOL Time Warner', *Financial Times*, 3 February.

38 See Kapadia, R. (2003) 'AOL, rivals, seek ways to curtail defections,' www.totaltele.com of 4 February.

39 See Larsen, P. (2003) 'Online troubles mar AOL's profits', http://news.ft.com of 23 July and Burt, T. (2003) 'AOL predicts drop in online sales', http://news.ft.com of 23 July.

40 In October 2003, AOL announced that it would itself be introducing a no-frills dial-up service, but using Netscape as its brand name.

41 AOL 9.0 boasted over 100 new features, including faster downloads, free e-mail

storage on AOL's computers and an easy way to keep online journals (blogs). Subscribers were also able to plug a handset into a computer and make free phone calls via AOL's instant messaging service – see 'AOL: Scrambling to halt the exodus', *BusinessWeek*, 4 August 2003, pp. 62, 64.

42 See Beard, A. (2003) 'AOL Time Warner drops the "AOL" name', http://news.ft. com of 18 September.

43 See Kapadia, R. (2003) 'AOL unveils new high-speed service, promises more', www.totaltele.com of 31 March.

10 The KirchGruppe

1 Which has parallels with the long-standing and overly protective Italian way of doing business discussed in the case study on Telecom Italia. It is of particular interest that it was the takeover bid for Telecom Italia by Deutsche Telekom which caused a major row between the respective governments as it was such a classic illustration of 'pots calling kettles black'.

2 The previous case study on Vivendi Universal demonstrates how mismanagement on a similar scale nearly brought down that company also.

3 Right to sell at a specified price at a specified future date.

4 See Tryhorn, C. (2002) 'Man at the Helm', *The Observer*, 7 April.

5 The so-called 'Vinkuliering' is a legal provision which permits the boards of certain German companies to prevent the buyer of a large stake from exercising the voting rights that would otherwise have come with the stake.

6 At the time, Springer's free float was only 10 per cent and its shares rarely traded, so the effect on the free float in a secondary offering by Deutsche Bank would be very significant.

7 See Benoit, B. (2002) 'Kirch attempt to sell Springer stake halted', http://news.ft. com of 3 September; 'Axel Springer considers link with Ringier', http://news.ft. com of 9 September; 'Kirch gains extension of Springer deadline', http://news. ft.com of 10 September; and 'Springer faces watershed but avoids abyss', http://news.ft.com of 11 September.

8 See Benoit, B. (2002) 'Springer, Ringier may form media giant', *Financial Times*, 20 September, p. 31 and 'Axel Springer talks with Ringier stall', http://news.ft. com of 29 September.

9 See http://news.ft.com of 11 September 2002 and 17 September 2002.

10 See Benoit, B. (2002) 'DT cable bidders eye Premiere', http://news.ft.com of 19 September.

11 See Benoit, B. (2002) 'Deutsche Bank to auction Springer stake', http://news.ft. com of 1 October.

12 See http://news.ft.com of 21 October 2002.

13 See http://news.ft.com of 9 December 2002.

14 See Benoit, B. (2002) 'Springer to exit TV and focus on print', http://news.ft.com of 18 December.

15 See Benoit, B. (2002) 'Permira steps in to control Premiere', http://news.ft.com of 19 December and 'Bid for Kirch's Premiere arm "on schedule",' http://news. ft.com of 21 January 2003.

16 See Benoit, B. (2002) 'KirchMedia assets to be sold to Bauer', http://news.ft.com of 22 December.

17 See Benoit, B. (2003) 'Kirch TV drama could run and run', http://news.ft.com of 21 January.

18 See Benoit, B. (2003) 'Saban closer to takeover of ProSiebenSAT.1', http://news. ft.com of 18 March.

19 It was noted that although Germany technically had no limitations on foreign ownership of media assets, Haim Saban was about to become the first foreigner to

actually achieve a takeover. In this respect he was favoured above both Rupert Murdoch and Silvio Berlusconi, insofar that he was perceived as a businessman rather than conservative ideologue looking for political outlets, but also above John Malone of Liberty Media – see Benoit, B. (2003) 'Saban gets green light for ProSiebenSAT.1', http://news.ft.com of 24 April.

20 See Benoit, B. (2003) 'Bankers give guarantee on ProSieben bid', http://news.ft.com of 11 May.

21 'Lex: Kirch Media', *Financial Times*, 4 June 2003.

22 Burt, T. (2003) 'Saban makes move on ProSieben investors', http://news.ft.com of 12 August.

23 See Harding, J. (2002) 'Reluctant Leo Kirch forced into the spotlight', *Financial Times*, 9 April, p. 28.

11 Cable & Wireless

1 See C&W Annual Report and Accounts 1998, pp. 72–3.

2 See Common Market Law Reports (1995) 'VebaCom: Cable & Wireless Europe', *CMLR Antitrust Reports*, September/October, p. 264.

3 See Curwen, P. (1997) *Restructuring Telecommunications: A study of Europe in a global context*, Basingstoke: Macmillan, pp. 163–5.

4 C&W subsequently felt itself unable to pursue its interests in both the UK and Germany, and decided to pull out of its German venture, selling its stake in Vebacom back to Veba for $1.3 billion. The alliance between C&W and Veba, C&W Europe, which covered Western Europe other than Germany, was not affected.

5 See Beesley, M. and B. Laidlaw (1989) *The Future of Telecommunications*, Research Monograph 42, London: IEA, pp. 22–4.

6 However, in March 1996, the government announced that it would issue new international licences, commencing in the latter part of 1996, as a major step in creating a fully liberalized market by 1 January 1998.

7 The golden share was given up in February 2002.

8 The structure of CWC was initially dominated by C&W (52.6 per cent), Bell Atlantic (18.5 per cent) and BCE, owner of Bell Canada (14.2 per cent), with roughly 12.5 per cent floated on the stock market. BCE sold its stake to institutional investors in June 1998, and, in August, Bell Atlantic issued an exchangeable bond permitting the buyers the option to acquire its CWC stake in August 2002 at a 28 per cent premium to the share price ruling four years previously.

9 C&W was floated in three stages with the government retaining a £1 'golden share'; 49.9 per cent was sold in November 1981 at 168p, fully paid, and trading opened at 203p. A further 22 per cent was sold in December 1983 by way of a tender at a minimum of 100p, part-paid, followed by a second instalment of 175p in February 1984. A final tranche was sold in two instalments: 300p in December 1985 plus 287p in March 1986. The number of shares was raised by a factor of 1.5 in October 1983 and by a factor of 2 in August 1986.

10 See the *Financial Times*, 3 October 1998, p. 20.

11 See the *Financial Times*, 13 May 1998, p. 29.

12 See the *Financial Times*, 21 August 1998, p. 19.

13 See the *Financial Times*, 16 November 1998, p. 26.

14 See the *Financial Times*, 16 April 1998, p. 25.

15 See the *Financial Times*, 14 July 1998, p. 21.

16 See the *Financial Times*, 12 November 1998, p. 33.

17 See the *Financial Times*, 14 May 1998, p. 31.

18 See the *Financial Times*, 29 May 1998, p. 1.

19 See the *Financial Times*, 17 July 1998, p. 26.
20 See the *Financial Times*, 27 July 1998, p. 25.
21 Fibre-optic cable laid in the ground but not yet activated by being connected to transmission equipment at both ends.
22 See the *Financial Times*, 17 November 1998, p.28.
23 See the *Financial Times*, 26 April 1999, p.1 and 27 April 1999, p. 23.
24 See the *Financial Times*, 29 March 1999, p. 24; 14 April 1999, p. 28; 17 April 1999, p. 22; 22 April 1999, p. 23; and 7 May 1999, pp. 22, 23.
25 See the *Financial Times*, 20 April 1999, p. 30; 4 May 1999, p. 22; and 13 May 1999, pp. 23, 26.
26 See the *Financial Times*, 1 June 1999, p. 1; 2 June 1999, p. 21; 3 June 1999, p. 24; and 10 June 1999, p. 22.
27 See the *Financial Times*, 1 June 1999, p. 26.
28 In mid-August, Pacific Century CyberWorks handed over $6.5 billion in cash and 4.5 billion shares amounting to a 19.1 per cent stake in PCCW. C&W immediately sold a 4.9 per cent stake for $1.3 billion. It pencilled in a further disposal of 7.5 per cent for February 2001 – see the *Financial Times*, 29 September 2000, p. 37.
29 See the *Financial Times*, 19 November 1999, p. 23.
30 Although previous financial data have been expressed in dollars as this is the most commonly understood currency, it is necessary to revert to pounds sterling in what follows. Broadly speaking, the pound/dollar rate has remained in the region of £1=$1.5.
31 See the *Financial Times*, 18 May 2000, p. 26.
32 See the *Financial Times*, 7 June 2000, p. 29.
33 See Biddlecombe, E. (2000) 'C&W and Nokia strike global wireless data deal', www.totaltele.com of 6 July.
34 See the *Financial Times*, 19 July 2000, p. 28 and www.totaltele.com of 18 July 2000.
35 See the *Financial Times*, 23 August 2000, p. 10.
36 The half-year results can be found in the *Financial Times*, 16 November 2000, p. 39.
37 See the *Financial Times*, 16 November 2000, p. 26.
38 See the *Financial Times*, 9 March 2001, p. 7 and www.totaltele.com of 7 April.
39 See the *Financial Times*, 21 February 2001, p. 34.
40 Having already made 1,500 workers redundant at the end of 2000.
41 See the *Financial Times*, 14 March 2001, p. 25.
42 See the *Financial Times*, 26 March 2001, p. 24.
43 See the *Financial Times*, 24 April 2001, p. 22.
44 See www.totaltele.com of 14 May 2001.
45 See the *Financial Times*, 20 September 2001, p. 26.
46 Although heavy reductions in the normal dividend payments meant that the total dividend for 2001 would be little higher than in 2000.
47 As reported in the *Financial Times*, 15 November 2001, p. 31.
48 See the *Financial Times*, 25 November 2001, p. 26.
49 See the *Financial Times*, 1 December 2001, p. 15. The deal was subject to Exodus emerging from Chapter 11 stripped of its $4.4 billion debts, and this was approved in January 2002. C&W also took advantage of the bankruptcy of ISP PSINet to pick up the assets of PSINet Japan for a rock-bottom price of $10.3 million.
50 See www.totaltele.com of 15 May 2002.
51 See www.totaltele.com of 13 November 2002 and *The Times*, 14 November 2002, p. 29.
52 That disclosure of lease liabilities was inadequate was well-known to accountancy bodies, especially in the UK where leases generally had a 25-year life. Nevertheless, it was permissible to omit mention of these in annual reports since, in

essence, all companies inevitably had property and leases did not present difficulties until one wanted to terminate them. Nevertheless, the financial markets were predictably outraged that, for example, the lease commitments of Exodus Communications were not revealed at the time of its acquisition.

53 For example, the 8.75 per cent sterling bond due August 2012 fell 25 percentage points to 68 per cent of its face value. Standard & Poor's did not respond until late January, but then cut C&W's rating by four points to a junk rating of BB compared to the two-point downgrade by Moody's to Ba1.

54 C&W paid no tax at the time despite making a £3.4 billion capital gain on the disposal, whereas MediaOne had paid £1.5 billion in tax.

55 It also triggered two lawsuits from groups of American and UK investors who alleged that they had been misled about the health of the company's balance sheet.

56 It was alleged that it received a £1.5 billion break-up bid from its smaller rival, Thus Group, backed by private equity firms, although neither party made this public and the value of C&W subsequently rose beyond the mooted break-up price.

57 See http://news.ft.com of 12 February.

58 See www.totaltele.com of 21 January 2003.

59 See http://news.ft.com of 5 February 2003 for several articles on the approach by PCCW.

60 At the end of May 2003, Fidelity reduced its stake further to 3.97 per cent – it had held over 9 per cent in December 2002 – in the run up to the annual results for 2003.

61 The full board changes were as follows: Departures – David Nash (31/12/02), Don Reed and Raymond Seitz (31/01/03), Sir Ralph Robins (02/03/03), Graham Wallace (04/04/03), Robert Lerwill (29/09/03), Sir Widifried Bischoff (25/07/03); Arrivals – Richard Lapthorne (10/01/03), Bernard Gray and Anthony Rice (21/01/03), Kevin Loosemore (02/04/03), Francesco Caio (04/04/03), Graham Howe and Kasper Rorsted (27/05/03), Lord Robertson (27/07/03).

62 These countries are discussed in detail in McClune, E. and J. Taaffe (2003) 'C&W to sell off European units', www.totaltele.com of 30 May which also analyses C&W's overall strategy.

63 A searing denouncement of the role of C&W's then board of directors is contained in Durham, P. (2002) 'Part-timers who let C&W waste £22 billion', *The Sunday Times*, 15 December, p. 8. Elsewhere, a top ten shareholder pointed out that the board had denied that there was anything else they needed to disclose well before the story broke about the effects of the debt downgrade, and the Association of British Insurers was so incensed that it asked the Financial Services Authority to determine whether C&W had infringed UK listing rules.

12 Marconi

1 'Reinventing Marconi', *The Economist*, 2 December 2000, pp. 46–7.

2 Cane, A. (2001) 'Heroic duo's reputation hit below waterline', *Financial Times*, 6 July 2001, p.18.

3 It is claimed by some that the decision to concentrate upon telecommunications was triggered by Siemens' decision not to take control of the joint venture. The many joint ventures set up by Lord Weinstock had certainly served to conserve cash, and could have been left to trundle on, but by this point in proceedings the kind of conglomerate built up by Lord Weinstock had become deeply unfashionable and George Simpson needed to restore market confidence by becoming more specialized.

4 Towards the end of 2000, George Simpson complained constantly that analysts seemed unable to distinguish between the likes of Lucent Technologies with its

numerous narrowband products and Marconi at the technological cutting edge. In particular, Marconi emphasized that it was a world leader in Synchronous Digital Hierarchy (SDH), known in the USA as SONET.

5 Optical switches are considerably cheaper than electronic switches to operate in a fibre-optic network.

6 Dickson, M. (2000) 'Market to Marconi: Have a not-so-happy birthday', *Financial Times*, 2 December, p. 17. In the event, he was half right but also, of course, half wrong. Interestingly, he was among the first to shout foul when Lord Simpson demanded his full contractual entitlement even when forced to retire in disgrace – see 'Marconi: This time let there be no rewards for failure', *Financial Times*, 8 September 2001, p. 15, although he continued to argue that it was inappropriate to claim that Lord Simpson and John Mayo had wilfully destroyed Marconi. In the end Lord Simpson walked away with £300,000 in cash and a seven-figure pension fund although Sir Roger Hurn refused to take any compensation.

7 Daniel, C. (2001) 'The wisdom of gate crashing the US when the bullish party is over', *Financial Times*, 7 April, p. 14.

8 Lord Simpson was once quoted as saying that 'cash in the bank offers a very low return and it does not say much about being a dynamic company. . . . I spent the cash as fast as I could.'

9 At the equivalent of $1.1 billion, this was somewhat below market expectations of up to $1.5 billion.

10 Many commentators took the view that the board should have risen at the crack of dawn and drawn up a statement by midday, thereby minimizing the time the shares were suspended. The revised forecast for the year ending March 2002 involved a 15 per cent reduction in sales, a halving of operating profits and £550 million of exceptional charges. An optimistic interpretation suggested that Marconi might just be able to avoid any increase in its borrowings – it anyway had an unused £4 billion credit facility, but only until 2003 – but not unless the dividend was sacrificed. However, if sales deteriorated faster than expected, as seemed quite possible, there could well be no operating profits left at all.

11 See, for example, the full page of analysis devoted to the issue in the *Financial Times* of 6 July and *The Sunday Times* of 8 July.

12 One must bear in mind, however, that Lord Weinstock held 50 million shares at the time and was sitting on a notional £500 million loss incurred since the share price peaked. Ironically, Lord Simpson had been awarded 1.5 million options at a strike price of 800p, but at least he had not borrowed money to take them up (in the manner of WorldCom's Bernie Ebbers).

13 It was suggested, half in jest, that the bankers still thought they were dealing with GEC – see Lex in the *Financial Times* of 5 September 2001.

14 As quoted in 'The mess at Marconi: Tell it straight', *The Economist*, 8 September 2001, pp. 84–85.

15 In which respect they were more or less right, but this hardly helped those who trusted their judgement and followed suit.

16 This was a particularly contentious matter since it emerged that news of the first-quarter loss was withheld from the non-executive directors on the board for a six-week period during which the AGM took place. Marconi's excuse was that it needed time to check the figures, but the London Stock Exchange was sufficiently convinced of the possibility that its listing rules in respect of 'full and timely disclosure' had been breached as to invite the Financial Services Authority to conduct an investigation.

17 A man seen as competent rather than visionary, and with a question mark hanging over his involvement in the events leading up to the profits warnings.

18 See, for example, the full-page spread in the *Financial Times* of 5 September 2001 and *The Sunday Times* of 9 September.

19 See Daniel, C. (2001) 'Marconi on target but warn on demand', *Financial Times*, 16 October 2001, p. 26.

20 See Daniel, C. (2001) 'Marconi writes off $4.5bn Fore goodwill' and 'Downbeat Marconi lays its bad news on the line', *Financial Times*, 14 November, pp. 25 and 27.

21 See Malkani, G. and V. Leboucq (2001) 'Marconi to sell stake in Hotpoint', *Financial Times*, 21 December, p. 23.

22 Mayo, J. (2002) 'Exploding some Marconi myths', *Financial Times*, 18 January, p. 18; 'How Marconi left investors hanging on', *Financial Times*, 19/20 January, p. 14; and 'Marconi under the microscope', *Financial Times*, 21 January 2002, p. 18. According to John Mayo, he and Lord Simpson basically did everything right, delivering huge benefits to shareholders who became fixated on the decline in Marconi's share price while forgetting the free shares in BAe, the generous dividends and the share repurchases.

23 For a sample response, see Plender, J. (2002) 'Mayo's handy guide to Marconi's road to ruin', *Financial Times*, 19 January 2000, p. 13.

24 As reported on the now defunct www.dljdirect.co.uk of 22 February.

25 See www.totaltele.com of 20 June 2002.

26 See Hunt, B. (2002) 'Marconi finalises debt restructuring deal', http://news.ft.com of 29 August and 'The end of the beginning for Marconi', *Financial Times*, 31 August, p. 12, and Marshall, S. (2002) 'Marconi aims for steady ship, keeps focus on SDH', www.totaltele.com of 5 September. Marconi Corporation would have one billion issued shares. Details of amendments to the restructuring plan can be found on the Marconi web site: press releases of 18/03/03. It is salutary to consider that the holder of 2,236 shares in Marconi Plc, worth almost £28,000 at their peak, ended up with four shares in Marconi Corp. worth under £3. Holders of fewer than five new shares were subsequently forced to sell them to Marconi Corp., thereby crystallizing the loss.

27 Grande, C. (2002) 'Marconi finalises £4bn restructuring plan', http://ft.news.com of 15 December.

28 Redall, B. (2003) 'Marconi delays debt swap completion', www.totaltele.com of 18 March.

29 The financial impact of the restructuring is set out in Marconi Corporation, Group Preliminary Financials, notes to the preliminary announcement at www.marconi.com. In effect, borrowings and creditors amounting to £4,818 million were written off during the restructuring. See also the Operating and Financial Review for the three months and twelve months ended 31 March 2003 at the same web site.

30 A one-year loan of £2 billion, extendable for a further year, was signed in May 2000 shortly before the first profits warning.

31 Readers are invited to draw up a short-list for themselves, but would be advised to start with a small piece of paper. It is noteworthy that it is Jack Welch at General Electric rather than the CEO of a TMT company who is usually rolled out when making invidious comparisons. However, Kirstie Hamilton in *The Sunday Times* makes the point that an analyst called Mustapha Omar of Collins Stewart was warning from the end of 1998 that GEC/Marconi was doing much worse than was generally believed. She notes that he expected that there could be worse to come. He was correct.

32 In April 2003, the FSA issued a statement censuring Lord Simpson (together with Sir Roger Hurn) for his conduct in relation to the suspension of the share price in November 2001. In accordance with its rulebook of the time – subsequently amended – the FSA had no power to impose fines, but its statement may well affect the class actions outstanding against Marconi in the USA.

References

Burnes, B. (2000) *Managing Change: A strategic approach to organizational dynamics*, 3rd edition. Harlow: Prentice Hall.

D'Cruz, J. and A. Rugman (1994) 'The Five Partners Model: France Telecom, Alcatel, and the global telecommunications industry,' *European Management Journal*, **12**(1), pp. 59–66.

Farkas, C.M. and S. Wetlaufer (1996) 'The way chief executives lead,' *Harvard Business Review*, **74**(May-June), pp. 110–23.

Financial Times (1999) '*Financial Times* survey – FT 500 Annual Review,' 28 January.

Financial Times (2000) '*Financial Times* survey – FT 500 Annual Review,' 4 May.

Financial Times (2001) '*Financial Times* survey – FT 500 Annual Review,' 11 May.

Financial Times (2002) '*Financial Times* survey – FT 500 Annual Review,' 10 May.

Financial Times (2003) '*Financial Times* survey – FT 500 Annual Review,' 27 May.

Finlay, P. (2000) *Strategic Management – An introduction to business and corporate strategy*. London: Prentice Hall.

Fransman, M (2002) 'The telecoms boom and bust, 1996–2002: puzzles, paradoxes, and processing', paper presented at the 14th Biennial Conference of the International Telecommunications Society, Seoul, South Korea, 18–21 August.

Howell, R. (2002) 'How accounting executives looked the wrong way,' *Financial Times*, 13 August, p. 11.

Johnson, G. and K. Scholes (2002) *Exploring Corporate Strategy – text and cases*, 6th edition. Harlow: Prentice Hall.

McKiernan, P. (1992) *Strategies of Growth – maturity, recovery and internationalization*, London: Routledge.

Pehrsson, A. (2001a) *Strategy in Emerging Markets: telecommunications establishments in Europe*. London: Routledge.

Pehrsson, A. (2001b) 'The Strategic States Model: optimum strategies to reach high performance,' *Management Decision*, **39**(6), pp. 441–7.

Porter, M. (1980) *Competitive Strategy: techniques for analysing industries and competitors*. New York: Free Press.

Porter, M. (1985) *Competitive Advantage: creating and sustaining superior performance*. New York: The Free Press

Rugman, A. and J. D'Cruz (2000) *Multinationals as Flagship Firms: regional business networks*. Oxford: Oxford University Press.

Stonehouse, G., J. Hamill, D. Campbell and T. Purdie (2000) *Global and Transnational Business: strategy and management*. Chichester: John Wiley.

Index

T - #0061 - 230425 - C0 - 234/156/18 - PB - 9780415342384 - Gloss Lamination